# A Comparative Study of Funding Shareholder Litigation

Wenjing Chen

# A Comparative Study of Funding Shareholder Litigation

Springer

Wenjing Chen
East China University of Political Science
and Law (ECUPL)
Shanghai
China

ISBN 978-981-10-3622-4 ISBN 978-981-10-3623-1 (eBook)
DOI 10.1007/978-981-10-3623-1

Library of Congress Control Number: 2017937116



Printed on acid-free paper

This Springer imprint is published by Springer Nature
The registered company is Springer Nature Singapore Pte Ltd.
The registered company address is: 152 Beach Road, #21-01/04 Gateway East, Singapore 189721, Singapore

# Acknowledgements

This book is mainly based on research conducted in Financial Law Institute, Ghent University, where it took shape under the guidance of my Ph.D. promoter Prof. Dr. Hans De Wulf. I would like to express my gratitude to Prof. Hans De Wulf for the guidance and support throughout the whole course of my research. I would also like to thank other members of my guidance committee, Prof. Stefaan Voet from KUL and Prof. Alain François from VUB for their insightful comments on my research. My sincere appreciation also goes to members of the Financial Law Institute for such great atmosphere for academic research. I would also like to acknowledge the funding provided by the China Scholarship Council to financially support my research in Ghent. Last but not least, my deepest gratitude goes to my family, especially to my husband Dr. Tiancheng Jiang who supported and encouraged me during my days in Ghent. The completion of this book would not have been possible without love and support from my family.

# Contents

# Abbreviations

| | |
|---|---|
| ABA | The American Bar Association |
| AFSL | Australian Financial Services Licence |
| ALF | The Association of Litigation Funders |
| ALI | The American Law Institute |
| ASIC | The Australian Securities and Investment Commission |
| ATE | After-the-Event insurance |
| ATLA | The American Trial Lawyers Association |
| BTE | Before-the-Event insurance |
| CA 2006 | Companies Act 2006 of the United Kingdom |
| CCL | Chinese Contract Law |
| CFA | Conditional Fee Agreement |
| CGFA | Contingency Fee Arrangement |
| CJC | The Civil Justice Council |
| CL | Company Law of the People's Republic of China |
| CPL | Civil Procedure Law of the People's Republic of China |
| CSRC | The China Securities Regulatory Commission |
| CWDF | The China Women's Development Foundation |
| DBA | Damages Based Agreement |
| FCA Act | The Federal Court of Australia Act |
| FRCP | Federal Rules of Civil Procedure |
| GDP | Gross Domestic Product |
| GPCL | The General Principle of the Civil Law of the People's Republic of China |
| ICJ | Institute for Civil Justice |
| ICL | The Israeli Company Law |
| ICO | Indemnity Cost Order |
| ISA | The Israel Securities Authority |
| JSLC | Joint Stock Limited Company |
| LEI | Legal Expenses Insurance |
| LFO | The Law Foundation of Ontario |

| | |
|---|---|
| LLC | Limited Liability Company |
| MALF | The Measures for the Administration of Lawyer's Fees of the People's Republic of China |
| MBCA | The Model Business Corporation Act |
| MPLC | Measures for the Payment of Litigation Costs of the People's Republic of China |
| NPO | Non-Profit Organization |
| PIOB | Public Interest Oversight Board |
| PRC | The People's Republic of China |
| RCSC | The Red Cross Society of China |
| SOE | State Owned Enterprise |
| SPC | The Supreme People's Court of the People's Republic of China |
| The PSLRA 1995 | The Private Securities Litigation Reform Act 1995 |
| TPLF | Third Party Litigation Funding |
| UK | The United Kingdom |
| US | The United States |
| U.S.C. | United States Code |

# Summary


Litigation is costly. The concern of high litigation costs would be greater than average in the context of shareholder litigation, where shareholder claimants would bear high financial risk when accessing to justice. In a collective lawsuit like shareholder litigation, litigation costs paid by shareholder claimants is highly likely to exceed benefits brought by a successful claim since proceeds must be distributed among group members, making such claims under-valued. To ensure the sound functioning of shareholder litigation and facilitate injured shareholders' claim for damages before the court, the study on how to remove funding obstacles with shareholder litigation is of importance. Shareholders' disincentives as a consequence of funding difficulties would, to a certain extent, negatively affect the functioning of shareholder litigation and further lead to a 'failure' on judicial approach to redress remedies.

Shareholder litigation in China is a good case to clarify the importance of funding issues for the functioning of shareholder litigation and the implementation of shareholders' right to sue. China introduced shareholder derivative litigation in 2006 but empirical research (2006–2013) suggests that the functioning of it is not good as expected. Shareholder class actions have similar problems. Through a comparative study, this book considers that funding difficulties confronted with potential shareholder claimants contribute to the 'failure' of shareholder litigation. Neither in China, nor has it been specified, in statutory provisions or case law of some other countries where shareholder litigation is adopted, how such actions should be properly funded. As a matter of fact, funding problems with shareholder lawsuits may largely discourage potential shareholder litigants who bear high financial risk in pursuing such a claim, while they may not have much to gain. In consideration of the lacks of incentives for shareholder claimants, effective funding techniques should be in place to avoid the 'death' of shareholder litigation. This book concentrates on examining, in a functionally comparative way, whether there are proper financing methods for shareholder plaintiffs to overcome financial obstacles, and also presents an in-depth analysis on how they work.

There are two main research questions this book will address: (1) how shareholder litigation is funded in selected countries; (2) which funding technique(s) is (are) applicable in China to finance shareholder litigation. This book attempts to, through a comparative way, investigate funding techniques in selected countries, including lawyer's funding (contingency fee arrangements and conditional fee agreements), company's funding (indemnity costs orders for shareholder derivative litigation in England and Wales), public funding (funding of private litigation by public authorities notably in Israel and Canada) and third party litigation funding. The aim of the book is to examine whether funding techniques investigated above are workable in financing shareholder litigation, potential problems caused in each technique, proper solution to such problems, and the potential of those funding methods for China in the context of its legal and social background.

In terms of funding techniques in selected countries, Chap. 4 contains an insightful analysis on public funding uniquely adopted by Israeli and Canadian (mainly in Ontario and Quebec) legal regime. Main finding in this regard is that public funding could be used to support shareholder litigant to pursue a lawsuit if several practical dilemmas, such as, the selection of a proper public authority administering public funding, designing a reimbursement system based on the gains of previous applicants, are solved. When public funding's potential for China is considered, it is extremely important to associate this issue with China's social and legal background. For instance, the concern of 'inside system' might largely contribute to the infeasibility of public funding in China. The interplay between the government and public authorities administering public funding might negatively affect the independent functioning of public funding, which is precisely the core requirement of this approach. A conclusion is drawn in this respect that public funding is not suitable to finance shareholder litigation in China currently, while it might be appropriate for China in the future in consideration of reforms on the political and judicial system that is likely to be conducted in the future or are already ongoing now.

Chapter 5 of this book mainly presents a comprehensive study on third party litigation funding (TPLF) and its potential for China. Cores issues in relation to the use of TPLF are analysed through a comparative study of the US, the UK and Australia, three countries where there already is some experience with this mechanism. The use of TPLF creates positive externalities, such as, facilitating the access to justice; indirectly deterring potential wrongdoers. On the other hand, concerns, such as the confusion of lawyer's duty of loyalty, are raised. In order to regulate the proper use of TPLF and meanwhile prevent negative effects brought by it, regulations should be adopted. The study of the practice of TPLF in Australia, the UK and the US demonstrates that codes on certain aspects, such as the funder's ethical issues, could be imposed to ensure the proper use of TPLF. This chapter then analyses its potential for China and reaches a conclusion that TPLF could be adopted to fund shareholder litigation in China, but with cautious. Reforms on PRC Contract law need to be carried out for solving potential problems brought by the use of TPLF.

Lawyers' funding (contingency fee arrangements, CGFAs and conditional fee agreements, CFAs) and company's funding (indemnity cost orders, ICOs) are investigated in Chap. 6 of this book. The main problem with ICOs lies in its procedural uncertainties. For instance, whether the eligibility of an ICO application contains the assessment of the applicant's financial capacity; under what circumstances could an ICO be awarded to the applicant. Since statutory rules do not set clear standards in relation to issues indicated above, ICO's practice in England generally refers to case law such as *Wallersteiner v. Moir* (No 2) and *Smith v. Croft*, which, however, easily make the procedure develop into a costly mini-trial. In terms of ICO's potential for China, this book proposes a reformed approach under which an ICO could be awarded if the court allows the claim to proceed as a derivative lawsuit. Two forms of lawyers' funding studied in this book are all based on the 'no win, no fees' principle, while CGFAs are associated with the damages granted by a successful suit and CFAs are only in relation to the outcome of a case (win or lose). Both of these two funding techniques have a common concern about lawyer's moral hazard, mainly referring to a condition where the lawyer's interests and clients' are divergent from each other. In addition, the risk of refusal to pay lawyer's fees was typically revealed in the *Grandall v. Weiguan* 2012 case. In China, lawyers might be further discouraged to conclude either a CGFA or a CFA with shareholder claimants to finance shareholder litigation considering the fact that Chinese courts are resistant to mass litigation. With regards to lawyers' funding, this book, in summary, argues that CGFAs and CFAs are not suitable to finance shareholder litigation in China.

Based on the functionally comparative studies on existing funding techniques, the principal conclusion of this book is reached that a reformed indemnity cost order and third party litigation funding could be used to finance shareholder litigation in consideration of China's existing legal and social context, while certain reforms should be carried out firstly to ensure the sound functioning of those funding mechanisms. Policy proposals about the potential use of indemnity cost orders and third party litigation funding are then specifically presented in Chap. 7 of this book.

# Chapter 1
# Introduction

In the very beginning of this book, a general evaluation of shareholder litigation would be presented to demonstrate the value of shareholder litigation and to prove why funding techniques should be adopted to make this mechanism functions.

## 1.1 A General Evaluation of Shareholder Litigation: Pros and Cons

### *1.1.1 Positive Externalities Brought by Shareholder Litigation*

Shareholder litigation plays an important role in enforcing corporate law.[1] Its beneficial effects could be summarized in three aspects:

(a) *Creating compensation*

For shareholders, successful shareholder litigation creates monetary compensation. For instance, a security fraud action could be launched by shareholders who

---

[1]This position has been widely indicated and confirmed in a wide range of legal literatures. For example, Roberta Romano, 'The Shareholder Suit: Litigation without Foundation?', *The Journal of Law, Economics and Organization*, (1991), Volume 7(1), 55; Jill E. Fisch, 'Teaching Corporate Governance through Shareholder Litigation', *Georgia Law Review*, (2000), volume 34, 745; Robert B. Thompson and Randall S. Thomas, 'The New Look of Shareholder Litigation: Acquisition-oriented Class Actions', *Vanderbilt Law Review*, (2004), Volume 57(1), 134; Ian Ramsay, 'Corporate Governance, Shareholder Litigation and the Prospects for a Statutory Derivative Action', *University of New South Wales Law Journal*, (1992), Volume 15(1), 149.



W. Chen, *A Comparative Study of Funding Shareholder Litigation*,
DOI 10.1007/978-981-10-3623-1_1

suffered losses caused by the company's misstatements.[2] A shareholder direct action could be commenced by shareholders to redress damage if their interests were infringed.[3]

A shareholder derivative lawsuit is initiated by shareholders on behalf of the company to redress remedies for the company's interests. For instance, if a director misappropriates the company's assets, a derivative claim can be commenced against the wrongdoer. Any damages brought by a successful derivative action belong to the company, which means that the company is compensated through the court's order.

(b) *Deterrence effects*

The deterrence effects are created by shareholder litigation indirectly. Potential wrongdoers might be deterred after being aware that they will be 'punished' if they engage in wrongdoing. At the same time, the court's judgment in a successful shareholder claim could guide company's directors (and other senior officers) on how to perform their legal obligations (i.e. fiduciary duties owed to the company).

(c) *Public significance*

Some court cases involving shareholder litigation may have effects on other parties than the litigants and company involved: precedents may be created, or (legal) problems that had not been noticed before could come to the surface. This may be called the public significance of certain cases. In fact, in terminology of law and economics, the production of a judgement in one case may have positive externalities in other cases or for society in general.

Some cases may have public significance even when they are not successful from the plaintiff's perspective. For instance, in a security fraud action involving a large number of investors, the court's decision might create an interesting precedent with wide influence even if this case is finally lost.[4] Such cases might drive legislators, legal scholars and legal practitioners to reconsider the problems under the current system.[5]

---

[2]For instance, the US securities fraud action, see *infra* 2.3.3; in China, collective litigation arising from securities fraud, see *infra* 2.3.1.

[3]See *infra* 2.2.

[4]For instance, ****shareholders v. HUANG Guangyu* (2012) in Beijing second intermediate court attracted wide public attention because it is the first securities fraud litigation alleging the defendant's inside-dealing behaviour. But, unfortunately, the plaintiff shareholders did not win the case because the causation between the investor's losses and inside dealing was not proved. However, this case was of significant importance (see http://finance.people.com.cn/stock/GB/217390/230095/index.html in Chinese, accessed on 24 July 2016).

[5]After the *HUANG Guangyu* case, many discussions about whether the security market should be better regulated were raised. http://www.360doc.com/content/08/1128/08/142_2009259.shtml (in Chinese, accessed on 16 July 2016).

### 1.1.2 *Potential Drawbacks of Shareholder Litigation*

(a) *Negative effects of frivolous or unmeritorious litigation*

Negative effects of frivolous or unmeritorious claims include two aspects. First, such claims may negatively affect the company's reputation. Second, for listed companies, the share price might by reduced because of the ongoing court proceeding.

(b) *Chilling effects on the directors' business behaviour*

Even though the directors' business activities could be protected by the business judgment rule (like in the US), this rule is not applied uniformly in practice, and is largely unknown in its "hard" form outside the US. The business judgment rule is regarded as 'one of the least understood concepts in the entire corporate field'.[6] It means that in practice under what circumstances the director's business decisions which cause a bad outcome for the corporation could be protected by the business judgment rule is vague.[7] Being afraid of being sued, directors might be more 'conservative' in making business decision than is optimal if they are to engage in 'optimal' levels of risk-taking on behalf of the company.

This book tries to solve funding difficulties with shareholder litigation, and several funding approaches will be investigated to figure out whether they could be used to fund shareholder litigation. The problem here is if shareholder litigation can be effectively financed, will those potential drawbacks of shareholder litigation become big concerns? It might be possible that with effective funding ways, the amount of shareholder litigation would increase. A similar finding in Australia shows that after the introduction of third party litigation funding, the number of lawsuits indeed did increase.[8] But there is no solid evidence demonstrating that the number of frivolous litigation increases.[9] In fact, it has been indicated that, for example, in China the current problem is not the abuse of the shareholder litigation mechanism.[10] The real concern is that the function of shareholder litigation is

[6]See Henry G. Manne, 'Our two corporation systems: law and economics', *Virginia Law Review*, (1967), Volume 53(2), 259, p. 270.

[7]Xiaoning Li, *A Comparative study of shareholders' derivative actions: England, the United States, Germany and China* (Kluwer, 2007), p. 146.

[8]See David S. Abrams and Daniel L. Chen, 'A Market for Justice: A First Empirical Look at Third Party Litigation Funding', *University of Pennsylvania Journal of Business Law*, (2013), Volume 15, 1075, p. 1090.

[9]Ibid.

[10]See Guanghua Yu and Junhai Liu, 'Legislation and the enforcement of law', (in Chinese), (理性立法和法律实施), commercial law forum no. 330, the minute of this forum could be available at (in Chinese) http://www.civillaw.com.cn/article/default.asp?id=43662 (accessed on 10 August 2016).

limited.[11] Also in the United Kingdom, one of the major obstacles in the path of commencing shareholder derivative litigation is the expensive litigation costs and the lack of effective funding ways.[12] Until now, no empirical evidence reveals that the mechanism of shareholder litigation has been abused due to the advent of effective funding methods. In fact, the American shareholder class actions were criticized for often being abused.[13] However, the reason for that is mainly because the existence of 'professional plaintiffs' who consistently 'purchase a few shares in troubled companies' in order to 'pursue a lawsuit',[14] but has nothing to with funding mechanisms.[15]

## 1.2 The Proposal of 'Funding Shareholder Litigation'

### *1.2.1 What Is the Funding Problem with Shareholder Litigation?*

Litigation is expensive.[16] Costs created in accessing justice may make potential litigants face funding problems. Particularly, the concern of high litigation costs may be greater than average in shareholder litigation[17] which often involves high monetary value. The shareholder plaintiffs would be confronted with even higher

[11]Ibid.

[12]See Arad Reisberg, *Derivative Actions and Corporate Governance: theory and operation*, (Oxford University Press 2007), pp. 222–223.

[13]See the House of Congress Report, Securities Litigation Reform, (No. 104-369), (1995), pp. 32–33.

[14]See John F. Olson, David C. Mahaffey and Brian E. Casy, 'Pleading Reform, Plaintiff Qualification and Discovery Stays Under the Reform Act', *Business Lawyer* (1996), Volume 51, 1101, p. 1105.

[15]The most common funding method for the American class actions is the 'common fund' which means that attorneys in a successful class action could collect reasonablefees from the entire monetary remedies after the court's discretion. If the action is lost (no common fund is generated), the class counsel get no fees.

[16]This conclusion is clearly supported by many authors. See for example, Christopher Hodges, Stefan Vogenauer and Magdalena Tulibacka, *The Cost and funding of Civil Litigation*, (Hart Publishing, 2010); Lord Jackson's Preliminary Report on Civil litigation (May, 2009); Lord Jackson's Final Report on Civil Litigation (December, 2009); James S. Kakalik and Nicholas M. Pace, *Costs and compensation paid in tort litigation*, (Rand Corporation, 1986); Craig Osborne, *Civil Litigation*, (Oxford University Press, 2004); Steven Shavell, *Foundations of Economic Analysis of Law*, (Harvard University Press, 2004), Part IV; And see articles, for instance, David M. Trubek, Austin Sarat, William L.F. Felstiner and Herbert M. Kritzer, 'The Costs of Ordinary Litigation', *UCLA Law Review*, (1984), Volume 31, 72; Leo Kevin and Denise Collier, 'Containing the Cost of Litigation', *Rutgers Law Review*, (1985), volume 37, 219.

[17]The term of 'shareholder litigation' in this book mainly covers four types of lawsuit: shareholder derivative actions, shareholder direct actions, shareholder class actions (this typically refers to securities fraud actions) and unfair prejudice remedies (under the British law).

financial risk when filing such a suit, which could result in the difficult implementation of shareholder protection through the judicial way.

### 1.2.2 *Why Funding Issue Is Crucial for Shareholder Litigation?*

Many countries where shareholder litigation is being used do not have clear statutory provisions or rules from case law regarding how such action should be funded properly.[18] Shareholder litigation is a procedural device to enable the court to do justice to compensate losses suffered by shareholder plaintiffs, however, without funding, how can a lawsuit be brought? The lack of funding may, to certain degree, make the device fail to function. Except for the function of wrongdoing correction, shareholder litigation also potentially exerts deterrence effects against potential wrongdoers.[19] But such effects may be weakened if injurers are aware of the fact that there is a lack of effective funding techniques to finance shareholder litigation.[20]

### 1.2.3 *How Will This Book Investigate Funding Issue of Shareholder Litigation?*

In order to bridge the funding gap in shareholder litigation, this book attempts to explore efficient funding ways for impecunious shareholder plaintiffs. Several funding techniques in civil litigation will be analysed from a functional and comparative perspective. Their potential for shareholder litigation will be examined. In addition to that, a focus will particularly rest on the discussion about whether shareholder litigation in China could be effectively financed through the funding methods examined in this book, considering the specific social and judicial context of China.

---

[18]For instance, shareholder derivative actions, shareholder direct actions and securities fraud actions are permitted in China but how should these claims be financed is not mentioned in current Chinese law. The absence of effective funding ways of shareholder litigation can also be found in other countries, including the US, the UK (only indemnity cost orders but practically problematic).

[19]See for example, Tom Baker and Sean J. Griffith, *Ensuring Corporate Misconduct, How Liability Insurance Underminies Shareholder Litigation*, (The University of Chicago Press, 2011), pp. 7–9; and see William B. Rubenstein, 'Why Enable Litigation? A Positive Externalities Theory of the Small Claims Class Action', *UMLC Law Review*, Volume 74, 709; and see Steven Shavell, 'The Social Versus the Private Incentive to Bring Suit in a Costly Legal System', *Journal of Legal Studies*, (1982), Volume 11, 333.

[20]The deterrence effects of litigation will be analysed in Sect. 4.1.1.2.

In order to conduct a more concrete investigation, the shareholder derivative action will be chosen as the main research topic in this book to elaborate the funding problems and how it could be funded in a proper way.[21]

## 1.3 The Structure of the Comparative Study

### *1.3.1 The Structure of the Book*

*The main research question of this book*

The main research question of this book is how to fund shareholder litigation. Based on this research question, this book investigates (almost) all funding approaches being currently used worldwide, including lawyer's funding (contingency fee arrangements and conditional fee agreements), company's funding (indemnity costs order for shareholder litigation), public funding,[22] and third party litigation funding.[23] Based on the examination of these funding techniques, the sub-questions come down to whether they are workable in funding shareholder litigation, potential problems caused by the use of them, possible solutions, and the potential of these funding methods for China in the context of its legal and social background.

*The structure of the book*

The first chapter of this book basically discusses the research question and the methodology (functionally comparative study) adopted by this book. Theoretical as well as practical analysis will be delivered in a selection of countries, including, among others, China, the US, the UK, Israel and Canada. The scope of the comparative study and the reason why those countries are chosen will also be illustrated in the first chapter of this book. Chapter 2 briefly studies 'what is shareholder litigation and several sorts of shareholder litigation'. In general, shareholder litigation is perceived to compensate infringed shareholders, and to deter managerial

[21]'Shareholder litigation' is not a concept defined in statute or elsewhere in the law. In fact, 'shareholder litigation' is a technical term used in academic research rather than a real legal concept applied in law; it generally refers to a sort of lawsuit involving shareholder litigants, and the filing of such an action is usually caused by the issue relevant to 'shareholder', 'company', 'director', or the relationship between these parties. For instance, shareholder derivative litigation is an action brought by shareholders on behalf of the company to redress losses caused by misbehaviours done by wrongdoers. The shareholder class action (securities fraud actions) permitted in the US and in China is brought to seek remedies caused by the misleading information about business profitability disclosed by the company.

[22]Legal aid is excluded.

[23]'Third party litigation funding' particularly refers to funding provided by professional litigation funders (not includes lawyers).

misconducts.[24] The term 'shareholder litigation' comprises all civil actions brought by shareholders against managerial wrongdoings within corporations in order to recover economic losses caused by them.[25] Almost in all countries, no law clearly provides what shareholder litigation is, therefore, the scope of it varies. This Part selects four sorts of actions to generally illustrate the nature and features of shareholder litigation, including shareholder derivative actions, shareholder direct actions and shareholder class actions (securities fraud litigation notably applied in the US).[26] A focus will particularly lie with the overview of shareholder derivative actions in China (my home country where derivative actions were introduced in 2006), the US (where derivative actions were flourished)[27] and the UK (where derivative actions were originated).[28]

Chapter 3 will present an introduction with regards to the general costs rules in civil litigation and general funding mechanisms applied to finance it. Through the investigation of the cost rules, the fact that litigation is expensive would be proved.[29] The concern of excessive litigation costs will be enhanced in the filing of shareholder litigation because of the high monetary value involved. Since a shareholder lawsuit is usually regarded as a 'property case', the court charges are calculated on an incremental basis in proportion to monetary value at stake. Under this circumstance, funding techniques financially supporting *bona fide* litigants need to be explored. The latter part of this chapter will examine several funding approaches of civil litigation in a general way.

Chapter 4 studies public funding (funding of private litigation by public authorities) notably used in Israel and Canada (Ontario and Quebec) to fund derivative actions and class actions respectively.[30] The working mechanism of

---

[24]See Paul Weitzel, 'The End of Shareholder Litigation? Allowing Shareholders to Customize Enforcement through Arbitration Provisions in Charters and Bylaws', *Brigham Young University Law Review* (2013), Issue 1, 65; and see Federico Pastre, *How Shareholder Litigations Deter Directors and Officers: US and Italy, a Comparative Analysis* (GRIN Verlag, 2013); See Patrick M. Garry, Candice Spurlin, Debra A. Owen, William A. Williams and Lindsay J. Efting, 'The Irrationality of Shareholder Class Action Lawsuits: A Proposal for Reform', *South Dakota Law Review*, (2004), Volume 49(2), 275.

[25]For instance, a shareholder derivative action is filed against wrongdoers (i.e. directors) on behalf of the company to redress remedies.

[26]And its counterpart in China—private securities litigation, but they are not entirely identical with respect to practical procedure and requirements.

[27]Xiaoning Li, *A Comparative Study of Shareholders' Derivative Actions*, (Kluwer, 2007), pp. 89–91 and 96–100; Robert B. Thompson and Randall S. Thomas, 'The Public and Private Faces of Derivative Lawsuits', Vanderbilt Law Review, (2004), Volume 57, 1747, pp. 1049–1051.

[28]Paul L. Davies, *Gower and Davies' Principles of Modern Company Law*, (Sweet&Maxwell, 7th edition, 2003), Part 4; Victor Joffe, David Drake and Giles Richardson, *Minority Shareholders: Law. Practice and Procedure*, (Oxford University Press, 2011), pp. 29–87.

[29]Christopher Hodges, Stefan Vogeauer and Magdalena Tulibacka, *The Cost and funding of Civil Litigation*, (Hart Publishing, 2010), pp. 11–29.

[30]Israel public funding of derivative actions (article 205A of Israeli Companies Law 1999); Ontario Class Proceedings Fund [Law Society Act (Ontario), s 59.1]; Quebec *Fonds d'aide aux recours collectifs* (section 23 of An Act Respecting the Class Action, RSQ, c R-2.1).

public funding will be investigated in detail, including what are the selection criterion before public funding is granted, how the public funding is financed (by the government or by the applicant who wins the funded case), which authority will take charge of public funding, and the relationship between the committee's decision on public funding and the court's permission for a case to proceed. Following that, the potential of public funding for China to fund shareholder litigation (mainly refers to shareholder derivative actions) will be examined in the context of China's legal and social background.

Chapter 5 will mainly focus on the discussion of third party litigation funding (TPLF), which is the most recent development in litigation funding industry. To conduct a comparative research in this respect, the use of TPLF in Australia (where it was originated),[31] the US and the UK (where it is being widely applied)[32] will be investigated respectively. Several concerns regarding TPLF, such as, the third party funder's moral hazard, the complicated lawyer-litigant-funder relationship, the traditional common law prohibition on champerty and maintenance, will be examined based on the empirical studies in those countries.[33] Subsequent to the comparative research, this chapter will switch to study whether TPLF could be introduced into China to fund shareholder litigation and what kind of reform on Chinese law should be carried out to facilitate the proper use of TPLF.

Chapter 6 will concentrate on analysing funding alternatives through fee or cost arrangements (other than public funding and TPLF) for shareholder litigation, including contingency fee arrangements (CGFAs), conditional fee agreements (CFAs) and indemnity cost orders (being used in England and Wales to fund derivative actions). The in-depth investigation mainly contains the discussion on the ethical concerns about the lawyer's role in CGFAs and CFAs, and the procedural requirements in indemnity cost orders. Following that, their potential for China will be examined also.

Chapter 7—Based on the investigations on several funding techniques, this chapter will, concretely, formulate a proposal for China regarding how to fund shareholder litigation, and how to design relevant statutory rules (or reform current law) to regulate the proper use of certain funding methods.

---

[31]Camille Cameron, 'The Costs and Funding of Civil Litigation: a National Report in Australia', in *The Cost and funding of Civil Litigation*, Christopher Hodges et al (eds), (Hart Publishing, 2010), 195, pp. 212–214; and see Marco de Morpurgo, 'A comparative legal and economic approach to third-party litigation funding', *Cardozo Journal of International and Comparative Law Review*, (2011), Volume 19, 343, pp. 390–393.

[32]Lord Jackson's Final Report on Civil Litigation (December, 2009), pp. 117–125; Vicki Waye, *Trading in Legal Claims*, (Presidian Legal Publications, 2008); Cento Veljanovski, 'Third Party Litigation Funding in Europe', *Journal of Law, Economics and Policy*, (2012), Volume 8, 405; Susan L. Martin, 'The Litigation Financing Industry: the Wild West of Finance Should be Tamed not Outlawed', *Fordham Journal of Corporate & Financial Law*, (2004), Volume 10(1), 55.

[33]Percy H. Winfield, 'History of Maintenance and Champerty', *Law Quarterly Review*, (1919), Volume 35, 50; Max Radin, 'Maintenance by Champerty', *California Law Review*, (1935), Volume 24(1), 48.

Chapter 8 of this book is 'conclusion', where main findings of the research question and proposals will be summarized.

## 1.3.2 *The Countries Chosen for the Comparative Study*

### 1.3.2.1 China

In my home country China where shareholder derivative actions were introduced in 2006, funding obstacles for minority shareholders who intends to commence a derivative lawsuit is observed. An empirical study shows that from 1 January 2006 to 30 August 2013, only 103 derivative actions were brought before Chinese courts.[34] Compared to the large number of registered companies in China (approximately 7.1 million in 2009), this relatively small figure (only 103 cases) is hardly to prove that the shareholder derivative action runs as a useful tool to discipline corporate management.[35] And also, considering the fact that there is no effective alternatives (for instance, unfair prejudice remedy is widely used to protect shareholders' interests in the UK) to redress misconduct and seek remedies, derivative actions ought to play a key role in discipline corporate management in China.[36] It has been rightly indicated that practical difficulties hamper the functioning of derivative actions. For instance, financial obstacles faced by shareholder litigants, namely, how a derivative lawsuit could be financed and whether there are incentives for potential shareholder claimants to bring such an action. That is why I chose the research topic 'funding shareholder litigation'. And also, comparative study regarding how to finance shareholder litigation is addressed in order to investigate whether funding problems with shareholder litigation in China could be solved through transplanting certain funding techniques being used in other countries and what kinds of reforms should be carried out in order to make it/them fits for China's context.

### 1.3.2.2 The United States

The comparative study covers the discussion of 'funding shareholder litigation' in the US. The reason why the US was chosen is that (1) shareholder litigation is very flourished in the US and the functioning of it does not seem to be hampered by

[34]See Shaowei Lin, "Derivative Actions in China: Case Analysis", (2014), *Hong Kong Law Journal*, Volume 44, 621, p. 638.

[35]An official report indicates that until the end of 2009, the number of enterprises in China was 7.1 million. See *National Economic Census 2009 (No. 2)*, (in Chinese), available at http://www.ce.cn/macro/more/200912/25/t20091225_20689923.shtml (accessed on 16 May 2016).

[36]See Shaowei Lin, "Derivative Actions in China: Case Analysis", (2014), *Hong Kong Law Journal*, Volume 44, 621, p. 640.

funding difficulties confronted by potential shareholder litigants; (2) funding techniques, such as contingency fee arrangements, third party litigation funding, are widely used in the US; Therefore, to study how shareholder litigation is financed in the US might be helpful to seek for solutions to funding problems with shareholder litigation in China.

#### 1.3.2.3 The United Kingdom

Shareholder derivative actions were originated since the establishment of the exceptions to *Foss* rule in the UK. Even though derivative actions are, in fact, relatively rarely initiated before the courts, this country has far more experience with this mechanism than other countries. The UK is also an interesting example in this regard because in 2006 the derivative action was fundamentally reformed after long debates, and because an important exercise was performed in thinking about litigation costs and litigation funding of the whole civil justice system (Lord Jackson's report). Since the enactment of the Access to Justice Act 1999, litigation funding market began to grow in the UK. A typical example in this respect is the development of third party litigation funding. And also, since April 2013, damages based agreements (identical with the US style contingency fee arrangements) were legally confirmed in the UK in order to providing the general public with more litigation financing approaches and facilitate the access to justice.

#### 1.3.2.4 Canada (Ontario and Quebec)

Ontario and Quebec are probably unique in having a public funding mechanism for civil litigation (mainly refers to class actions). Ontario Class Proceeding Fund and Quebec Class Action Assistance Fund (*Fonds d'aide aux recours collectifs*) are, in nature, funding provided by public authorities to facilitate the access to justice for individuals having financial difficulties in bringing certain actions before the courts. The study of the Canadian case in this book intends to explore the working mechanism of public funding and to examine common problems when public funding is used through the empirical research.

#### 1.3.2.5 Israel

Like Canada, Israel is also unique in having public funding particularly for financing shareholder class actions and shareholder derivative actions. Public funding (introduced in Israeli Company Law since 2011) in Israel is provided by Israel Securities Authority (ISA) to fund certain cases 'reveal public interest and importance'. The main practical problems regarding the functioning of Israel public funding is the relationship between the decision made by the ISA and the court's judgment in the funded case.

#### 1.3.2.6 Australia

The reason why this book chooses Australia as a case study is because third party litigation funding was originated in Australia in 2006 through the *Fostif* case before the Australian High Court. In fact, the growth and evolution of TPLF has been one of the most significant developments in the litigation market since its legal confirmation in 2006. The examination of the Australian case in TPLF could help to understand and analyse the evolution of TPLF industry, and try to observe practical problems when this technique is applied. For instance, how to regulate third party litigation funder.

## 1.4 The Scope of the Comparative Study

This book covers all of the typical techniques being used in financing shareholder litigation in the current world, including public funding, third party litigation funding, lawyer's funding (contingency fee arrangements and conditional fee agreements) and company's funding (indemnity cost orders).

### *1.4.1 Public Funding*

The term of public funding in this book excludes the traditional 'legal aid'. In this book, 'public funding' refers to a sort of funding provided by a public authority to finance civil litigation meeting given requirements laid down by the authority. First of all, it should be indicated that public funding is not a widely-used technique across the world. Typical examples are found in Israel (Israel public funding) and Canada (Ontario Class Proceeding Fund and Quebec Class Action Assistance Fund). The examination of public funding in this book aims at analysing its working mechanism, its function in facilitating the access to justice for potential claimants in shareholder litigation and whether this technique could be introduced to China in consideration of Chinese social and legal background.

### *1.4.2 Third Party Litigation Funding (TPLF)*

Third party litigation funding (TPLF), since for the first time, legally approved by Australian High Court in *Campbells Cash and Carry Pty Ltd v Fostif* [2006], the industry of TPLF has grown rapidly with a number of funders entering into the market of litigation financing in many countries, such as, United States, New Zealand, Singapore. Along with its development, however, concerns are raised. For example, the challenge to the privileged lawyer-and-client relationship, the funder's moral risk and whether TPLF encourages frivolous and unmeritorious claims. With regards to TPLF, this book will firstly investigate current practice of it in Australia, the US and the UK where this technique is flourished. Following that, the potential for TPLF in China to finance shareholder litigation will be studied and policy advice with regards to the introduction of TPLF will also be given.

### *1.4.3 Lawyer's Funding*

Lawyer's funding in this book mainly refers to contingency fee arrangements (CGFA) and conditional fee agreements (CFAs).

#### 1.4.3.1 Contingency Fee Arrangements (CGFAs)

A contingency fee arrangement (CGFA) is, in nature, based on the 'no win, no fee' basis, where the litigant shares damages granted by the court with the lawyer. This technique is allowed to use in many countries, while it is banned in many countries, particularly, in continental Europe. CGFA is quite frequently used in the US to finance civil litigation, and the UK formally adopted CGFA in April 2013. In China, CGFAs were allowed to use since 2006, and the contingent rate should be capped at 30% of the damages. But CGFA is not allowed to fund mass litigation in China. This book will study the practice of CGFA mainly in the US, the UK and China respectively, and it is then concluded that using CGFAs to fund shareholder litigation is probably not feasible.

#### 1.4.3.2 Conditional Fee Agreements (CFAs)

Like the CGFA, the nature of a CFA is also 'no win, no fee'. Lawyers are paid both normal fees and an amount of success fees only if the case is won. CFAs are typically used in the UK, where the success fee is allowed to be 100% of the basic fee in commercial cases. Both CFAs and CGFAs are based on the same principle, however, the success fee in a CFA is determined in the contract up front, while the amount of contingent fee varies in each case depending on the amount of damages granted in a favourable outcome. A common concern regarding the use of CFA is the conflict of interests between lawyers and funded litigants. This book will study the working mechanism of CFAs and further investigate whether it could be used to fund shareholder litigation in China.

### 1.4.4 Company's Funding (Indemnity Cost Orders, ICO)

Indemnity cost orders was originated in the UK. It is, essentially, a sort of litigation funding provided by the company to finance a derivative lawsuit. It refers to such a case that the court may order a company to indemnify the claimant against the liability for costs incurred in a derivative lawsuit which was brought on the name of the company. In China, the Fourth Judicial Interpretation of the Supreme People's Court on Some Issues Regarding the Application of PRC Company Law, Consultation Paper 2016 proposed a model under which the shareholder plaintiffs could be indemnified by the company if the case is won under the court's discretion. However, under what circumstances the court could order the company to indemnify the claimant are not stated in this consultation paper. The study of the practice of indemnity cost order in the UK might be help to illustrate certain practical aspects that have not been mentioned in the consultation paper.

# Chapter 2
# An Overview of Shareholder Litigation

## 2.1 Introduction

Shareholder litigation is traditionally perceived as being about compensating shareholders for infringements of their rights or for losses they suffered as a result of negligent behaviour by the company and its directors, or by third parties. For a long time now, an additional function of shareholder litigation has been put forward: to deter managerial misconduct.[1] The term 'shareholder litigation' comprises all civil actions brought by shareholders against managerial wrongdoings within companies in order to recover economic losses caused by them.[2] Plaintiffs in shareholder litigation are obviously shareholders of a company. But defendants vary depending on different forms of shareholder litigation; they include companies, majority shareholders, directors, other senior managers in companies and third parties that are involved with the company (suppliers, bankers and other creditors, government agencies…).[3] With regards to the causes of actions, as indicated before,

[1]See Paul Weitzel, 'The End of Shareholder Litigation? Allowing Shareholders to Customize Enforcement through Arbitration Provisions in Charters and Bylaws', *Brigham Young University Law Review* (2013), Issue 1, 65, pp. 67–68; And see Federico Pastre, *How Shareholder Litigations Deter Directors and Officers: U.S. and Italy, a Comparative Analysis* (GRIN Verlag, 2013), pp. 3–4.

[2]See Patrick M. Garry, Candice Spurlin, Debra A. Owen, William A. Williams and Lindsay J. Efting, 'The Irrationality of Shareholder Class Action Lawsuits: A Proposal for Reform', *South Dakota Law Review*, (2004), Volume 49(2), 275, pp. 276–277.

[3]For example, in a shareholder derivative action, the nominal defendant is the company where the misconduct occurs. In a shareholder direct action, the defendants are generally the wrongdoers. In an unfair prejudice remedy, the defendants are the members of the company who commit wrongdoings (they can include majority shareholder, directors, or other members).



W. Chen, *A Comparative Study of Funding Shareholder Litigation*,
DOI 10.1007/978-981-10-3623-1_2

they are mainly caused by wrongdoings within companies resulting in financial losses.[4] The following sections will introduce three types of shareholder actions that could be used to claim for damages, including shareholder direct actions, shareholder derivative actions, and shareholder class actions.

## 2.2 Shareholder Direct Actions

Shareholder direct actions are, in nature, 'personal claims' not brought on behalf of companies. It is, in many cases, compared with shareholder derivative actions which are commenced by shareholders on behalf of the company for the losses suffered by the company. Practically, to distinguish derivative actions from direct ones, it depends on the answers to two questions—who suffers the alleged injury? (the company as a whole or the individual shareholder)—and who will receive the recoveries ordered by the court?[5] Actually, in a derivative action, the company suffers financial losses because of wrongdoings, and the shareholder plaintiff suffers reflective losses in that case. But in a direct action, injuries are done to the shareholder plaintiff individually. One of the fundamental differences between those two actions may be that injuries in a direct action must be a special injury which does not equally affects all shareholders of the company.[6] Furthermore, an action cannot be a derivative one if the shareholders' injuries are separate and distinct from that suffered by others.[7] But in case law, the courts in Delaware and New York hold that an action should still be considered as a direct one if the principal injury is done to the company, but special injuries remain with the individual shareholders.[8] Fundamentally, close attention should be given to the issue whether a particular

[4]As for financial losses in shareholder litigation, they differ in different type of shareholder litigation. For example, in a shareholder derivative action, the cause of action must be that the company's interests have been infringed by wrongdoings, and under this circumstance, shareholder plaintiffs may suffer 'reflective losses' (the term of 'reflective loss' is a concept use in the English company law, which means that reflective losses of an individual shareholder are inseparable from general losses of the company). In a direct action, the cause of action should be that the shareholder plaintiffs suffer a special injury which does not infringe the interests of other members of the company. It is also the main point distinguishing derivative actions from direct actions. And also in the U.S., shareholder class action is a sort of shareholder litigation, in which the shareholder plaintiffs are financially harmed because they pay the inflated prices for their stock. See Patrick M. Garry et al., 'The Irrationality of Shareholder Class Action Lawsuits: A Proposal for Reform', *South Dakota Law Review*, (2004), Volume 49(2), 275, p. 277.

[5]Andreas Cahn and David C Donald, *Comparative Company Law: text and cases on the laws governing corporations in German, the UK and the USA*, (Cambridge University Press, 2010). pp. 602–603.

[6]See American Law Institute (ALI), *Principle of Corporate Governance: Analysis and Recommendations* (American Law Institute Publisher, Minnesota, 1994), Volume 2, pp. 17–22.

[7]Ibid.

[8]*Elster v. American Airlines, Inc.*, 34 Del. Ch. 94, 100A.2d 219, 222 (1953); 12b Fletchers Cyclopedia Corps., S 5912, p. 431 (Perm. Ed., Rev. Vol. 1984), see American Law Institute (ALI),

right of claim belongs more to the company or to the shareholders.[9] If it belongs more to the company, it should be a derivative action. Otherwise, it is a direct action.[10]

## 2.3 Shareholder Derivative Actions

Up till now, shareholder derivative actions have been legally confirmed in many jurisdictions (for instance, the UK, the US, China, Japan, Singapore).[11] Actually, the derivative action was originated in the UK as an exception to the proper plaintiff principle (the *Foss* Rule[12]) which means that an action brought because of wrongdoings to the company should be pursued by the company itself and the damages should also be awarded to the company. Derivative actions enable (certain) shareholders to redress the company's losses on behalf of the company in the event that the company (the proper plaintiff) is not able to bring a suit by itself.[13] For instance, when the company is substantially controlled by the wrongdoers. In this case, wrongdoings done to the company can be redressed by shareholders representing the company instead of the company per se, which could be regarded as a fundamental justification for the existence of derivative actions.[14]

---

(Footnote 8 continued)

*Principle of Corporate Governance: Analysis and Recommendations* (American Law Institute Publisher, Minnesota, 1994), Volume 2, p. 19.

[9]See Joseph Bishop, *The Law of Corporate Officers and Directors: Indemnification and Insurance*, (Clark Boardman Callaghan, 1981), pp. 3–10.

[10]Actually, there are overlaps of direct and derivative actions. In many cases, the line between a direct and a derivative action is hazy. For example, while it is generally agreed that actions for declared dividends are direct actions, there have been disagreements as to compelling dividends. In this case, the claim might be direct and individual since 'the right to dividends is an incident of stock ownership, and shareholders were injured directly due to the failure of distribution of dividends', On the other hand, a derivative action is also justified on the ground that the corporation also suffered losses due to 'punitive excess retain-earnings taxes or the retained earnings will otherwise be used improvidently'. See James D. Cox and Thomas Lee Hazen, *Corporations* (Aspen Publishers, 2nd edition, 2002), p. 421.

[11]In most of countries in continental Europe, derivative actions are legally allowed (e.g. Germany, Spain, Sweden, Austria, Slovenia, Italy). But Dutch law does not permit derivative actions.

[12]In fact, in the Foss rule, two main principles have been identified: one is the majority rule principle and the other one the proper plaintiff principle. The majority rule principle states that the alleged wrongdoing can be ratified by a simple majority of company's members in a general meeting, then the court will not interfere. *Foss v Harbottle* (1843) 67 ER 189.

[13]See Xiaoning Li, *A Comparative Study of Shareholders' Derivative Actions: England, the United States, Germany and China*, (Kluwer, 2007), p. 1.

[14]See Xiaoning Li, *A Comparative Study of Shareholders' Derivative Actions: England, the United States, Germany and China*, (Kluwer, 2007), p. 2 and pp. 22–23.

The shareholder plaintiffs' right to sue, in fact, derives from the company's right to commence a lawsuit.[15] Because of the very nature of the derivative action (an exception to the general principle), it can only be applied in limited circumstances. For instance, a derivative action could only be brought for a certain range of causes of actions.[16] And from the procedural perspective, in some jurisdictions like the UK and the US, the court's discretion on allowing a derivative suit is expressed in several procedure requirements specially designed for such litigation.[17] The derivative nature of this litigation also explains the fact that, if the action is for damages, any award will be paid to the company, and not to the shareholders who brought the action on behalf of the company.

## 2.3.1 *Shareholder Derivative Actions in China*

### 2.3.1.1 Introduction and Development of Shareholder Derivative Actions

For quite a long time, Chinese companies have been conceived as having what one could call a block-holder model of shareholder structure, where the state or the Communist Party controls the general operation of the company.[18] But since the opening and reform policy initiated in early 1980s, the planned economy has been gradually transformed into a market economy and a large amount of economic entities began to emerge at that time. Given this background, the demand for regulations on corporate governance and relevant issues increased. Hence, the first PRC Company Law was born in 1993 (CL 1993). After more than ten years' development, it had become clear that this law did not succeed in solving disputes

[15]Ibid.

[16]For example, in the US, the shareholder plaintiff should demonstrate that the company is in the "wrongdoers' control", and the derivative action would have been commenced by directors in good faith. And in the UK, a derivative action could be brought only in respect of a cause of action arising from an actual or proposed act or omission involving negligence, default, breach of duty or breach of trust by a director of the company (section 260(3) of UK Companies Act 2006).

[17]For example, in the UK, since 1 October 2007, the procedures in respect of all derivative claims have been set out in the Civil Procedure Rules 1998 (CPR) Parts 19.9 to 19.9F, Practice Direction 19C and UK Companies Act 2006 Part 11. Generally, the permission to continue the claim is a two-stage procedure (At the first stage, the shareholder plaintiff should present evidence to demonstrate the case is a *prima facie* one, otherwise, the claim will be dismissed by the court. And at the second stage, the court carries out a comparatively high degree of judicial discretion). See A. M. Gray, 'The statutory derivative claim, an outmoded superfluousness', *Company Lawyer*, (2012), Volume 33(10), 295, p. 297.

[18]See Flora Xiao Huang, 'shareholder revolt? The statutory derivative action in China', *Comparative Research in Law & Political Economy. Research Paper No. 49/2009.* pp. 4–5 http://digitalcommons.osgoode.yorku.ca/clpe/157 (accessed on 10 August 2016).

between directors and shareholders, and also failed to meet the demand of balancing the interests of controlling shareholders and minority ones.[19]

Given that, the CL 2006 introduced a series of techniques aimed at achieving such balance, including the introduction of shareholder derivative actions.[20] These are expected to promote corporate governance, enhance the protection of minority shareholders and build an investor-friendly legal regime in response to the rapid economic growth in China. In fact, prior to the introduction of it in 2006, there were legal practices and judicial discussions regarding derivative actions because conflicts between controlling shareholders and minority ones had begun to become a common issue in corporate governance.[21] There were several significant cases regarding some forms of ‘derivative actions’ even though the concept was not dealt with in the law at that time. For example, Mr. Shao, a shareholder of Sanjiu Medical & Pharmaceutical Co., Ltd., used it against the director of that company in April 2003, claiming that around 96% of the company’s assets had been inappropriately usurped by the director and controlling shareholders. Mr. Shao required the court to order the wrongdoers to make amends towards the company. Unfortunately, the Shenzhen Intermediate People’s Court dismissed Mr. Shao’s appeal, stating that a derivative action should represent the legal interests of all shareholders of the company, and Mr. Shao must obtain consent from all of them prior to the commencement of such a lawsuit.[22] In fact, Li Guoguang, the deputy president of the Supreme People’s Court (SPC) indicated that courts should accept derivative actions in a meeting concerning China’s court adjudication work for civil and commercial affairs on December 11th 2002. However, Mr. Li’s view was not adopted by the court because his speech could only be considered as a reference but not a rule with binding effects.[23,24]

---

[19]See Xudong Zhao, ‘The aim of the amending of the Company Law 1993’, (in Chinese), (公司法修改的价值取向), *Legal Forum* (法学论坛), 2004(6), 11; see Junhai Liu, ‘The amendment and interpretation of the Company Law 1993’, (in Chinese), (公司法的修改与解释), *The Application of Law* (法律适用), 2005(3), 2, p. 3; Min’an Zhang, *The Balance of Interests in the Company Law 1993*, (Peking University Press, 2003).

[20]Those new techniques include the introduction of independent directors, the application of a cumulative voting system and the use of shareholder derivative actions.

[21]See Peizhong Gan, ‘The Potential for Shareholder Derivative Actions in China’, (in Chinese), (论股东派生诉讼在中国的有效适用), *The Journal of Peking University (Philosophy and Social Science)*, 2002, 39(5), 17, pp. 18–19; Yunqiu Yan, ‘The Theoretical and Statutory Aspects of Shareholder Derivative Actions’ (in Chinese) (公司利益相关者派生诉讼的理论逻辑与制度构建), *Studies in Law and Business*, 2006, 22(6), 24, pp. 26–27.

[22]See Guojie Xu, ‘The first derivative lawsuit was refused by the court due to the absent of consent from all company’s shareholders’, (in Chinese), China Securities Journal (中国证券报), (April 22nd 2003).

[23]Ibid.

[24]Except for *Sanjiu* case, before 2006, there were several significant cases regarding the similar issue, which could also be regarded as milestones in the development of shareholder derivative actions. For example, *Li Kai v. Lianhua Weijing* (May 2004); *Xie Guangxue, Yao Jun* et al. *v. Pan Shiyi* (August 2004, and the disputed value of the case is amounted to 1.05 Billion RMB); *Daqing Lianyi Case* (2004). These casea are not officially published, but articles discussing them could be

After 2003, several rules concerning derivative actions were issued by High People's Courts. For instance, Shanghai High People's Court promulgated its *Opinion on Some Issues in Trials for Legal Actions Related to Company Dispute (No 1)*, where the legality of derivative actions was confirmed by a Chinese court for the first time.[25] On top of that, Jiangsu High People's Court issued its *Opinion on Some Issues in Trials for Legal Actions Applied with Company Law (Provisional Rules)*,[26] which set up rules for shareholder representative actions (股东代表诉讼) largely equivalent to the common law definition of shareholder derivative actions.[27,28]

On the national level, the SPC in 2003 published the first draft of *Regulations on Some Issues Concerning Trials for Company Disputes (consultation paper)*, which includes five articles concerning derivative actions.[29] Article 43 of it provides causes of derivative actions.[30] Article 44 stipulates two preconditions for a commencement of a derivative claim, including the 'contemporaneous ownership requirement'[31] and the 'threshold requirement'. Article 45 is about the status of

(Footnote 24 continued)

found. See, for example, (*Li Kai v. Lianhua Weijing*) http://finance.sina.com.cn/y/20040731/1844916842.shtml; (in Chinese, accessed on 16 July, 2016); http://www.cctv.com/news/financial/inland/20040729/101495.shtml (in Chinese, accessed on November 16th, 2014); For the case (*Xie Guangxue, Yao Jun* et al. *v. Pan Shiyi*), see, for example, http://www.china.com.cn/chinese/law/660372.htm (in Chinese, accessed on 16 July 2016); http://news.163.com/05/0519/02/1K35GSLN0001122D.html (in Chinese, accessed on 16 July 2016).

[25]Article 5(1) of it states that the court cannot refuse a derivative claim on the ground that the plaintiffs are ineligible.

[26]Article 17 of it provides that the court should accept derivative actions. And defendants in such claims are wrongdoers, while the company should be listed as 'a third person' in the litigation. PRC Civil Procedure Law (CCPL) indicated that 'a third person' is a party whose interests will be affected by the result of a case. See article 56 of the CCPL.

[27]See Flora Xiao Huang, 'shareholder revolt? The statutory derivative action in China', *Comparative Research in Law & Political Economy. Research Paper No. 49/2009*. p. 9 http://digitalcommons.osgoode.yorku.ca/clpe/157 (accessed on 10 August 2016).

[28]In addition, Zhejiang High People's Court in 2002 (Understandings on Several Difficult Issues Regarding the Application of the Company Law) and Beijing People's High Court in 2004 (The Guiding Opinions of Beijing High People's Court on Several Issues on Adjudicating Corporate Disputes Cases) respectively issued similar judicial opinions concerning the use of shareholder derivative actions.

[29]'Regulations on Some Issues Concerning Trials for Company Disputes' (关于审理公司纠纷案件若干问题的规定), articles 43–47 (in Chinese).

[30]Shareholder could launch a court proceeding if a director, supervisor or senior officer breaches his or her obligation of loyalty to the company, or if controlling shareholders abuse their position, which cause losses to the company.

[31]The 'contemporaneous ownership requirement' means that qualified shareholder plaintiffs should hold continuously the company's shares when the misconducts infringing the company's interest occur. And the 'threshold requirement' means that a complaint shareholder should hold at least 10% of a limited liability company's total shares or 1% of a joint stock limited company.

other parties in a derivative lawsuit.[32] And article 47 indicates that under certain circumstances the court could order the shareholder plaintiffs to post security for costs.[33] Although this draft by the SPC was only a consultation paper and had no binding effects on judicial practice, it did demonstrate the efforts to unify the rules on shareholder derivative actions.[34]

In 2006, the new Companies Legislation formally granted minority shareholders the right to protect the company's interests (and shareholders' interests as well) by initiating shareholder derivative actions. Neither the statutory provisions concerning derivative actions in the CL 2006 nor those rules in the subsequent judicial interpretations of it by the SPC[35] have offered practical guidance (for instance, the problem in the 'demand requirements', see the following sections in this regard), which might be partly responsible for the comparatively unsuccessful functioning of derivative actions after 2006.[36] The following sections will attempt to investigate the practical difficulties when derivative actions are used.[37]

#### 2.3.1.2 Anatomy of Derivative Actions Under the PRC Company Law 2014[38]

##### 2.3.1.2.1 General Statutory Provisions

For a better explanation of the legal framework of derivative action in China, the overall rules for them can be summarized in four steps. First of all, there should be an actual wrongdoing to the company, which causes damage. Second,

---

[32]For example, the status of other shareholders who also file an action and the status of the injured company.

[33]For example, if the derivative claim was suspected to be a strike suit, a financial deposit by the shareholder plaintiff would be necessary.

[34]See Xiaoning Li, *A comparative study of shareholders' derivative actions: England, the United States, Germany and China*, (Kluwer, 2007), p. 272.

[35]There are three judicial interpretations on CL 2006 in total, which were issued in 2006, 2008, 2010.

[36]Actually there are opinions supposing that the use of derivative actions in China was not a success because compared to the large amount of companies, derivative actions were rarely used. See Dan Wang, *Theoretical analysis on shareholders' derivative actions*, (in Chinese), (公司派生诉讼论), China legal publishing house (中国法制出版社), (2012), p. 325; And it was also indicated that the unsuccessful function of shareholder derivative actions are due to the defects on Chinese judicial system and special social background. See Donald C. Clarke and Nicholas C. Howson, 'Pathway to minority shareholder protection: derivative actions in the People's Republic of China', in Dan W. Puchniak, Harald Baum and Michael Ewing-Chow (eds), *The derivative action in Asia: a comparative and functional approach*, (Cambridge University Press, 2012), 243.

[37]For example, the funding difficulties and the ambiguous procedures.

[38]The latest version of PRC Company Law is CL 2014, but the rules concerning shareholder derivative actions are the same with those in CL 2006. So in this book, for convenience, when discussing derivative actions in China, the law usually refers to the CL 2014.

shareholders[39] cannot commence a derivative action immediately: they should first ask the board of supervisors in writing to file a lawsuit in the court. Third, if the board of supervisors finds itself in the circumstances (for instance, the company's director breaks law and causes losses to the company) as stated in Article 149 of CL 2014,[40] the aforementioned shareholders may require the board of directors in writing to initiate a lawsuit. And fourth, eligible shareholders could bring a derivative action provided that the board of directors refuses to commence a derivative action or it fails to file such a lawsuit within 30 days after receiving the shareholders' request. In addition to that, in case of emergency, eligible shareholders can initiate a derivative action without any prior request.[41] It should be noted that the 'wrongdoings' mentioned before could have been committed by directors, supervisors[42] and other senior officers of a company as well as outsiders to the company who infringe the lawful rights and interests of the company.[43]

#### 2.3.1.2.2 Standing to Sue

In general, who is qualified to commence a derivative action on behalf of a company depends on the type of the company involved in the lawsuit. There are two main types of companies under Chinese law—limited liability companies (LLCs) and joint stock limited companies (JSLC).[44] In a LLC, all shareholders are eligible to initiate a derivative action, while in a JSLC only those who separately or aggregately hold one percent or more of the total shares in the company for more than 180 consecutive days are entitled to file a derivative lawsuit.[45] Given that, it can be said that the law imposes stricter requirements for shareholders of JSLCs to launch derivative lawsuits.[46]

[39]The CL 2014 provides that eligible shareholders in a derivative action only include (a) in a joint stock limited company, shareholders who separately or aggregately hold 1% or more of the total shares of the company; (b) in a limited liability company, all shareholders are eligible to commence a derivative action.

[40]Article 150 provides when performing their duties, directors, supervisors and senior managers should comply with laws, administrative regulations and the company's articles of association. If their illegal behaviors cause losses to the company, they should be held liable for such losses.

[41]The emergency case refers to a circumstance that the failure to bring up a derivative action will cause unrecoverable damages to the company.

[42]Companies must establish a board of supervisors (for small-scaled companies with a small number of shareholders, one or two supervisors without a 'board' form is also allowed under Chinese law). Supervisors must be selected representatives from shareholders and the staffs of the company. No directors and senior officers of the company could be selected as supervisors (article 117 of PRC company law 2014).

[43]Article 151 of CL 2014 defines the scope of defendants in derivative actions.

[44]The formation and operation of these two types of companies differ. Generally, requirements regarding the formation of a JSLC are more that those when a LLC is established. Issues concerning LLCs are provided in this chapter and Chap. 3 of CL 2014, and Chaps. 4 and 5 present statutory provisions regarding JSLCs.

[45]Article 151 of CL 2014.

[46]See Hui Huang, 'The statutory Derivative Action in China: Critical Analysis and Recommendations for Reform', *Berkeley Business Law Journal* (2007), Volume 4, 227, p. 236.

An important reason can be identified to account for the different standing rules is that the risk of strike suits in the case of a LLC might be lower than that in a JSLC where a third party can purchase shares more easily to become a shareholder just for the purpose of obtaining the standing to sue.[47] Moreover, disgruntled shareholders can easily leave JSLCs by selling their shares in the stock market while due to the closely-held nature of LLCs, a consent from at least half of all shareholders is required prior to a member selling his shares.[48] Furthermore, compared to LLCs, the performance of JSLCs is supervised by various regulatory authorities, such as the China Securities Regulatory Commission (CSRC) and relevant stock exchanges.[49] Therefore, improving corporate governance by derivative actions might be more relevant to LLCs than to JSLCs.[50] Empirical research has found that from 2006 to 2011, the number of derivative actions brought against directors in LLCs is much higher than that of derivative lawsuits involving JSLCs.[51]

#### 2.3.1.2.3 Demand Requirement

Article 151 of CL 2014 sets out the preconditions that should be met prior to the commencement of a derivative lawsuit by providing that:

> If a director or senior manager is under the circumstances as mentioned in article 149[52] of this law.....eligible shareholders may require the board of supervisors or the supervisor of LLCs with no board of supervisors in writing to file a lawsuit in the court. If the supervisor is under the circumstance as stated in article 149 of this Law, qualified shareholders may require the board of directors or the executive director of LLCs with no board of directors in writing to initiate a lawsuit in the court.
>
> ........
>
> If the board of supervisors, or supervisor of a LLC with no board of supervisors, or the board of directors or the executive director refuses to file a lawsuit after it/he receives a written request as mentioned above, or if it/he fails to initiate a lawsuit within 30 days after it receives the request, or if, in an emergency, the failure to lodge a lawsuit immediately will cause unrecoverable damages to the interests of the company, qualified shareholders may, on their own behalf, directly file a lawsuit in the court.[53]

---

[47]Limitations on stock transfer in a JSLC are only for directors and senior managers but not for general shareholders. But the stock transfer to an outside person in a LLC needs to get the consent of half of the shareholders (article 71 of CL 2014).

[48]Article 71(2) of CL 2014.

[49]See Hui Huang, 'The statutory Derivative Action in China: Critical Analysis and Recommendations for Reform', *Berkeley Business Law Journal* (2007), Volume 4, 227, p. 236.

[50]See Hui Huang, 'The statutory Derivative Action in China: Critical Analysis and Recommendations for Reform', Berkeley Bus. LJ 4 (2007), 227, p. 236.

[51]From 2006 to 2011, only two derivative actions sued directors of JSLCs. See Dan Wang, *Theoretical analysis on shareholders' derivative actions*, (in Chinese) (公司派生诉讼论), (China legal publishing house, 2012), p. 325; It should be indicated that the argument that there is a greater need of derivative actions for LLCs that that for JSLCs could not be provided as the only reason to explain the disequilibrium. For other reasons, see *infra* 4.4.

[52]Article 149 of CL 2014 provides that directors, supervisors and senior managers should make compensation where they violate laws, administrative regulations or the articles of association and the interests of the company are infringed because of violation.

[53]Article 151 of CL 2014.

According to these statutory requirements, eligible shareholders could lodge a derivative action after making a demand to the board of directors, or otherwise they should demonstrate that any delay in bringing the lawsuit would cause irreparable damage to the company,[54] which means that the derivative action is the last resort only applied when all internal remedies are exhausted.[55,56]

However, it is found that these rules might be problematic. According to preconditions provided in article 151, eligible shareholders could commence a derivative action after the demand is refused by the company or the company does not respond to the shareholders' application. The law does not give an answer to the question—if the company refuses the demand in order to prevent a strike suit, whether the shareholder could still bring a derivative lawsuit after the rejection. In light of the statutory provisions, unless the company brings the action by itself, it cannot stop a suit from being brought even though it is a case without merits.[57] Even though an unmeritorious case can be rejected after the court's investigation, it might waste judicial resources and might hurt the company's reputation. In this regard, it is suggested if a derivative action brought in a court was previously refused by a company, the court should be informed of the reasons of the rejection, be provided with relevant evidence and take them into account.

#### 2.3.1.3 Problems and Recommendations for Reform

##### 2.3.1.3.1 The Issue of Legal Expenses

The functioning of the derivative lawsuit could be largely impacted by litigation costs. Litigation costs of a derivative action may be high given its commercial

[54]See Flora Xiao Huang, 'shareholder revolt? The statutory derivative action in China', *Comparative Research in Law & Political Economy. Research Paper No. 49/2009.* p. 9 http://digitalcommons.osgoode.yorku.ca/clpe/157 (accessed on 10 August 2016).

[55]Ibid.

[56]Preconditions for the filing of a derivative lawsuit could also be found in other jurisdictions. For instance, the American law similarly provides that prior to the initiation of a derivative action, demand needs to be made on the company (Rule 23.1 of the Federal Rules of Civil Procedure); Normally, a company is allowed to make a decision within 90 days after receiving the shareholder's demand. But if the shareholder can prove that the delay would generate unrecoverable damages to the company, the period could be shorter (Section 7.42 of Model Business Corporation Act. This act does not have mandatory effect but many states have adopted this rule, such as, Connecticut, Iowa, Michigan). The Australian law similarly provides that at least 14 days before an application of a derivative lawsuit is granted by the court, the shareholder applicant must give a written notice to the company of the intention and reasons why the application is made, in order to screen out vexatious or frivolous suits (Section 237(2) of Australian Corporation Act 2001), for the Australian case, see also Hui Huang, 'The statutory Derivative Action in China: Critical Analysis and Recommendations for Reform', Berkeley Bus. LJ 4 (2007), 227, p., p. 239. And see P.M. Choo, *'The Statutory Derivative Action in Singapore: a Critical and Comparative Examination'* (2001) 13 Bond L. Rev. 64, pp. 72–73.

[57]Hui Huang, 'Shareholder Derivative Litigation in China: Empirical Findings and Comparative Analysis', *Banking and Finance Law Review*, (2012), Volume 27, 619, p. 639.

nature.[58,59] Generally, litigation expenses for a derivative lawsuit are composed of at least two parts: the court's charges (including the case acceptance fees paid to the court before the suit and the case application fees incurred during or after the hearing of the case) and the lawyer's fees.[60] Thus, a rational would-be shareholder plaintiff in a derivative lawsuit would take the success rate of the case, the risk involved and the legal costs into consideration when deciding whether or not to file such a lawsuit.

In addition to that, according to article 29 of *Measures on the Payment of Litigation Costs* (2006), the losing party should be liable for the winning party's litigation costs excluding lawyer's fees.[61] Considering that, the prospective shareholder plaintiff's concern about high litigation costs may be further enhanced. In fact, even if the shareholder plaintiff finally wins the case, the lawyer's fees, which might be a considerable amount of money, should be borne by himself. What could be even worse is that the successful shareholder plaintiff may suffer from substantial financial losses if the defendant goes bankrupt or refuses to pay back the court charges.[62] Under this circumstance, the winning shareholder plaintiff should plead for an obligatory enforcement of the court's judgment, but the cost of such a pleading should be paid by the shareholder.[63]

From the perspective of the monetary benefits brought by a successful shareholder lawsuit, it is an essential feature of derivative actions that the recoveries, actually belong to the company rather than the shareholder plaintiff.[64] But nevertheless it is the plaintiff who faces a substantial financial risk when commencing a derivative claim, which is disproportion to the benefits. Therefore, from the perspective of cost-and-benefit analysis, plaintiffs lack direct incentives to bring a derivative action because they 'have nothing to gain, but much to lose'.[65] In order to make derivative actions function, funding from other sources must be obtained.

With regards to funding issues of derivative actions, article 35 of the Fourth Judicial Interpretation of the Supreme People's Court on Some Issues Regarding

---

[58]According to the calculation method under Chinese civil procedure rule, litigation expenses are generally proportionate to the value of the dispute. See article 13 of the Measures on the Payment of Litigation Costs (2006).

[59]Why litigation costs for a derivative action is high is explained in *infra* 3.1.1 (Costs arising).

[60]See *infra* 3.1.1 (costs arising).

[61]It could be understood as a partial cost-shifting rule. For further discussions, see *infra* Part II, Chapter I 2 ('the cost-shifting rule').

[62]See Flora Xiao Huang, 'shareholder revolt? The statutory derivative action in China', *Comparative Research in Law & Political Economy. Research Paper No. 49/2009.* p. 9 http://digitalcommons.osgoode.yorku.ca/clpe/157 (accessed on 10 August 2016).

[63]Article 10 of the Measures on the Payment of Litigation Costs (2006).

[64]The shareholder plaintiffs just benefit from the recoveries through an indirect way. For example, the derivative suit may correct wrongdoings of the directors and promote the corporate governance, thus the probable rise of the share value in the stock market is beneficial to all shareholders of the company.

[65]*Wallersteiner v. Moir (No.2)* [1975] QB 373, at 392.

the Application of PRC Company Law, Consultation Paper 2016 stated that the shareholder plaintiffs could be indemnified by the company if the case is won under the court's discretion. The proposal in this consultation paper might be helpful to solve the funding problems confronted with prospective shareholder claimants in derivative lawsuit, but the problem is the consultation paper did not mention under what circumstances the court could order the company to indemnify the claimant.

#### 2.3.1.3.2 Shareholder Derivative Actions or Shareholder Direct Actions

The 2014 CL also grants the shareholders the right to bring a direct lawsuit when his legal right or interest is infringed. Article 22 and article 152 of CL 2014[66] are both concerned with shareholder direct actions.

##### 2.3.1.3.2.1 Claims for Nullification

Article 22 provides that

> The resolution of the shareholders' meeting, shareholders' general meeting or board of directors of a company violating any law or administrative regulation should be invalid.
>
> If the procedure for convening or the method of voting at a shareholders' meeting, shareholders' general meeting or meeting of the board of directors violates any law, administrative regulations or the company's articles of association, a shareholder may, within 60 days as of the day when the resolution is made, request the people's court to revoke it.
>
> If a shareholder brings a lawsuit in accordance with the preceding paragraph, the people's court may, at the request of the company, require that the shareholder provide financial guarantee.
>
> .........

According to article 22, shareholders can commence a lawsuit to nullify and withdraw a void[67] or voidable resolution[68] of the shareholders' meeting or that of the board of directors. But whether or not such judicial requests should be based on the fact that interests (including the shareholders' interests and the company's interests) are infringed by the defective resolution is not mentioned in the law. In fact, article 22 only grants shareholders the right to request the court to nullify defective resolutions.[69] If such defective resolution causes damages to the company or the shareholders, a claim for damages may not be brought under article 22.[70] Therefore, the function of article 22 is not concerned with redress of damages.

---

[66]Article 22 of CL 2014 is the same with article 22 of CL 2006 and article 111 of CL 1994. And article 152 of CL 2014 is the same as article 153 of CL 2006.

[67]A void resolution refers that the content of the resolution violates mandatory rules (laws and administrative regulations). And this sort of resolution is invalid from its inception.

[68]A voidable resolution means that the formation procedure of this resolution violates laws administrative regulations or the company's articles of association.

[69]See Xiaoning Li, *A comparative study of shareholders' derivative actions: England, the United States, Germany and China*, (Kluwer, 2007), p. 279.

[70]Ibid.

#### 2.3.1.3.2.2 Claims for Compensation (Article 20 and Article 152 of CL 2014)

The shareholder derivative action under article 151 is a lawsuit in which damages are claimed as compensation. Article 152 is also concerned with this issue by stating that

> If any director or senior manager damages the shareholders' interests by violating any law, administrative regulation or the articles of association, the shareholders may file a lawsuit in the people's court.

Compared to article 151 regarding shareholder derivative actions, actions brought under article 152 could be regarded as a direct lawsuit. There are no procedural preconditions to be met for such a direct lawsuit prior to its commencement. However, several practical problems arise because article 152 is not clear enough. For example, it does not indicate what kinds of infringement of shareholders' interests could generate a cause of a direct action. When a company's interests are harmed and shareholders suffer indirect losses, is it feasible for the shareholder to initiate a direct lawsuit under article 152?[71] In a comparative perspective, it is found that shareholders' reflective losses are usually not regarded as a tenable ground on which a direct lawsuit could be brought. Generally, under this circumstance, a shareholder derivative action must be initiated for the redress of shareholders' reflective losses.[72] Considering that, the CL 2014 should have made a clear distinction between shareholder derivative actions (article 151) and shareholder direct actions (article 152), indicating on the base of which kinds of infringement a given lawsuit can be commenced. But the law is not that clear on this issue.

The second problem is that article 152 states that a direct suit could only be brought where the shareholder's interests are infringed by the company's directors or senior managers. If a controlling shareholder not holding the position as a director or a senior manager harms the shareholder's interests, a direct suit cannot be initiated under article 152 against the guilty controlling shareholder, which may lead to the result that the shareholder who is the victim of another shareholder cannot redress his loss through the courts.[73]

#### 2.3.1.3.2.3 Conclusion

Through the comparison between derivative actions and direct actions under CL 2014, dilemmas can be found. As indicated before, when a shareholder's personal interests are infringed by the controlling shareholders, he is not able to bring a lawsuit against the wrongdoers to claim for compensation. CL 2014 only provides in article 20(2) that:

---

[71] See Li Xiaoning, *A comparative study of shareholders' derivative actions: England, the United States, Germany and China*, (Kluwer, 2007), p. 280.

[72] *Johnson v Gore Wood & Co* [2002] 2 AC 1 at 19.

[73] Under this condition, it is also not feasible for the harmed shareholder to commence a derivative action because his own interests instead of the company's are infringed by the controlling shareholder.

> Where the abuse of shareholders' rights causes any loss to the company or other shareholders, such abusive shareholder shall be liable for compensation in accordance with the law.

It could be found in article 20(2) that it does not explicitly grant the injured shareholder the right to commence an action. A lawsuit cannot be brought under article 20(2) when an infringed minority shareholder is oppressed by a majority one. And also, in this case, a derivative action is not applicable because the loss of the shareholder's personal interests is not a cause of a derivative action.

CL 2014, subsequent judicial interpretations and consultation paper do not clearly mention the distinctions between derivative actions and direct actions.[74] It is very vague under what circumstances a derivative action or a direct action could be brought. As indicated in the last section, the American case law draws the distinctions between derivative actions and direct ones mainly based on the 'special injury' test,[75] meaning that a claim could be commenced without showing an injury or breach of duty to the corporation should be treated as a direct lawsuit.[76] Furthermore, the American Law Institute (ALI) also points out that an action cannot be a direct one if all of the shareholders are equally affected by the infringement.[77] Sometimes, both the company and the individual shareholder suffer an injury at the same time and it is not easy to distinguish one from the other. Under this condition, an additional 'special duty' test could be used—to whom the defendant owes the duties?[78] For instance, when the defendants are directors or senior managers of the company, it is particularly important to identify the party to whom the defendants owed the relevant duty, because they own duties to both the company as an entity and to the shareholders as individuals.[79] In this regard, Chap. 6 of the CL 2014 is concerned with the duties of directors and senior managers owed to the company,

---

[74]Three judicial interpretations and one consultation paper on CL were issued in 2006 (available in http://vip.chinalawinfo.com/newlaw2002/slc/slc.asp?db=chl&gid=219133), 2008 (available in http://vip.chinalawinfo.com/newlaw2002/slc/slc.asp?db=chl&gid=219131), 2010 (available in http://vip.chinalawinfo.com/newlaw2002/slc/slc.asp?db=chl&gid=219132) and 2016 (consultation paper) (http://www.legaldaily.com.cn/index_article/content/2016-04/12/content_6583564.htm?node=5955) respectively (in Chinese, accessed on 16 August 2016).

[75]This test provides if a shareholder alleges a 'special injury', he is entitled to state a direct action. A special injury was alleged if the wrong was inflicted only upon that shareholder or where the shareholder complained of a wrong affecting a particular right. See *Tooley v. Donaldson, Lufkin & Jenrette, Inc.*, 845 A.2d 1031 (Delaware 2004), 1038.

[76]American Law Institute (ALI), *Principles of Corporate Governance: Analysis and Recommendations*, (American Law Institute Publishers, 1994), S6.11.

[77]Ibid.

[78]Stepben M. Bainbridge, *Corporation Law and Economics*, (Foundation Press, New York, 2002) p. 363.

[79]Ibid.

and other shareholders.[80] However, the law elaborates the duties owed to the company by the controlling shareholders, the directors and the senior managers,[81] while their duties owed to the shareholders are rarely touched upon. It is only briefly mentioned that the directors and senior managers of a company are not allowed to harm the shareholder's interests by violating the law, administrative regulations or the articles of association of the company, which is vague. In view of that, it is suggested that the law needs to indicate what kinds of director's duties owed to the shareholders in a clear way rather than stating a general term. Furthermore, it should be noted that certain misconducts can breach duties owed to the company as well as those owed to individual shareholders.[82] For instance, inside trading can violate both a duty owed to the company as an entity and a separate duty owed to the shareholder who is selling their securities.[83]

**2.3.1.3.3 The Practical Development of Derivative Actions (2006–2016) in the Chinese Context**

In addition to the already indicated difficulties, for instance concerning funding, there are other reasons why the practice of derivative actions is up till now not a great success in China. The unique Chinese judicial system and social background also account for the 'failure' of derivative actions.[84] For instance, the lack of judicial independence means that the courts are hardly shielded from the influences of the local government and the Communist Party, making it difficult for the court to independently judge derivative actions involving SOEs or significant enterprises.[85] In addition to that, the general resistance of courts to mass litigation may also contribute to the failure of derivative actions. For instance, the SPC issued instructions to lower courts to strictly limit the acceptance of the private securities claims in order to prevent the potential turmoil brought by a mass lawsuit where a group of injured people may join and the result of which may affect the general

---

[80] Article 146–152 of the CL 2014.

[81] For instance, article 148 provides that the directors and the senior managers are not allowed to misappropriate the company's funds.

[82] American Law Institute (ALI), *Principles of Corporate Governance: Analysis and Recommendations*, (American Law Institute Publishers, 1994), S7.01(c).

[83] Ibid.

[84] See Donald C. Clarke and Nicholas C. Howson, 'Pathway to minority shareholder protection: derivative actions in the People's Republic of China', in Dan W. Puchniak, Harald Baum and Michael Ewing-Chow (eds), *The derivative action in Asia: a comparative and functional approach*, (Cambridge University Press, 2012), 243.

[85] If a derivative action involved a highly profitable enterprise in a given region, the court might be reluctant to side with shareholder plaintiffs. Because the local government may attach much importance to the tax turned by this enterprise, and may interfere any negative decision on the enterprise by the court. See *infra* 4.4.3 ('typical characteristics and deficiencies in Chinese judicial system').

public in a given area.[86,87] Additionally, the court may not be willing to hear the derivative lawsuit even when it has not been explicitly prohibited by these legal documents. In theory, a derivative action could be filed by an individual shareholder, however, in fact, the result of a derivative lawsuit may influence the interests of a large number of shareholders even if they are not nominal plaintiffs.[88] Since in China, including in the courts, a lot of importance is attached to 'the harmonious society', this may be why the Chinese courts were not active in hearing corporate and securities cases.[89]

#### 2.3.1.4 Summary

In China the introduction of derivative actions was as such a milestone in corporate governance and shareholder protection. Nevertheless, as the comparative overview in this section has made clear, having statutory rules on derivative actions as such is of course no guarantee of their effectiveness as a governance mechanism. We criticised several statutory rules regarding derivative actions in China. For example, the demand requirements in article 151 of the CL 2014. It provides that eligible

[86]Supreme People's court's notice on temporarily not accepting securities cases involving civil suits for damages, ('最高人民法院关于涉证券民事赔偿案件暂不予受理的通知'), issued on September 21st, 2001, available at www.law-lib.com/law/law_view.asp?id=16373 (accessed on 10 August 2016); Also see Supreme People's court's notice on issues relating to the acceptance of civil cases in tort arising out of false representations in securities markets, ('最高人民法院关于受理证券市场因虚假陈述引发的民事纠纷案件有关问题的通知'), issued on January 15th, 2002, available at www.law-lib.com/law/law_view.asp?id=16956 (accessed on 10 August 2016); And see Supreme People's court's several provisions on the adjudication of civil suits for damages arising out of false representations in securities markets, ('最高人民法院关于审理证券市场因虚假陈述引发的民事赔偿案件的若干规定'), issued on January 9th, 2003, available at www.law-lib.com/law/law_view.asp?id=42438 (accessed on 10 August 2016); One judicial document issued in May 2007 has to be mentioned is that it guided the courts internally to broaden the scope of permissible claims to include market manipulation and inside trading, however, other procedure hurdles established by the aforementioned documents still apply, see Peixin Luo, Difficulties over whether to eliminate or keep the precondition procedure, ('前置程序去留困境'), Caijing (Finance), 19(2007), 28.

[87]The concept of 'harmonious society' (和谐社会) is highly valued in Chinese society. Thus, a lawsuit with lots of participants is, normally, thought to have the potential for turmoil. See Supreme People's Court, *Notice of the Supreme People's Court on Issuing Some Opinions of the Supreme People's Court about Providing Judicial Protection for the Construction of Socialist Harmonious Society*, (in Chinese), (最高人民法院关于为构建社会主义和谐社会提供司法保障的若干意见), (2007-01-15).

[88]Donald C. Clarke and Nicholas C. Howson, 'Pathway to minority shareholder protection: derivative actions in the People's Republic of China', in Dan W. Puchniak, Harald Baum and Michael Ewing-Chow (eds), *The derivative action in Asia: a comparative and functional approach*, (Cambridge University Press, 2012), 243, pp. 279–280.

[89]See Xin Tang, 'Protecting Minority Shareholders in China: A Task for Both Legislation and Enforcement', in Hideki Kanda, Kon-sik Kim, and Curtis Milhaupt (eds.), *Transforming Corporate Governance in East Asia* (New York: Routledge, 2008), pp. 141–167.

shareholders may commence a derivative action after the demand is refused by the company or the company does not respond to the shareholders' application. But the law does not indicate whether the shareholder could still bring a derivative lawsuit after the company's rejection. According to article 151, unless the company brings the action by itself, it cannot stop a suit from being brought even though it is a case without merits. Another problem is the unclear criteria in China to distinguish between direct actions and derivative actions. Rules about shareholder direct actions are mainly incorporated in article 20 and article 152 of the CL 2014. The former one is about the injunctive relief (in particular to nullify a resolution of a shareholders' meeting) while the latter one is dealing with claims for damages (i.e. a shareholder's interests are infringed and causes monetary losses to him). Article 152 only provides that if the shareholder's interests were infringed by the board of directors or senior managers, a direct action against the wrongdoers could be commenced by the victim. The problem is if a controlling shareholder, who does not hold the position of director or senior managers, infringes a minority shareholder's interests, article 152 does not grant the victim the right to sue the wrongdoer directly. In this case, obviously, the victim cannot launch a derivative lawsuit because the individual shareholder but not the company suffers losses. The second problem of article 152 is that it does not indicate what kinds of infringement of shareholders' interests could generate a cause of a direct action. The law does not mention if a shareholder suffers reflective losses, he can initiate a direct or a derivative lawsuit, which might create uncertainty in practice.

As the law stands now, derivate actions cannot really become a success in China. Except for the problems in statutory rules in the CL 2014, the lack of effective funding ways also contributes to the failure of derivative actions. Shareholder plaintiffs (particularly minority ones) need to pay lots of money to sustain an expensive derivative action. But on the other hand, damages created in a successful case belong to the company but not the shareholder plaintiffs. They would only indirectly benefit from remedies through the potential rise in the share price on a *pro rata* basis. However, in light of the shareholder's (except for majority ones) small stakes in the company, in financial terms, an economically rational shareholder may not be incentivized to launch a shareholder derivative claim. In addition to that, a prospective shareholder claimant may have strong incentives to leave the claim for someone else to sue after being aware that the company and other shareholders will free ride on his efforts.[90] However, the latest Fourth Judicial Interpretation of the Supreme People's Court on Some Issues Regarding the Application of PRC Company Law, Consultation Paper 2016 proposed a model under which the shareholder plaintiffs could be indemnified by the company if the case is won under the court's discretion. But further details such as under what

[90]Arad Reisberg, *Derivative Actions and Corporate Governance: Theory and Operation*, (Oxford University Press, 2007), pp. 222–223.

circumstances such indemnification could be awarded to the shareholder plaintiff are not mentioned in the consultation paper.

Additionally, problems are also caused by the unique judicial system and social background in China. For example, the lack of judicial independence makes it difficult for the court to independently judge a derivative action involving SOEs or significant enterprises. Moreover, there is general resistance of the courts to mass litigation. The court may not be willing to hear derivative action cases as such cases may be likely to break the principle of 'maintaining the harmonious society' held by the Chinese society and judicial system. In fact, Chinese courts are not proactive in hearing corporate and securities cases.

## 2.3.2 *Shareholder Derivative Actions in the United Kingdom*

### 2.3.2.1 The Traditional *Foss* Rule and Its Exceptions

In the UK, the traditional common law derivative actions were developed from the *Foss v. Harbottle* rule and its exceptions. The main principle of this rule was where a wrong is done to a company, only the company per se was considered to be the proper plaintiff to bring a lawsuit to redress losses (the proper principal rule). An individual shareholder could bring a derivative claim in exceptional situations.[91] In fact, the *Foss* rule received quite a lot of criticism.[92] The most significant criticism was that this rule scarcely grants minority shareholders any effective mechanisms to protect themselves or the company, and to discipline corporate governance.[93] In view of that, the introduction of statutory derivative actions in the UK was suggested. Currently, the rules governing statutory derivative actions are incorporated in Part 11 of the UK Companies Act 2006 (CA 2006), under which a member of a company could commence, under certain conditions, a derivative action against the directors in case of negligence, default, breaches of duties or breaches of trust.[94] The shareholder plaintiff in the action should, at the time when the conduct being challenged took place, have been a member of the company.[95]

---

[91]For example, the 'wrong control' exception, which allows the shareholder to commence a derivative action in the event that the company was controlled by the wrongdoers. For more exceptions to the *Foss* rule, see Xiaoning Li, *A comparative study of shareholders' derivative actions: England, the United States, Germany and China*, (Kluwer, 2007), pp. 23–27.

[92]See Gower & Davies, *Principles of Modern Company Law*, (Sweet&Maxwell, 2012), pp. 647–648.

[93]Ibid.

[94]Section 260(3) of CA 2006.

[95]Section 260(4) of CA 2006.

#### 2.3.2.2 The Legal Framework of Statutory Derivative Actions Under the CA 2006

Rules regarding statutory derivative actions in CA 2006 reflects the recommendations of the Law Commission that 'a new statutory derivative procedure with more modern, flexible and accessible criteria for determining whether a shareholder can pursue an action'.[96,97] In line with this recommendation, statutory derivative actions will only be available in case of negligence, default, breaches of duties or breaches of trust by a director of the company,[98] even if the director does not benefit from these conducts personally.[99] On top of that, plaintiffs in a derivative action should demonstrate that the director committing misbehaviours substantially controls the company.[100]

##### 2.3.2.2.1 Standing to Sue

CA 2006 indicates who are entitled to commence a derivative claim. Only the members of a company are entitled to launch a derivative claim.[101] A former member of the company cannot initiate such an action even if the issued complained of was occurred during his membership.[102] However, it should be noted that there is an important statutory extension of the notion of 'member'.[103] Even though a person has not entered into the registration procedure to officially become the company's member, he could also be considered to hold a valid membership to bring a derivative action if his shares have been transferred or transmitted by operation of law (for instance, through succession).[104] According to section 260 of CA 2006, a member of the company could bring a derivative action where the alleged wrongdoing arose before he enters into the company.[105]

##### 2.3.2.2.2 Permission to Continue: A Three-Step Test

Previously, under the regime of common law derivative actions, the criteria used in determining whether a claim can be brought before the court is vague. The commencement of a derivative claim relied on the exceptions to the *Foss* rule. The only important exception of that rule was 'fraud on the minority', under which individual shareholders are allowed to bring an action on behalf of the company.[106]

---

[96]See Law Commission, Shareholder Remedies (LC 246), para. 6.15.

[97]The Foss rule is not used in practice. See Gower & Davies, Principles of Modern Company Law, (Sweet&Maxwell, 2012), p. 654.

[98]Section 260 (3) of CA 2006.

[99]See Saleem Sheikh, *A guide to the Companies Act 2006*, (Routledge-Cavendish publisher, 2007), p. 1043.

[100]For instance, the director controls the decision-making procedure. Ibid.

[101]Section 260 of the CA 2006.

[102]Ibid.

[103]See Gower & Davies, Principles of Modern Company Law, (Sweet&Maxwell, 2012), p. 655.

[104]Section 260(5)(c) of the CA 2006.

[105]Section 260(4) of the CA 2006.

[106]See Zhong Zhang, *The derivative action and good corporate governance in China: Economic theories and legal rules*, (Lambert Academic Publishing, 2011), p. 114.

'Fraud on the minority' contains two elements: fraud and wrongdoers control.[107] It means that a shareholder can bring a derivative action only if the complained wrongdoing should be a fraud and meanwhile the wrongdoers substantially control the company.[108] Moreover, it must be stated that the wrong here is actually done to the company, but not to the individual shareholder. However, unfortunately, those requirements are vague under English common law.[109]

In order to make the rules clear, the Law Commission proposed to reform shareholder derivative actions. Generally, it was suggested that the court has the power to decide whether a shareholder could lodge a derivative action by considering:

> (1) whether the shareholder is in good faith; (2) whether the action would be in the interest of the company; (3) whether the alleged wrong has been, or may be, approved by the company at a general meeting; (4) whether the general meeting has resolved not to pursue the wrong; (5) the views of an independent organ; and (6) the availability of alternative remedies.[110]

In addition, it was also suggested that ratification of a wrongdoing by a shareholders' meeting could bar the commencement of a derivative action, unless this shareholders' meeting was under the support or the influence of wrongdoers.[111]

In fact, these reform proposals were largely accepted by the CA 2006. Under the current law, a shareholder intending to bring a derivative action has to apply to the court for permission to continue the action.[112] The factors which should be taken into consideration by the courts in deciding whether to grant a leave to the action are mainly consistent with those recommendations proposed by the Law Commission.[113] All breaches of directors' duties generate causes of actions, unless there was an actual authorization or ratification.[114] The authorization or ratification is valid only if it is made by a shareholder's meeting without the influence of directors who allegedly committed misbehaviours and persons that may involve in such misconducts.[115]

---

[107]Ibid.

[108]*Prudential Assurance Co. Ltd. v. Newman Industries Ltd.* (No.2) (the Court of Appeal), [1982] Ch. 204, at 210F-211B.

[109]See Xiaoning Li, *A comparative study of shareholders' derivative actions: England, the United States, Germany and China*, (Kluwer, 2007), p. 19.

[110]See Law Commission, Shareholder Remedies (LC 246), para. 6.75–6.92.

[111]See DTI, *Modern company law for a competitive economy: completing the structure,* (London, DTI, 2000), para. 7.46.

[112]Section 260 (1) of the CA 2006.

[113]Section 263 of the CA 2006.

[114]Section 263 (2) of the CA 2006.

[115]Section 239 (3) & 239 (4) of the CA 2006.

Regarding the leave granted by the court, the CA 2006 formulates a three-stage test.[116] First, the plaintiff must present evidence to demonstrate there is a *prima facie* case. Otherwise, the claim will be dismissed by the court.[117] For the second stage, the court carries out a higher degree of judicial scrutiny.[118] Permission must be refused by the court at the second stage if the defendant performed his duty in line with section 172 of CA 2006[119] to promote the general success of the company.[120] Or, if the issue in question was ratified or authorized in a proper way,[121] the application by the claimant will not be accepted by the court.[122] In the event the claim can overcome the first two tests, the court will then take into the six factors listed in section 263 (3) of the CA 2006 into consideration to decide whether the claim should proceed.[123]

At the first stage, the main question is what kind of standard should be adopted by the court to decide the claim is a *prima facie* one. The CA 2006 does not provide any concrete rules in this respect. While in the case law, a typical example is the *Wishart v. Castlecroft Securities Ltd.*[124] case, in which the Scottish Court of Session (Inner House) appeared to place a low threshold for the plaintiff by indicating:

> The question is not whether the application and supporting evidence disclose a *prima facie* case against the defendant, but whether there is no *prima facie* case disclosed for granting the application for permission. And on onus is placed on the claimant to satisfy the court that there a *prima facie* case: rather, the court is to refuse the application if it is satisfied that there is not a *prima facie* case.[125]

---

[116]See Victor Joffe, David Drake, Giles Richardson and Daniel Lightman, *Minority shareholders, law, practice and procedure*, (Oxford University Press, 2011), p. 46.

[117]Section 261(2) of the CA 2006.

[118]See A.M. Gray, 'The statutory derivative claim, an outmoded superfluousness', *Company Lawyer*, (2012), Volume 33(10), 295, p. 297.

[119]Section 172 of CA 2006 explains what constitutes duty to promote the success of the company.

[120]Section 263(2)(a) of the CA 2006.

[121]Section 239(3) & 239(4) of the CA 2006.

[122]Section 263(2)(b) of CA 2006.

[123]Section 263(3) of CA 2006. The six consideration factors include: (a) whether the member is acting in good faith in seeking to continue the claim; (b) the importance that a person acting in accordance with section 172 (duty to promote the success of the company) would attach to continuing it; (c) where the cause of action results from an act or omission that is yet to occur, whether the act or omission could be, and in the circumstances would be likely to be—(i) authorized by the company before it occurs, or (ii) ratified by the company after it occurs; (d) where the cause of action arises from an act or omission that has already occurred, whether the act or omission could be, and in the circumstances would be likely to be, ratified by the company; (e) whether the company has decided not to pursue the claim; (f) whether the act or omission in respect of which the claim is brought gives rise to a cause of action that the member could pursue in his own right rather than on behalf of the company.

[124]*Wishart v. Castlecroft Securities Ltd.* [2010] BCC 161.

[125]*Wishart v. Castlecroft Securities Ltd.* [2010] BCC 161, per Lord Reed Opinion at 31.

In contrast, in *Iesini v. Westrip Holdings Ltd*,[126] a stricter standard was used.[127] Lewison J pointed out that two aspects had to be satisfied simultaneously in order to prove a *prima facie* claim[128]: the company should have a good cause of action; and the cause of action arises from a directors' default or a breach of duty.[129]

In light of that, whether the claimant will overcome the first stage seems to depend largely on the standard employed by the court. In this regard, it is supposed that the English court would be cautious to grant the leave for the claimant because a conservative manner has been applied for long by the English courts.[130]

For the second stage, one of the major concerns is about the ratifiable wrongdoings.[131] It means that a ratifiable wrongdoing that has not actually been ratified will no longer generate a bar to the filing of a derivative action. Even though the court is required to take into account the possibility that the wrongdoing will be ratified by the company, such possibility could not be regarded as a block to the commencement of a derivative action.[132] Furthermore, not all wrongdoings that have been ratified by the company will definitely constitute a bar to a derivative action.[133] Ratification will be invalid if it concerns certain misbehaviours, such as expropriation of the company's property by the majority.[134]

Furthermore, section 239 of the CA 2006 highlights the issues regarding ratification.[135] To ratify a director's negligence, default, a breach of duty or a breach of trust (causes of a statutory derivative action), the votes of the persons who are personally interested in this ratification should be excluded. Given that, the requirements for achieving a valid ratification become stricter, and it seems that

---

[126] *Iesini v. Westrip Holdings Ltd.* [2010] BCC 420.

[127] See Victor Joffe QC et al., Minority shareholders, law, practice and procedure, (Oxford University Press, 2011), p. 48.

[128] *Iesini v. Westrip Holdings Ltd.* [2010] BCC 420. at 75, 81–83.

[129] Ibid.

[130] See Arad Reisberg, 'Corporate law in the UK after recent reforms: the good, the bad, and the ugly', *Current Legal Problems*, (2010), Volume 63(1), 315, p. 349.

[131] See Gower & Davies, Principles of Modern Company Law, (Sweet&Maxwell, 2012), p. 657.

[132] Ibid.

[133] There are a few cases to support this point of view. In *Franbar Holdings Ltd v. Patel* [2008] BCC 885, William Trower QC confirmed that the CA 2006 did not alter the common law position that certain wrongs were unratifiable. In *Eastford Ltd v. Gillespie* [2012] BCC 303, Lord Hodge indicated 'I see nothing in the statutory provisions which suggests that Parliament intended to alter the pre-existing rules on ratification by a board of a director's unauthorized acts' (para. 15).

[134] In *Cook v. Deeks* [1916] 1 AC 554, the directors concluded a contract for the interests of themselves instead of for the company, and tried to ratify their misconduct by proposing resolutions in a general meeting of the company (because the majority votes were held by those directors). In the case, the Privy Council indicated that the resolutions, which had been passed by virtue of the votes of the wrongdoers who held a majority of the votes, were not valid. *Cook v. Deeks* [1916] 1 AC 554, at 564.

[135] See Victor Joffe QC et al., *Minority shareholders, law, practice and procedure*, (Oxford University Press, 2011), pp. 27–28.

those directors committing wrongdoings are not able to make use of the ratification procedure any longer.

**2.3.2.2.3 Procedural Innovations in Section 262 and 264 of the CA 2006**

Section 262, for the first time, innovatively permits a member of a company to apply for permission to continue a claim, which has been brought by the company, as a derivative action under several circumstances.[136] The cause of this derivative action commenced by the shareholder is identical to that of the previous action brought by the company. Additionally, section 264 permits a member to apply for permission to continue a derivative action brought or continued by another member under certain conditions.[137]

The main purposes of these two innovative procedural devices in the CA 2006 could be summarized as follows

(i) The goal is to preclude the possibility that a company not having a real intention of achieving a proper resolution brings up an action with a purpose to prevent its members from commencing a derivative action.[138]

(ii) Another goal is to prevent a member of the company, who is not *bona fide*, from bringing a derivative action just with the purpose to stop another member from initiating the action, or to allow another member of the company to continue the derivative action in some circumstances.[139] For example, if the member who brought the action is in short of funding to support the court proceeding, another member would be permitted to continue the action.

### 2.3.2.3 Comments on the Statutory Derivative Actions Under the CA 2006

Before the enactment of the CA 2006 which allows statutory derivative actions, the common law derivative actions actually did not effectively discipline corporate

---

[136]Section 262(2) provides that the member of a company may apply to the court for permission to continue the action as a derivative on the ground that: (a) the manner in which the company commenced or continued the claim amounts to an abuse of the process of the court; (b) the company has failed to prosecute the claim diligently; and (c) it is appropriate for the member to continue the claim as a derivative claim.

[137]Those conditions provided in section 264 are similar to that in section 262(2). However, as for the first condition, section 264 uses the expression 'the manner in which the proceedings have been commenced or continued by the claimant amounts to an abuse of the process of the court', which has been regarded as a comparatively higher threshold to overcome. See Victor Joffe QC et al., *Minority shareholders, law, practice and procedure*, (Oxford University Press, 2011) p. 61.

[138]See Law Commission, Shareholder Remedies (LC 246), para. 6.63. And in para. 6.63, the Law Commission points out that the reason why they do not want individual shareholders to apply to take over current litigation being pursued by their company is that they are not satisfied with the progress being made.

[139]See Victor Joffe QC et al., Minority shareholders, law, practice and procedure, (Oxford University Press, 2011), p. 62.

management and protect the interests of the company since it was practically difficult to initiate a derivative action under the common law.[140] The introduction of statutory derivative lawsuits in the CA 2006 was expected to facilitate the commencement of derivative actions and make relevant rules more clear and practical. Unlike the vague cause of a common law derivative actions (fraud on the minority), the CA 2006 lists a clear scope of the causes of an action including the director's negligence and breaches of duties.[141] Moreover, the law also facilitates derivative actions by prohibiting the directors from ratifying their own wrongdoings.[142] It is thought that the law provides a delicate balance between promoting corporate governance and shielding director's sound business judgment from liabilities.[143] Counter-arguments, however, state that the law is in favour of protecting directors in the sense that the filing of a derivative action is still subject to 'tight judicial control at all stages'.[144] Shareholder plaintiffs in a derivative claim may still face the traditional suspicion of the English courts.[145] Thus, it is doubted whether the statutory rules succeed in facilitating derivative claims. To further investigate this issue, we first discuss the first stage in the permission procedure–how could a plaintiff prove a *prima facie* case.

**2.3.2.3.1 The Problematic Test of *prima facie* Case at the First Stage**

At this step, the shareholder applicant is required to provide evidence to prove the claim is a *prima facie* case.[146] The main difficulty for the individual shareholder, at this stage, is how to collect information to prove misconducts by directors who are more familiar with the operation of the company than the minority shareholders. It is hard to imagine that minority shareholders could access to the company's key documents (for example, accounting books). In consideration of that, it might be difficult for the shareholder plaintiff to overcome this stage in most of cases.

The criteria applied in proving a *prima facie* case is also criticized to be vague.[147] To what extent a case could be considered as a *prima facie* case? It was indicated that to prove a *prima facie* case was merely required to show that this case

---

[140]See Xiaoning Li, *A comparative study of shareholders' derivative actions: England, the United States, Germany and China*, (Kluwer, 2007), p. 33.

[141]Section 260 of the CA 2006.

[142]Section 239 of the CA 2006 provides that directors are no longer able to vote on their own wrongdoings.

[143]Brenda Hannigan, *Company Law*, (Oxford University Press, 2009), p. 229. David Gibbs, 'Has the statutory claim fulfilled its objectives? A *prima facie* case and the mandatory bar: Part 1', *Company Lawyer*, (2011), 32(2), 41, p. 42.

[144]See Arad Reisberg, 'Corporate law in the UK after recent reforms: the good, the bad, and the ugly', *Current Legal Problems*, (2010), Volume 63(1), 315, p. 348.

[145]Arad Reisberg, 'Shadows of the past and back to the future: Part 11 of the UK Companies Act 2006 (in) action', *European Company and Financial Law Review*, (2009), Volume 6, Issue 2–3, 219, pp. 224–225.

[146]Section 261 of the CA 2006.

[147]Julia Tang, 'Shareholder remedies: demise of the derivative claims?', *UCL Journal of Law and Jurisprudence*, (2012), Volume 1, 178, p. 183.

had more than 0 percent of success.[148] On the other hand, another approach suggested that the shareholder applicant must establish a good cause of action to convince the court that there is a serious question that must be dealt with before the court.[149] The unclear standard in the '*prima facie*' test would easily make the first stage develop into a mini-trial.[150] In view of that, a recent trend is that the English courts try to combine the '*prima facie*' test into the second and third parts of the permission stage.[151]

**2.3.2.3.2 The Ratification and Authorization of the Claimed Wrongdoing**

The CA 2006 provides that a permission to continue a derivative action should be denied in the event that the challenged act has been authorized or ratified by the company. The new law also stresses that interested directors can no longer vote on their own misconducts, which was allowed in the common law regime.[152] This change in the law aims at vanishing the irrational ratification and authorization by wrongdoers.[153] In practice, this approach is, however, only workable in small companies.[154] For large public companies, where proxy vote is widely applied, it might be difficult to identify disinterested members.[155] In *Prudential Assurance Co Ltd. v Newman Industries*,[156] Vinelott J, in first instance, proposed that in a large public company the directors who commit misconducts 'might be able to determine the outcome of a resolution in general meeting in their own favour by the use of proxy votes.'[157] In addition to that, 'shareholder alliance' (shareholders influenced

[148]This doctrine was derived from *Australian Broadcasting Corporation v Lenah Game Meats Pty Ltd*, [2001] 208 CLR 199 (High Court of Australia), see David Gibbs, *'Has the statutory claim fulfilled its objectives?* A *prima facie* case and the mandatory bar: Part 1', Company Lawyer, (2011), 32(2), 41, p. 44.

[149]David Gibbs, *'Has the statutory claim fulfilled its objectives?* A *prima facie* case and the mandatory bar: Part 1', Company Lawyer, (2011), 32(2), 41, p. 44.

[150]See Law Commission, Shareholder remedies, 1996, Consultation Paper No.142, para. 16.22, available at http://lawcommission.justice.gov.uk/docs/cp142_Shareholder_Remedies_Consultation.pdf (accessed on 10 August 2016).

[151]In recent cases, the *prima facie* test was bypassed or telescoped because of its defects. For example, in *Mission Capital plc v Sinclair* [2008] BCC 866, the permission procedure was telescoped into one; In *Franbar Holdings Ltd v Patel* case [2008] BCC 885, counsel for the defendants had accepted that 'it would be appropriate... to deal with the entirety of the application for permission to continue at a single hearing.' See Julia Tang, 'Shareholder remedies: demise of the derivative claims?', *UCL Journal of Law and Jurisprudence*, (2012), Volume 1, 178, pp. 182–183.

[152]Section 239 of the CA 2006.

[153]See J. Paul Sykes, *'The continuing paradox: a critique of minority shareholder and derivative claims under the Companies Act 2006'*, Civil Justice Quarterly, (2010), 29(2), 205–234, p. 223.

[154]In a strict sense, not all small companies could be able to implement this provision. For example, in some family-run companies, most of the members belong to the same family. Therefore, there is usually no clear distinction between interested members and disinterested ones.

[155]See Julia Tang, *'Shareholder remedies: demise of the derivative claims?'*, p. 200.

[156]*Prudential Assurance Co Ltd v Newman Industries* [1981] Ch 257.

[157]*Prudential Assurance Co Ltd v Newman Industries* [1981] Ch 257, at 324.

by wrongdoers) in large public companies is also difficult to be identified, which makes it not easy to find 'disinterested members'.[158]

**2.3.2.3.3 Funding Derivative Actions**

For shareholder plaintiffs (especially, minority ones), how to fund a derivative action is a big concern when they decide whether or not to commence such a lawsuit. Traditionally, the indemnity cost order (the company indemnifies the claimant for the costs incurred in the derivative claim)[159] is assumed to be an effective way to financially assist shareholder plaintiffs. It was, for the first time, illustrated in *Wallersteiner v. Moir (No.2)*,[160] in which the Court of Appeal ordered the company to indemnify Mr. Moir his costs incurred and to be incurred in the forthcoming proceeding. The rationale behind the court's order is that a company should indemnify a plaintiff in a derivative lawsuit because the plaintiff is acting on behalf of the company and the company will directly benefit from a successful suit.[161] The eligibility of this indemnity depends on whether the plaintiff is in good faith and whether the action is for the company's interests.[162] The outcome of the action has no direct impact on the granting of the indemnity. Even if the action is lost, the plaintiff may still be entitled to be indemnified. Generally, the award of an indemnity cost order would be subject to the court's discretion at the permission stage or, under certain circumstances, at the end of the court proceeding.[163] This funding technique could also help to discourage frivolous and unmeritorious claims for the reason that at the very beginning there is no a guarantee for an indemnity cost order.

Rule regarding indemnity cost orders were further illustrated in *Smith v. Croft (No.1)*,[164] where Walton J supposed that the rule of the indemnity cost order formulated in *Wallersteiner v. Moir* was somewhat unfair to the defendant. He further proposed that a plaintiff should only be indemnified provided that he was genuinely in need (a mean test).[165] Along with that, Walton J also clarified the standard of the test by indicating that the court should satisfy that an independent board of directors would consider the action under certain circumstances.[166]

The common law rules about indemnity cost orders also have reflection in the statutory law. The Civil Procedure Rules (Rules and Directions) provide that the court may order a company to indemnify the plaintiff for the costs incurred in the

[158] Pearlie Koh, 'Directors' Fiduciary Duties: Unthreading the Joints of Shareholder Ratification' *Journal of Corporate Law Studies*, (2005), volume 5, 363, p. 389.

[159] Civil Procedure Rule 19.9 E.

[160] *Wallersteiner v. Moir (No.2)* [1975] QB 373.

[161] Zhong Zhang, The derivative action and good corporate governance in China: Economic theories and legal rules, (Lambert Academic Publishing, 2011), p. 204.

[162] Ibid.

[163] *Wallersteiner v. Moir (No.2)* [1975] QB 373, *per* Scarman L.J at 408.

[164] *Smith v. Croft (No.1)* [1986] 2 All ER 551.

[165] *Smith v. Croft (No.1)* [1986] 2 All ER 551, Walton J at 597.

[166] Ibid.

derivative action.[167] However, this provision does not specify any further procedures for the parties and the court to follow, not to mention the conditions or tests for awarding an indemnity cost order. Therefore, guidance is only sought from the common law.[168] In this regard, the CA 2006 does not make any improvements to make the rules of the indemnity cost order more clear and detailed.

#### 2.3.2.4 Summary

As to the development of the English company law, the replacement of the ambiguous standing requirements in the *Foss* rule by provisions in Part 11 of the CA 2006 was a step forward. It was expected that the reform of derivative actions in 2006 could introduce new statutory derivative actions with 'modern, flexible and accessible criteria'. However, as analysed before, problems still exist in the existing statutory derivative action regime. For example, the interpretation of several technical terms at the permission stage remains controversial.[169] Moreover, funding difficulties with derivative claims still remain as burdens for shareholder plaintiffs. Unfortunately, the CA 2006 has not made significant progress in tackling with this issue.

### 2.3.3 *Shareholder Derivative Actions in the United States*

#### 2.3.3.1 Introduction and Development of Shareholder Derivative Actions in the US

In the US, the law regulating derivative actions is incorporated in both state law and federal law. Although rules about derivative actions vary from state to state, several principles are generally accepted. The following sections will try to discuss these general principles and state law (e.g. Delaware law) on derivative actions will be investigated also. To give a comprehensive overview of derivative actions, analysis

---

[167]Rule 19.9 (E) of CPR, available at http://www.justice.gov.uk/courts/procedure-rules/civil/rules/part19#19.9E (accessed on 16 August 2016). This rule indicates that the costs could be indemnified by the company include fees incurred in the permission application or in the course of the derivative claim or both of them.

[168]Recent cases suggest that the English courts, actually, hold a pragmatic attitude towards indemnity costs orders. In *Kiani v Cooper* [2010] BCC 463, Proudman J made a limited indemnity costs order in favour of the applicant, and further proposed that the applicant should undertake part of the litigation risk. *Kiani v Cooper* [2010] BCC 463, Proudman J at 49. See Zhong Zhang, *The derivative action and good corporate governance in China: Economic theories and legal rules*, (Lambert Academic Publishing, 2011), pp. 84–85.

[169]For instance, how to prove a *prima facie* case.

on the rules incorporated in the Model Business Corporation Act (MBCA)[170] and principles suggested in the American Law Institute's Principles of Corporate Governance: Analysis and recommendations (the ALI Principles)[171] will also be examined.[172]

In the course of the development of derivative actions, it could be observed that at the beginning, a lenient approach was applied.[173] However, it did not mean that any shareholder is qualified to bring a derivative action without limits. In fact, the exhaustion of internal remedies had already been considered as an important principle during that period.[174] Prior to launching a derivative lawsuit, the shareholder plaintiff should request the board of directors to correct the alleged wrongdoings.[175] Now it has been established in MBCA and state rules that the shareholder plaintiff is obliged to make a demand on the board of directors before a derivative claim is initiated.[176]

The lenient approach did not continue to dominate in the later development of derivative actions because it gave rise to strike suits.[177] New York became the first state to adopt the 'security-for-expenses' statute, which was enacted to deter strike suits. This rule requires a shareholder or shareholders who do not possess the statutorily required minimum interest in the corporation to post security for expenses, when prosecuting a derivative action.[178] However, this rule did not have the expected effects in the following years. The plaintiffs could easily circumvent it

---

[170]The Model Business Company Act (MBCA) is a model set of law prepared by the Committee on Corporate Laws of the Section of Business Law of the American Bar Association and is followed by twenty-four states. It was created due to variation in how states defined companies after World War II in 1950. The variation and uncertainty resulted in many lawsuits in which a promoter was sued personally for obligations ostensibly incurred in the name of the nascent company. The widespread adoption of the MBCA brought some clarity to such confusion and other corporate law issues. Most states are now guided by the Revised Model Business Company Act (RMBCA), a revised version of the MBCA.

[171]American Law Institute, *Principle of Corporate Governance: Analysis and recommendations*, St. Paul, Minnesota: American Law Institute Publishers (1994).

[172]Although MBCA and ALI's Principles are not law and have no binding effects, they reveal basic principles and rules of corporate law.

[173]George D. Hornstein, 'The Shareholder's Derivative Suit in the United States', *Journal of Business Law*, (1967), 282–289.

[174]In *Dodge v. Woolsey* 18 How. (59 U.S.) 331 (1855), the shareholder plaintiff requested the board of directors to prevent the alleged corporate wrongdoings prior to the filling of the lawsuit. See Xiaoning Li, *A Comparative study of shareholders' derivative actions* (Kluwer, 2007), p. 91.

[175]*Dodge v. Woolsey* 18 How. (59 U.S.) 331, 341–344 (1855).

[176]Section 7.42 of MBCA and Section 327.4.3 of Delaware General Corporation Law.

[177]'Strike suits' refer to claims which were brought without substantial merits in law or in fact, but simply for the benefits from a settlement. See A.J. Boyle, *Minority Shareholders' Remedies*, (Cambridge University Press, Cambridge, 2002), p. 41.

[178]Ralph C. Ferrara, Kevin T. Abikoff and Laura Leedy Gansler, *Shareholder derivative litigation: besieging the board*, (Law Journal Seminars-Press, 2013), Section 4.06.

by pleading a federal cause of action.[179] And also, plaintiffs may urge other shareholders to join in the suit in order to satisfy the percentage threshold.[180] Consequently, by the late 1960s there was a revival of derivative actions.[181] Between 1956 and 1966 the number of reported derivative actions increased dramatically compared to the previous decade.[182]

During the mid-1970s, in the wake of economic development, the balance between the protection of minority shareholders and the power of corporate management was reconsidered.[183] As the 'security-for-expenses' statute gradually lost its effects in preventing strike suits, a new strategy to prevent the abuse of derivative actions came into play. A special litigation committee consisting of disinterested directors could investigate a plaintiff's claim and recommend whether the litigation should be brought.[184] It should be stressed that those disinterested directors should not be the defendants of the lawsuit. If all of the directors were named as defendants, the board might appoint outside directors who had no personal financial interest in the challenged transactions to the committee.[185] This strategy was first applied by the Federal District Court of New York in *Gall v. Exxon Corp.*,[186] and later by the Federal Supreme Court in *Burks v. Lasker*[187] and the New York Court of Appeals in *Auerbach v. Bennett.*[188] At present, the 'special litigation committee' approach is still being used by many US courts, at state level as well as federal level.

### 2.3.3.2 The Legal Framework of Derivative Actions in the US

#### 2.3.3.2.1 A Direct Action or a Derivative Action

To determine whether an action is direct or derivative, two questions should be answered: who suffered the alleged injury (the company as a whole or the suing shareholder individually); who would receive the remedies?[189] With regards to

---

179American Law Institute (ALI), *Principles of Corporate Governance: Analysis and recommendations*, (American Law Institute Publishers, 1994), S7.04(c), comment at 91.

180Ibid.

181John C. Coffee and Donald E. Schwartz, 'The Survival of the Derivative Suit: an Evaluation and a Proposal for Legislative Reform', *Columbia Law Review*, Volume 81(2), 261, pp. 261–262.

182Daniel J. Dykstra, 'The Revival of the Derivative Suit', *University of Pennsylvania Law Review*, (1967), Volume 116, 74, pp. 74–75.

183Xiaoning Li, *A Comparative study of shareholders' derivative actions: England, the United States, Germany and China,* (Kluwer, 2007), p. 94.

184Robert C. Clark, *Corporate Law* (Little, Brown, The United States, 1986), p. 645.

185Ibid.

186418 F Supp 508 (United States District Court, SDNY, D.C.N.Y. 1976).

187*Burks v. Lasker* 441 U.S. 471 (1979).

188*Auerbach v. Bennett* 47 N.Y.2d 619.

189Andreas Cahn and David C Donald, *Comparative Company Law: text and cases on the laws governing corporations in German, the UK and the USA* (Cambridge University Press, Cambridge, New York, 2010), pp. 602–603.

these two questions, the Delaware Supreme Court used a 'special injury' test, providing if a shareholder alleged a 'special injury', he could bring a direct action.[190] A 'special injury' is manifested if the wrong is inflicted only upon the shareholder rather than the company as a whole.[191] But the Delaware Supreme Court disregards the 'special injury' test and attempts to consider all facts of the complaint because, in some cases, the alleged wrongdoing would be very complicated and just using one simple standard to test it is not sufficient enough.[192]

Sometimes both the company and the individual shareholder suffer an injury at the same time and it is not easy to distinguish one from another. Under this circumstance, an additional criterion should be introduced: to whom the defendant owes the duties?[193] When the wrongdoers are directors or senior managers of the company, it is particularly important to identify the party to whom the wrongdoers owe the relevant duties since they owe duties to both the company as an entity and each shareholder individually. In consideration of that, if the directors or managers violate such kind of duty, the shareholders may bring a direct action to redress their own injuries, and they can also commence a derivative action on behalf of the company to seek recoveries.[194] For instance, insider trading violates a director's fiduciary duty owed to the company and a separate duty owed to the shareholder who is selling securities.[195]

##### 2.3.3.2.2 Substantial Limitations on the Filing of a Derivative Action

Except for the procedural requirements, the business judgment rule shielding the internal business activities from external interference is a significant substantial restriction on the commencement of a derivative lawsuit. Although the statutory rules do not explicitly indicate that the business judgment rule should be functioned as an exception to the cause of a derivative action, the courts, in fact, hold it as a basic doctrine to avoid judicial interference with the business issues within a company.[196] If the directors and senior officers, performing in good faith and for the company's interests, still cause losses to the company by their business judgments, they should be exempted from being charged.

---

[190] *Tooley v. Donaldson, Lufkin & Jenrette, Inc.*, 845 A.2d 1031 (Delaware 2004), at 1038.

[191] Ibid.

[192] Edward P. Welch, Andrew J. Turezyn and Robert S. Saunders, *Folk on the Delaware General Corporation Law,* (Aspen publishers, 2010), p. 919.

[193] American Law Institute (ALI), *Principles of Corporate Governance: Analysis and recommendations*, (American Law Institute Publishers, 1994), S7.01(c).

[194] American Law Institute (ALI), *Principles of Corporate Governance: Analysis and recommendations*, (American Law Institute Publishers, 1994), S7.01(c).

[195] Ibid.

[196] For example, in *Aronson v. Lewis*, the Delaware court held that 'it is a presumption that in making a business decision the directors of a corporation acted on an informed basis, in good faith and in the honest belief that the action taken was in the best interests of the company'. *Aronson v. Lewis*, 473 A.2d 805, at 812 (Delaware 1984); The same rule could also be found in *Smith v. Van Gorkom*, 488 a.2d 858, at 872 (Delaware 1985); *Brehm v. Eisner*, 746 A.2d 244, at 264 (Delaware 2000).

#### 2.3.3.2.3 Procedural Requirements on Plaintiffs to Initiate Derivative Actions

##### 2.3.3.2.3.1 The Qualification of Shareholder Plaintiffs

###### 2.3.3.2.3.1.1 The Contemporaneous Ownership Rule

The contemporaneous ownership rule requires that the shareholder plaintiff in a derivative action should be holding shares when the complained transaction is happening, or shareholders entitling to launch a derivative lawsuit should be the ones whose shares were devolved by operation of law (for instance, through succession).[197] The rule is designed to prevent abuse of derivative actions and in particular to avoid the purchasing of shares just in order to maintain a derivative action attacking a transaction that occurred prior to the purchase of the share.[198] However, this rule also creates a dilemma. If a person bought the shares after the misconduct had been committed but before the misconduct was disclosed, does he meet the requirement of contemporaneous ownership rule and is he entitled to commence a derivative action? In practice, this condition is not rare in publicly-held companies for the reason of information asymmetry in capital market.[199] On this issue, the ALI's principles recommends to grant the standing to persons who acquired their shares before the material facts are disclosed to the public.[200]

When implementing the contemporaneous ownership rule, some states adopt liberal approaches. For instance, Pennsylvania allows a non-contemporaneous shareholder to initiate a derivative action in order to correct serious wrongdoings.[201] California adopts several exceptions to the application of the contemporaneous ownership rule, such as, a strong *prima facie* case, absence of similar action elsewhere, acquisition of shares before the disclosure of the misconducts.[202]

###### 2.3.3.2.3.1.2 The Continuous Ownership Rule

The continuous ownership rule requires the shareholder plaintiff to hold shares in the corporation continuously till the delivery of judgment.[203] Once the plaintiff, for whatever reason, ceases to be a shareholder, he would lose the standing to continue a derivative action.[204] This rule is designed to prevent speculative suits and to ensure that the derivative action is brought with merits. However, it may cause problems in certain circumstances such as merger and acquisition. Thus, several states have developed exceptions to this rule. For instance, under Delaware law there are two exceptions to the continuous ownership rule. First, if a merger is

---

[197]Section 327 of Delaware General Corporation Law.

[198]*Lewis v. Anderson*, 477 A.2d 1040, at 1046 (Delaware 1984).

[199]Stepben M. Bainbridge, *Corporation Law and Economics*, (Foundation Press, New York, 2002), p. 374.

[200]American Law Institute (ALI), *Principles of Corporate Governance: Analysis and recommendations*, (American Law Institute Publishers, 1994), S7.02(a)(1).

[201]Section 1782(b) of the Pennsylvanian Business Corporation Law (PBCL).

[202]Section 800 of the California Corporation Code 1977 (CCC).

[203]American Law Institute (ALI), *Principles of Corporate Governance: Analysis and recommendations*, (American Law Institute Publishers, 1994), S7.02(a)(2).

[204]Lewis v. Anderson, 477 A.2d 1040, at 1049 (Delaware 1984).

conducted merely to deprive shareholders of standing to bring a derivative action. Second, if the merger is in reality merely a reorganization which does not affect the plaintiff's ownership in the company.[205]

**2.3.3.2.3.2 The Demand Requirement**

**2.3.3.2.3.2.1 Demand on the Board Requirement**

The demand on the board requirement means that a shareholder does not have the right to initiate a derivative action without making a demand on the board first unless he can demonstrate that such a demand is futile. The demand requirement grants the board an opportunity to consider the disputes before the shareholders bring them to the court.[206] The rationale of this requirement is largely based on an important principle of company law that the power to manage corporate business, including the power to make a litigation decision, is granted to the board of directors rather than individual shareholders.[207] After receiving a demand, the board of the company may respond in three ways: refusing the demand; accepting the demand and allow the litigation to proceed; resolving the matter internally without judicial interference.[208]

**2.3.3.2.3.2.2 Demand Refused Cases**

In a demand refused case, the board usually states that the law was not violated and the cause of the derivative action could not be established on tenable grounds. For instance, the exception of business judgment rule. In a vast majority of cases, shareholders may allege that the board made the 'refusal decision' is 'personally involved or interested in the alleged wrongdoing in a way calculated to impair their exercise of business judgement on behalf of the company, or that their refusal to sue reflects bad faith or breach of trust in some other way'.[209] Since whether or not to pursue a claim could also be considered as the board's business judgment, it can only be challenged before a court on the ground that it is irrational. But the interpretation of 'irrational' is greatly subject to the court's discretion. The court will apply its own standard to decide whether the challenge is rational or not. If the shareholder's challenge is successful, the derivative action would then be permitted to proceed.

It needs to be indicated that in the challenge the burden of proof belongs to the shareholder plaintiffs. Normally, they should prove that the directors who made the refusal decision were not independent or disinterested. However, in some states,

---

[205]Edward P. Welch, Andrew J. Turezyn and Robert S. Saunders, *Folk on the Delaware General Corporation Law,* (Aspen publishers, 2010), p. 928.

[206]Blair L. Lockwood and Karen L. Barsch, 'United States', in Dennis Campbell and Sheila Buckley (eds), *Protecting Minority Shareholders*, (Kluwer, 1996), 656, pp. 667–669.

[207]Xiaoning Li, *A Comparative study of shareholders' derivative actions: England, the United States, Germany and China* (Kluwer, 2007), p. 161.

[208]Stepben M. Bainbridge, *Corporation Law and Economics*, (Foundation Press, New York, 2002), p. 394.

[209]Robert C. Clark, *Corporate Law* (Little, Brown, The United States, 1986), p. 644.

(for example Delaware) the inside documents are not available to general shareholders and it is difficult for them to acquire necessary evidence.[210] For the reason of that, the Delaware law has made effort to facilitate the access to certain corporate books and records for shareholders.[211] New Jersey law allocates the burden of proof to the company's board by requiring it to prove that it was disinterested and independent and the refusal decision was made in good faith and with due care.[212]

**2.3.3.2.3.2.3 Demand Accepted Cases**

When a demand is accepted by the board, there will be two possibilities. The first one is the board accepts the demand and prosecutes the action. The other one is that the board intends to solve the issue internally without resorting to the court. In the former situation, the board would notify the shareholders that it plans to take some measures on the demand. Normally, investigations on the complained issues may be conducted by the company thereafter. Then, the company may either go ahead with the lawsuit or make a settlement.[213] It should be noted that the parties who attempt to make a settlement must comply with the judicial approval requirement listed in FRCP 23.1 or its relevant state counterparts.[214] While in the latter case, the company resolves the complained issues through a settlement, and the judicial approval requirement in FRCP 23.1 or its relevant state counterparts does not apply.[215] One question that might be raised in this regard is when the board accepts the demand and then a settlement is made without resorting to the court, what could the shareholders do if they are not satisfied with the settlement? Generally, shareholders, under this circumstance, are entitled to commence a derivative action on the same ground.[216]

**2.3.3.2.3.2.4 Demand Excused Cases**

In some cases, the shareholders could commence a derivative action without making a demand on the board.[217] A typical example in this regard is when the demand is excused as futile, the shareholder could initiate a derivative claim directly.[218]

---

[210] Deborah A. DeMott, *Shareholder Derivative Actions: Law and Practice*, (Thomson West Press, 2003), Section 5.11.

[211] Section 220 of DGCL.

[212] *In re PSE & G Shareholder Litigation*, 173 N.J. 258, 286, (2002).

[213] Arthur R. Pinto and Douglas M. Branson, *Understanding Corporate Law* (LexisNexis 3rd edition, 2009), p. 479.

[214] Stepben M. Bainbridge, *Corporation Law and Economics*, (Foundation Press, New York, 2002), p. 394.

[215] Ibid.

[216] Ibid.

[217] There are several circumstances under which the case could be regarded as 'demand excused'. For instance, among others, the company is threatened with irreparable harm; the company has taken an extraordinarily long period of time and make no responses.

[218] Arthur R. Pinto and Douglas M. Branson, *Understanding Corporate Law* (LexisNexis 3rd edition, 2009). p. 480.

A demand could be futile if the shareholder plaintiff supposes that a fair hearing by the board of the company would not be given upon the demand. For instance, if a majority of directors were involved in the alleged wrongdoing and a sound litigation decision could hardly be made, it would be futile for the shareholder plaintiff to make a demand on the board.

In state law, a widely-accepted doctrine is the Delaware Supreme Court's opinion in *Aronson v. Lewis*,[219] stating that in deciding whether a demand on the board is futile, two issues should be considered: whether the directors were disinterested and independent; and whether the challenged transaction was a product of a valid exercise of business judgment.[220]

The *Aronson* test seems to provide a fairly liberal standard and most of the state law as well as the Federal Rules of Civil Procedure adopt this principle by requiring that a shareholder plaintiff pleading demand futility must plead with particularized facts to prove that the *Aronson* standards have been met.[221] For example, if the plaintiff only indicated the facts that the directors were nominated or elected by the defendant, or the majority of the board approved of the challenged transaction, it would not be sufficient to render a demand futility.[222] This requirement to plead with particularized facts indeed imposes a significant burden on the plaintiff because normally the plaintiff is not allowed discovery at this stage.[223]

In the mid-1970s, after a drastic increase in the number of derivative lawsuits, an independent body within company boards (the special litigation committee) was established to make the litigation decision for the company. Generally, a special litigation committee is comprised of two or three directors who were not named as defendants in the litigation.[224] If all of the directors were named as defendants, the board might appoint outside directors who had no personal financial interest in the challenged transactions to the committee.[225] If the special litigation committee decides that the commencement of a derivative action is not in the company's best interest, its decision may have a binding effect.[226]

According to the business judgment rule, a litigation decision made by the company or the special litigation committee is considered as business judgment which could be exempted from judicial review. Therefore, such a decision made by the special litigation committee, in nature, bars any derivative action initiated by

---

219 *Aronson v. Lewis*, 473 A.2d 805 (Delaware 1984).

220 *Aronson v. Lewis*, 473 A.2d 805, at 814 (Delaware 1984).

221 Ralph C. Ferrara, Kevin T. Abikoff and Laura Leedy Gansler, *Shareholder derivative litigation: besieging the board*, (Law Journal Seminars-Press, 2013), Section 6.02.

222 *Aronson v. Lewis*, 473 A.2d 805, at 814–815 (Delaware 1984).

223 See Carol B. Swanson, 'Juggling Shareholder Rights and Strike Suits in Derivative Litigation: the ALI Drops the Ball', *Minnesota Law Review*, (1993), Volume 77, 1339, pp. 1376–1377.

224 Robert C. Clark, *Corporate Law* (Little, Brown, 1986) p. 645.

225 Ibid.

226 The 'binding effect' will be discussed below.

shareholders.[227] With regards to this issue, it is argued that the decision made by the special litigation committee should not have a binding effect because of the 'structural bias' problem.[228] The members of a special litigation committee are normally appointed by the board and have a close relationship with the directors, which makes it difficult to for the committee to maintain independence when making litigation decision. They tend to perceive their role 'as that of a buffer by which to shelter and protect management from hostile and litigious shareholders'.[229] The 'structural bias' problem could be proved by the fact that a substantial number of decisions made by the special litigation committee are not to initiate a derivative claim.[230]

From the practical perspective, several questions in relation to the 'structural bias' problem could also be raised, such as, to what extent should the court defer to the 'not to sue' decision made by the special litigation committee; how would the business judgment rule be applied when the court reviews the committee's decision? If the court adopts a strict approach to review the merits of the case, it may deprive the special litigation committee of the power to decide corporate issues, which is, to a certain degree, not in line with the business judgment rule. On the other hand, if the courts simply stick to the business judgment rule and completely defer to the committee's decision, the 'structural bias' problem cannot be solved. Regarding this issue, there are generally three approaches adopted by state courts.

The first approach entirely adheres to the business judgment rule, which is a loose standard. For example, the New York Court of Appeals in *Auerbach v. Bennett*[231] in 1979 (this was a demand-excused case) allowed only minimal review of the committee's decision.[232] In this case, the court held that the business judgment rule would protect the special litigation committee's decision from being reviewed by the court.[233] Only if the plaintiff can demonstrate that the members of the committee were not truly independent and disinterested or that they did not act in good faith or in the company's best interest, the decision by the committee could be reviewed by the court.[234] In fact, the *Auerbach* approach has been criticized for

[227]John C. Coffee and Donald E. Schwartz, 'The Survival of the Derivative Suit: an Evaluation and a Proposal for Legislative Reform', *Columbia Law Review*, (1981), Volume 81, 261, pp. 262–263.

[228]Xiaoning Li, *A Comparative study of shareholders' derivative actions: England, the United States, Germany and China*, (Kluwer, 2007), p. 169.

[229]John C. Coffee and Donald E. Schwartz, 'The survival of the derivative suit: an evaluation and a proposal for legislative reform', Columbia Law Review, (1981), Volume 81(2), 261, p. 283.

[230]Ralph C. Ferrara, Kevin T. Abikoff and Laura Leedy Gansler, *Shareholder Derivative Litigation: Besieging the Board*, (Law Journal Seminars-Press, 2013), Section 8.01.

[231]*Auerbach v. Bennett,* 47 N.Y.2d 619 (N.Y. 1979).

[232]*Auerbach v. Bennett,* 47 N.Y.2d 619, at 621 (N.Y. 1979).

[233]Ibid.

[234]*Auerbach v. Bennett,* 47 N.Y.2d 619, at 623–624 (N.Y. 1979).

over-deferring to the special litigation committee's decision.[235] It is argued that the courts should employ greater scrutiny to eliminate the 'structural bias' problem.[236]

In contrast to the New York approach, the Iowa Supreme Court took a strict approach when reviewing a committee's decision. In *Miller v. Register & Tribune Syndicate, Inc.*,[237] the court held that under no circumstances should the special litigation committee's decision not to sue be deferred to.[238] In the court's point of view, where the majority of the board is incapable of making a litigation decision, it has no authority to delegate such power to a special litigation committee.[239] However, like the New York loose approach, the Iowa approach is also criticized for the reason that it imposes a heavy burden on the court and may waste judicial resources.[240]

In practice, most states take a position between New York and Iowa. For instance, Delaware adopts a standard indicating that the committee's decision should be deferred to a certain degree, but judicial review should also be conducted when necessary.[241] The Delaware standard is well illustrated by the *Zapata corporation v. Maldonado*[242] case, in which a two-step test was used to review the committee's decision. At the first stage, the court should 'inquire into the independence and good faith of the committee and the bases supporting its conclusions'.[243] In this step, the company should prove that the committee's decision was made independently, with good faith and after reasonable investigation.[244] If the court finds that the committee did not meet the above-mentioned requirements, the decision by the committee should be dismissed.[245] If the court is satisfied with all the procedural requirements, the case may proceed to the next step.[246] At the second stage, the court could, at its discretion, decide whether or not to dismiss the suit.[247] In this step, special consideration to matters of law and public policy should be taken by the court.[248] Like the two approaches mentioned before, the Delaware approach has also been criticized for granting too much flexibility to the court.[249]

---

[235]Ralph C. Ferrara et al., *Shareholder Derivative Litigation: Besieging the Board*, (Law Journal Seminars-Press, 2013), Section 8.02.

[236]Ibid.

[237]*Miller v. Register & Tribune Syndicate, Inc.* 336 N.W.2d 709 (Iowa 1983).

[238]*Miller v. Register & Tribune Syndicate, Inc.* 336 N.W.2d 709, at 714 (Iowa 1983).

[239]Ibid.

[240]Kenneth B. Davis, 'Structural bias, special litigation committee, and the vagaries of director independence', 90 *Iowa Law Review*, (2005), Volume 90, 1035, p. 1041.

[241]Ibid.

[242]*Zapata corporation v. Maldonado* 430 A.2d 779 (Delaware 1981).

[243]*Zapata corporation v. Maldonado* 430 A.2d 779, at 788 (Delaware 1981).

[244]Ibid.

[245]Ibid.

[246]*Zapata corporation v. Maldonado* 430 A.2d 779, at 789 (Delaware 1981).

[247]*Zapata corporation v. Maldonado* 430 A.2d 779, at 789 (Delaware 1981).

[248]Ibid.

[249]Kenneth B. Davis, 'Structural bias, special litigation committee, and the vagaries of director independence', 90 *Iowa Law Review*, (2005), Volume 90, 1035, p. 1045.

#### 2.3.3.2.4 Settlements

The federal rule (FRCP 23.1) provides that derivative actions should not be dismissed or compromised without the approval of the court and that notice of a proposed settlement or dismissal must be given to the shareholders in the manner the court directs.[250] Normally, the proponents of a settlement have the burden of convincing the court that the settlement is in the best interests of the company and its shareholders, when the court's hearing is held.[251]

In fact, due to many reasons, a majority of cases are terminated with settlements rather than judgment in the US.[252] For instance, the plaintiff's attorney would be strongly inclined to settle rather than go to trial because the first option is less risky for him.[253] For the defendants, they also prefer to reach a settlement rather than to wait for the trial for the reason that most of them are directors or senior officers of a company who are afraid of potential harm to their career and reputation in case of losing. Additionally, if a significant public company loses at trial, people would easily lose confidence in the company and it may negatively affect the share price in the stock market.

In consideration of the reasons indicated before, the settlement is of great importance in a derivative action. It is necessary for the court to hold judicial control over it to a certain degree. However, the standard of such judicial control should be moderate. If the judicial control is too far-reaching, it would essentially deprive litigation parties of the freedom to reach a settlement or compromise. On the other hand, if it is just a procedural device not touching the substantial issues involved in the settlement, it would, like before, not be possible to avoid suspect settlements.[254]

### 2.3.3.3 Summary

In the US, both state law and federal law have rules regarding shareholder derivative actions. Although state law concerning derivative lawsuit varies, several principles are generally accepted. For instance, settlement agreements concluded by parties in a derivative lawsuit should be approved by the court in order to prevent suspect agreement and protect the company's interests. With regards to 'standing to sue', shareholders should adhere to 'contemporaneous ownership rule' and

[250] Section 23.1 of the Federal Rule of Civil Procedure (FRCP).

[251] Robert C. Clark, Corporate Law (Little Brown, 1986), p. 657.

[252] Robert C. Clark, Corporate Law (Little Brown, 1986), p. 652.

[253] Through a settlement, the lawyer will get an amount of money for sure. But in a court's trial, the attorney will not be paid in case of losing through a contingency fee arrangement which is widely applied in the US.

[254] In earlier times, it was not the case that settlements had to be approved by the court. Consequently, many suspect settlements not in the company's best interests occurred. To ensure the company's interests, the judicial control by the courts is introduced in order to eliminate such settlements.

'continuous ownership rule' at the same time, meaning that shareholders entitled to initiate a derivative action should hold shares at the time of the complained issue is happening and should hold shares continuously until the judgment is delivered. Demand requirements before a derivative lawsuit is commenced under the U.S. law is also important procedural rules that potential shareholder claimants should notice. For instance, under certain circumstances, demand is not needed if the potential shareholder claimant could prove that the board in not independent and disinterested in the challenged issue.

## 2.4 Shareholder Class Actions

A particular type of shareholder class action is the litigation brought by shareholders against their company, alleging that the company misrepresents its profitability[255] and the shareholders thus purchase stocks at an inflated price.[256] When the true profitability of the company is revealed, the stock price plummets.[257] In other words, plaintiffs in shareholder class actions (also named 'securities fraud actions') sue the company and its officers on behalf of investors who have paid too much for their shares caused by the corporation's misrepresentation.[258,259] On top of compensating injured investors and deterring future fraud, shareholder class actions also attempt to improve the functioning of the financial markets.[260] However, shareholder class actions are commonly perceived as 'lawyers-driven' in nature, meaning that those actions are essentially initiated and controlled by plaintiffs' lawyers.[261]

---

[255]See Patrick M Garry et al., 'The Irrationality of Shareholder Class Action Lawsuits: A Proposal for Reform', *South Dakota Law Review*, (2004), Volume 49(2), 275, pp. 276–277.

[256]Ibid.

[257]Ibid.

[258]See Adam C. Pritchard, 'Markets as Monitors: A Proposal to Replace Class Actions with Exchanges as Securities Fraud Enforcers', *Virginia Law Review*, (1999), Volume 85, 925, p. 928.

[259]In shareholder class actions, the corporation's misstatements can take various forms, including fraudulent filings with the Securities and Exchange Commission, public statements by corporate officers, or press releases issued by the corporation. See Patrick M Garry et al., 'The Irrationality of Shareholder Class Action Lawsuits: A Proposal for Reform', *South Dakota Law Review*, (2004), Volume 49(2), 275, pp. 278–279.

[260]'Fraud on market' could jeopardize the stock transaction in free market, and further has negative effect on the whole market system and damage the investors' confidence. The mechanism of shareholder class actions could, in this regard, prevent the fraud behaviour and moreover protect the interests of investors.

[261]See Patrick M Garry et al., 'The Irrationality of Shareholder Class Action Lawsuits: A Proposal for Reform', *South Dakota Law Review*, (2004), Volume 49(2), 275, pp. 283–285; and see Jill E. Fisch, 'Class Action Reform: Lessons From Securities Litigation', *Arizona Law Review*, (1997), Volume 39, 533, pp. 533–534.

## 2.4.1 Class Actions in China

### 2.4.1.1 A General Overview

The Chinese law allows collective actions (共同诉讼) and representative actions (代表人诉讼). Relevant statutory rules are mainly incorporated in article 53–55 of the Civil Procedure Law (CPL).[262] In general, there are basically two types of collective lawsuits: (A) essential collective litigation (必要的共同诉讼)[263]; (B) ordinary collective litigation (普通的共同诉讼). The ordinary group litigation can be further divided into two sub-catalogues: (A) representative collective litigation in which the number of litigants is fixed at the time the case is filed (人数确定的代表人诉讼); (B) representative collective litigation in which the number of litigants is not fixed at the time the case is filed (人数不确定的代表人诉讼).

### 2.4.1.2 Rules Concerning Essential Collective Litigation

Under the CPL, essential collective litigation is a claim where participating parties (two or more persons) are involved in the same disputed matter and thus may not be separated.[264] Generally, only certain types of collective actions could be considered as essential collective actions, while others not identified in statutory laws are within the category of ordinary collective litigation.[265] Essential collective litigation is, in nature, inseparable, meaning that persons having the same disputed issue

---

[262]The PRC Civil Procedure Law was enacted in 1991. Amendments to the CPR came out in 2007 and 2012 respectively. Provisions with regards to collective actions and representative actions are not changed by these two amendments.

[263]In fact, the essential group litigation could also be a representative lawsuit. The act of the representative in the litigation should be valid for the party he represents (except for a few particular acts, e.g. modification or waiver of the claim). See article 53 of the CPL. According to the 'inseparable' nature of essential group actions, group members who do not agree with the result of the representative selection should join in the whole procedure personally. See article 60 of the Opinions of the Supreme People's Court on Some Issues Concerning the Application of the Civil Procedure Law of the PRC (最高人民法院关于适用中华人民共和国民事诉讼法若干问题的意见).

[264]See Xiaoming Xi (ed), Annotations to the Provisions in the New Civil Procedure Law (新民事诉讼法条文释义), (3rd edition, Beijing: People's Court Press 2010).

[265]The type of cases that could be regarded as essential group litigation are listed in art 43, 46, 47, 50, 52, 55 and 56 of the Opinions and in art 124 to 128 of the Judicial Interpretation of the Supreme People's Court on Some Issues Regarding the Application of Security Law of the PRC (最高人民法院关于适用中华人民共和国担保法若干问题的解释). For example, litigation arising from joint credit or joint liability; litigation arising from joint succession property. And see Michael Palmer and Chao Xi, 'Collective and representative actions in China', National Report to the University of Oxford Centre for Social-Legal Studies and Stanford Law School Joint Project on the Globalization of Class Actions. (2007), p. 3.

should jointly sue or be sued.[266] If one or some members of them refuse to join in an essential collective action, the lawsuit cannot be initiated. By contrast, parties in an ordinary collective action have claims concerning disputed matters of the same kind instead of 'the same disputed matter'. In an essential collective action, aggregated parties have to select one or several representatives through the consent of all members.[267] If a member is not satisfied with the selected representative(s), under Chinese rules he still needs to join the action, but as a separate party to the proceedings.[268] In addition to that, the inseparability of an essential collective action is also reflected in the provision that there should be just one final outcome of the case (a judgment or a settlement).[269]

#### 2.4.1.3 Rules Concerning Ordinary Collective Litigation

Unlike essential collective actions, ordinary collective litigation is 'separable'. Aggregated parties are not treated as an integrated group. Instead, joint parties in an ordinary collective action do not rely on each other, and each group member could commence a claim respectively. Combining their claims together as a collective one is, perhaps, in order to increase judicial efficiency. The CPL suggests that one or several representatives could be selected to represent the whole litigation group. On this issue, if a consensus could not be reached, the representative would be determined by the court through consultation with the group members.[270] It should be stressed that under the CPL, the act of the representative in ordinary collective litigation would be valid for all persons he represents (except for a few particular acts, e.g. modification or waiver of the claim).[271]

**2.4.1.3.1 The Fixed-Member Representative Collective Litigation**

The fixed-member representative collective litigation refers to a lawsuit where all group members have been confirmed when the lawsuit is filed with the court. The number of group member is generally 'large' (The *Opinions* provides that

---

[266]In fact, essential group litigation could be divided into two categories: the positive essential group litigation and the passive essential group litigation. The former one means that two or more persons joint together to sue a single defendant, while the latter one indicates that two or more defendants are jointly sued by a single plaintiff.

[267]See article 53 of the CPL, and article 60 of the Opinions of the Supreme People's Court on Some Issues Concerning the Application of the Civil Procedure Law of the PRC (最高人民法院关于适用中华人民共和国民事诉讼法若干问题的意见).

[268]See article 60 of the Opinions of the Supreme People's Court on Some Issues Concerning the Application of the Civil Procedure Law of the PRC (最高人民法院关于适用中华人民共和国民事诉讼法若干问题的意见).

[269]In an ordinary group action, the final result (the judgment or the settlement) could vary from one member to another. See Xiaoming Xi (ed), Annotations to the Provisions in the New Civil Procedure Law.

[270]See article 54 (2) of the CPL.

[271]See article 53 of the CPL.

'large' number means ten or more than ten persons).[272] In such cases, two to five representatives could be selected to represent the whole group to participate the court proceeding.[273]

**2.4.1.3.2 The Unfixed-Member Representative Collective Litigation**

'Unfixed-member representative collective litigation' refers to a lawsuit where not all group members have been confirmed when the lawsuit is filed with the court. The general procedure of an unfixed-member representative collective action is that the court handling the lawsuit issues a notice, specifying the circumstances of the lawsuit and instructing all persons whose interests are similarly affected to come forward and register with the court within a given period (the period should generally not be less than 30 days).[274] Potential participants who intend to register with the court should demonstrate that their interests have been similarly affected and they have suffered damage as a result.[275] Persons failing to do so can launch independent claims with the same or similar cause of action within (around) 2 years.[276] The court's final decision on an unfixed-member representative collective has binding effect on all registered group members.[277] The court's decision is also valid for those people who do not register with the court but bring similar claims as indicated above.[278]

#### 2.4.1.4 Rules and Practice Regarding Collective Litigation Arising from Securities Fraud

The main question in this regard is which sort of collective action can be used when a securities fraud action is filed with the court (an essential collective action, a fixed-member representative collective litigation, or an unfixed-member representative collective litigation). To answer this question, we should first give a brief introduction to the development of securities fraud litigation in China.

On 20 September 2001, 363 disgruntled investors in the York point Science & Technology Co (亿安科技) (a Chinese listed company) simultaneously filed lawsuits with Intermediate People's Courts in Beijing, Shanghai and Guangzhou, alleging large-scaled market manipulation by the company. But unfortunately, courts in Beijing, Shanghai and Guangzhou refused to accept the *York point* case for the reason that on 21 September 2001, the Supreme People's Court (SPC) issued

---

272 See article 59 of the CPL Opinions.

273 See article 62 of the CPL Opinions.

274 See article 55 of the CPL, and article 63 of the CPL Opinions.

275 See article 64 of the CPL Opinion.

276 See article 135 of General Principles of the Civil Law of the People's Republic of China (中华人民共和国民法通则, 'zhonghua renmin gongheguo minfa tongze').

277 See article 54 (4) of the CPL.

278 Ibid.

a temporary notice (SPC 2001 notice) to instruct lower courts not to accept private securities lawsuits.[279]

This temporary bar set by SPC received heavy criticism. It was stated that the court's refusal to private securities fraud cases would fundamentally harm the development of the Chinese stock market and damage investors' confidence.[280] In January 2002, the SPC lifted the temporary bar to allow lower courts to accept private securities litigation in which the cause of the case was false statements (SPC 2002 notice).[281] On top of that, in January 2003, SPC further issued interpretations (SPC 2003 interpretation) to provide specific guidance on the trial of private securities lawsuits.[282]

The 2002 Notice ruled out the use of a group action (集团诉讼), which is largely equivalent to the unfixed-member representative collective litigation under Chinese law, to establish a private securities fraud lawsuit arising from false statements.[283] It further provides that injured investors are allowed to sue the company individually or collectively.[284] In addition to that, the 2003 interpretation suggests that injured investors could bring a fixed-member representative collective action to redress the losses caused by the company's false statements,[285] but the number of the plaintiffs must be ascertained before the commencement of the trial.[286] Furthermore, the 2003 interpretation also stipulates that the court may require individual claimants to join other aggrieved investors who choose to sue collectively.[287] The court may also choose to combine several collective claims (brought by different groups of victimized investors arising from the same false statement) into one single collective action.[288] With regards to representatives in securities fraud actions, the 2003 Interpretation expands the scope of representative's delegation power to a wider extent, including, such as, the power of modification or waiver of the claim that is

---

[279]The Supreme People's Court: *Notice of the Supreme People's Court on Refusing to Accept Civil Compensation Cases Involving Securities For the Time Being* (关于涉证券民事赔偿案件暂不予受理的通知).

[280]See Bin Luo, *Researchs on Securities Class Actions*, (Law Press, China, 2011); and see Ren Zili, *Securities Class Actions: International Experience And China's Way Out*, (Law Press, China, 2008).

[281]The Supreme People's Court: *Notice of the Supreme People's Court on the Relevant Issues concerning the Acceptance of Cases of Disputes over Civil Tort Arising from False Statement in the Securities Market* (关于受理证券市场因虚假陈述引发的民事侵权纠纷案件有关问题的通知) (2002).

[282]The Supreme People's Court: *Some Provisions of the Supreme People's Court on Trying Cases of Civil Compensation Arising from False Statement in Securities Market*, (关于审理证券市场因虚假陈述引发的民事赔偿案件的若干规定) (2003).

[283]See article 4 of the 2002 Notice.

[284]See article 4 of the 2002 Notice and article 12 of the 2003 Interpretation.

[285]See article 13 of the 2003 Interpretation.

[286]See article 14 of the 2003 Interpretation.

[287]See article 13 of the 2003 Interpretation.

[288]Ibid.

not authorized by the CPL.[289] But the rule in the 2003 interpretation concerning the representative's power contradicts with the articles regarding lawyer's power in civil litigation in the CPL. Considering the hierarchy system of Chinese law, the level of the CPL is higher than that of the 2003 Interpretation, meaning that the power held by representatives in securities fraud litigation should be in line with the provisions under the CPL. In light of that, the power to approve certain issues (for instance, modification or waiver of the claim, admission of the claim of the other party) still remains with all group members rather than the representatives. But in reality, injured investors in securities fraud actions are widely dispersed, making it difficult to gather consent from all of the members to authorize delegation power to the representatives. In consideration of the practical difficulty, it is suggested that the power to determine special issues would better to be remained with litigation representatives instead of the widely-dispersed victimized investors, provided that the representatives always act for the best interests of the group.

## 2.4.2 *Class Actions in the United Kingdom*

Even though the UK has certain forms of collective litigation, there are no specific shareholder class actions (securities fraud litigation).[290]

[289] See article 15 of the 2003 Interpretation and article 53 of the CPL.

[290] Actually the British law adopts procedures by which claimants with similar claims may group together to bring collective claims against the same defendants (Part 19 of the Civil Procedure Rule UK). Under the Civil Procedure Rules (CPR), two types of collective actions could be brought by claimants. One is a group litigation order (GLO) made by the court, which permits a number of claims concerning common or related issues to be managed collectively (Part 19 of the Civil Procedure Rule UK). Under the GLO mechanism, once it is issued, a register of group claims must be established, and a court which will manage the claims (the management court) has to be specified as well [19.11 (2) (a) and 19.11 (2) (c) of the Civil Procedure Rule, and its Practice Direction 19B (6)]. The other approach is through representative actions. Under this mechanism, a claim where more than one person has the same interests could be begun or continued by representatives selected from this group of persons (Part 19 II of the Civil Procedure Rule). In a representative proceeding, any order of the court is binding on all persons represented in the claim (19.6 of the Civil Procedure Rule). In fact, the mechanism of representative actions is infrequently used in the UK because of narrow interpretations by the courts. Theoretically, the mechanism of representative actions allows a person to take legal action on behalf of persons who had 'common issues' arising from 'the same interest' in a claim against the same defendant. But the 'same interests' requirements has proven to be the most problematic aspect of the rule. Much of its controversy arises from the meaning of 'same interests' (See Rachel Mulheron, The Class Action in Common Law Legal System, a Comparative Perspectove, Hart Publishing 2004, p. 78). A relatively broad interpretation of representative litigation was given in the House of Lords decision Duke of Bedford v. Ellis in 1901. In this case, Lord MacNaughten held that the requirement of 'the same interest' is satisfied if the representative can show a common interest or common grievance and that the relief sought is beneficial to all. However, in a series of later cases, the requirement of common interest was used to give the rule a more restrictive application. And representative proceedings were therefore not available where the sole relief sought involved

## 2.4.3 *Class Actions in the United States*

### 2.4.3.1 Rules 23 of the Federal Rules of Civil Procedure

#### 2.4.3.1.1 Rule 23(a)

In the US, all sorts of class actions in the federal courts are governed by Rule 23 of the Federal Rules of Civil Procedure.[291] Rule 23(a) sets out four preconditions that need to be met before the commencement of a class lawsuit:

(1) the class is so numerous that joinder of all members is impracticable;
(2) there are questions of law or fact common to the class;
(3) the claims or defenses of the representative parties are typical of the claims or defenses of the class; and
(4) the representative parties will fairly and adequately protect the interests of the class.

---

(Footnote 290 continued)

damages: these would have to be proved individually (Edward F. Sherman, 'Group Litigation under Foreign Legal Systems: Variations and Alternatives to American Class Actions', *DePaul Law Review* (2003) Volume 52, 401, p. 422). In the framework of representative lawsuits, damages cannot be awarded without reference to the particular loss suffered by members of the class (see Neil Andrews, 'Multi-Partv Proceedings in England: Representative and Group Actions', *Duke Journal of Comparative and International Law* (2001) Volume 11, 249, p. 253). These limitations on damages awards were reflected in case laws. For example, in E.M.I. Records Ltd. v. Riley, the court indicated that the damages in a representative claim could be awarded only when '(1) the class members' losses can be readily ascertained at the time of the judgment; (2) the class members have waived their rights to individual receipt of damages and wish their compensation to be paid to a body enjoying care of their interests' [E.M.I. Records Ltd. v. Riley, 1 W.L.RI 923 (Ch. 1981)]. Given the shortcomings of English representative claims and their practical difficulties, amendments to CPR were made in 2000 to permit the use of GLOs in order to facilitate case management for claims concerning related issues of fact or law. In a GLO, each individual claimant has to start his own proceeding, and parties who want to join in the group must choose to 'opt in' [19.11 (2) (a) of the Civil Procedure Rule, and its Practice Direction 19B (6.2)]. It means that litigants have to choose affirmatively to litigate by entering their names on the group register [19.11 (3) (a) of the Civil Procedure Rule, however, claimants can apply for their claims to be removed from the register, see 19.14 (a) of the CPR]. For the management court, the scope of its power ranges over a wide field. For example, it may vary the GLO issues, it may appoint the solicitor of one or more parties to be the lead solicitor for the claimants or defendants (19.13 of the Civil Procedure Rule). In addition, any judgment or order given on a GLO issue is binding upon other parties on the group register, and the court may give directions as to the extent to which that judgment or order is binding on the parties to any claim which is subsequently entered on the group register [See 19.12 (1) of the Civil Procedure Rule]. Moreover, the management court may give directions for the trial of common issues as well as the trial of individual issues, and the latter ones may be heard from another court whose locality is convenient for the parties [Practice Direction 19B (15.1 and 15.2)]. In October 2015, the US-style class action was introduced into UK by the Consumer Rights Act 2015, making it far easier for groups of consumers to seek compensation from firms that have fixed prices and formed cartels.

[291]There are several typical categories of class actions in the US. For example, shareholder class actions, consumer class actions.

These four prerequisites are often referred to as *numerosity, commonality, typicality, and adequacy of representation.*[292,293]

**2.4.3.1.2 Rule 23(b)**

An additional requirement set in Rule 23(b) is that the action must fall within the categories specifically indicated in Rule 23(b). This rule has three subdivisions, and the first subdivision Rule 23(b)(1) is further broken down into two parts: Rule 23(b)(1)(A) and Rule 23(b)(1)(B). The first part permits a class action when the prosecution of separate actions by class actions would create a risk of creating incompatible standards of conduct generated by individual adjudications. For instance, an action to enjoin state officers from terminating unemployment compensation without a hearing.[294]

As for the second part [Rule 23(b)(1)(B)], it permits a class lawsuit when individual litigation would impair the ability of class members to protect their rights and interests. For example, when a defendant's fund is too limited to financially afford the claims brought by many individual claimants.[295]

Rule 23(b)(2) provides that a class may be certified when a party opposing the class has acted (or refused to act) by the same way to a definable group, thus a final injunctive relief or corresponding declaratory relief is appropriate to be delivered to the class as a whole.

The last division of Rule 23 is the most common ground on which to base a class lawsuit. In practice, most class actions claiming monetary compensations are brought under Rule 23(b)(3).[296] This rule provides that, in addition to the criterion provided in Rule 23(a), a class action must meet two further requirements set out in this subdivision. First, do the common issues 'predominate' over issues affecting

---

[292]See Robert H. Klonoff, Edward K.M. Bilich and Suzette M. Malveaux, *Class Actions and Other Multi-Party Litigation: Cases and Materials*, (Second Edition, Thomson/West 2006), pp. 68–70. Janet Cooper Alexander, 'An Introduction to Class Action Procedure in the United States', Presented Conference: Debates over Group Litigation in Comparative Perspective, Geneva, Switzerland, (July 21–22, 2000), pp. 4–5.

[293]As a matter of fact, these four requirements are key battleground in the grant of class certification. For instance, the 'numerosity' requirement. What should the court take into consideration when assessing whether or not the class meets this requirement? Does it mean that the court only needs to focus on the number? In fact, some courts have emphasized that it is wrong to focus on numbers alone. 'Sometimes, joinder may be impracticable even where the relative size of the potential class is small', Hernandez v. Alexander, 152 F.R.D. 192, 194 (D.Nev.1993). It is indicated that the court must look at numbers as well as 'all other relevant factor'. See Robert H. Klonoff, Edward K.M. Bilich and Suzette M. Malveaux, *Class Actions and Other Multi-Party Litigation: Cases and Materials*, (Second Edition, Thomson/West 2006), pp. 78–82.

[294]Crow v. California Department of Human Resources., 325 F. Supp. 1314 (N.D.Cal. 1970).

[295]See Robert H. Klonoff, Edward K.M. Bilich and Suzette M. Malveaux, *Class Actions and Other Multi-Party Litigation: Cases and Materials*, (Second Edition, Thomson/West 2006), pp. 166–167.

[296]Janet Cooper Alexander, 'An Introduction to Class Action Procedure in the United States', Presented Conference: Debates over Group Litigation in Comparative Perspective, Geneva, Switzerland, (July 21–22, 2000), pp. 4–5.

only individual members?[297] Second, is class treatment of an action 'superior' to other alternatives for adjudicating the controversial issue?[298]

For the first 'predominate' requirement, the Advisory Committee pointed out that only where the questions common to the class predominate over the questions affecting individual members, is it possible to achieve the economies that the device of class action pursues.[299] It further suggests that the predominance analysis involves a two-stage test:

> First, once the threshold determination has been made that common questions predominate sufficiently to support overall class treatment; second, the predominance criterion acts as a guide to the judge in molding and defining the class.....It is appropriate to consider simply the degree to which the common questions may be decisive of the issues to be dealt with in the separate phase of the action, in order to judge the efficiency of the arrangement.[300]

In addition to predominance, Rule 23(b)(3) requires the court to assess whether the class treatment is 'superior to other available methods for fairly and efficiently adjudicating the controversy'. In determining the superiority, the court needs to consider the factors listed in Rule 23(b)(3)(A)-(D):

(A) the class members' interests in individually controlling the prosecution or defense of separate actions;
(B) the extent and nature of any litigation concerning the controversy already begun by or against class members;
(C) the desirability or undesirability of concentrating the litigation of the claims in the particular forum; and
(D) the likely difficulties in managing a class action.

For example, when the individual damages are too small for individual lawsuits to be economically feasible, an aggregated class action is superior to other methods of handling such claims.[301] However, by contrast, cases involving mass accidents or mass torts (for instance, birth defects caused by prescription drugs, tobacco-related diseases caused by smoking) are not considered suitable for class actions.[302]

---

[297]John Bronsteen and Owen Fiss, 'The Class Action Rule', Notre Dame Law Review (2002), Volume 78, 1419, pp. 1423–1424; Robert H. Klonoff, Edward K.M. Bilich and Suzette M. Malveaux, *Class Actions and Other Multi-Party Litigation: Cases and Materials*, (Second Edition, Thomson/West 2006), p. 245.

[298]Ibid.

[299]Notes of Advisory Committee on Rules—1966 Amendment, available at http://www.law.cornell.edu/rules/frcp/rule_23 (accessed on 21 July 2016).

[300]See James William Moore *et al*, *Moore's Federal Practice*, para 23.45(2), at 323–333, (third edition, 1997).

[301]Janet Cooper Alexander, 'An Introduction to Class Action Procedure in the United States', Presented Conference: Debates over Group Litigation in Comparative Perspective, Geneva, Switzerland, (July 21–22, 2000), p. 5.

[302]Ibid.

#### 2.4.3.1.3 Rule 23(c) (Class Certification)

This rule directs the court to determine whether the case could be maintained (certified) as a class action. The judge needs to give its permission, as it were, for the case to proceed as a class action. This is called certification. Certification should take place 'at an early practicable time' after the case is filed.[303] The 'early practicable time' indicated the moment when the court has sufficient information to decide whether or not the case meets the requirements listed in Rule 23(a) and 23(b).[304]

If the court decides the action could be maintained as a class lawsuit, the certification must be delivered to class members.[305] The key factor in the court's notice is the 'opt-out' right for class members. Rule 23(c)(2)(B)(v) provides that in a class action permitted according to Rule 23(b)(3), the members have the right to choose not to take part in the class (to "opt out" of the class). Those who do not opt out will be bound by the effects of the court's judgement or settlement reached between two parties.

#### 2.4.3.1.4 Rule 23(e) (Class Action Settlements)

This rule provides that no class action could end in settlement unless the court approves the settlement agreement.[306] Sometimes, the settlement agreement is reached even before the class is certified.[307] Under this circumstance, the settlement agreement still needs to be approved by the court. In addition to applying the criteria listed in Rule 23(e) about the approval of settlement agreement, the court also needs to make sure that the class meets the conditions for certification.[308] However, this issue has been debated, for many years, by courts and commentators whether the strict requirements for certifying a class action for litigation purpose need also to be applied in the situation that the certification is sought only for validating a settlement agreement.[309] On this issue, the federal law and some state law adopt different approaches. The former one requires that except for the requirement that the court should consider 'the likely difficulties in managing a class action', all requirements for certifying a litigation class listed in Rule 23(b)(3) should be applied for the approval of a class settlement agreement.[310] However,

---

[303]The term 'At an early practicable time' takes place of the previous term 'as soon as practicable' after the 2003 amendment.

[304]See Robert H. Klonoff, Edward K.M. Bilich and Suzette M. Malveaux, *Class Actions and Other Multi-Party Litigation: Cases and Materials*, (Second Edition, Thomson/West 2006), p. 311.

[305]Rule 23(c)(2) of Federal Rules of Civil Procedure.

[306]Rule 23(e) of Federal Rules of Civil Procedure.

[307]American Law Institute, *Principles of the Law: Aggregate Litigation*, (American Law Institute Publishers, 2010), pp. 212–213; John Bronsteen and Owen Fiss, 'The Class Action Rule', *Notre Dame Law Review* (2002), Volume 78, 1419, p. 1443.

[308]John Bronsteen and Owen Fiss, 'The Class Action Rule', *Notre Dame Law Review* (2002), Volume 78, 1419, p. 1443.

[309]American Law Institute, *Principles of the Law: Aggregate Litigation*, (American Law Institute Publishers, 2010), p. 213.

[310]Ibid.

some state law adopts a relaxed approach where strict requirements for certifying a class action are not used for the approval of settlement agreement.[311]

In the court's approval of settlement of a case which is certified according to Rule 23(b)(3), the opt-out rule is also applicable.[312] In the context of the approval of class action settlement, it is called a second opt-out opportunity. Under this rule, the class members have an opt-out right to leave the class if the content of the settlement agreement does not satisfy them.[313] But this rule has not exerted a substantial effect and is only applied as a matter of discretion by the court.[314] In fact, few courts have ordered such second opt-out right.[315]

**2.4.3.1.5 Rule 23(g) and (h) (The Class Counsel and Attorney's Fees in Class Actions)**

According to Rule 23(g), the court normally appoints class counsel when the class is certified after considering several relevant factors.[316] In general, the court must select the counsel who can best represent the interests of the class when there is more than one applicant.[317] The selection criteria include, among others, counsel's experience in handling class actions and counsel's knowledge of the applicable law.[318]

To fund a class action, a contingency fee arrangement is not commonly used.[319] Rather, the 'common fund doctrine'[320] is of significant importance in financing class actions, where attorneys in a successful class action could collect reasonable

---

[311]For example, La. Code Civ. Proc. Ann. art. 591(B)(4) (1997), see American Law Institute, *Principles of the Law: Aggregate Litigation*, (American Law Institute Publishers, 2010), pp. 213–216.

[312]Rule 23(e)(4) of Federal Rules of Civil Procedure.

[313]The first opt-out right appears in the certifying procedure of a class action, see Rule 23(c)(2)(B)(v) of Federal Rules of Civil Procedure.

[314]American Law Institute, *Principles of the Law: Aggregate Litigation*, (American Law Institute Publishers, 2010), p. 242.

[315]See for instance, *Denney v. Deutsche Bank AG*, 2006 WL 845727, at 12 (2d Cir. Mar. 31, 2006); and see *Hicks v. Morgan Stanley & Co.*, 2005 U.S. Dist. LEXIS 24890, at 17 (S.D.N.Y. Oct. 24, 2005); and see *In re Visa Check/Mastermoney Antitrust Litig.*, 297 F. Supp. 2d 503, 518 (E.D.N.Y. 2003). In all those cases, the second opt-out rights are denied by the courts. For more, see Robert H. Klonoff, Edward K.M. Bilich and Suzette M. Malveaux, *Class Actions and Other Multi-Party Litigation: Cases and Materials*, (Second Edition, Thomson/West 2006), pp. 706–707.

[316]Rule 23(g)(1)(2) of Federal Rules of Civil Procedure.

[317]Rule 23(g)(2) of Federal Rules of Civil Procedure.

[318]The issues must be taken into consideration and may be considered by the court when such a selection is made are incorporated in Rule 23(g)(1)(A) and Rule 23(g)(1)(B) of Federal Rules of Civil Procedure.

[319]Janet Cooper Alexander, 'An Introduction to Class Action Procedure in the United States', Presented Conference: Debates over Group Litigation in Comparative Perspective, Geneva, Switzerland, (July 21–22, 2000), p. 10; and also see Rachael Mulheron, The Class Action in Common Law Legal Systems: a Comparative Perspective, (Hart Publishing, 2004), pp. 469–470.

[320]The common fund doctrine was endorsed for federal class actions in *Boeing Co. v. Van Gemert*, 444 U.S. 472 (1982).

fees from the entire monetary remedies after the court's discretion.[321] If the claim is lost (no common fund is generated), the class counsel get no fees.

#### 2.4.3.2 Securities Fraud Actions in the US

In the US, most shareholder class actions (securities fraud litigation) are substantially based on fraud as provided in section 10 (b) of the Securities Exchange Act of 1934 (15 U.S.C S78j) implemented by Securities Exchange Commission Rule 10b-5. The Private Securities Litigation Reform Act 1995 introduced several procedural rules to combat abuses or practical difficulties in securities class litigation.[322] In order to establish a securities class action under Rule 10b-5, a plaintiff has to prove that a defendant made a misrepresentation of material fact, upon which the plaintiff justifiably relies.[323] The plaintiffs should suffer financial losses when transacting stocks, which is directly caused by the company's misstatement.[324] Empirical research demonstrates that securities class actions have been widely applied in the US, with a total number of 3641 filings between 1 Jan 1996 and 30 June 2013.[325]

#### 2.4.3.3 The Private Securities Litigation Reform Act of 1995 (The PSLRA 1995)

The PSLRA 1995 imposed restrictions on private securities actions by aiming at preventing frivolous securities class actions, which were filed by lawyers desiring high amounts of lawyers' fees.[326] In Congress's views, the biggest winners in

[321]In practice, the successful lawyer must submit a request to the court to claim reasonable lawyer's fees, which are paid out of the class compensation (the common fund).

[322]See Robert H. Klonoff, Edward K.M. Bilich and Suzette M. Malveaux, *Class Actions and Other Multi-Party Litigation: Cases and Materials*, (Second Edition, Thomson/West 2006), pp. 996–997. See Donna M. Nagy, Richard W. Painter and Margaret V. Sachs, *Securities Litigation and Enforcement: Cases and Materials*, (Thomson/West 2003), pp. 2–11.

[323]Securities Exchange Commission Rule 10b-5.

[324]Ibid.

[325]The Stanford Law School Securities Class Action Clearinghouse in cooperation with Cornerstone Research has identified this figure, available at http://securities.stanford.edu (accessed on 11 August 2016).

[326]Patrick M. Garry, Candice Spurlin, Debra A. Owen, William A. Williams and Lindsay J. Efting, 'The Irrationality of Shareholder Class Action Lawsuits: A Proposal for Reform', South Dakota Law Review, (2004), Volume 49(2), 275, pp. 281–282; and see Jill E. Fisch, 'Class Action Reform, Qui Tam, and the Role of the Plaintiff', Law and Contemporary Problems, (1997), Volume 60, 167, p. 168; and see Susan P. Koniak and George M. Cohen, 'Under Cloak of Settlement', *Virginia Law Review*, (1996), Volume 82,1051; and see Jonathan R. Macey and Geoffrey P. Miller, 'The Plaintiffs' Attorney's Role in Class Action and Derivative Litigation: Economic Analysis and Recommendations for Reform', *University of Chicago Law Review*, (1991), Volume 58, 1.

securities class actions appear to be plaintiffs' lawyers because they can simply facilitate settlements and collect lawyers' fees.[327,328] The PSLRA 1995 provides a 'safe harbour' standard, authorizing three independent bases for dismissals of fraud actions involving forward-looking statement.[329] The first ground is based on the Bespeaks Caution Doctrine, requiring that forward-looking statements should be 'identified as a forward-looking statement, and be accompanied by meaningful cautionary statements identifying important factors that could cause actual results to differ materially from those in the forward-looking statement.'[330] The second ground provides that forward-looking statements should be 'immaterial' as a matter of law.[331] And the third ground authorizes the dismissal when the plaintiff fails to prove that a forward-looking statement is made 'with actual knowledge' by the defendant.[332]

The PSLRA 1995 brought new procedural requirements in securities fraud actions. For example, the selection of a lead plaintiff.[333] This procedural change was aimed at preventing 'professional plaintiffs', who own a few shares of stock in a large number of companies just for the purpose of attaching their names to the issues complained, from being lead plaintiffs in securities class actions.[334] Congress worried that class action lawyers would 'hire' professional plaintiffs to be lead plaintiffs, thereby encouraging frivolous litigation just for high lawyers' fees.[335] The PSLRA designed new provisions against 'professional plaintiffs'.[336] The most important rule probably is normally the court will appoint a class member with the highest monetary stake in the case as the lead plaintiff. Another rule is that, during a three-year period, the same lead plaintiffs are not allowed to act in this role in more than 5 class actions.[337] Lead plaintiffs are required to file a sworn certification

---

[327]See Donna M. Nagy, Richard W. Painter and Margaret V. Sachs, *Securities Litigation and Enforcement: Cases and Materials*, (Thomson/West 2003), p. 9.

[328]Moreover, Professor John C. Coffee's article states that 'The present structure of securities class actions benefits a trio of interest groups—corporate officials, plaintiff's attorneys, and insurers but not shareholders'. See John C. Coffee, 'Reforming the Securities Class Action: An Essay on Deterrence and Its Implementation', Columbia Law Review, (2006), Volume 106(7), 1534, p. 1535.

[329]See Section 21(E)(c) of the PSLRA 1995.

[330]See Section 21E(c) (1) (A) (i) of the PSLRA 1995.

[331]See Section 21E(c) (1) (A) (ii) of the PSLRA 1995.

[332]See Section 21E(c) (1) (B) of the PSLRA 1995.

[333]See Section 27 (a) (3) of the PSLRA 1995.

[334]See R. Chris Heck, 'Conflict and Aggregation: Appointing Institutional Investors as Sole Lead Plaintiffs Under the PSLRA', *University of Chicago Law Review*, (1999), Volume 66(4), 1199, p. 1202.

[335]See the House of Congress Report, Securities Litigation Reform, (No. 104-369), (1995), p. 31.

[336]See Donna M. Nagy, Richard W. Painter and Margaret V. Sachs, *Securities Litigation and Enforcement: Cases and Materials*, (Thomson/West 2003), p. 398.

[337]See Section 27 (a) (3) (B) (vi) of the PSLRA 1995.

stating that—the plaintiff has reviewed the complaint and authorized its filing. The plaintiffs, if necessary, are required to provide testimony at deposition and trial.[338]

#### 2.4.3.4 The Problematic Role of Plaintiffs' Lawyers in Securities Class Actions

An important criticism of American securities fraud actions relies on the allegedly problematic role of plaintiffs' lawyers.[339] In practice, it is common that each class member is only compensated with a small fraction of their monetary losses through a settlement or a judgment in favour of him, while plaintiffs' lawyers appear to be the biggest winners in class litigation.[340] A survey conducted by the National Economic Research Associates (NERA) in this regard reveals that damages paid to class members just amounted to approximately 5% of their losses.[341] It was once indicated plaintiffs' lawyers, in practice, face little scrutiny of their performance on behalf of class members because the group of plaintiffs in class actions are, in most cases, 'diffuse and unorganized'.[342]

As a matter of fact, the 'lawyers-driven' procedure is not unique to class actions, but could also be found in any sort of litigation on account of the existence of the divergent interests between lawyers and the clients.[343] The concern of 'lawyer-driven' procedure might be further enhanced by the fact that procedures in securities fraud class actions are on average much more complicated than simple civil lawsuits (for instance, contract disputes).[344] For this reason, the role of

[338]Section 21D (a) (2) (A) (i) to 21D (a) (2) (A) (vi) lists several requirements for the certification of the lead plaintiff.

[339]Patrick M. Garry, Candice Spurlin, Debra A. Owen, William A. Williams and Lindsay J. Efting, 'The Irrationality of Shareholder Class Action Lawsuits: A Proposal for Reform', *South Dakota Law Review*, (2004), Volume 49(2), 275, pp. 276–278; see Jill E. Fisch, 'Class Action Reform, Qui Tam, and the Role of the Plaintiff', *Law and Contemporary Problems*, (1997), Volume 60, 167, pp. 169–170; Susan P. Koniak and George M. Cohen, 'Under Cloak of Settlement', *Virginia Law Review*, (1996), Volume 82,1051; and see Jonathan R. Macey and Geoffrey P. Miller, 'The Plaintiffs' Attorney's Role in Class Action and Derivative Litigation: Economic Analysis and Recommendations for Reform', *University of Chicago Law Review*, (1991), Volume 58, 1.

[340]See Patrick M. Garry, Candice Spurlin, Debra A. Owen, William A. Williams and Lindsay J. Efting, 'The Irrationality of Shareholder Class Action Lawsuits: A Proposal for Reform', *South Dakota Law Review*, (2004), Volume 49(2), 275, pp. 275–276.

[341]See James D. Cox, 'Making Securities Fraud Class Actions Virtuous', *Arizona Law Review*, (1997), Volume 39, 497, p. 501.

[342]In theory, the class members own the class action, however, lawyers control and conduct the entire proceeding. The separation of ownership and control would easily lead lawyers to 'monopolize' the whole litigation proceeding. Adam C. Pritchard, 'Markets as Monitors: A Proposal to Replace Class Actions with Exchanges as Securities Fraud Enforcers', *Virginia Law Review*, (1999), Volume 85, 925, p. 928.

[343]Further analysis in this regard will be in Sects. 6.2 and 6.3 of this book.

[344]Simple civil disputes (e.g. contract dispute) are generally not multi-party actions, where complex procedures like 'opt-in', 'register with the court' are not applied.

plaintiffs' lawyers would be more significant in conducting the whole litigation proceeding because general class members are not experts in monitoring complex litigation. In fact, shareholder class actions are criticized for becoming an industry for lawyers specializing in class actions to earn huge lawyers' fees.[345]

Before the enactment of PSLRA, lots of lawyers 'race to the courthouse' to sue in the wake of the disclosure of unfavourable information or a drop in stock price.[346] To facilitate speedy filings of class actions before courts, a common approach for lawyers is to retain a list of potential plaintiffs and their shareholdings,[347] and seek help from these 'professional plaintiffs' before the class litigation is initiated.[348] In this regard, the 'most adequate plaintiff' provisions in the PSLRA 1995 try to make shareholders in the securities fraud class actions function more actively, by encouraging them to become lead plaintiffs in lawsuits.[349] The rationale behind this rule is that a class action where the role of the shareholders is active would be more in line with the shareholders' interest than a class action essentially driven by lawyers.[350]

[345]Patrick M. Garry, Candice Spurlin, Debra A. Owen, William A. Williams and Lindsay J. Efting, 'The Irrationality of Shareholder Class Action Lawsuits: A Proposal for Reform', *South Dakota Law Review*, (2004), Volume 49(2), 275, p. 284.

[346]Donna M. Nagy, Richard W. Painter and Margaret V. Sachs, *Securities Litigation and Enforcement: Cases and Materials*, (Thomson/West 2003), p. 399.

[347]See Elliot J. Weiss and John S. Beckerman, 'Let the Money do the Monitoring: How Institutional Investors Can Reduce Agency Costs in Securities Class Actions', *Yale Law Journal*, (1995), Volume 104, 2053, p. 2061.

[348]See Elliot J. Weiss and John S. Beckerman, 'Let the Money do the Monitoring: How Institutional Investors Can Reduce Agency Costs in Securities Class Actions', *Yale Law Journal*, (1995), Volume 104, 2053, p. 2060.

[349]See 27 (a) (3) (B) of the PSLRA 1995. For example, the most adequate plaintiff shall select and retain counsel to represent the class; [27 (a) (3) (B) (v)].

[350]Janet Cooper Alexander, 'Do the Merits Matter? A Study of Settlements in Securities Class Actions', *Stanford Law Review*, (1991), Volume 43, 497, p. 535.

# Chapter 3
# Rules on the Costs and Funding of Shareholder Litigation

## 3.1 General Rules on the Costs of Shareholder Litigation

Different forms of shareholder litigation, including shareholder derivative actions, shareholder direct actions and shareholder class actions, are all considered to fall within the scope of civil litigation. In many jurisdictions the procedural requirements for these actions are mainly incorporated in civil procedure rules.[1] In this chapter, general rules on the costs of shareholder litigation will be studied by investigating relevant statutory provisions in the general civil procedure regime.

### *3.1.1 Costs Arising*

Each jurisdiction has its rules regulating litigation costs. Generally, there are three components of litigation costs—the court charges, the lawyers' fees and evidential costs for witnesses and experts.[2]

#### 3.1.1.1 The Court Charges

Normally, the two parties in a lawsuit will be charged an amount of money for dispute resolution service by the court. Although the amount of the court charges

[1]For example, in the United States, the procedural requirements of the derivative action are incorporated in Rule 23.1 in Federal Rules of Civil Procedure; In the United Kingdom, such kind of provisions are found in Part 19.9 of Civil Procedure Rules. And in China, article 3 of the PRC Civil Procedure law provides that 'the provisions of this law is dealing with civil litigation arising from disputes on property and personal relations between citizens, legal persons or other organizations'.

[2]Christopher Hodges, Stefan Vogenauer and Magdalena Tulibacka, *The Cost and funding of Civil Litigation*, (Hart Publishing, 2010), p. 12.

 
W. Chen, *A Comparative Study of Funding Shareholder Litigation*,
DOI 10.1007/978-981-10-3623-1_3

differs in each jurisdiction, most of the countries charge court fees from the plaintiffs who initiate a claim, and sometimes from defendants who have taken certain steps in the court proceeding.[3] However, France, Sweden and eight countries in Latin America are exceptions to this rule, where people could access to the court without paying any fees.[4] Generally, the court fees vary according to the type of the court, the proceeding and the case. Many countries use 'a tariff system'[5] to reduce the unpredictability of the court charges.[6]

#### 3.1.1.1.1 The Chinese Rules on Court Charges

China is one of the countries where a tariff system is applied. After decades of no court charges, in 2007 China introduced rules on court fees by enacting *Measures for the Payment of Litigation Costs* (the MPLC).[7] The court charges are divided into three main categories: (A) the case acceptance fees; (B) the application fees; (C) other expenses.

##### 3.1.1.1.1.1 The Case Acceptance Fees

The case acceptance fee has to be paid in advance when a court formally accepts the case.[8] Article 7 of the MPLC provides that in most of cases, the case acceptance fee is applied when the cases are accepted by the court of first instance, by the court of second instance or for certain types of retrial proceedings.[9] Article 20 of the MPLC provides that the case acceptance fee should be prepaid by the plaintiff, a third party with an independent claim,[10] or by the appellant.

As for the amount of the court fees that should be charged, article 13(1) of the MPLC states that, for disputes over monetary issues, the case acceptance fees are charged based on the monetary value in a particular case. The fees are in direct proportion to the disputed amount.[11] Moreover, article 15 provides that the case

---

[3]Christopher Hodges, Stefan Vogenauer and Magdalena Tulibacka, *The Cost and funding of Civil Litigation*, (Hart Publishing, 2010), p. 13.

[4]Ibid.

[5]'A tariff system' refers to rules on how much fees could be charged from litigation parties by the court and how the fees are calculated.

[6]The importance of predictability of the cost will be discussed later.

[7]诉讼费用交纳办法(Measures for the Payment of Litigation Costs), (2007), English version is available at http://www1.lawinfochina.com/display.aspx?lib=law&id=5765 (accessed on 13 July 2016).

[8]Article 20 of the MPLC.

[9]The 'retrial proceeding' (再审程序) indicates a court proceeding where litigation parties could apply for a new proceeding on a case which has been adjudicated before. Article 177 of the PRC Civil Procedure Law.

[10]'A third party with an independent claim' (有独立请求权第三人) refers to a person who has an independent claim to the object of the current action. Article 56 of the PRC Civil Procedure Law.

[11]

| The monetary value of the case (RMB) | The case acceptance fee to be charged (RMB) |
|---|---|
| Lower than 10,000 | Fixed fee of 50 |
| From 10,000 to 100,000 | 50 + 2.5% (A-10,000) |

(continued)

acceptance fee could be charged at half rate where the claimants or appellants withdraw the pleadings. The 'half rate rule' also applies in the summary proceedings, or in the situation where the case is settled through mediation.[12]

**3.1.1.1.1.2 The Application Fees**

Article 10 of the MPLC provides that a litigant has to pay application fees when he applies for any of the following proceedings: (1) enforcement by the court of a legally effective judgment or ruling, enforceable deed, or arbitral award; (2) preservation measures; (3) a payment warrant; (4) a public summons[13]; (5) revocation of an arbitral award or affirmation of the effectiveness of an arbitration agreement; (6) bankruptcy proceedings; (7) certain types of application under the 1999 PRC Special Maritime Procedure Law; or (8) recognition and enforcement of a foreign judgment or foreign arbitral award.

The rate of the application fees depends on the type of the application. For cases involving monetary value, similar to the calculation method used in the case acceptance fees, the application fee is in direct proportion to the financial value involved in the claim.[14] Just like the case acceptance fee, the application fee has to be paid prior to making such application to the court. Unless a fee remission is granted under the judicial aid system, unfulfilled payment would lead to the rejection of the application.

---

(Footnote 11 continued)

(continued)

| The monetary value of the case (RMB) | The case acceptance fee to be charged (RMB) |
|---|---|
| From 100,000 to 200,000 | 2300 + 2% (A-100,000) |
| From 200,000 to 500,000 | 4300 + 1.5% (A-200,000) |
| From 500,000 to 1,000,000 | 8800 + 1% (A-500,000) |
| From 1,000,000 to 2,000,000 | 13,800 + 0.9% (A-1,000,000) |
| From 2,000,000 to 5,000,000 | 22,800 + 0.8% (A-2,000,000) |
| From 5,000,000 to 10,000,000 | 46,800 + 0.7% (A-5,000,000) |
| From 10,000,000 to 20,000,000 | 81,800 + 0.6% (A-10,000,000) |
| More than 20,000,000 | 141,800 + 0.5% (A-20,000,000) |

[12]Article 15 of the MPLC.

[13]Under article 193(1) of the 2007 Civil Procedure Law, the holder of transferable negotiable instruments may apply for a public summons where such negotiable instruments are stolen, lost or destroyed. The effect of a public summon is to nullify such negotiable instruments and protect the interest of the holder of it.

[14]The calculating method is stipulated in article 14(1)(2)(3)(6) of the MPLC. And the application fees for preservation measures and for insolvency proceedings are capped at RMB 5000 and RMB 300,000, respectively. According to subsection (4)(5)(7) of this article, with regards to public summons, revocation of arbitral awards, confirmation of effectiveness of arbitral awards, and certain types of applications under 1999 PRC Special Maritime Procedure Law, the application fees are fixed, ranging from 100 RMB to 10,000 RMB.

#### 3.1.1.1.1.3 The Role of the 'Court Charges' in Chinese Civil Litigation

Undoubtedly, the court charges impose a financial burden upon potential litigants. For instance, in a case with high monetary value, the litigant has to prepay a large amount of case acceptance fees to the court and bears big financial risk in case of losing.[15] It, in practice, creates disincentives for potential litigants who intend to commence actions.

Particularly, for the reason that shareholder litigation (for example, derivative actions) usually involves high monetary value, potential litigants would take it into account before filing such lawsuits. Empirical studies suggest that the number of derivative actions in China is comparative small, which may be partly attributed to the disincentives brought by the high litigation costs.[16]

Therefore, it was suggested that court charges for derivative actions would not be calculated in the same way as that of 'monetary cases'.[17] It is suggested that the court charges for these cases should be fixed at a certain level, irrespective of the financial value involved.[18] Also in this respect, it was further proposed that, instead of a fixed rate, a more flexible charging standard could be introduced to decide the rate of the case acceptance fees in a derivative lawsuit.[19] It was proposed the court charges for a derivative action should be proportionate to the registered capital of the company regardless the form of the company.[20,21] For example, a shareholder from a company which holds a registered capital of less than 1 million RMB should pay 1000 RMB as the case acceptance fees when commencing a derivative lawsuit. Similarly, if the company's registered capital is between 1 million RMB and 10 million RMB, the case acceptance fees would amount to 5000 RMB. The general rule in calculating case acceptance fees is like 'more registered capital, more court

---

[15]Chinese law provides that the losing party in a civil lawsuit should be liable for the winning party's court charges (article 29 of the MPLC).

[16]From 2006 to 2011, there were just 60 derivative lawsuits brought into the courts. Dan Wang, *Theoretical analysis on shareholders' derivative actions*, (in Chinese) (公司派生诉讼论), (China legal publishing house, 2012), p. 325.

[17]Changwu Zuo and Guanghua Yu, 'The rationality of legislation and the efficiency of the law enforcement: begin with the analysis of derivative actions' (in Chinese) (理性立法和法律实施的效率: 从分析公司派生诉讼机制开始), http://hub.hku.hk/handle/10722/136717 (accessed on 10 August 2016).

[18]Ibid. The reason for the proposal about fixed court charges for derivative actions might be that, from the points of view of this book, derivative actions demonstrate boarder public significance than ordinary civil litigation. It could have deterrence effects for potential wrongdoers and set as an example for good corporate governance.

[19]Peizhong Gan, 'An overview of shareholder derivative actions in Chinese company law', (in Chinese, 简评中国公司法对股东派生诉讼制度的借鉴 'jianping zhongguo gongsifa dui gudong paisheng susong zhidu de jiejian'), http://www.civillaw.com.cn/Article/default.asp?id=25127 (accessed on 10 August 2016).

[20]Ibid.

[21]The current Chinese company law provides two main company forms—limited liabilities companies (LLC) and joint stock limited companies (JSLC), which are provided respectively in Chaps. 2 and 4 of PRC company law.

charges'. But this proposal could not fundamentally remove disincentives for *bona fide* shareholders to commence a derivative claim because they may still face high litigation costs in the event that the company has a high registered legal capital. In this regard, a fixed small amount of court charges would be more desirable. It is true that low rates might encourage strike suits or frivolous claims. However, it is observed in current practice shareholders are reluctant to commence derivative actions while the abuse of litigation mechanism has not been a big concern.[22] From a comparative perspective, it is found that in Japan derivative actions are considered as 'non-monetary cases' and the filing fees are fixed at ¥ 8200 (about $75), which facilitates the use of derivative actions in Japan.[23]

#### 3.1.1.1.2 The Rules on Court Charges in the UK and the US

The English courts also charge courts fees. For instance, a range from 30 lb (for a case of less than 300 lb) to 1530 lb (for a claim of 300,000 lb or above) will be charged as court fees when a litigant initiates a civil claim. Similar to the Chinese rule, court fees in the UK are also calculated on an incremental basis. In the UK, the civil justice system is not mainly financed by the state from the general taxation but is predominantly funded by the court fees charged from litigants.[24] Normally, court fees constitute approximately 80% of the funding for civil justice system, while the remaining 20% is covered by taxpayers (through the Ministry of Justice budget).[25] This high proportion of 'self-funding' could be considered as a key reason for the excessive court charges in the UK, which has been criticized for long.[26] Therefore, when the issue of costs was considered as part of the reform of the English civil justice system, Lord Jackson's preliminary report proposed that taxpayers should deliver a larger part of the funding for the court system to ensure the access to civil justice.[27,28] It was also proposed that one of the reasons for the expensive courts

---

[22]See Guanghua Yu and Junhai Liu, 'Legislation and the enforcement of law', (in Chinese), (理性立法和法律实施), commercial law forum no. 330, the minute of this forum could be available at (in Chinese) http://www.civillaw.com.cn/article/default.asp?id=43662 (accessed on 10 August 2016).

[23]It demonstrates after the fees reduction for derivative claims, there was a rise in the filing of such actions in Japan. Dan W. Puchniak, 'The complexity of Derivative Actions in Asia: an Inconvenient Truth', in *The Derivative Action in Asia: a Comparative and Functional Approach*, Dan W. Puchniak et al. (eds), (Cambridge University Press, 2012), 90, pp. 144–145.

[24]Christopher Hodges et al., The cost and funding of civil litigation, (Hart Publishing, 2010), p. 295.

[25]Lord Jackson, Review of Civil Litigation Costs: Preliminary Report, (the preliminary report), May 2009, p. 63.

[26]Lord Jackson, Review of Civil Litigation Costs: Preliminary Report, (the preliminary report), May 2009, p. 63–65.

[27]Lord Jackson, Review of Civil Litigation Costs: Preliminary Report, (the preliminary report), May 2009, p. 63.

[28]In Lord Jackson's preliminary report 2009, he indicated that taxpayer afforded around 20% of the funding of the court system. A document of Ministry of Justice in 2012 showed that the taxpayer paid 18% of the funding of court system. Therefore, it seems that Lord Jackson's

charges in English Supreme Courts is because the long procedure for facts statement that prolongs the oral hearing in the court.[29]

In the US, the fees to file a civil claim in the federal court were raised from $250 to $350.[30] In state courts, court fees may be set by state or local statute and may differ depending on the type of the case.[31] For example, the Delaware Supreme Court charges a non-refundable $450 filing fee and a $10 court security assessment fee. For civil actions in the court of chancery, the filing fee for a new case would be $250, $350 or $600 based on different circumstances.[32] The filing fees indicated above could increase or decrease by the court of chancery for good causes.[33]

Similar to the English civil litigation costs, litigation charges in the US is always blamed for being too expensive. High litigation costs in the US is mainly caused by civil discovery,[34] such as the procedure to discover and present evidence. Empirical study shows that courts and litigation parties do not limit discovery on their own, and the lack of controlling on the discovery procedures generates costly consequences.[35] Civil discovery normally supports truth-seeking, however, the absence of control mechanism over the discovery procedure may lead to the abuse of it. Respondents to a survey conducted by Federal Judicial Centre (FJC) demonstrate that discovery is abused commonly in federal courts.[36]

#### 3.1.1.1.3 Rethinking the Rule of 'Higher Value, Higher Court Charges'

As mentioned before, in many countries, the court fees for a property case generally depend on the monetary value at dispute.[37] However, is it rational that

(Footnote 28 continued)

proposal has not been adopted. See 'Why we charge court fees', (March, 2012), available at http://www.justice.gov.uk/courts/fees/why-we-charge (accessed on 14 August 2016).

[29]Andrew Le Sueur, 'A Report on Six Seminars About the UK Supreme Court' (December 2008), p. 26. QueenMary School of Law Legal Studies Research Paper No. 1/2008, Available at SSRN: http://ssrn.com/abstract=1324749 or http://dx.doi.org/10.2139/ssrn.1324749 (accessed on 10 August 2016).

[30]Deborah R. Hensler, 'The national report on cost and funding of civil litigation in the United States of America', in Christopher Hodges et al. (eds), *The Cost and funding of Civil Litigation*, (Hart Publishing, 2010) 535, p. 539.

[31]Ibid.

[32]For more details about the filing fee in court of chancery in Delaware, http://courts.delaware.gov/help/fees/chanceryfees.stm#civilaction (accessed on 10 August 2016).

[33]ibid.

[34]Institute for the Advancement of the American Legal System, *'Preserving access and identifying excess: areas of convergence and consensus'*, (2010), p. 13.

http://civilconference.uscourts.gov/LotusQuickr/dcclMain.nsfl$defaultview/7B6BO47956592D3A8525771900011F6A/$File/IAALS,PreservingAccess_and_IdentifyingExcess.pdf (accessed 10 August 2016).

[35]Institute for the Advancement of the American Legal System, *'Preserving access and identifying excess: areas of convergence and consensus'*, (2010), p. 14.

[36]Ibid.

[37]See Christopher Hodges et al., The Cost and funding of Civil Litigation, (Hart Publishing, 2010), p. 71.

'higher value implies higher court charges'? Do high-valued cases need to use more judicial resources? In other words, will the court spend more time and use more personnel in a high-valued case than in a case which has less value? Only linking the value of the case and the amount of the court costs is not rational. Therefore, in China, the amount of the 'case acceptance fee' depends both on the value of the case and the type of case. For example, article 13(d) of the MPLC states that in labour disputes, regardless of the monetary value involved, the 'case acceptance fee' is 10RMB. This is an exception where the case acceptance fee mainly depends on the type of the case rather than the value of the case. Also, for patent cases, trademark disputes and maritime cases, the amount of the case acceptance fee is 100 RMB for each in spite of the financial value at stake. 100 RMB would be charged as the case acceptance fee for each administrative case. Apart from those cases mentioned above, the case acceptance fees for cases involving a basically monetary claim ('property cases') are proportionate to the value at stake. But this system is still criticized as unreasonable, because how many judicial resources would be used for each case may have many determinants and the 'double standard' (the value at stake and the case type) in MPLC is still too general and vague. A much more detailed case classification should be introduced. For instance, it was suggested in doctrine that the rate of the case acceptance fee could be determined according to different trial procedures. There are generally two types of trial procedures for cases in the first instance under PRC Civil Procedure Law—the summary procedure (简易程序, Chapter 13 of the CPL) and the ordinary (non-summary) procedure (普通程序, Chapter 12 of the CPL). The former one is applied to cases where the facts are simple and obligations of the two parties are well defined, while the ordinary procedures are used for cases with complexities and the court needs to investigate the facts and carefully define the rights and obligations for each party. It has been recommended that a big difference between the summary procedure and the ordinary procedure should exist in terms of the case acceptance fees in the sense that these two procedures consume different amounts of judicial resources.[38] It was also suggested that, compared to the case ending in a judgment, a lower case acceptance fee should apply to the case ending in a settlement in exchange for the judicial resources it has saved.[39]

[38]Yong'an Liao, *A Research on Litigation Costs*, (诉讼费用研究), (Press of China University of Political Science and Law, 中国政法大学出版社, 2006), pp. 31–32.

[39]For example, article 84 of the Civil Procedure Rule of Taiwan provides if the case is ended with a settlement, half of the case acceptance fees could be refunded. And see Yong'an Liao, *A Research on Litigation Costs*, (诉讼费用研究), (Press of China University of Political Science and Law, 中国政法大学出版社, 2006), pp. 33–34. (it stated that Chinese courts encourage litigation parties to achieve a settlement through negotiation in order to save judicial resources and maintain the social harmony).

#### 3.1.1.2 The Lawyers' Fees

Compared to court charges which might be known in advance through the 'tariff system', lawyers' fees are unpredictable, which contributes to the unpredictability of the overall litigation costs.

In almost every country, the fees between lawyers and client can be agreed freely. Irrespective of the overwhelming application of the principle of free agreement, lawyers' fees are also controlled by various mechanisms—rules on ethics of lawyers, complaint mechanisms available to clients, and court assessment of the cost reasonability in given cases.[40]

For instance, in China, the Measures for the Administration of Lawyers' Fees (MALF) enacted in 2006 provides the guidance for the setting of lawyer's fees. Because of the disequilibrium of economic development and different level of commodity price among districts, the law authorizes each province to set lawyer's fee based on the local economic development and commodity price.[41]

As for the lawyers' fees in a given case, many countries have regulations on the setting of the rate. These rules usually enumerate a series of factors that should be taken into account when deciding the amount of lawyer's fees in a given case, which usually includes the case complexity, the risk involved and the workload.[42]

---

[40]See Christopher Hodges et al., The Cost and funding of Civil Litigation, (Hart Publishing, 2010), p. 16.

[41]The self-determined power is still subject to government's guidance. Article 6 of the MALF provides that 'the benchmark price and the floating range of market-regulated price shall be determined by the competent department of price of the people's government of each province, autonomous region or municipality directly under the central government together with the judicial administrative department at the same level'.

[42]Like in Article 9 of the MALF, it provides: The following main factors shall be taken into account when a law firm is consulting about the lawyers' fees with its clients: (1) time to be spent on the work; (2) complexity of the legal affair; (3) affordability of the clients; (4) risks and responsibilities the law firm might assume; and (5) social reputation and working level, etc. of the lawyers. http://www.chinalawinfo.com/ (accessed on 10 August 2016)

And the United States of America, article 1.5 of the Model Rules of Professional Conduct (the MRPC) adopted by American Bar Association (ABA) provides a similar standard that '(a) A lawyer shall not make an agreement for, charge, or collect an unreasonable fee or an unreasonable amount for expenses. The factors to be considered in determining the reasonableness of a fee include the following: (1) the time and labour required, the novelty and difficulty of the questions involved, and the skill requisite to perform the legal service properly; (2) the likelihood, if apparent to the client, that the acceptance of the particular employment will preclude other employment by the lawyer; (3) the fee customarily charged in the locality for similar legal services; (4) the amount involved and the results obtained; (5) the time limitations imposed by the client or by the circumstances; (6) the nature and length of the professional relationship with the client; (7) the experience, reputation, and ability of the lawyer or lawyers performing the services; and (8) whether the fee is fixed or contingent.'http://www.americanbar.org/groups/professional_responsibility/publications/model_rules_of_professional_conduct/rule_1_5_fees.html (accessed 10 August 2016).

### 3.1.2 The Cost-Shifting Rule

Many countries have the cost-shifting rule, where losers pay the litigation costs not only of themselves, but also of their adversary who wins the case.[43] An important exception is the United States (except for Alaska),[44] where each side bears its own costs.[45] However, in a country where the cost-shifting rule is adopted, if any unmeritorious conduct by the parties, such as falsifying evidence, occurs during the proceeding, the cost-shifting rule could be modified by judges as a sanction.[46] A refusal to award costs could be made to punish the unmerited conducts by litigation parties.[47] Therefore, the court discretion over the grant of costs can provide an incentive for proper conducts during the proceeding.

It should be noted that the cost-shifting rule in principle means the losing party should pay both the winning party's court fees and lawyer's fees. However, in several countries (for instance, China, Russia, Japan and France), the shifted fee only includes court charges, but not lawyer's fees.[48]

It could be said that the cost-shifting rule raises the unpredictability of the litigation cost. A potential plaintiff should figure out how much he should pay for the court fees, lawyer's fees, other relevant costs (like evidential costs for witnesses and experts) and also the opposite party's litigation costs in case of losing. In

---

43Many countries adopt the cost-shifting rule. For instance, China (but loser is only liable for the winning party's court charges); Japan (only shifts the court charges to the losing party, the same like China's cost-shifting rule); The Netherlands (a mitigated cost-shifting rule where the shifting lawyer's fees are based on tariff is applied); Spain; Switzerland. See Christopher Hodges et al., *The Cost and funding of Civil Litigation*, (Hart Publishing, 2010), pp. 187–545 (the Party of 'National Reports').

44Christopher Hodges et al., *The Cost and funding of Civil Litigation*, (Hart Publishing, 2010), p. 17.

45Fewer countries and arears adopt the US non cost-shifting rule. Examples of non cost-shifting rule could be found in British-Columbia in Canada for collective redress litigation. (British Columbia Class Proceedings Act, s. 37).

46Christopher Hodges et al., *The Cost and funding of Civil Litigation*, (Hart Publishing, 2010), p. 80.

47Ibid.

48However, Chinese legislators may adopt the shifting of lawyer's fees and other relevant costs (reimbursement of witnesses and expert's fees) might be adopted in the future (article 29 of the MPLC). A consultant paper in this regard was issued to collect opinions from the general public. The consultant paper proposed that the losing party should bear the lawyers' fee as well as other relevant costs (such as reimbursement of witnesses and experts' fee). According the responses from the public, some people support this amendment while other people oppose it. The people who support it hold that expanding the scope of 'shifted cost' would prevent frivolous cases. People opposing it argue that this amendment might deter some claimants who are impecunious. And the expanding of the scope of 'shifted cost' would make litigation riskier. All-China Lawyers Association, 'Proposed amendments to Chinese Civil Procedure Law, A Consultation Paper', (中华全国律师协会,民事诉讼法修正案修改意见稿), (2011), (in Chinese), available at http://www.legaldaily.com.cn/index_article/content/2011-12/01/content_3150583.html (accessed on 14 August 2016).

consideration of that, a rational claimant may be very cautious to evaluate the financial risk before bringing a lawsuit. To mitigate risk, the cost-shifting rule may probably encourage settlements, or even earlier settlements.[49]

From the economic perspective, incentives to sue for claimants may be affected by the cost-shifting rule.[50] First, for potential plaintiffs, the cost-shifting rule may encourage them to bring claims with high possibilities to win, because the legal expenses could be paid by the defendants in case of winning.[51] On the other hand, cases with low success rates may be discouraged by the rule, particularly, when the litigation costs in these cases are high.[52]

Also, greater litigation costs may be caused by the cost-shifting rule.[53] Parties concerned in an action may hold a point of view that investing more money (for example, spend more money to hire a good lawyer) to the action could yield more benefits (remedies could be obtained in case of winning). From the perspective of economics, the trial expenditure added by the parties is a 'marginal cost' and the benefits increased through a favourable judgement could be considered as 'marginal benefit'.[54] From the economic theory, the result is optimal where the marginal cost equals the marginal benefit, which may result in the increase of litigation costs.[55] The 'greater expenditure effect' was, actually, empirically verified through the data collected from the State of Florida from 1980 to 1985 where the rule of cost shifting was used during that period.[56] On the part of defendants, it was found that the cost-shifting rule led to an increase in defence expenditures of 108% and 150% for litigated and settled claims respectively.[57] But, fortunately, restrictions on litigation

[49]Christopher Hodges et al., *The Cost and funding of Civil Litigation*, (Hart Publishing, 2010), p. 78.

[50]Steven Shavell, *Foundations of Economic Analysis of Law*, (Harvard University Press, 2004), p. 429.

[51]Ibid.

[52]Ibid.

[53]Tom Schepens, 'Bridging the funding gap-the economics of cost shifting, fee arrangements and legal expenses insurance and their prospects for improving the access to civil justice', *German Working Papers in Law and Economics*, (volume 7, article 1, 2007), p. 8. http://www.core.kmi.open.ac.uk/download/pdf/6541012.pdf (accessed on 10 August 2016).

[54]The marginal cost of an activity is the increase in total cost that results from carrying out one additional unit of an activity. The marginal benefit of an activity is the increase in total benefit that results from carrying out one additional unit of activity. From the economic perspective, it is thought that 'marginal cost equals marginal benefit is an optimal condition'. See Robert H. Frank and Ben S. Bernanke, *Principles of Economics*, (Mcgraw-Hill Irwin, 2001), p. 12.

[55]Ibid.

[56]For a comprehensive overview of the empirical literature on cost shifting, see Herbert M. Kritzer, 'Lawyer Fees and Lawyer Behaviour in Litigation: What Does the Empirical Literature Really Say?', *Texas Law Review*, (2002) 1946, p. 1952.

[57]Edward A. Snyder and James W. Hughes, 'The English rule for allocating legal costs, evidence confronts theory', *Journal of Law, Economics and Organization* (1990), Volume 6, 345, p. 374.

costs mitigating the greater expenditure effect is found. For example, in England, cost awards are limited to a reasonable level.[58] The German *Bundesrechtsanwalts-gebuhrenordnung* (BRAGO) imposes restrictions on the level of lawyer's fees.[59] Such restriction is reasonable for both of the parties because if a party holding a case with a high success rate tries to 'invest' more money in the suit, the financial risk of this payment will easily be transferred to the opposite party. For example, without a restriction, a claimant holding a case with more than 95% of winning probabilities may hire a very expensive lawyer (even though it is unnecessary) and make the defendant cover the lawyer's fees under the cost-shifting rule is the case is won.

Unlike many other countries where the cost-shifting rule is adopted, the US employs an approach that 'each party bears his own litigation costs'. The purpose and rationality of the American rule could be best explained by the critical role it plays in enabling and promoting the 'private enforcement' of law.[60] Traditionally, the American regulatory system depends largely on a wide range of regulators, including private parties, rather than rely only upon a centralized bureaucracy, while in most of other countries, enforcement of public norms is mostly reserved for public agencies rather than private parties.[61] The American private enforcement theory encourages private parties to seek out and rectify wrongdoings.[62] In line with this theory, the US adopts a rule that parties in a lawsuit do not face the risk of paying the opposite party's litigation costs in case of losing.

For shareholder litigation, the cost rules might significantly affect the incentives for shareholder plaintiffs. For example, plaintiffs in a derivative action are usually minority shareholders with limited, non-corporate financial means at their disposal. Irrespective of the opposite party's litigation costs under the cost-shifting rule, commencing a shareholder lawsuit might be costly per se, which might deter *bona fide* claimants without sufficient financial resources to bring such an action.

---

[58]James W. Hughes and Edward A. Snyder, 'Allocation of litigation costs: American and English rules', in Peter Newman (ed.), *The new palgrave dictionary of economics and the law*, (Palgrave Macmillan, 2004), 51.

[59]Matthias Kilian 'Alternatives to Public Provision: The Role of Legal Expenses Insurance in Broadening Access to Justice: The German Experience', *Journal of Law and Society*, (2003), Volume 30(1), 31, p. 42.

[60]Maria Glover, 'The structural role of private enforcement mechanisms in public law', *William & Mary Law Review*, (2011), volume 53, 1137, pp. 1138–1139.

[61]Christopher Hodges et al., *The cost and funding of civil litigation*, (Hart Publishing, 2010), p. 79.

[62]For example, in corporate governance, minority shareholders could supervise and rectify misbehaviours of directors and other senior managers through private enforcement.

### *3.1.3 Shareholder Litigation Is Expensive and It Lacks Incentives for Litigants*

It could be regarded as a generally acknowledged fact that shareholder litigation is expensive.[63] The cause of shareholder litigation is usually concerned with commercial issues. For instance, a shareholder derivative claim could be brought on a ground that the director misuses an amount of company's assets which damages the interests of the company. For a securities class action, it is usually commenced if a company's false statements cause the financial losses to tens of thousands of shareholders (collective actions arising from securities fraud in China and US securities fraud actions). Considering that, court charges, which are generally proportionate to the monetary value involved in a case (except for Japan's rule of court charges for derivative actions) are high. The Lawyer' fees (if charged on an hourly rate basis)[64] and potential adverse fees under the cost-shifting rules also contribute to the high litigation costs in shareholder lawsuits.

Thinking of the damages for a shareholder plaintiff, it might not be proportionate to the litigation costs he paid before. For example, in a shareholder derivative action, monetary remedies go to the company directly. The shareholder plaintiff who bears litigation risk only indirectly benefits from the potential rise in his share

---

[63]The fact that shareholder litigation is expensive has been confirmed by legal scholars and legal practioners in many countries. For instance, for US, see Roberta Romano, 'The Shareholder Suit: Litigation without Foundation?', *The Journal of Law, Economics and Organization*, (1991), Volume 7(1), 55; Daniel J. Morrisey, 'Shareholder Litigation After the Meltdown', *West Virginia Law Review*, (2011), Volume 144, 531; Randall S. Thomas, 'A Theory of Representative Shareholder Suits and its Application to Multijurisdictional Litigation', *Northwestern University Law Review*, ((2012), Volume 106(4), 1753; Mark J. Loewenstein, Shareholder Derivative Litigation and Corporate Governance, Delaware Journal of Corporate Law, (1999), Volume 24(1), 1; Jacob Gershman, 'Losing a shareholder lawsuit could soon become more expensive', (May, 2014), available at http://blogs.wsj.com/law/2014/05/19/losing-a-shareholder-lawsuit-could-soon-become-more-expensive/ (accessed on 14 August 2016); For the UK, see Joan Loughrey, 'Directors' Duties and Shareholder Litigation: the Practical Perspective', in *Derectors' Duties and Shareholder Litigation in the Wake of the Financial Crisis*, Joan Loughrey (eds), (Edward Elgar, 2013), p. 239; Arad Reisber, Derivative Actions and Corporate Governance: Theory and Operation, (Oxford University Press, 2007), p. 222; William Kaplan and Bruce Elwood, 'The derivative action: a shareholder's bleak house?', University of British Columbia Law Review, (2003), Volume 36, 443; For China, see Lei Hao, Study on the Practical Aspects of Shareholder Litigation, (股东诉讼的实施问题研究), (China Legal Publisher, 2012); Guiqing Liu, A Study on Shareholder Litigation: from the Perspective of Corporate Governance, (公司治理视角中的股东诉讼研究), (China Fangzheng Publisher, 2005); Jun He, 'Will the Company pay for the Shareholder Litigation', (股东代表诉讼,公司"埋单"?), (2007), available at http://finance.sina.com.cn/stock/t/20070131/03341189782.shtml (accessed on 15 August 2016); Kaixiang Liu, 'Judicial Enforcement of Shareholder Litigation', (股东代表诉讼的司法适用和立法完善), (2008), available at http://www.chenglawyer.com.cn/ShowArticle.shtml?ID=20114918262598297.htm (accessed on 15 August 2016).

[64]Lawyer's fees charged on a contingent basis could not be regarded as a financial burden on the litigant. In fact, it appears like a reduction on the litigant's compensation in a successful case because the litigant must share proceeds with the lawyer.

value on a *pro rata* basis.[65] When we compare costs and benefits, it is easily found that shareholders (particularly minority ones) will usually lack incentives to initiate an action. For a shareholder class action, for instance, securities fraud litigation, a group of shareholder plaintiffs shares the damages in a successful lawsuit, which is different from derivative claims. But the lengthy court proceedings[66] and the case complexities create big risk for litigants because whether or not their 'investment' (litigation costs) could be recouped is far from certain, which may disincentivize them to commence such claims.

## 3.2 How to Fund Shareholder Litigation: General Funding Techniques

This section will introduce general funding techniques of civil litigation. Features of shareholder litigation which might make the funding approach different from that of general civil litigation would be taken into account when the study is delivered.[67]

### *3.2.1 Funding Regimes in General*

Generally, shareholder litigation could be funded in several ways as follows:

- Personal funding where litigants cover litigation costs from their own pocket
- Legal aid provided by the government to help impecunious litigants
- Lawyers funding typically includes contingency fee arrangements, conditional fee agreements and success fees

[65]In fact, this potential rise in share value is not certain because a derivative action could negatively affect a company's reputation which may reduce its share price. See Arad Reisberg, *Derivative Actions and Corporate Governance*, (Oxford University Press, 2007), p. 222.

[66]For instance, the length of the court proceeding for each class action differs, but a typical class action will take 2–3 years. (data from a US law firm specializing in representing class actions, available at http://www.rgrdlaw.com/cases-questions.html, accessed on 16 August 2016); In China, shareholder class actions generally have a lengthy court proceeding. For instance, a recently settled shareholder class action in China (Investors v. Wuliangye Company) has lasted for 5 years before being settled. See Wenliang Liu, '141 investors in Wuliangye are compensated with 13 million RMB', (in Chinese), (October, 2014), available at http://finance.people.com.cn/stock/n/2014/1011/c67815-25809971.html (accessed on 16 August 2016).

[67]This section only attempts to deliver a general introduction regarding general funding ways. Chapters 4, 5 and 6 of this book will discuss, in detail, how these funding ways function and potential problems with them.

- Public funding[68] provided by a public authority[69]
- Third party litigation funding (TPLF) provided by a professional litigation funder who is not a litigation party[70]
- Legal expenses insurance including before-the event insurance (BTE) and after-the-event insurance (ATE).

### 3.2.2 *Self-funding*

Of course there is nothing against self-funding: it is the normal state of affairs. But as mentioned in the first section of this Chapter, litigation costs in a shareholder lawsuit is generally high and may exceed the personal financial ability of the litigant. Considering the topic of this book is how can the law help in funding shareholder litigation. The issue of self-funding as such needs no further exploration.

### 3.2.3 *Legal Aid*

Legal aid is applied in almost all of the countries around the world.[71] A remarkable example in this regard is the UK, where legal aid has been applied for more than 60 years. When the legal aid scheme was established, approximately 80% of the population was eligible for civil legal aid.[72] Before the twenty-first century, this figure remained at a comparatively high level.[73] For instance, in 1986, around 63% of the population was eligible for civil legal aid.[74] But after the start of the 21st century, the figure began to drop from 50% in 2000 to 29% 2007.[75,76] The legal aid is, actually, available for certain sorts of litigation in the UK, in particular, medical

---

[68]'Public funding' discussed in this book excludes legal aid.

[69]'Public funding' investigated in this book includes public funding provided by a public authority (for instance, the Israeli Securities Authority) and public funding provided by a non-profit organization (for instance, Ontario law foundation). See *infra* Chap. 4.

[70]The scope of the professional litigation funder in third party litigation funding does not include lawyer, public funding provider and legal insurer.

[71]Christopher Hodges, Stefan Vogenauer and Magdalena Tulibacka, *The Cost and funding of Civil Litigation*, (Hart Publishing, 2010), p. 22.

[72]Lord Jackson, Review of Civil Litigation Costs: Final Report, (the final report) (2009), p. 68.

[73]Ibid.

[74]Ibid.

[75]Ibid.

[76]The influence brought by the downturn of the state economy on the legal aid budget and the increase on people's income both contribute the downside on the number of eligible people. See Lord Jackson, Review of Civil Litigation Costs: Final Report, (the final report) (2009), pp. 68–69.

negligence, housing cases and judicial review.[77] Shareholder litigation cannot be funded by legal aid.

In China too, legal aid has been provided by the state government[78] to financially assist people with financial difficulties in order to facilitate the access to justice since mid-1990s.[79] Most of the legal aid programmes are established by the Ministry of Justice (司法部) and local justice bureaus (司法局), and those legal aid programmes are mainly funded by the state budget.[80] A small part of legal aid schemes is provided by the legal aid centre based in law faculties of universities, which could be regarded as non-governmental legal aid providers.[81] The *legal aid review 2009*[82] states that 82.2% of the legal aid is funded by local governments, 7.9% of it is financed by the central governments and 9.9% is paid by the provincial government. In view of the regional economic disequilibrium in China, each provincial government has its own financial budget on legal aid, leading to different levels of legal aid. Article 10 of the 2003 Regulations on Legal Aid (2003 regulation) authorises the provincial governments to make local rules regarding the eligibility of the legal aid applicant, which may lead to a disequilibrium of the level of legal aid where people in wealthy provinces can access to justice more easily than those in undeveloped provinces.[83] In consideration of that, the Ministry of

[77]See Lord Jackson, Review of Civil Litigation Costs: Final Report, (the final report) (2009), pp. 68–69.

[78]Most of the legal aid schemes are provided by the government, while a small part of them can be provided by the legal aid centre based in the law school of a university.

[79]See generally Benjamin L. Liebman, 'Legal Aid and Public Interest Law in China,' *Texas international Law Journal* (1999), volume 34, 211; Benjamin L. Liebman, 'Lawyers, Legal Aid, and Legitimacy in China' in WPALford (ed) *Raising the Bar: The Emerging Legal Profession in East Asia* (East Asian Law Studies, Harvard Law School, 2007), 211. Legal aid is delivered in a number of ways in China, and is varied in each province. Namely, first, a full time legal aid lawyer scheme; second, an arrangement allocating work to lawyers (for example, by requiring a law firm to offer various legal services annually); and third, a system of legal aid centres staffed by lawyers from law firms and legal aid workers. Legal aid typically involves either the provision of free legal advice or the allocation of a lawyer or an employee (who may or may not be a lawyer). Regulations on Legal aid (PRC, 2003) (法律援助条例), article 2, 21 and 25.

[80]Article 3 of the 2003 Regulations on Legal Aid.

[81]A well-known legal aid centre in Shanghai is based in East China University of Political Science and Law (ECUPL), see its website (in Chinese) http://www.hzfy.ecupl.edu.cn/ (accessed on 5 August 2016).

[82]See http://www.chinalegalaid.gov.cn/China_legalaid/content/2010-08/26/content_2260702.htm (In Chinese) (accessed on 5 August 2016).

[83]In some wealthy province, such as Guangdong Province, few restrictions are placed on eligibility of potential applicants. See, *Guangdong Provincial Rules on Legal Aid*, http://www.chinalegalaid.gov.cn/China_legalaid/content/2010-08/24/content_2257106.htm?node=24970 (in Chinese) (accessed on 5 August 2016). And in Shanghai, the municipal government heightened the minimum income eligibility level for legal aid to let more people access to the court. http://www.shanghai.gov.cn/shanghai/node2314/node2319/node2404/node28669/node28670/u26ai29887.html (in Chinese) (accessed on 5 August 2016).

Justice states that the central government would provide more financial support to legal aid to mitigate such disequilibrium between regions by issuing the 'general developing plan for the year 2011–2015'. However, it should be noted legal aid is only available to a given range of cases, including state compensation, social insurance and minimum living standards guarantees, survivor's pension and relief funds and etc. (article 10 of the 2003 Regulation) Shareholder litigation cannot be funded through legal aid.

In the US, given the popularity of lawyer's funding (for instance, contingency fee arrangements), individual plaintiffs in tort and other litigation seeking damages mostly choose to conclude contingency fee arrangements with lawyers instated of resorting to legal aid.[84] However, there are still situations where lawyers decline to act on the contingent basis (for instance, in injunction cases).[85] It is indicated that the demand from low-income Americans for free legal aid service is still unmet.[86] Legal assistance for many routine civil matters (for example, housing eviction, divorce and welfare claims) is available to low income Americans from a combination of publicly and privately funded legal service providers, however, present research suggests that the population who has got such kind of service is relatively low.[87] A report by *Legal Service Corporation* (LSC) states that 'there was a significant shortage of civil legal assistance available to low-income Americans'.[88] The report also indicates that less than 20% of the legal needs of low income Americans are being met.[89] Although state and private support for legal assistance to the poor has increased in the last two decades, comparatively low level of (or declining after factoring in inflation) federal funding and an increased poverty population have served to increase the unmet demand.[90]

---

[84]Christopher Hodges, Stefan Vogenauer and Magdalena Tulibacka, *The Cost and funding of Civil Litigation*, (Hart Publishing, 2010), p. 22.

[85]Deborah R. Hensler, 'The Cost and Funding of Civil Litigation: A National Report on the United States of America', in *The Cost and funding of Civil Litigation*, Christopher Hodges et al. (eds), (Hart Publishing, 2010), 535, pp. 539–541.

[86]The unmet rate was as large as 80% in 2005. See Legal Service Corporation, 'Documenting the Justice Gap in America', (2005), www.lsc.gov/press/documents/LSC%20Justice%20Gap_FINAL_1001.pdf (accessed on 5 August 2016).

[87]Deborah R. Hensler, 'The Cost and Funding of Civil Litigation: A National Report on the United States of America', in *The Cost and funding of Civil Litigation*, Christopher Hodges et al. (eds), (Hart Publishing, 2010), 535, p. 537.

[88]Legal Service Corporation, Documenting the Justice Gap in America, (2005), available at www.lsc.gov/press/documents/LSC%20Justice%20Gap_FINAL_1001.pdf (accessed on 10 August 2016).

[89]Ibid.

[90]Ibid.

## 3.2.4 *Funding by Lawyers*

### 3.2.4.1 Contingency Fee Arrangements (CGFAs)

A CGFA is, in nature, based on the 'no win, no fee' basis, where the litigant shares the monetary recoveries brought by a successful claim with the lawyer. If the funded case is lost, neither the funded litigant nor the lawyer will get any money. If the case is won, the plaintiff's lawyer would get a part of the proceeds awarded by the court to the plaintiff.

The CGFA is allowed in many countries, while it is banned in a certain number of other countries, particularly, in continental Europe.[91] A most typical example is the US where CGFAs are frequently adopted to finance lawsuits.[92,93] Several other jurisdictions also allow the use of CGFAs. For instance, the UK formally adopted CGFA in 2013.[94] And also, in China, CGFAs were allowed to use since 2006, and the law also further indicates that contingent rate should be capped at 30% of the

[91]For instance, CGFAs are permitted in the US, UK (just from 2013), China, Canada. But they are banned in, for instance, Denmark. Christopher Hodges, Stefan Vogenauer and Magdalena Tulibacka, *The Cost and funding of Civil Litigation*, (Hart Publishing, 2010), pp. 25–26.

[92]CGFA is used in the US to fund, mostly, civil damage cases. For instance, 87% of people in personal injury litigation choose to sign CGFAs with lawyers. See Deborah R. Hensler et al., *Compensation for Accidental Injuries in the United States*, (RAND Corporation Reports, 1991), Table 5.11, p. 136.

[93]Contingency fee arrangements are, in principle, illegal in Germany. The judgement by the German Constitutional Court (1 BvR 2576/04) explored an exception to the general rule. But the requirements laid down in this case is very high, which leads to a fact that in practice contingency fees still do not play a significant role in German civil litigation. It generally requires that if the client, without the contingency fee arrangement, was not able to enforce or defend his or her rights in a proper manner for personal financial reasons, such agreement would have been allowed. Eric P. Polten, 'Rules for costs and fees for lawyers—a comparison of German law and the lawof the province of Ontario/Canada', (Feb 2011), pp. 8–9, available at http://www.poltenassociates.com/Resource-Links/Legal-Fees-English.pdf (accessed on 16 August 2016); For more, see also Bernhard Schmeilzl (attorney at law, Munich Bar), 'How expansive is a German lawsuit?', (November, 2013), available at http://www.crosschannellawyers.co.uk/how-expensive-is-a-lawsuit-in-germany/#more-502 (accessed on 16 August 2016). In France, the same as that in Germany, contingency fee arrangements are in principle banned. But they are allowed to be used in the combination with another method, such as lawyer's hourly fee and flat fees. For more details, see 'French attorneys and legal fees', available at http://www.french-business-law.com/french-attorneys-and-legal-fees-page21.html (accessed on 16 August 2016).

[94]CGFAs were formally adopted in the UK since 2013, and it is known as Damaged Based Agreements (DBAs), see http://www.justice.gov.uk/civil-justice-reforms/main-changes (accessed on 5 August 2016).

damages.[95] But several sorts of cases are prohibited to be funded by CGFAs under Chinese law, such as mass litigation[96,97]

In nature, in a CGFA, the funded litigant gives up a portion of his reward in exchange for the elimination of litigation risk. On the other hand, the lawyer 'invests' his time and professional knowledge in a case to expect a reward in the event that the case is won. The lawyer, normally, is able to diversify the investment risk through a portfolio of cases, meaning that he may lose this case but win another one.[98] In this sense, the CGFA could be a way to distribute litigation risk between the litigant and the lawyer, which could help to facilitate the access to court for financially disadvantaged litigants.

One of the most serious concerns with regards to the use of CGFAs might be the potential conflict of interests between lawyers and funded litigants. For instance, a lawyer may prefer to accept a favourable settlement, by which he could obtain a share of damages more surely without investing additional time to request for a court trial.[99] And also, the conflict of interests may appear in other situations. For instance, a settlement offer which is optimal for the litigant may not always be ideal for the lawyer.[100] In an economic sense, the lawyer's net proceeds depend on the share of damages under a CGFA minus his time and efforts done in the case, while the litigant's net proceeds are recoveries minus the part shared by the lawyer. Considering of the different determinants in the economic model, the decision on whether or not to accept a settlement offer may diverge between the lawyer and the litigant. Particularly, the concern of conflict of interests will be further enhanced in shareholder litigation funded by a CGFA because such litigation is usually concerned with complicated case details and professional commercial issues which shareholder litigants may not be familiar with. It may therefore be difficult for shareholder claimants to monitor the conflict of interests and to decide whether the lawyer's behaviour is in the client's best interest.

---

[95]Article 13 of the MALF.

[96]Article 12 of the MALF provides that administrative cases, collective actions, criminal cases and state compensation claims should not be funded through CGFAs.

[97]The reason why collective actions are banned to be funded through CGFAs may be in line with the court's resistance to mass litigation. See *infra* 4.4.3.3.

[98]Jonathan T. Molot, 'A Market in Litigation Risk', *University of Chicago Law Review*, (2009), Volume 76, 367, pp. 408–409.

[99]See GP Miller, 'Some Agency Problems in Settlement' (1987) 16 *The Journal of Legal Studies*, 189, pp. 192–193; T Thomason, 'Are Attorneys Paid What They Are Worth? Contingent Fees and the Settlement Process' (1991) 20 *The Journal of Legal Studies*, 187, pp. 191–193.

[100]Hugh Gravellea and Michael Waterson, *No win, No fee: Some Economics of Contingency Legal Fees, The Economic Journal*, (1993), Volume 103 (420), 1025, p. 1026.

#### 3.2.4.2 Conditional Fee Agreements (CFAs)

Similar to CGFA, the nature of CFA is also 'no win, no fee'. Lawyers are paid both normal fees and an amount of success fees in the event that the case is won. In case of losing, the client may just pay a reduced amount of normal fees or even do not have to pay, subject to the terms in a CFA agreed by the two parties previously. CFAs are typically used in the UK,[101] where the success fee is allowed to be 100% of the basic fee in commercial cases, but the success fee in personal injury claims should be capped at 25% of the normal fee.[102] As indicated before, both CFAs and CGFAs are based on the same principle, however, the success fee in a CFA is determined in the contract up front. The amount of contingent fee varies in each case depending on the amount of monetary recoveries brought by the favourable outcome, making that the conflict of interests in a case funded by a CGFA might not be more serious than that in a case funded by a CFA.[103]

### *3.2.5 Public Funding*

A public agency could financially assist a lawsuit by covering court charges, lawyer's fees and adverse fees under the cost-shifting rule. To obtain public funding, applicants should meet certain preconditions generally including a requirement that the case should demonstrate public interests.[104] The concerns raised regarding public funding usually includes, among others, the neutrality of the public sector when dealing with politically sensitive application, how public funding should be financed.[105]

### *3.2.6 Third Party Litigation Funding (TPLF)*

The most recent development in litigation funding is third party litigation funding (TPLF), which is the provision of funds by someone (the funder) who is not a litigation party to enable the litigant to pursue an action. The funding may cover the client's litigation costs (court charges and lawyer's fees) and the adverse costs in

---

[101]CFAs are also allowed in other countries, such as Greece and Australia.

[102]In April 2013, the 25% cap came into effect. http://www.justice.gov.uk/civil-justice-reforms/personal-injury-claims (accessed on 5 August 2016).

[103]The success fee in a case is fixed, therefore, the incentive for the lawyer is just to win the case, while in a case funded by a CGFA, both a favourable outcome and the extent of the success make sense.

[104]Through the investigation on public funding in this book, it is found that the both the Ontario Fund and the Israeli public funding have the 'public interests' requirement. See *infra* 4.2 and 4.3.

[105]See *infra* 4.2.3.3.

case of losing under the fee-shifting rule. The funder usually has a contract with each individual litigant (plaintiff), creating immediate difficulties of applying the traditional TPLF model to class actions. TPLF is considered as a non-recourse loan provided by the third party funder. Potential proceeds for the funder are based on a 'no win, no fee' principle, meaning that the recoveries brought by a favourable outcome are shared between the funder and the funded litigant, while in case of losing the funder will get no compensation. In practice, TPLF has already spread to several countries, such as Australia, the UK and the US.

Like lawyer's funding, TPLF could be regarded as a tool for the litigant to share litigation risk with a third party. For the funder, risk can be externalized through a portfolio of funded cases, particularly, for big funders, the distribution of risk would be more effective.[106] For potential wrongdoers who are aware that the victims could be funded by TPLF to overcome the financial obstacle to file a lawsuit might be 'deterred' by TPLF.[107]

#### 3.2.6.1 Concerns About Unmeritorious Claims and Frivolous Litigation

TPLF is criticized that it encourages frivolous cases and unmeritorious litigation.[108] Providing funding for plaintiffs makes litigation cheaper and, accordingly, may lead to the increase of the volume of litigation. And even, it has also been argued that 'third-party financing particularly increases the volume of questionable claims'.[109] In practice, however, as a professional litigation funding provider, the funder conducts a cost-and-benefit analysis prior to financing a case.[110] Rational litigation funders will engage in due diligence when evaluating the potential investment and are likely to choose those lawsuits with good prospect of success which could recoup its investment on the case.[111] An empirical study done by IMF (the biggest Australian litigation funding company) shows that cases being funded have grown

[106]Steven Shavell, *Foundations of Economic Analysis of Law*, (Harvard University Press, 2004), p. 177.

[107]Marco de Morpurgo, A Comparative Legal and Economic Approach to Third-party Litigation Funding, Cardozo Journal of International and Comparative Law Spring 2011, p. 5.

[108]U.S. Chamber Institute for Legal Reform, 'Selling Lawsuits, Buying Trouble: Third Party Litigation Funding in the United States', (October 2009), pp. 5–7. Available at http://www.instituteforlegalreform.com/sites/default/files/thirdpartylitigationfinancing.pdf (accessed on 5 August 2016).

[109]U.S. Chamber Institute for Legal Reform, 'Selling Lawsuits, Buying Trouble: Third Party Litigation Funding in the United States', (October 2009), p. 5.

[110]U.S. Chamber Institute for Legal Reform, 'Selling Lawsuits, Buying Trouble: Third Party Litigation Funding in the United States', (October 2009), p. 19.

[111]As some data presented, the selection of litigation to be funded is quite stringent. For example, in Australia, the largest litigation funding company (IMF) only funded 5% among the funding applications during 2001–2010. Similarly, in the US, the Juridica Capital Management only funded 6% of the cases considered. See RAND ICJ conference in Washington D.C. Conference:

riskier over the past several years.[112] But there is no evidence revealing that third party funders will accept truly frivolous or unmeritorious cases because there are few possibilities for funders to recoup investment.[113]

#### 3.2.6.2 Potential Increase in Case Volume Before the Court

Along with the availability of TPLF, an important question whether it results in the increase of case volume before the court is raised.[114] Lawsuits, which would otherwise be dropped because of the prohibitive litigation expenses and the high litigation risk, would be filed with the financial assistance from a third party funder.[115] It is true that the number of case indeed increases, but it cannot be directly concluded that 'bad' cases are encouraged. If those lawsuits are not frivolous and based on good merits, the increase in the case volume would not be regarded as a negative issue for the reason that more illegal behaviours might be corrected and wrongdoers might be held liable.[116] The increase in case volume could also be justified through the economic analysis: if the general benefits and potential deterrence effect outweigh litigation costs, TPLF is socially desirable.[117] Otherwise, it is undesirable. In light of this theory, whether an externality brought by the introduction of TPLF is positive or negative does not depend on just one element (for example, the case volume), and it is, actually, determined by the comparison between the totals benefits and costs occurred.

#### 3.2.6.3 Ethical Concerns in TPLF

Like CGFAs and CFAs, ethical concerns are also raised in TPLF. Generally, if a third party (no matter he is a lawyer or a third party litigation funder) participates in a traditional plaintiff-and-defendant relationship in a lawsuit, agency problems will

(Footnote 111 continued)

'Alternative litigation finance in the U.S—where are we and where are we headed with practice and policy?', Washington, D.C., May 20–21,2010.

[112] David S. Abrams and Daniel L. Chen, 'A Market for Justice: A First Empirical Look at Third Party Litigation Funding', *University of Pennsylvania Journal of Business Law*, (2013), Volume 15, 1075, p. 1091.

[113] Ibid.

[114] See Paul H. Robin, 'Third-party financing of litigation', *Northern Kentucky Law Review*, (2011), Volume 38, 673, p. 682.

[115] See Jason Lyon, 'Revolution in Progress: Third-Party Funding of American Litigation', *UCLA Law Review* (2011) Volume 58, 571, p. 590.

[116] See Kevin Pennell, 'On the assignment of legal malpractice claims: a contractual solution to a contractual problem', *Texas Law Review* (2004), Volume 82, 481, pp. 494–496.

[117] See Steven Shavell, 'The social versus the private incentive to bring suit in a costly legal system', *Journal of Legal Studies*, (1982), Volume 11, 333, p. 335.

come into being. As indicated before, there is conflict of interests between the lawyer and the client in a case funded by a CGFA.[118] In a TPLF-funded case, the conflict of interests will be much more complicated considering the participation of the third party funder. The triple relationship brings new concerns, such as, who substantially controls the litigation, whether the lawyer owes the loyalty duty to the funder or to the litigant.

First, in the funder-and-litigant relationship, the two parties are not at an even level in terms of financial ability. Unscrupulous funders may take advantage of vulnerable litigants by imposing unfair terms on them in funding agreements, or even purposely failing to fully disclose all relevant aspects of funding agreements to funded litigants.[119] And also, with regards to the conflict of interests between these two parties, the funded litigant's interests may be subordinated to that of the funder's.[120] For instance, the funder would prefer to an early settlement to speed up the cash flow.

Second, to whom the lawyer owes his loyalty duty? In an ordinary case not funded by TPLF, lawyer's duty of loyalty is supposed to be owed to the litigant (his client). Even in a TPLF-funded case, theoretically this principle should not be changed. However, in reality, the funder rather than the litigant pays the lawyer's fees. In consideration of that, it is highly possible that the traditional principle will be damaged because we cannot neglect the fact that most lawyers are incentivized by financial rewards.[121] It might be possible to conclude that the lawyer may serve more for the funder's interests.[122] Moreover, both the lawyer and the funder are repeat players in litigation market, making that the lawyer may stand more closely with the funder than with the litigant.[123]

Third, the right to access to confidential information by the funder is practically difficult to enforce. As indicated before, a rational funder must conduct due diligence to evaluate the success rate of a case before funding it. Apparently, the assessment on a case is hardly to be completed without certain information or even confidential documents. Particularly, in shareholder litigation which is usually concerned with complicated case details and, perhaps, confidential business documents. In such a case, the funding is generally higher than average considering its commercial nature. If the access to necessary documents could not be provided, the

---

[118]See *infra* 6.3.1 ('the conflict of interests and the agency problem under a CGFA').

[119]The Standing Committee of Attorneys-General in Australia, 'Litigation Funding in Australia: Discussion Paper', (May, 2006), p. 8 http://www.imf.com.au/docs/default-source/site-documents/discussionpaperstandingcommitteeofattorneysgeneral_may2006 (accessed on 5 August 2016).

[120]See Wayne Attrill, 'Ethical issues in litigation funding', (Feb 16th, 2009), p. 8 http://www.imf.com.au/docs/default-source/site-documents/ethical-issues-paper-imf09—globalaw-conference (accessed on 5 August 2016).

[121]*Oliver v. Board of Governors*, 779 S.W. 2d 212, at 215 (Kentuky 1989) ('an attorney's primary loyalty will, as a practical matter, rest with the person or entity who pays him.').

[122]Further analysis in this regard, see *infra* 5.1.3.

[123]See *infra* 5.1.3.2.

funder might be reluctant to fund such a case since the potential risk is unpredictable. Thus, the lack of necessary documents may make meritorious cases underfunded.

### 3.2.7 Legal Expenses Insurance

Legal insurance is used to eliminate litigation risk for litigants, particularly for those in countries where litigation costs are hard to predict up front.[124] After-the-Event insurance (ATE) and Before-the-Event insurance (BTE) are two main sorts of legal insurance. BTE means that the insurance product is bought before the 'event' (the event which triggers a legal action) in order to cover potential litigation costs (including court charges, lawyers' fees and any adverse fees in case of losing under the cost-shifting rule), which is wide-spread in civil law systems, except for Germany and Austria.[125,126] On the other hand, ATE is a sort of insurance product that is purchased after the event which triggers a legal claim in order to cover litigation cost including court charges and lawyer's fees on his own side and the opponent's court's and lawyer's fees if the case is lost under the cost-shifting rule, which arose and is now mainly found in England and Wales.[127] In England and Wales, ATE is usually used as a supplementary way to cover the risk of adverse fees under the cost-shifting rule when a CFA is applied.[128] But the supplementary function of ATE insurance might be difficult to be realized mainly due to the prohibitive price.[129]

[124]For instance, in countries applying tariff, litigation costs are predictable to a certain extent. (such as Germany).

[125]For definition, see http://www.lawsociety.org.uk/for-the-public/faqs/before-the-event-insurance/ (accessed on 19 August 2016.

[126]Christopher Hodges, Stefan Vogenauer and Magdalena Tulibacka, *The Cost and funding of Civil Litigation*, (Hart Publishing, 2010), p. 21.

[127]For definition, see http://www.lawsociety.org.uk/for-the-public/faqs/after-the-event-insurance/ (accessed on 19 August 2016).

[128]ATE arose in England and Wales from 1995 to insure plaintiff against adverse costs which are not covered by CFAs. See Christopher Hodges, 'England and Wales: Summary of the Jackson Cost Review', in *The Cost and Funding of Civil Litigation*, Christopher Hodges et al. (eds) (Hart Publishing, 2010), 303, pp. 305–306.

[129]Jackson's final report (2009), pp. 82–86.

# Chapter 4
# Funding Shareholder Litigation: Public Funding

To solve funding problems, public funding could be an option. 'Public funding' in this book refers to an approach where the state (e.g., a government agency) provides funding to support private civil litigation.[1] This chapter will discuss two countries, Israel and Canada (Quebec and Ontario), that have ample experience with this technique in order to conduct a comparative study to investigate the public funding mechanism *per se*, how it functions, and problems caused by the use of it. After the case studies on Israel and Canada, the potential for public funding to finance shareholder actions in China will be examined.

## 4.1 An Overview of Public Funding

### *4.1.1 The Analysis of 'Public Interest' Element*

Before public funding is awarded, the 'public interests' requirement should be met. For example, both in Israel and Canada, publicly funded cases are required to demonstrate that they involve public interests.[2] When discussing the applicability of

---

[1]Theoretically, the scope of civil litigation is broad. For example, it includes derivative actions, class actions, and commercial litigation. Given that, public funding could be provided to finance class actions, derivative actions or other sort of civil litigation. In Israel and Canada, public funding has been, indeed, provided to fund derivative actions and class actions. These practical examples will be analysed further in this chapter.

[2]Article 205A of the Israeli Company Law 1999 (the ICL) provides that prior to awarding public funding, two cumulative preconditions should be met, and one of them is 'there is a public interest in bringing the case'. And in Ontario and Quebec, public interest is also applied as a selection criterion when the application for public funding is considered. Arad Reisberg, 'Access to Justice or Justice Not Accessed: Is There a Case for Public Funding of Derivative Suits?', *Brooklyn Journal of International Law*, (2012), Volume 37, No. 2, 1037, p. 1042; David Collins, 'Public Funding of Multi-party Litigation', *Manitoba Law Journal*, (2010), Volume 31, 211, pp. 232–235.



W. Chen, *A Comparative Study of Funding Shareholder Litigation*,
DOI 10.1007/978-981-10-3623-1_4

public funding of shareholder litigation, we should examine whether it concerns public interests.

#### 4.1.1.1 From the Perspective of Corporate Governance and Business Activities

The cause of shareholder litigation is usually the infringement of shareholders' interests or companies' interests.[3] It is generally concerned with corporate governance and the company's business operation.[4] Thus, to investigate the public feature of shareholder litigation, a fact should be justified that corporate governance and business operation in a given company must be concern with public interests.

Apparently, a company is considered as a profit maximize, and the company's directors ought to make the company profitable and distribute profits to shareholders.[5] Thus, it is generally thought that a company, particularly a private company, is mainly concerned with private gains and has no connection with 'public interests'. The modern economic theory, however, has overturned this viewpoint by stating that an individual company cannot make a clear distinction from the whole economic system.[6] A company, no matter it is a publicly-listed corporation or a private firm, has influence, to some extent, on the public system and society by means of affecting the market price of certain 'products', such as labour force and the raw materials.[7] And also, the 'public interests' theory could be justified by the fact that corporate governance within a company, especially a publicly-listed company, is no longer an internal issue, and it, indeed, attracts public concerns.[8] As a unit in the whole economic system, each company is expected to share responsibility to maintain a rational market order.[9] Short-sighted behaviours by the management, such as opportunistic practice and manipulation of account, may harm the whole public system.[10] A typical case in this regard is the Enron Incident, where the deceptive accounting, dishonest company's books and records

[3]For instance, a shareholder derivative action is brought to protect the interest of the company as well as that of the shareholder. And a shareholder class action is filed to go against the company's misleading disclosure on business profitability which harms the shareholders' interests.

[4]For example, the derivative lawsuit and shareholder direct litigation may be designed to promote corporate governance and facilitate shareholder protection. And shareholder class action is always concerns that company's misleading disclosure of business profitability.

[5]Randall S. Kroszner and Louis Putterman, *The Economic Nature of the Firm*, (Cambridge University Press, third edition, 2009), p. 7.

[6]Randall S. Kroszner and Louis Putterman, *The Economic Nature of the Firm*, (Cambridge University Press, third edition, 2009), p. 80.

[7]Ibid.

[8]Ibid.

[9]Stephen M. Bainbridge, *Corporate Governance after the Financial Crisis*, (Oxford University Press, 2012), pp. 155–156.

[10]Ibid.

almost make the general public lose confidence on the company's audit service and even the US system of corporate governance.[11]

As for public companies, in consideration of its important role in the whole market, professor Brenda Hannigan indicates that excellent corporate governance in public companies just by effective control of shareholders proves to be overoptimistic. Therefore, a public interest oversight board (PIOB) is proposed to be established to fill lacuna in the current arrangement as there is not a permanent organ within a company to tackle issues concerning public interests.[12]

#### 4.1.1.2 From the Perspective of the Function of Litigation

Filing a case before a court will bring externalities.[13] As Posner explains, litigation 'establishes rules of conduct designed to shape future conduct, not only the present disputants' but also other people's',[14] conduct code set up in the proceeding will not diminish when the court procedure terminates. The principle established in the case would be served as 'public good' followed by successors.[15] This function would be enhanced in the common law jurisdictions, where the *stare decisis* doctrine is applied. Potential effects of precedents could also be found in statute-law countries. For example, in China, courts are allowed to refer to precedents to obtain guidance when making trials, although judicial decisions are made mostly based on statutory rules.[16]

---

[11]*See* Margaret M. Blair, "Post-Enron Reflections on Comparative Corporate Governance", (2002), Georgetown University Law Center 2002 Working Paper Series in Business, Economics, and Regulatory Law Working Paper No. 316663, available at http://papers.ssrn.com/paper.taf?abstract_id=316663 (accessed on 27 August 2016).

[12]Brenda Hannigan, 'Board Failures in the financial Crisis: Tinkering with codes and the need for wider corporate governance reforms: Part 2', *Company Lawyer*, (2012), 33(2), 35, p. 38.

[13]William B. Rubenstein, 'Why Enable Litigation: A Positive Externalities Theory of the Small Claims Class Action', 74 *Umkc Law Review* (2006), 709, pp. 720–728.

[14]Richard A. Posner, *Economic Analysis of Law* (Aspen Publisher, 2003), pp. 530–531.

[15]William B. Rubenstein, 'Why Enable Litigation: A Positive Externalities Theory of the Small Claims Class Action', 74 *Umkc Law Review* (2006), 709, p. 726.

[16]There has been a typical example to illustrate the effect of precedent in Chinese judiciary. As early as 1990s, when the regime of derivative action had not been introduced in the law system officially, the Wuxi Nancheng Real Estate Development Company (WX Company) and Shanghai Pudong State-owned Assets Investment and Management Company (SH Company) suited Hengtong Groups (HT). In this suit, the two plaintiffs were minority shareholders in Xinjiangnan Company (XJN), while HT was holding shareholder and held an overpowering control in XJN. The plaintiffs claimed that the defendant dealt with the XJN's assets without authorization and harmed the interests of XJN as well as shareholders. Even though in this case, the company (XJN) was listed as 'a third party' but not plaintiff under the law of that time, it was regarded as the rudiment of current derivative action. It was the first time the court accepted a case in which the minority shareholders suited the majority shareholder on the basis of the harm to the company cause by defendant's behaviour. Notwithstanding until 2006 the derivative action was first time officially established in Chinese company law, the XJN case in late 1990s was served as a

Like general litigation, shareholder litigation may also produce 'public good' to the society and enhance public norms. Professor Cox indicates that few shareholder lawsuits only dispose of breaches of private contracts between the claimants and the defendants.[17] Instead, breaches of fiduciary duties or even fraud involving public norms are main causes of shareholder claims.[18] A similar viewpoint in this regard could also be found in case law. For example, in *Zapata Corporation v. Maldonado*, the court held an opinion that 'it should, when appropriate, give special consideration to matters of law and public policy in addition to the corporation's best interests.'[19] The well-known *Wallersteiner v. Moir* (*No.* 2)[20] case also has public significance because subsequent cases with similar condition could all benefit from the plight made by Mr. Moir.[21] In the US as well, there are ample evidence to justify the 'public good' theory. In *Rosenfeld v. Black*,[22] it established a behaviour code on mutual fund advisor, which could be considered as a contribution to the public norm in mutual fund industry.[23]

In realizing the 'public function' of shareholder litigation, a court plays its role like an adjudicator to private interest and a preacher to public norms. In other words, the court steers the private business activity to an appropriate degree in accordance with some public norms when a demand by plaintiffs is made.[24] It is

(Footnote 16 continued)

precedent for legislators and company's participators. The case had its potential implication to the future legal amendment and corporate governance.

[17]James D. Cox, 'The social Meaning of Shareholder Suits', 65 *Brooklyn Law Review* (1999), 3, p. 11.

[18]Ibid.

[19]*Zapata corporation v. Maldonado* 430 A.2d 779 (Delaware 1981).

[20]*Wallersteiner v. Moi* (*No. 2*) (1975) Q.B.373.

[21]In this case, Mr. Moir, as a minority shareholder sued against Wallersteiner (majority shareholder of the company) on the ground that Wallersteiner bought Hartley Baird Ltdwith money from the company itself, which was in contravention of the prohibitions on financial assistance (under Companies Act 1948s 54 and 190). Actually, Mr. Moir's plight is beneficial to all shareholders of the company, because if the final judgment is in favour of Mr. Moir, a sum of monetary remedy will go to the company directly, and the shareholders of it will benefit from the remedy indirectly.

[22]*Rosenfeld v. Black* 445 F.2d 1337 (2d Cir.1971).

[23]Many other notable cases can be found as well, such as, *Perlman v. Feldmann*, 219 F.2d 173 (2d Cir. 1955), *Moses v. Burgin*, 445 F.2d 369 (1st Cir.1971), *Fogel v. Chestnutt*, 533 F.2d 731 (2d Cir. 1975). None of these cases involved big sum of monetary recoveries, whereas they were of immeasurable significance to the enhancement of the level of corporate governance by setting conduct code for corporate governors. See Arad Reisberg, 'Access to Justice or Justice Not Accessed, is there a case for public funding of derivative claims?', *Brooklyn Journal of International Law*, (2012), Volume 37(3), 1021, p. 1048.

[24]One point should be noted that the steering activities by the courts should remain passive that distinct from the governments or the administrators which can govern and standardize the business activities through initiative methods, such as, bringing vetting procedures and formulating regulations.

also indicated that once private disputes are presented before the public courtroom, a certain portion of public interests must be taken into account in the proceeding.[25] But it would not be reasonable to give an overwhelming preference to public factors regardless of the private essential. The public norm regulation may be produced as a side effect of a shareholder action which is traditionally deemed as a claim resolving private disputes within a company. Nevertheless, the court is just a public organ providing remedies *ex post facto*. Principal authorities maintaining and reinforcing public norms should be legislators and administrators taking measures on their own initiatives to, for instance, make and enforce law.

Shareholder litigation could provide deterrence effects to future misconducts. The deterrence effect, which is difficult to be quantified precisely, is easily neglected in empirical studies.[26] For example, gains to shareholders resulted from the future deterred misconduct could not be easily evaluated.[27] However, a successful derivative claim can show other companies what kind of misconducts will be considered to be illegal and those companies which intended to commit such wrongdoings may be deterred.[28] Even if the proceeding of a shareholder claim creates litigation costs, the benefits brought by the positive externalities would exceed the legal costs. Because the shareholders, the directors of the company and the managements in other companies may modify their behaviours after the awareness of the outcome of the case.[29]

Shareholder litigation also promotes private enforcement of law.[30] By enabling shareholder actions, it strikes a structural balance of the law enforcement between traditional public agencies and initiative private sectors, and a significant quantity of the enforcement shifts to private scope.[31] Even though the private enforcement of law has its own problem, such as, agency problem between lawyers and clients,

[25]John C. Coffee, 'Litigation and Corporate Governance: An Essay on Steering between Scylla and Charybdis', 52 *George Washington Law Review* (1983), 789, p. 817.

[26]Robert Thompson & Randall S. Thomas, 'The Public and Private Faces of Derivative Lawsuits', 57 *Vanderbilt Law Review*, (2004), 1747, p. 1749.

[27]John C. Coffee, 'New Myths and Old Realties: The American Law Institute Faces the Derivative Action', *The Business Lawyer*, Volume 48, Issue 4, (1993), 1407, p. 1428.

[28]In this respect, Shavell explains that the social benefits of litigation could exceed the private benefits in some instances. An illustration would be where the action generates some beneficial deterrent effects that cause others to desist from a course of conduct that would impose externalities on society. Steven Shavell, 'The Social Versus the Private Incentive to Bring Suit in a Costly Legal System', Journal of Legal Studies, (1982), Volume 11, 333, p. 334.

[29]For example, a study in the United States has shown that the "impact of decisions in derivative cases like Caremark, Disney, and Oracle goes well beyond the outcome of the cases themselves. These decisions changed the rules for future legal practice by forcing companies to accept better conduct and procedures." Robert Thompson & Randall S. Thomas, 'The Public and Private Faces of Derivative Lawsuits', 57 *Vanderbilt Law Review*, (2004), 1747, p. 1749.

[30]Arad Reisberg, 'Access to Justice or Justice Not Accessed, is there a case for public funding of derivative claims?', *Brooklyn Journal of International Law*, (2012), Volume 37(3), 1021, p. 1048.

[31]William B. Rubenstein, 'Why Enable Litigation: A Positive Externalities Theory of the Small Claims Class Action', 74 *Umkc Law Review* (2006), 709, p. 727.

however, the diversity of law enforcement, indeed, breaks through the monopolistic law enforcement by public authorities.[32] Compared to private enforcement, public enforcement seems less 'motivated'. There are no direct incentives for public employees who generally receive a fixed salary and do not gain directly from enforcing the law. Nevertheless, private enforcers, who are usually direct victims of the violation of law, are clearly aware of the details of infringement.[33] For instance, in a shareholder class action, shareholders are victims of the misleading information about the company's profitability disclosed by the company. The advantages of private enforcement could be enhanced by the fact that public authorities shoulder many responsibilities in administrating the whole society, while private enforcers could focus more on certain sectors, such as, corporate governance. In this regard, it is more logical to enhance private enforcement of affairs concerning corporate governance in the sense that issues concerning corporate governance are subject more to the free market rather than public interventions.[34]

It should be noted that in shareholder litigation, cases are often settled instead of going through the entire proceeding ending in a judgement. The question therefore arises whether there is any 'guidance effect' from settlements. Do settlements produce similar positive externalities as judgements? As a matter of fact, settlement resulting from an action will have similar positive 'settlement effects'.[35] When a case is filed before the court, the court oversees and monitors the settlement agreement. For instance, in China, Chapter Eight of PRC Civil Procedure Law provides that once an agreement has been made by the two parties, the court will scrutinize the legality of it and give ratification to make the settlement agreement get the same legal force as that in a judgement,[36] meaning that a settlement agreement comes into force only if the court proves that it is consistent with law. Similar judicial control on the settlement agreement can also be found in other countries, such as Rule 23 of the Federal Rules of Civil Procedurein the US.[37] Even though a settlement and a judgement are not generated through the same procedure,

---

[32]Barton H. Thompson, 'The Continuing Innovation of Citizen Enforcement', *University of Illinois Law Review*, 185, p. 206.

[33]Lars Klöhn, 'Private Versus Public Enforcement of Laws—A Law & Economics Perspective', p. 9. (Ludwig-Maximilians-Universität Munich Working Paper 2010), available at http://papers.ssrn.com/sol3/papers.cfm?abstract_id=1730308. Mitchell Polinsky and Steven Shavell, 'The Theory of Public Enforcement of Law', *Handbook of Law and Economics*, (2007), Volume 1, 403, p. 406.

[34]Public enforcement always requires lengthy procedures, including application by individuals, approval by public authorities and then essential reaction. It usually lasts long and costs more in a public enforcement procedure than private ones which involve only private individuals and institutions without bureaucracy.

[35]William B. Rubenstein, 'Why Enable Litigation: A Positive Externalities Theory of the Small Claims Class Action', 74 *Umkc Law Review* (2006), 709, p. 724.

[36]Article 89–91 of PRC Civil Procedure Law.

[37]For instance, in the US, the courts still retain jurisdiction over settlements. Under Rule 23 of the Federal Rules of Civil Procedure, in class actions, all settlements are subject to approval by the court. In the UK and Israel, there are also such kinds of 'court oversight' over settlements.

they are endowed with the same legal force by the court.[38] Although settled cases may be inferior to adjudicated cases in terms of guidance effects,[39] they still shed some lights on future cases.[40]

## 4.2 Public Funding of Derivative Actions: The Israeli Case

### *4.2.1 Statutory Provisions Under the Israeli Law*

The ISA stated in its 2011 annual report that, for the reason that private enforcement of securities laws was undeveloped and relatively limited in Israel, it would remove barriers to private enforcement and promote the filing of justified derivative actions by providing funding for shareholder plaintiffs with financial difficulties.[41] In line with the ISA's proposal, amendment 16 to Israel Company Law (ICL) was introduced in 2011, stating that similarly with funding of representative actions,[42] funding for shareholder plaintiffs in derivative lawsuits would be provided by the ISA.[43] With regards to practical details, amendment 16 only mentions that they are similar to those of public funding of representative actions provided in Section 209 of ICL:

> (a) Any plaintiff, who wishes to bring a derivative action in the name of a public company or a private company, and who meets the criterion under section 171(a), is allowed to request the Israel Securities Authority to bear his costs.
> (b) If the Israel Securities Authority is convinced there is a public interest in bringing the case and there is a reasonable prospect the court would grant leave for the action to continue as a derivative action, the Authority may bear the plaintiff's costs, on such sums and conditions as it thinks fit; the Authority's decisions according to this section cannot be used as an evidence and it is not possible to submit them before the court.
> (c) If the court decided in favour of the company, the court may in its judgment provide for the company to reimburse the Israel Securities Authority for its expenses.[44]

Section 205A clearly indicated two cumulative preconditions that should be met before the public funding is awarded (1) the case to be brought needs to

[38]William B. Rubenstein, 'Why Enable Litigation: A Positive Externalities Theory of the Small Claims Class Action', 74 *Umkc Law Review* (2006), 709, p. 724.

[39]Unlike the judgment, settlements are rarely published. For example, in China, if the cases are settled finally, the conciliation statements (调解书) are normally not published.

[40]For example, if a case attracted lots of public attention, the result of this case may have great effect even though it is settled finally. Or a significant enterprise involves in a lawsuit, the settlement of it will have potential effect.

[41]Israel Securities Authority Annual Report 2011, pp. 109–110, http://www.isa.gov.il/sites/isaeng/1489/1512/Documents/IsaFile_7037.pdf (accessed 30 August 2016).

[42]Section 209(a)–(c) of ICL provides that representative actions could be financed by ISA.

[43]Section 9.2 of Amendment No. 16 to Israeli Companies Law.

[44]Israeli Company Law S 205(a)–(c).

demonstrate public interests; (2) there should be a reasonable prospect that the case would be granted leave as a derivative action by the court.[45] The public funding introduced in Section 205A is expected to provide a supplementary financial incentive for plaintiffs who were deterred by financial difficulties.[46]

At first glance, the introduction of public funding facilitates plaintiff shareholders (particularly for those who have financial difficulties) to file derivative actions and further to improve corporate governance. Additionally, the Explanatory Notes to amendment 16 indicate two important points of view. First, the commencement of a derivative lawsuit, except for benefiting the claimant shareholders themselves, will be beneficial to all other shareholders who are in the similar position within a company. Second, it states that enforcement and supervision of the financial markets would be strengthened by this Amendment.[47] For a shareholder derivative action, the primary problem inherent is how the fees involved in the action could be afforded by shareholders who normally do not possess adequate money. Besides the provisions concerning public funding, a wide range of plaintiffs-friendly amendments regarding derivative suits have been included in Amendment 16 to facilitate and encourage the use of derivative actions.[48]

### *4.2.2 Rethinking Section 205A*

As the law provides, before the public funding is granted, two preconditions should be met: (1) there is a reasonable prospect that the court would grant leave for the action to proceed as a derivative action; (2) the case is concerned with public interests.

---

[45] Arad Reisberg, 'Access to Justice or Justice Not Accessed, is there a case for public funding of derivative claims?', *Brooklyn Journal of International Law*, (2012), Volume 37(3), 1021, p. 1038.

[46] Companies Act, (amend. no. 16), 19 (explanatory notes) 2011.

[47] The early version of this Amendment stated that the funding incentive provided to plaintiff shareholders in respect of derivative action would enforce the corporate governance as well as the directors' duties.

[48] The other two rectifications are as follows: first, under section 194 of the company law, the plaintiff shareholder is no longer required to make a demand on the board before filing the suit, and if the board has a personal interest in the suit or is subject to the suit or a disclosure to the board may damage the relief sought by the plaintiff. Unlike the similar 'demand requirement' in most of other jurisdictions, the plaintiff shareholders in Israel could directly submit the claim to the court without referring to the board of directors in advance. Second, under section 198 of the company law, given that the asymmetries exist between the shareholders and the company, it confers the informative right on the shareholder applicants. With this informative right, the shareholder applicants could acquire the documents relating to the leave to proceed of the derivative action with the help of court's order. However, this informative right should be based on the condition that the shareholder claimants can provide an initial evident to convince the court.

#### 4.2.2.1 The First Precondition

The first precondition incorporated in Section 205A is nothing innovative in the sense that the court's approval of the continuance of a derivative action is statutorily required in many countries.[49] For instance, the Section 263 of the UK Company Act 2006 is about the courts' decisions on whether or not to grant permission to the continuance of a derivative action. The general principle of the court's permission could be summarized as a two-stage test: (a) the case has to be proved to be a *prima facie* case by the claimant and the evidence in support of it has also to be disclosed to the court[50]; (b) a series of criteria stipulated in Section 263(3) of CA, such as, 'the member is acting in good faith to seek to continue the claim'. At the first stage, the court can set different levels of threshold for a claimant because requirements listed in statutory rules are vague. For example, in *Wishart v Castlecroft Securities Ltd*,[51] the Court placed a low threshold for a shareholder plaintiff by pointing out that

> The question is not whether the application and supporting evidence disclose a prima facie case against the defendants, but whether there is no prima facie case disclosed for granting the application for permission. Additionally, the claimants are not obliged to satisfy the court that there is a prima facie case, inversely, the court is to refuse the application if it proves that there is not a prima facie case.[52]

In *Iesini v Westrip Holdings Ltd*,[53] Lewison J took a stricter approach by indicating that a prima facie case for granting leave should be required to demonstrate both (A) the company has a good cause of action; (B) the cause of action arises out of a director's default or his breach of duty.[54] In this case, the court also applied some of the factors provided in Section 172 of CA 2006 to decide whether or not to grant leave to this case to proceed as a derivative action.[55] Therefore, the standard at the first stage is not clear, which is greatly subject to the court's discretion. For example, if the court has a tendency to restrain the application of derivative actions,

---

[49]For example, in the UK, section 263 of the Company Act 2006 (CA 2006) deals with the permission made by the court when an application of the continuance of a derivative action by the plaintiff shareholder is brought. See section 263(2)(a) ('Permission (or leave) must be refused if the court is satisfied—(a) that a person acting in accordance with section 172 (duty to promote the success of the company) would not seek to continue the claim.'). And an analogue can also be found in section 168(B) (C) of the Hong Kong Companies Ordinance that has a similar provision to the English regulation. Additionally, in New Zealand companies Act 1993, section 165(1)(b) requires the courts' permission prior to the continuance of the derivative actions.

[50]See section 261(2) of the CA 2006.

[51]*Wishart v Castlecroft Securities Ltd* (2010) BCC 161.

[52]*Wisbart v Castlecroft Securities Ltd* (2010) BCC 161, per Lord Reed (Inner House Opinion), at 31.

[53]*Iesini v Westrip Holdings Ltd* (2010) BCC 420.

[54]*Iesini v. Westrip Holdings Ltd* (2010) BCC 420. at 75, pp. 81–83.

[55]Reisberg Arad, '*Access to Justice or Justice Not Accessed*', p. 1040.

a higher threshold at stage one may be set,[56,57] which would make many rational shareholders give up at this stage in view of complexities involved.[58]

The first vague precondition in Section 205A of the ICL may have the similar problem with that in the English case, making it largely depend on the ISA's discretion. As mentioned before, beyond the Section 205A regarding public funding of derivative actions, a wide series of plaintiffs-friendly amendments to facilitate derivative lawsuits was also brought into current legal regime. It might be possible to conclude that the ISA might hold a plaintiffs-friendly attitude to set a comparatively low threshold, making it easier for shareholder applicants to satisfy the first precondition in Section 205A. The main question in this regard is what are the comparatively relaxed standards adopted by the ISA when it considers whether the case would have a prospect to be permitted to proceed as a derivative action. A question is further raised that, as a public authority not specialising in judicial issues, how well and how professional the ISA can scrutinise these issues like a court.[59] For the court, to decide whether a derivative action could be allowed to proceed is greatly subject to discretion, where clear rules are lacking. In terms of the appraisal of case merits, the courts might be superior to other board of officials for the reason that courts have a long history of analysing and determining whether a case has tenable grounds to proceed as a derivative claim, as opposed to ISA.[60]

Even though ISAs expertise can be gradually improved over time, it raises another question as to how ISAs opinion should be treated. If ISA approves a

---

[56]In the UK, the Law Commission admits that "a list of criterion may appear to be a set of hurdles which applicants have to overcome and which would deter them. It could easily be seen as maintaining a policy of not favouring derivative actions and as a signal of an over-restrictive approach to shareholders which would over-deter them." Consultation Paper, para 16.43. Arad Reisberg, 'Derivative Claims Under the Companies Act 2006: Much Ado About Nothing?', in *Rationalityin Company Law: Essay in Honour of DD Prentice*, (J. Armour eds), (Hart Publishing, 2009), 17, p. 29.

[57]In the UK, the Law Commission admits that "a list of criterion may appear to be a set of hurdles which applicants have to overcome and which would deter them. It could easily be seen as maintaining a policy of not favouring derivative actions and as a signal of an over-restrictive approach to shareholders which would over-deter them." Consultation Paper, para 16.43. Arad Reisberg, 'Derivative Claims Under the Companies Act 2006: Much Ado About Nothing?', in *Rationalityin Company Law: Essay in Honour of DD Prentice*, (J. Armour eds), (Hart Publishing, 2009), 17, p. 29.

[58]Arad Reisberg, 'Access to Justice or Justice Not Accessed, is there a case for public funding of derivative claims?', *Brooklyn Journal of International Law*, (2012), Volume 37(3), 1021, p. 1040.

[59]Arad Reisberg, 'Access to Justice or Justice Not Accessed, is there a case for public funding of derivative claims?', *Brooklyn Journal of International Law*, (2012), Volume 37, Issue 3, 1021, pp. 1040–1041.

[60]Ian Ramsay, 'Corporate Governance, Shareholder Litigation and the Prospects for Statutory Derivative Action', *University of New South Wales Law Journal*, (1992), Volume 15(1), 149, pp. 173–174; John C. Coffee and Donald E. Schwartz, 'The Survival of the Derivative Suit: An Evaluation and a Proposal for Legislative Reform', *Columbia Law Review*, (1981), Volume 81(2), 261, pp. 282–283.

funding application by a shareholder claimant, would it affect the court's decision about whether or not allow the derivative action to be continued?[61] Normally, ISA should act a role as an unbiased public funding provider, whose decision is not expected to have potential influence on that of the court. However, the fact is not fully in line with this expectation. In consideration of the trend of the efficiency principle's dominance in Israeli courts, the court may easily side with the ISA in order to save judicial resources and accelerate the efficiency of the trial.[62] It might be possible to imagine that the court would be partly influenced by the ISAs positive decision of awarding public funding to finance a derivative action or *vice versa*.

#### 4.2.2.2 The Second Precondition

The 'public interests' theory has been analysed in Sect. 4.1.1.

### *4.2.3 Dilemmas in Public Funding of Derivative Actions*

As pointed out before, the use of derivative action can be considered as a sort of private enforcement of law. Shareholder plaintiffs are private law enforcers correcting and deterring wrongdoings in corporate governance. When observing the very nature of Section 205A of the ICL, we can find that there are several 'public' factors: (1) the authority taking charge of granting public funding is ISA, which is a public institute; (2) the ISA should take the 'public interest' requirement into account when scrutinizing the application from shareholder applicants. Thus, public funding of shareholder derivative actions may have a dual-identity of private and public enforcement of law.

#### 4.2.3.1 The 'Market Failure' Theory

A combination of public and private factors in public funding of derivative actions could be considered as an analogy to the phenomenon of 'public intervention in free

[61] Arad Reisberg, 'Access to Justice or Justice Not Accessed, is there a case for public funding of derivative claims?', *Brooklyn Journal of International Law*, (2012), Volume 37, Issue 3, 1021, pp. 1042–2043.

[62] See Orna Rabinovich-Einy, 'Beyond Efficiency: the Transformation of Courts through Technology', *UCLA Journal of Law and Technology*, (2008), Volume 12(1), 1, pp. 1–3. Even though this article mainly complains that the courts excessively rely on the modern technology for the sake of judicial efficiency, there are reasons to believe that Israeli courts lay emphasis on judicial efficiency to a great extent.

markets'. The traditional market theory holds that the free market is operated by the 'invisible hand'.[63] A general justification for the public intervention frequently quoted by mainstream economists mostly relies on the view when a particular market fails to achieve 'public interest' objectives, the market failure should be corrected by the 'invisible hand'.[64] This theory could also be applied to explain the nature of public funding of derivative actions. If the sound functioning of derivative actions is assumed as a free market, public funding provided by ISA can be considered as the public intervention. An ideal market movement in this respect should be: derivative actions are commenced when necessary by *bona fide* shareholder plaintiffs without any financial deterrence. Funding difficulties with prospective shareholder plaintiffs in filing such an action could be regarded as a 'market failure'. To realize a desired market order, the ISA, as a public authority, comes out to regulate this market by providing public funding to impecunious shareholders when necessary.

Although it seems quite reasonable to interpret the rationality of Section 205A in the 'market failure' and 'public intervention' system, there are still fundamental problems in policing its practice, for instance, the expected unbiased role of the ISA,[65] the interplay between the courts and the ISA.

#### 4.2.3.2 The Infrequency of Derivative Actions

After the reform of introducing public funding of derivative actions, there are currently few derivative actions filed in Israel by private plaintiffs, which might disappoint people who had hoped to see a rise in the number of such cases.[66] The low number of derivative claims in Israel is very much like that in the UK, where there has not been an increase in the number of derivative claim after the 2006 reform.[67] A similar case could be found in China where statutory derivative actions were formally introduced in 2006, but the number of it remains small (just 103 derivative lawsuit from 2006 to 2013).[68] Despite practical issues, the Chinese long-existing legal culture of 'resistance to lawsuits' could be interpreted as one of the main reasons why the commencement of derivative actions remains infrequent.

---

[63]Adam Smith, *The Wealth of Nations*, (New York, Collier, 1902).

[64]John Blundell and Colin Robinson, 'Regulation without the State', (2000), pp. 1–3. http://www.iea.org.uk/sites/default/files/publications/files/upldbook12pdf.pdf (accessed on 2 August 2016).

[65]See *supra* 4.2.3.3.

[66]Arad Reisberg, 'Access to Justice or Justice Not Accessed, is there a case for public funding of derivative claims?', *Brooklyn Journal of International Law*, (2012), Volume 37, Issue 3, 1021, p. 1050.

[67]Ibid.

[68]*See* Shaowei Lin, 'Derivative Actions in China: Case Analysis', *Hong Kong Law Journal*, (2014), Volume 44, 621, p. 638.

In Canada too, it was concluded that statutory derivative actions failed to exert a significant impact given the infrequency of such proceedings.[69]

However, when a reform on facilitating derivative actions is carried out, only looking at the number of such claims to evaluate whether the reform is successful might not be reasonable. For example, even though, as mentioned before, derivative actions were not frequently filed in Canada, there were still influential cases which set examples regarding corporate governance and further positively influence it.[70,71] Therefore, only associating the number of derivative actions with the success of a reform in this respect and the function of derivative actions might be a misleading methodology. Other elements, such as the traditional cultural resistance to litigation in China and perhaps in other Asian countries that are also influenced by Confucius, have to be taken into account. The function of the derivative action mechanism does not only cover that the plaintiffs can sue a case before the court and claim for a trial. Its deterrent effects could be realized in a much more economical way, since wrongdoers might be deterred if they are aware that potential shareholder plaintiffs could be financially supported by the ISA to sue against them by launching derivative claims. Therefore, in practice, few derivative action filed in the courts cannot be strong evidence to demonstrate the failure of this mechanism.

Furthermore, the reason why there are few derivative actions in practice can also be explained by the nature of this device. Derivative actions originated in the common law world, and the *Foss* rule is a milestone in this regard. At the time of the exception to the *Foss* rule was established, the cause of a derivative lawsuit was regarded as 'exceptional'. In fact, common law derivative claims are largely based on the *Foss* rule and its exceptions.[72] Therefore, from the very origin of the derivative action, it was found to be *exceptional* in nature. After the introduction of statutory derivative actions in the 2006 reform, the circumstances under which a derivative lawsuit could be filed were broadened, it was, however, specifically stated that the reform was not intended to lead to a large increase in shareholder litigation.[73,74] Moreover, in countries such as the UK, where public rather than private legal enforcement dominates the practice of corporate law, the most typical

---

[69]Brian R. Cheffins and Janet M. Dine, 'Shareholder Remedies: Lessons from Canada', *Company Lawyer*, (1992), Volume 13, 89, p. 94.

[70]*Jenkins v Enterprise Gold MinesNL* (1992) 6 ACSR 539; *Niord Pty Ltd v Adelaide PetroleumNL* (1990) 2 ACSR 347. See Arad Reisberg, 'Access to Justice or Justice Not Accessed, is there a case for public funding of derivative claims?', *Brooklyn Journal of International Law*, (2012), Volume 37, Issue 3, 1021, p. 1050.

[71]Companies and securities advisory committee, 'report on a statutory derivative action', pp. 6–7. http://www.camac.gov.au/camac/camac.nsf/byHeadline/PDFFinal+Reports+1993/$file/Statutory_Derivative_Action,_July_1993.pdf (accessed on 10 August 2016).

[72]Ibid.

[73]UK Law Commission, *Shareholder Remedies*, LC 246 (London: TSO, 1997), p. 77.

[74]Actually, limitations on the commencement of derivative actions can be found in almost every country where it is applied. Similar to the English rule, the American and Chinese law also provide strict procedural and factual requirements on shareholder plaintiffs who intend to file a derivative claim in the court (2.3.2).

enforcement agencies concerning corporate governance are the Takeover Panel, the Financial Reporting Review Panel, and the Financial Services Authority, all of which provide *ex ante* preventive measures.[75] Derivative actions, as private enforcement of law, are, indeed, supplementary methods to promote sound corporate governance. Thus, a small quantity of derivative actions is of no surprise.[76] It is, nevertheless, likely that derivative actions, even if not be presented in the courtrooms frequently, might have an impact on issues concerning corporate governance in a long run as a supplement to public enforcement.[77]

Derivative actions are designed, principally, to promote the level of corporate governance and director's performance of companies. If the realization of this purpose only relies on the legal system, it is not economically and socially desirable, because the legal system is a very expensive social institution.[78] From the perspective of economics, a drastic increase in the amount of derivative actions cannot be entirely regarded as a positive signal for the reason that it is not sure benefits brought by court proceedings will exceed the costs caused by them.[79] In nature, the device of derivative action just provides shareholders with a 'last resort'[80] to redress losses and protect interests instead of encouraging them to commit every dispute to the court in spite of the high legal costs.[81]

---

[75]J Armour, 'Enforcement Strategies in UK Corporate Governance: A Roadmap and Empirical Assessment' in *The Law and Economics of Corporate Governance: Changing Perspectives*, (Alessio M. Pacces eds), Chap. 5.

[76]Another reason why the number of derivative actions in the UK remains small is because there are other substitutes for shareholder remedies, such as unfair prejudice remedy. (Section 994 of UK CA 2006) Compared to derivative actions, unfair prejudice remedy focuses more on the interests of shareholders, but not the interests of a company as a whole, which can be easily observed from section 994(1)(a) of CA 2006. Therefore, a shareholder, from the perspective of economy theory, will tends to choose the unfair prejudice remedy rather than the derivative action to compensate his monetary loss. As an individual shareholder, especially minority ones, it is reasonable to rest more on self-interest than on the company's benefits and its long-term development. For minority shareholders, particularly in some listed companies, they transact their shares mainly for making 'quick money'. Therefore, the level of corporate governance and the real interest of a company is not the first priority to them. Additionally, for the high financial risk involved in a derivative lawsuit and low proceeds generated in case of success, minority shareholders are not motivated to do so. They may prefer to bring unfair prejudice petition, under which monetary compensation can go directly to the shareholders' pockets. Given all that, unfair prejudice remedy may be superior to derivative actions in terms of compensating minority shareholders' monetary losses.

[77]Arad Reisberg, 'Access to Justice or Justice Not Accessed, is there a case for public funding of derivative claims?', *Brooklyn Journal of International Law*, (2012), Volume 37, Issue 3, 1021, p. 1052.

[78]See Steven Shavell, 'The Level of Litigation: Private Versus Social Optimality of Suit and of Settlement', 19 *International Review of Law and Economics*, (1999), Volume 19, 99, pp. 99–100.

[79]See Steven Shavell, 'The Social Versus the Private Incentive to Bring Suit in a Costly Legal System', *Journal of Legal Studies*, (1982) Volume 11, 333, pp. 333–339.

[80]For instance, Chinese law sets pre-procedures for shareholder plaintiffs to meet prior to a commencement of a derivative action. (Article 151 of the PRC Company Law 2014) (2.3.1).

[81]UK Law Commission, *Shareholder Remedies*, LC 246 (London: TSO, 1997), p. 77.

#### 4.2.3.3 The Problematic Authority

In theory, a desirable public intervention to adjust the market failure should be carried out by a 'perfect' public authority adhering to the principle of pursuing 'public interests'.[82] A completely altruistic public institute will detect the market failure and perform the duty of adjustment.[83] However, this expectation is hardly to be realized due to practical problems. Sometimes, public interests may contradict the self-interests of a public authority, or may not be in line with political considerations.

From a theoretical perspective, it might be difficult or even unrealistic for a public regulator to be entirely shielded from pressures of political and interest groups.[84] When performing regulatory measures which are not completely consistent with interest groups' considerations, the public authority may confront practical difficulties.[85] A distorted outcome may appear that the regulatory agency serves the private interests of powerful groups rather than the supposed goal of promoting public interests. Even worse, government officials could hardly put aside self-interests, such as salaries and career prospects, to fully devote themselves to pursue the 'public interests', if there is any contradiction between their own interests and the performance of job duties. The public authority is not expected to be almighty because, to a certain extent, it is subject to its leading body at a higher level in terms of budget allocation and personnel arrangement.[86] Thus, it is a fallacy to expect the government officials to become the completely disinterested purveyors of public interests.[87] A similar viewpoint concerning the defects of public enforcers is mentioned in the A.L.I's recommendations.

> when the legal system assigns an enforcement role [(or alternatively leaves room for) private enforcers (i.e., through litigation of derivative actions)] there is less need to rely on public agencies and in turn the tendency of such public agencies … to determine, sometimes arbitrarily or for political reasons, not to enforce rights or duties it had previously guarded is likely to be higher.[88]

---

[82]John Blundell and Colin Robinson, 'Regulation without the State', (2000), pp. 3–4. http://www.iea.org.uk/sites/default/files/publications/files/upldbook12pdf.pdf (accessed on 2 August 2016).

[83]Ibid.

[84]John Blundell and Colin Robinson, 'Regulation without the State', (2000), pp. 74–75 http://www.iea.org.uk/sites/default/files/publications/files/upldbook12pdf.pdf (accessed on 2 August 2016).

[85]See Brian R. Cheffins, *Company Law: Theory, Structure and Operation*, (Oxford University Press, 1997), Chap. 4.

[86]The Chinese case on this concern will be elaborated in the last section of this chapter.

[87]John Blundell and Colin Robinson, 'Regulation without the State', (2000), p. 34. http://www.iea.org.uk/sites/default/files/publications/files/upldbook12pdf.pdf (accessed on 2 August 2016).

[88]American law institute, *Principles of Corporate Governance: Analysis and Recommendations*, Part VIII, (1994), pp. 220–221.

Returning to the study of the derivative action, it has been considered to be a principal constraint on directors' mismanagement for quite a long time.[89] It seems to be feasible to correct director's performance through derivative actions which can be regarded as a sort of shareholders' private enforcement.[90] However, in the Israeli case, situations are changed because derivative actions can be funded publicly by a public authority (the ISA). It might raise a concern when a public institute intervenes in the shareholders' private enforcement, how can it be guaranteed that the public authority's consideration is in line with that of the private enforcers'? Except for the pursuit of public interests, enforcement by the public authorities is easily affected by many other factors, such as political influence, interest of powerful groups and public officials' self-interests as pointed out before. In contrast, the aim of a derivative action is to safeguard the shareholders and the company's interests, which is much simpler and straightforward. Therefore, when a public institute interposes in a derivative action, the conflict of interests among different participants will be likely to arise, making the realization of sound corporate governance through the derivative actions become complex. In the Israeli case, since the ISA's public funding was recently established in 2011, it is too early to judge whether the theoretical 'public authority' concern really happens. The ISA's annual reports from 2011 to 2014 (Report on the Activities of the Israel Securities Authority) suggest that the ISA's public funding indeed enhance the private enforcement by individual shareholders, and no solid evidence has been found to prove that the 'public authority' concern has been manifested.[91] What we stress in this regard is that the functioning of public funding largely depends on the role of the regulatory public authority. A problematic authority will easily lead to a failure of public funding.[92]

[89]Robert B. Thompson and Randall S. Thomas, 'The Public and Private Faces of Derivative Lawsuits', *Vanderbilt Law Review*, (2004), Volume 57(5), 1747, p. 1756.

[90]Mathias Siems, ' Private Enforcement of Directors' Duties: Derivative Actions as a Global Phenomenon' in *Collective Actions: Enhancing Access to Justice and Reconciling Multilayer Interests?* Stefan Wrbka, Steven Van Uytsel and Mathias Siems (eds), (Cambridge University Press, 2012), 93, pp. 96–99.

[91]It was indicated in the ISA's 2014 annual report that there was a growing number of public funding application, and this trend was expected to continue in 2015. ISA's annual report of 2011, available at http://www.isa.gov.il/Download/IsaFile_7037.pdf (accessed on 30 August 2016), pp. 109–119; ISA's annual report of 2012, available at http://www.isa.gov.il/Download/IsaFile_7850.pdf (accessed on 30 August 2016), pp. 132–141; ISA's annual report of 2013, available at www.isa.gov.il/sites/ISAEng/1489/1512/Documents/ISA_Report__2013.pdf (accessed on 30 August 2016), pp. 153–162; ISA's annual report of 2014, available at http://www.isa.gov.il/sites/ISAEng/1489/1512/Documents/ISA%20Annual%20Report%202014.pdf (access on 30 August 2016).

[92]When analysing the potential for public funding in China in 4.4 of this Chapter, we will discuss whether the 'public authority concern' exists.

## 4.3 Public Funding of Class Actions: The Canadian Case

### *4.3.1 Introduction*

Class action plaintiffs in Canada could seek funding from a variety of sources.[93] The most common approach to fund a class action is to resort to a lawyer to get financial assistance out of their pockets in terms of a contingence fee arrangement.[94] In practice, in Canada, entrepreneurial lawyers have become the main impetus behind class actions.[95] It is not rare that in a class action, the plaintiff's lawyer treats the lawsuit as a 'potentially lucrative action'[96] and put the representative plaintiff in the position of a 'figurehead' for the litigation.[97] The real function of the representative plaintiff is usually to get the certification from the court and to facilitate the discovery procedure.[98] Plaintiffs also have an option to seek financial supports from third party investors to cover litigation costs and lawyer's fees.[99] However, the application of litigation funding provided by a third party may violate the old common law prohibition of champerty and maintenance.[100] Given that, the third party litigation funding is not permitted in all jurisdictions. For instance, until 2012, third party funding of class actions was only legalized in some Canadian provinces, such as Alberta, Nova Scotia and Ontario, while in Australia, England and the United States, third party litigation funding has been legally recognized and has developed for long.[101]

The following section of this chapter will focus on investigating the Canadian innovation with regards to public funding of class actions, mainly including the Ontario Class Proceedings Fund and the Class Action Assistance Fund (*Fonds d'aide aux recours collectifs*) in Quebec. In discussing these two funding ways, the examination of rationalities, application requirements and working mechanisms will be presented respectively.

---

[93]Glenn M. Zakaib and Jeremy M. Martin, 'International Class Actions in the Canadian Context: Standing, Funding, Enforceability and Trial', *Defense Counsel Journal* (2012), Volume 79, 296, p. 309.

[94]Ibid.

[95]Thomas D. Rowe, 'Shift Happens: Pressure on Foreign Attorney-Fee Paradigms from Class Actions', *Duke Journal of Comparative and International Law*, (2003), Volume 13, 125, p. 128.

[96]Ibid.

[97]Ibid.

[98]Ibid.

[99]The third party litigation funding (TPLF) will be discussed in Chap. 5 of this book.

[100]Poonam Puri, 'Financing of Litigation by Third-Party Investors: A Share of Justice', *Osgoode Hall Law Journal*, (1998), Volume 36, 515, p. 519.

[101]Glenn M. Zakaib and Jeremy M. Martin, 'International Class Actions in the Canadian Context: Standing, Funding, Enforceability and Trial', *Defense Counsel Journal* (2012), Volume 79, 296, p. 309.

### 4.3.2 Ontario Class Proceeding Fund

The creation of the Ontario Class Proceeding Fund in 1992 was in response to the concern that private litigants face big financial difficulties in initiating class actions.[102] The Fund was described as 'the most attractive method of supporting class proceedings'.[103] This Fund is particularly important for cases where injunctive relief is claimed, because those cases, even if they are successful, cannot create monetary incentives for lawyers working under contingency fee arrangements.[104,105] On the other hand, the Fund has been criticized by the Ontario Law Reform Commission mainly for the reason that public money should not be used for private litigants to pursue class litigation.[106] In addition to that, concerns about the function of regulatory authority of the Fund were also raised.[107]

As stated in the Law Society Act, *bona fide* plaintiffs in a class action are qualified to apply for the Fund to cover disbursements[108] occurred during the proceeding, but lawyer's fees would not be covered by the Fund.[109] In litigation where the representative plaintiff has been awarded with the Fund, the adverse fees will be indemnified by the Fund in the event that the funded claim is lost.[110] For the sake of future *bona fide* applicants, the Committee favours cases demonstrating broad public importance, or cases having impact on the improvement of the situation of people who have been historically disadvantaged in the society.[111] From

[102]Ontario Law Foundation, 'Class Proceeding Fund: 20 Years in Review', (2012), p. 1, available at http://www.lawfoundation.on.ca/wp-content/uploads/CPF-Brochure-2013.pdf (accessed on 30 August 2016).

[103]Federal Court of Canada, the Rules Committee, Class Proceedings in the Federal Court of Canada—A Discussion Paper, (June 9, 2000), p. 102.

[104]Federal Court of Canada, the Rules Committee, Class Proceedings in the Federal Court of Canada—A Discussion Paper, (June 9, 2000), pp. 102–103.

[105]Contingency fee arrangements are legally allowed in Ontario, http://www.attorneygeneral.jus.gov.on.ca/english/about/contingency/ (accessed on 30 August 2016).

[106]Ontario Law Reform Commission, Report on Class Actions (1982), Volume III, p. 713.

[107]Ibid.

[108]See Law Society Act (Ontario), s 59.3(1)(2) provides that the Class Proceedings Fund are to be used for 'disbursements related to the proceeding' and 'shall not include a claim in respect of solicitor's fees.' Disbursements include the usual sort of fees that are common in all litigation. For example, filling fees, transcript costs, expert fees. Disbursements for special expenses that only arise in class actions (for example, the cost of class notice) are also covered by this Fund.

[109]In contrast to Ontario's practice, the Special Fund (Le fonds d'aide aux recours collectives) available in Quebec is more generous than Ontario's Fund. The Quebec Fund is able to pay for both lawyers' fees and disbursements.

[110]This rule is provided in s 59.4(1) of the Law Society Act; since the establishment of this principle, there has been practical application. For example, Garland v Consumers' Gas Co (1998), 165 DLR (4th) 385, 40 OR (3d) 479 (SCC).

[111]Collins David, 'Public Funding of Multi-Party Litigation', *Manitoba Law Journal*, (2010), Volume 31, 211, pp. 230–231.

this perspective, it appears that the Committee prefers to rectify systemic wrongs rather than to compensate individual victims.[112]

The Ontario Fund is financed by two parts (1) its initial funding came from a $500,000 grant by the Law Foundation of Ontario; (2) in the event that the funded case is won, a ten percent of the court-ordered award or settlement amount should be repaid to the Fund.[113] Actually, the Ontario Fund heavily relies on self-financing (the ten percent charging), because the seed funds provided by the government is thought to be insufficient.[114] The low government's contribution may partly be that, as mentioned before, the Ontario Law Reform Commission opposes using the public money for settling disputes between private individuals.[115]

In deciding whether or not to provide public funding, the Ontario Class Proceedings Committee should also scrutinize

> (1) the merits of the case; (2) whether or not the plaintiff made reasonable efforts to raise funds from other sources; (3) whether or not the plaintiff has made a clear and reasonable proposal for the use the funds; and (4) whether or not the plaintiff has appropriate financial controls to ensure that the funds are spent for the purpose of the grant.[116]

It is indicated that, normally, the Committee prefers to finance a case with more than 50% possibilities of success.[117] Even though the statutory rules do not require the Committee to fund cases with high success rates, due to the 'self-financing' nature, it is rational for the Committee to prefer such cases in order to receive the 10% 'repayment' by funded plaintiffs. It appears that in 2013, the total amount of 10% levying on favourable settlements and awards was approximately $2.8 million, while funding provided (cover the disbursements plus costs awards in favour of defendants) was amounted at around $4.3 million.[118] In 2014, however, the

---

[112] Ibid.

[113] http://www.lawfoundation.on.ca/class-proceedings-fund/ (accessed on 30 August 2016).

[114] The low start-up fund has been criticized by many scholars. For instance, see Rachael Mulheron, *The Class Action in Common Law Legal Systems: A Comparative Perspective*, (Hart Publishing, 2004), p. 457; Garry D. Watson, 'Class Actions: The Canadian Experience', *Duke Journal of Comparative and International Law* (2001), Volume 11, 269, p. 276; Collins David, 'Public Funding of Multi-Party Litigation', Manitoba Law Journal, (2010), Volume 31, 211, p. 227; See Donald Bisson and David I. W Hamer, *Defending Class Actions in Canada*, (CCH Canadian, Toronto, 3rd, edition, 2011), p. 300.

[115] Ontario Law Reform Commission, Report on Class Actions (1982), Volume III, p. 713.

[116] See section 59.3(4) of the Law Society Act, RSO 1990, c L-8 s 59.3, see http://www.e-laws.gov.on.ca/html/statutes/english/elaws_statutes_90l08_e.htm#BK140 (accessed on 30 August 2016).

[117] Collins David, 'Public Funding of Multi-Party Litigation', *Manitoba Law Journal*, (2010), Volume 31, 211, p. 230. The chance of success here does not mean that every funded case should have a 50% chance of success. It is an average concept meaning that in general the Committee can make a balance on all of the funded cases in terms of their rates of success.

[118] See the Law Foundation of Ontario, Annual Report 2013, pp. 8–9, available at http://www.lawfoundation.on.ca/wp-content/uploads/LFO-2013-Annual-Report-English-final-E-Web-4.pdf (accessed on 30 August 2016).

situation was quite different from that of 2013, where the 10% levies received ($10.3 million) exceeds the total amount of funding awarded ($2 million).[119]

As indicated above, on the part of the Committee, strong cases with good chance to win would be preferred. Considering the fact that contingency fee arrangements have been legally permitted in Ontario, a plaintiff's lawyer with good business sense may suggest the client to conclude a contingency fee arrangement with him if the case has a strong possibility of success.[120] For rational plaintiffs in such 'strong' cases, he may prefer to contract with the lawyer rather than to apply for the Fund because in the latter case the plaintiff needs to afford the lawyer's fees (which is not covered by the Fund) and contribute 10% of the monetary rewards if the case wins, while under a contingency fee arrangement the successful plaintiff only needs to pay for the lawyer. From the economic perspective, plaintiffs and lawyers may not be incentivized to resort to public funding if the case is with a high rate of success.

On the part of potential applicants and lawyers, the Committee's demanding requirements (e.g., a written statement of the merits of the case, a proposal for the use of the fund) for the Fund may further discourage them from applying for public funding.[121] Particularly, for the lawyer, the incentive to apply for the Fund might be even less than the plaintiffs because the Fund cannot help to mitigate the risk of the non-payment of lawyer's fees. If a funded case is lost, the Fund would not cover the lawyer's fees, meaning that the lawyer's fees are still subject to the payment by the plaintiffs. If the plaintiff refuses to pay for the attorneys on the pretext of financial difficulty, the Fund, under this circumstance, cannot function like a 'back-up' for the lawyer.

Conversely, provided that a case is won, the lawyer would be paid for an amount of money, either in the form of a percentage-of-recovery from court-ordered awards under a contingency fee arrangement or the basic hourly fees.[122] The Ontario

---

[119]See the Law Foundation of Ontario, Annual Report 2014, p. 18, available at http://www.lawfoundation.on.ca/wp-content/uploads/2014_LFO_Report_EN.pdf (accessed on 30 August 2016).

[120]Lawyer's contingency fee arrangements have been permitted in Ontario since 2002, http://www.attorneygeneral.jus.gov.on.ca/english/about/contingency/ (accessed on 30 August 2016); and see Ontario Class Proceedings Act 1992 (S.O. 1992, Chap. 6), S. 33.

[121]See section 59.3(4) of the Law Society Act, RSO 1990, for an applicant, at least, he has to prepare four kinds of materials to convince the committee. They include a written statement of the merits of the case; a statement to show the application for the Fund is the last resort for the applicant; a proposal for the use of the fund; and finally a statement to ensure the proper use of the fund; see Jacob Ziegel, 'Class Actions to Remedy Mass Consumer Wrongs: Repugnant Solution or Controllable Genie? The Canadian Experience', *Penn State International Law Review*, (2009), Volume 27, 879, p. 890.

[122]As a matter of fact, the types of contingent fees in Ontario varies, including a certain percent of court-ordered compensation, lawyer's hourly fees, or a 'multiple' to be applied to a base fee. See Ontario Class Proceedings Act 1992 (S.O. 1992, Chap. 6), S. 33; The act does not explicitly state the type of a percentage-of-recovery contingent fees, but the use of it does exist in Ontario. Evidence in this regard could be found in case law and academic commentary. For instance, see Rachael Mulheron, *The Class Action in Common Law Legal Systems: A Comparative Perspective*, (Hart Publishing, 2004), p. 475; see Kirk M. Baert and Jonathan Bida, 'Fee Approval Hearing in

statute even contemplates to provide more incentives for the class counsel working under contingent basis by conferring them the right to make a motion to the court to request an increase on the basic fees (hourly rates) by a multiplier.[123] The court, after receiving the motion, may determine the amount of attorney's basic fees and the potential multiplier to be added under certain circumstances.[124] If there is, indeed, a 'fair and reasonable compensation to the solicitor for the risk incurred in undertaking and continuing the proceeding under an agreement for payment only in case of success',[125] the lawyer's request for increasing the basic fees by a multiplier will be supported by the court.[126] Hence, an entrepreneurial lawyer's willingness to invest in a highly risky case might be further enhanced by the potential 'multiplier' to the basic lawyer's fees.

The lawyer's and the plaintiff's preference to contingency fee arrangements in 'strong' cases plus the Committee's cautious cost-and-benefit analysis would lead to a 'vicious circle' that a sluggish periodic fund flow may make the self-financing Fund easily fall into funding shortage. Even though it appears that the Ontario Fund does not show a financial deficit now, the reason for that might be contingency fee arrangements were legally confirmed in Ontario in 2002, while the Ontario Fund dates back to 1992. It might be possible that from 1992 to 2002, without the availability of contingency fee arrangements, 'strong' cases chose the Fund, and the 10% levying during that period financially contributed to the Fund's budget. But after 2002, the advent of lawyer's funding may negatively affect the Fund's attractiveness for applicants with 'strong' cases. It is observed that in the Committee's annual reports from 2010-2013, financial deficit appeared while in 2014, this situation was changed.[127]

As early as the year of 2001, Professor Garry D. Watson[128] pointed out that the Ontario Class Proceedings Fund was a failure. His conclusion was made based on

(Footnote 122 continued)

Class Proceedings', in the Sevens National Symposium on Class Actions, (Aprial 29–30, 2010), p. 3, available at http://www.kmlaw.ca/site_documents/Fee%20Approval%20Hearings%20-%20Class%20Proceedings_18jun10.pdf (accessed on 30 August 2016); For case law in this regard, see, for example, Pelletier v Baxter Health Care Co (SCJ, 9 Jul 1999); Nantais v Telectronics Pty (Canada) Ltd (1996), 134 DLR (4th) 470.

[123]Ontario Class Proceedings Act 1992 (S.O. 1992, Chap. 6), S. 33(3) & (4).

[124]Ontario Class Proceedings Act 1992 (S.O. 1992, Chap. 6), S. 33(7).

[125]Ontario Class Proceedings Act 1992 (S.O. 1992, Chap. 6), S. 33(7)(b).

[126]In *Gagne v Silcorp Ltd* (1998), 41 OR 3d (417) (CA), the Ontario Court of Appeal considered the factors concerns the reasonable multiplier. In the court's opinion, the degree of risk assumed by the lawyers and the degree of success achieved were both consideration factors by the court. In this case, the court allowed a multiplier of two to a base fee. In this decision, the Ontario Court of Appeal stated that the upper limit of the multiplier in the 'most deserving case' would be three or four. Christopher Hodges, *Multi-Party Actions*, (Oxford University Press, 2006), pp. 233–234.

[127]Annual reports of Class Proceedings Fund from 2010–2014 could be found in http://www.lawfoundation.on.ca/class-proceedings-fund/resources-reports/ (accessed on 30 August 2016).

[128]Garry D. Watson is a professor of law in Osgoode Hall Law School, York University, Toronto. And also Professor Watson had been a member of the committee administering the Fund.

the fact that the Fund had inadequate financing resources. However, the article did not attempt to investigate the failure of the Fund from the perspective of those reasons stated above, such as the lawyer's preference to contingency fee arrangements. Professor Watson mainly attributed the failure to the inadequate financial resource and problematic supplementary funding mechanism.[129] However, it should be mentioned that the Professor Watson's article was published in 2001. The question here is whether the Fund has been improved and functions better than 15 years ago? The Ontario Class Proceedings Fund still works and it appears from the annual report that the number of the funded cases as well as the number of applications is increasing.[130] However, unfortunately, positive appraisals are hardly to be found in recent publications. For example, in a recent publication by Professor Kalajdzic, who was once a member of the five-person Class Proceedings Committee considering all funding applications, a negative view was delivered regarding the practice of the Fund.[131] In this article, the author holds an opinion that the Ontario Fund is less attractive than contingency fee arrangements. Since other litigation funding techniques, such as third party funding (TPLF)[132] also available, the Class Proceedings Fund seems to be the least attractive means to fund class actions.[133,134] In Kalajdzic's article, she reveals the result of an interview regarding which kind of litigation funding is preferred to class action lawyers. The result demonstrates that most of class action lawyers (5 out of 8) choose to enter into contingency fee arrangements, while only one respondent states that he may try to apply for the Class Proceedings Fund for riskier cases.[135]

---

[129]Ibid.

[130]See Class Proceedings Fund: 20 Years Review, available at http://www.lawfoundation.on.ca/wp-content/uploads/CPF-Brochure-2013.pdf, (accessed on 30 August 2016).

[131]Jasminka Kalajdzic, Peter Cashman and Alana Longmoore, 'Justice for Profit: A Comparative Analysis of Australian, Canadian and U.S. Third Party Litigation Funding', *American Journal of Comparative Law* (2013), Volume 61(1), 93, pp. 118–119.

[132]For third party funding, see Rachael Mulheron, *The Class Action in Common Law Legal Systems: A Comparative Perspective*, (Hart Publishing, 2004), pp. 459–461; Paul G. Karlsgodt, *World Class Actions, A Guide to Group and Representative Actions around the Globe*, (Oxford University Press, 2012), pp. 102–103; Poonam Puri, 'Financing of Litigation by Third-Party Investors: A Share of Justice', *Osgoode Hall Law Journal*, (1998), Volume 36, 515, pp. 519–210.

[133]Jasminka Kalajdzic, Peter Cashman and Alana Longmoore, 'Justice for Profit: A Comparative Analysis of Australian, Canadian and U.S. Third Party Litigation Funding', *American Journal of Comparative Law* (2013), Volume 61(1), 93, p. 118.

[134]Compared to the public funding, the third party litigation funding (TPLF) is more attractive for applicants in some cases. For example, normally, the application procedure of the TPLF will be shorter than that of the public funding. Material the applicant has to prepare is simpler in the application for the TPLF.

[135]Jasminka Kalajdzic, Peter Cashman and Alana Longmoore, 'Justice for Profit: A Comparative Analysis of Australian, Canadian and U.S. Third Party Litigation Funding', *American Journal of Comparative Law* (2013), Volume 61(1), 93, p. 118.

The Class Proceedings Fund has drawbacks in the working mechanism *per se*.[136] A most significant problem is that the 10% levy is too excessive.[137] Professor Watson suggests in his article that a much lower levy rate should be set (for example, one or two percent) to all class actions, no matter whether or not those cases were previously financially assisted by the Fund.[138] The criticism of the 10% levy could also be observed in case law. In *Parsons v The Canadian Red Cross*,[139] the plaintiffs did not choose to apply for the Class Proceedings Fund due to the excessive 10% levy.[140] It was stressed that in this case, if the case were funded by the Committee, $63,550,000 would have been levied, which was rather excessive.[141]

Watson's article also indicates that a single cost award for an unsuccessful representative plaintiff to pay the adverse fees may use up the Fund because of the inadequate financing ability.[142] This concern could be further enhanced by the fact that the court has not taken into the financial ability of the Fund as a matter of judicial concern.[143] In response to the Law Foundation's request that the court should consider whether an award on adverse fees exceeds the financial ability of the Fund, the courts held the opinion that such kind of issue should be considered by the Committee when the funding scheme was recommended, but not contained in the courts' discretion.[144] Actually, the court's refusal to scrutinize the rationality

---

[136]Rachael Mulheron, *The Class Action in Common Law Legal Systems: A Comparative Perspective*, (Hart Publishing, 2004), p. 457.

[137]Rachael Mulheron, *The Class Action in Common Law Legal Systems: A Comparative Perspective*, (Hart Publishing, 2004), p. 457; Garry D. Watson, 'Class Actions: The Canadian Experience', *Duke Journal of Comparative and International Law* (2001), Volume 11, 269, p. 277; see Garry D. Watson, 'Is the Price Still Right? Class Proceedings in Ontario', The Administration of Justice in Commercial Disputes Conference, Toronto, October 15–18, (1997), pp. 32–33; W.A. Bogart, Jasminka Kalajdzic and Ian Matthews, 'Class Actions in Canada: A National Procedure in a Multi-Jurisdictional Society?', A report prepared for The Globalization of Class Actions Conference, (Oxford University, December 2007), p. 30.

[138]Garry D. Watson, 'Class Actions: The Canadian Experience', *Duke Journal of Comparative and International Law* (2001), Volume 11, 269, p. 277; it has also been indicated that the success of the Quebec Fonds is partly due to the leving on all successful cases whether or not they were publicly funded before, see W.A. Bogart, Jasminka Kalajdzic and Ian Matthews, 'Class Actions in Canada: A National Procedure in a Multi-jurisdictional Society?', A report prepared for The Globalization of Class Actions Conference, (Oxford University, December 2007), p. 30.

[139]*Parsons v The Canadian Red Cross* [1999] OJ No 3572.

[140]Rachael Mulheron, *The Class Action in Common Law Legal Systems: A Comparative Perspective*, (Hart Publishing, 2004), pp. 457–458.

[141]Ibid.

[142]Garry D. Watson, 'Class Actions: The Canadian Experience', *Duke Journal of Comparative and International Law* (2001), Volume 11, 269, p. 276.

[143]Rachael Mulheron, *The Class Action in Common Law Legal Systems: A Comparative Perspective*, (Hart Publishing, 2004), p. 458.

[144]*Edwards v Law Society of Upper Canada* (2000), 188 DLR (4th) 613, 48 OR (3d) 329 (CA) [52]; *Garland v Consumers' Gas Co* (1995), 22 OR (3d) 767 (Gen Div) [46]. Rachael Mulheron, *The Class Action in Common Law Legal Systems: A Comparative Perspective*, (Hart Publishing, 2004), p. 458.

of the order of adverse fees might further enhance the Committee's risk-averse attitude.[145]

The under-utilization of the Funds also caused by certain procedural requirements.[146] According to the Committee's rule, an application for the Fund will not be considered until a statement of defence of an action has been delivered, which deters the plaintiff's funding application.[147] Normally, the defendants would withhold the filing statement until the certification motion has been determined.[148] But in practice, the availability of the litigation funding will be taken into consideration when the court decides whether the certification motion will be granted.[149] Therefore, the Committee's rule makes it unpractical for plaintiffs who need financial assistance to satisfy the certification requirement before they get funded.[150] In contrast, the Quebec approach is much more applicant-friendly in this respect. The applicants can submit the application for the Quebec *Fonds* in the very beginning, and even before the initiation of a class action,[151] which is more practical than the Ontario's approach.

### *4.3.3 The Quebec Fonds D'aide Aux Recours Colleftifs (the Quebec* Fonds*) and Its Comparison with the Ontario Class Proceedings Fund*

Compared to the Class Proceedings Fund in Ontario, the functioning of the Quebec *Fonds* appears more successful. One of the reasons for the more frequent use of the Quebec *Fonds* may be that the Quebec approach reimburses the lawyer's fees which are not covered by the Ontario Fund. In addition to the wider scope of reimbursement of the *Fonds*, the requirements under which the financial assistance can be granted in Quebec are easier to be satisfied.[152] For instance, there is no requirement for the case to demonstrate broad public importance; the *Fonds* does

[145]Rachael Mulheron, *The Class Action in Common Law Legal Systems: A Comparative Perspective*, (Hart Publishing, 2004), p. 458.

[146]Ibid.

[147]Ibid.

[148]Ibid.

[149]Ibid.

[150]Rachael Mulheron, *The Class Action in Common Law Legal Systems: A Comparative Perspective*, (Hart Publishing, 2004), pp. 458–459.

[151]See the official website of the Quebec *Fonds d'aide aux recours collectifs*, http://www.farc.justice.gouv.qc.ca/ (accessed on 30 August 2016).

[152]In section 23 of *An Act Respecting the Class Action, RSQ, c R-2.1*, it provides that 'In order to determine whether to grant assistance, the *Fonds* shall assess whether the class action may be brought or continued without such assistance; in addition, if the status of representative has not yet been ascribed to the applicant, the *Fonds* shall consider the probable existence of the right he intends to assert and the probability that the class action will be brought'.

not require the applicant to prepare materials such as a proposal for the use the funds, which is included in the application requirements of the Ontario's Fund.

Moreover, the financial resources in Quebec *Fonds* are more adequate than that in the Ontario Class Proceedings Fund. The *Fonds* is an ongoing financial responsibility of the Quebec government and the government plays an active role in financially supporting the *Fonds*.[153] Apart from the government's assistance, the *Fonds* is also entitled to collect a certain percent of court-ordered recoveries from *any* judgment or settlement in class lawsuits even if those cases were not previously funded by the *Fonds*. The levying rate varies and mainly depends on the different method of recoveries by the class. For example, if the final recovery is in a collective form, the *Fonds* can charge a range from 30 to 70% of the balanced account (court-ordered recoveries minus litigation costs);[154] if the monetary remedies have been distributed to individual claimants, the *Fonds* can charge a range from 50 to 90 of each plaintiff's balanced account.[155] It needs to be mentioned that the *Fonds*, like the Ontario Fund, covers adverse fees in an unsuccessful funded case. However, a different point is that, unlike the Ontario's approach, the *Fonds* can take the successful defendant's position and claim the reimbursements of the adverse fees from the adverse party (the losing plaintiff).[156]

In fact, the Quebec's approach demonstrates continuous vigour and acts dynamically like an important role of promoting the access to justice.[157] Before the twenty-first century, the *Fonds* had made 995 decisions with 79% of cases being financially assisted by it.[158] From 2002 to 2012, approximately 230 cases, in total, were funded,[159] while only 50 cases were financed by the Class Proceedings by the Ontario Fund from 2001 to 2010.[160]

---

[153]Jocob Ziegel, 'Class Actions to Remedy Mass Consumer Wrongs: Repugnant Solution or Controllable Genie? The Canadian Experience', *Penn State International Law Review*, (2009), Volume 27, 879, p. 891. Unlike the Ontario Class Proceedings Fund, the clear amount of money that the Quebec government provided to support the *Fonds* was not indicated. However, almost all literatures states that the financial support the Quebec government provided to the *Fonds* was comparatively adequate and the government plays an active role in financially supporting the *Fonds*. Alan Riley, '*Damages in EC Antitrust Actions: Who Pays the Piper*?', European Law Review, (2006), 31(5), 748, p. 759.

[154]See also Regulation Respecting the Percentage Withheld by the Fonds d'aide aux recours collectifs, R.R.Q. c. R-21, r. 2. S1(2).

[155]See also Regulation Respecting the Percentage Withheld by the Fonds d'aide aux recours collectifs, R.R.Q. c. R-21, r. 2. S1(1).

[156]See *An Act Respecting the Class Action, R.S.Q. c. R-21, s. 31.*

[157]Paul G. Karlsgodt, *World Class Actions, A Guide to Group and Representative Actions around the Globe*, (Oxford University Press), 2012, p. 102.

[158]*Fonds D'Aide Aux Recours Collectifs Rapport Annuel* 2011–2012, pp. 10–11. (in French) http://www.farc.justice.gouv.qc.ca/doc/RapportAnnuel2011-2012.pdf (accessed on 30 August 2016).

[159]Ibid.

[160]Annual Report of the Ontario Class Proceedings Fund, http://www.lawfoundation.on.ca/who-we-are/annual-reports/ (accessed on 30 August 2016).

## 4.4 The Potential for Public Funding in China

### *4.4.1 Introduction*

Shareholder litigation, including shareholder direct actions, shareholder derivative actions and shareholder class actions, is legally permitted in China. But Chinese law does not, specifically, mention how to fund shareholder litigation. For instance, shareholder derivative actions were first introduced in 2006, while the PRC Company Law, even after the recent 2014 amendment, does not indicate any effective funding ways to finance such actions. The absence of a proper funding mechanism makes individual shareholder(s) face high litigation risks when filing shareholder litigation before the court.[161] Normally, a rational shareholder is mostly driven by the potential benefits brought by the litigation. If the litigation costs are likely to exceed the potential benefits, the rational shareholder(s) may prefer to sell his shares rather than to initiate a financially risky lawsuit. After investigating the public funding applied in Israel and Canada, the following sections of this chapter will focus on examining its potential for China. It needs to be pointed out that the Chinese social background and the cultural tradition cannot be neglected when we consider the possibility of transplanting public funding into China. More specifically, features of Chinese judicial system, the current situation of Chinese public sectors and judicial attitude to shareholder litigation should be taken into account.

### *4.4.2 Shareholder Litigation in China: How Does It Function*

#### 4.4.2.1 The Unique 'Inside System' (体制内), 'Local Protectionism' (地方保护主义) and the Characteristics of Shareholder Litigation in China

Shareholder litigation is a broad concept that cannot be found in statutory law,[162] in order to investigate the characteristics of shareholder litigation, we will mainly take

[161] The reason why litigation costs for shareholder claims are usually high is mainly because that they are, in nature, property claims. Accordingly, litigation costs in such claims are calculated in proportionate with the monetary value involved in the cases, which are generally high.

[162] Within the framework of this book, shareholder litigation refers to claims for damages mainly in the forms of shareholder derivative actions, shareholder direct actions and shareholder class actions. The Chinese law, up till now, has allowed the first three types of shareholder litigation. In nature, shareholder class actions (private securities litigation under Chinese law) and shareholder derivative actions are both mass litigation which may involve a group of shareholder litigants and, perhaps, bring significant social impact. In this sense, they share similar grounds and the judicial attitude towards them might be similar to a certain degree. What we try to discuss in this chapter regarding the features and the current practice of derivative actions and the judicial attitude to them could be applied to Chinese shareholder class actions.

the shareholder derivative action as a research topic to make the investigation more concrete. Shareholder class actions (private securities litigation under Chinese law) will also be mentioned.

As Professor Clarke indicates, the rules of derivative actions in China cannot be simply interpreted from their literal meaning, and there are further complexities in this regard:

> In China the actual implementation of a derivative action mechanism has implications going beyond mere corporate governance concerns. Many corporate entities in the PRC are dominated by insiders who have—or represent—significant political power that exceeds their formal economic or management power. Leading directors and officers at large corporatized state-controlled enterprises are often Communist Party *nomenklatura* appointments or representatives of central government institutions. The same is true of insiders at enterprises controlled by local governments or subordinate Party levels. And even if insiders are not directly tied to the Party or state, they are often part of a system (系统 'xitong') of connected actors with overwhelming political and economic power.[163]

In China, corporate management and the company's business activities cannot be shielded from political power over the past few decades.[164] In early 1980s, after the reform and opening up policy by Deng Xiaoping, policy-makers began to make effort to reform Chinese State-owned Enterprises (SOEs), which were plagued by low productivity, inefficient management and superfluous staffs.[165] During that period, the manager accountability system was introduced to enhance the level of enterprise management, which, indeed, increased productivity.[166] However, this reform created another managerial problem: the promotion of the status of managers without effective supervisory boards results in an even stronger position for managers (the manager's block power).[167] Under this circumstance, even if a manager committed misconducts, they would not be sanctioned. This condition did not change until the enactment of the 1993 Company Law (1993 CL) which introduced a series of measures to supervise the company's management.[168] However, the supervision measures in the 1993 CL did not prove to be effective to restrain managers' power.[169] After that, the 2006 Company (2006 CL) brought a key change in this regard by introducing shareholder derivative actions mechanism

---

[163]Donald C. Clarke and Nicholas C. Howson, 'Pathway to minority shareholder protection: derivative actions in the People's Republic of China', in Dan W. Puchniak, Harald Baum and Michael Ewing-Chow (eds), *The derivative action in Asia: a comparative and functional approach*, (Cambridge University Press, 2012), 243, pp. 243–244.

[164]Ibid.

[165]Peizhong Gan, 'Overview on Shareholder Derivative Action in Chinese Company Law', (in Chinese) (简评中国公司法对股东派生诉讼制度的借鉴), http://www.civillaw.com.cn/Article/default.asp?id=25127 (accessed on 30 August 2016).

[166]Ibid.

[167]Ibid.

[168]For example, the 1993 Company Law introduced board of supervisors for the first time to reinforce the supervision of corporate management.

[169]Donald C. Clarke and Nicholas C. Howson, 'Pathway to minority shareholder protection: derivative actions in the People's Republic of China', in Dan W. Puchniak, Harald Baum and

by which shareholders could directly launch actions on behalf of the company to redress manager's wrongdoings and enhance corporate governance. Seemingly, the Chinese legislators has made essential progress in supervising corporate managers and protecting shareholders.

However, after 2006, derivative lawsuits did not function as effectively as expected. from 1 January 2006 to 30 August 2013, only 103 derivative actions were brought before Chinese courts.[170] It is observed that among these cases, very few of them were initiated against the directors in joint stock limited companies (JSLC).[171] During those years (from 2006 to 2013), no derivative actions involving public companies were launched.[172] In other words, derivative actions were used to settle disputes between minority shareholders and directors in LLCs rather than that in JSLCs.[173] The reason why the use of derivative actions in LLCs is much more popular than that in JSLCs may be that in China the number of LLCs is much greater than that of JSLCs and public companies. However, this reason cannot fully explain why derivative action rarely happen in Chinese public companies after its introduction in 2006. In fact, the ownership of the shares held by minority shareholders in a public company or a JSLC is usually widely dispersed, and the amount of shares held by those shareholders is usually small, making that there are few incentives for them to commence derivative actions.[174] In practice, lawsuits brought by these public shareholders (公众股东) are mostly direct actions rather than derivative actions.[175] Another reason why derivative lawsuits are more frequently

(Footnote 169 continued)

Michael Ewing-Chow (eds), *The derivative action in Asia: a comparative and functional approach*, (Cambridge University Press, 2012), 243, pp. 260–263.

[170]*See* Shaowei Lin, "Derivative Actions in China: Case Analysis", (2014), *Hong Kong Law Journal*, Volume 44, 621, p. 638.

[171]Ibid.

[172]Ibid.

[173]Rules concerning LLCs are mainly incorporated in chapter two of the 2014 Company Law. The law provides that a LLC should be established through joint investment by no fewer than 2 but no more than 50 shareholders. Actually, a LLC under Chinese company law is similar to a close company in common law countries. See Douglas K. Moll, 'Minority Oppression and the Limited Liability Company: Learning (or Not) from Close Corporation History', *Wake Forest Law Review*, (2005), Volume 40, 883, pp. 888–892; Under Chinese law, the number of shareholders and the registered capitals requirements for a JSLC are much more than those for a LLC. Normally, in China, public companies fall within the scope of JSLC.

[174]Minority shareholders in a public company are usually private investors (散户). They purchase and sell shares just to make 'quick money', but not carefully mind the corporate governance of the company. If corporate governance in that company is not sound, those minority shareholders prefer to sell their shares rather than to bring derivative actions. See Dan Wang, *Theoretical analysis on shareholders' derivative actions*, (in Chinese) (公司派生诉讼论), (China legal publishing house, 2012), p. 325.

[175]Dan Wang, *Theoretical analysis on shareholders' derivative actions*, (in Chinese) (公司派生诉讼论), (China legal publishing house, 2012), p. 325; Lei Hao, *Practical aspects of shareholder litigation in China*, (in Chinese), (股东诉讼的实施问题研究), (China Legal Publishing, 2012), p. 137.

used by shareholders in LLC might be that disgruntled shareholders in a LLC could only choose to opt out of the company in limited circumstances,[176] while the mobility of shares is much higher in a JSLC or in a public company. Disgruntled shareholders in a JSLC or a public company can sell their shares more easily and opt out of the company without strict limitations, which might explain the infrequent use of derivative actions by shareholders in JSLCs and public companies.

Besides reasons analysed before, another important reason for the infrequent use of derivative actions in JSLCs and public companies might be caused by the unique judicial system and social background.

First, the 'local protectionism' theory, holding that the local government and local judicial authorities (for instance, local courts) may be very *protective* of local enterprises and avoid orders that may negatively affects these enterprises' profitability, could be regarded as a typical feature of the China's judicial system.[177] The reason for this 'local protectionism' could be explained as follows. A local government's fiscal budget largely depends on the tax turned over by local enterprises, which is generally in proportion to their incomes. Considering that, what the local government concerns most might be the enterprise's profitability. Orders that would negatively affect the company's profitability may not be favoured by the local government. Local courts cannot ignore the influences from the local government because they heavily rely on the financial allocation from the government at the same level (for instance, a Provincial Higher People's Court is financially supported by the provincial government).[178] In nature, they are both controlled and led by the Communist Party.[179] The reality of the unique 'inside system' in current China may suggest that it is difficult for the court to act independently, and its judicial decisions

[176]Article 75 of CL 2014 provides three circumstances under which disgruntle shareholders can choose to opt out and request the company to purchase his shares at a reasonable price: (1) The company that has made profits for five consecutive years has failed to distribute any dividends to the shareholders for 5 consecutive years and conforms to the profit distribution conditions as prescribed in this Law; (2) The company is going to merge with others, to be split up, or transfer the major properties of the company to others; (3) When the business term as specified in the bylaw expires or other reasons for dissolution as prescribed in the bylaw occur, the shareholders' meeting makes the company exist continuously by adopting a resolution to modify the bylaw.

[177]For instance, a court's judgment which fines a company a big sum of money and negatively affects its reputation might influence the company's profitability and its business cooperation with others.

[178]Besides the financial reliance on government, the appointment of the court's personnel is partly determined by the government. For instance, the court's staff recruitment is basically through the 'civil servant exam' (公务员考试), which means that staffs in the courts (judges) are civil servant in nature. The third plenary session of the 18th Central Committee of the Communist Party of China in 2013 (第十八届三中全会) suggested a mode of 'vertical governance' of the judicial system, holding that courts at each level should be financed by a special fund by the central government. But, until now, no enforcement in this regard has been found.

[179]'Courts are led by the Communist Party' is a unique ideology in Chinese judicial system. Even if the Communist Party (the central government) has stressed that a round of 'judicial reform' needs to be launched to guarantee the judgers' independence in dealing with cases (it has been stated consecutively in the third and fourth plenary session of the 18th Central Committee of the

are easily affected by the government at the same or upper levels,[180] which may further enhance the concern of 'local protectionism'. In a company, the directors and controlling shareholders, compared to minority shareholders, substantially operate the company and control its profitability. In consideration of the 'local protectionism' and 'inside system', it might be possible to conclude that in a shareholder derivative lawsuit, the local court might be reluctant to side with minority shareholders even though directors indeed committed wrongdoings.

On the other hand, it might be true that if a derivative action only involves a small company with low profitability, the concern about 'local protectionism' is not justified, because such a company is less important for the local economy and tax income. However, for the small-scale company with only a few shareholders, the most feasible way to solve disputes between minority shareholders and directors is not to file a lawsuit. They may prefer to solve the disputes through personal negotiation or other internal ways rather than to resort to the costly judicial system.[181] If a company has more shareholders and is more profitable, it might be safe to conclude that a derivative action involving such a company will confront judicial resistance due to the 'local protectionism' and 'inside system' theory, as indicated before.

'Local protectionism' also influences the enforcement of judgment. Sometimes, a local court refuses the civil judgment made by courts of other provinces.[182] The law directly indicates that the courts have the obligation to enforce valid judgments, local courts, however, may evade such obligations as a result of the 'local protectionism'.[183] The lack of judicial independence and the interplay between

(Footnote 179 continued)

Communist Party of China in 2013 and 2014), the Communist Party never explicitly declared that courts should be independent from the Party's lead.

[180]For a Provincial Higher People's Court, the provincial government is the government at the 'same level'. The central government is the government at the upper level.

[181]In China, a big portion of small companies are family-run enterprises, shareholders and directors are usually members from the same family. It is nature that the most common way to solve disputes between them is through personal negotiation. For example, in Wenzhou, family-run private companies are very flourishing. Filing lawsuits is not a common way to solve conflicts in these companies. Dispute resolution is generally realized by internal negotiation between family members. See Xiangqian Yu, *The governance of family-run enterprises: the Wenzhou example*, (in Chinese) (家族企业治理，传承及持续成长：基于温州的实证研究), (Zhejiang University Press, 2010), pp. 78–79 & 114–116.

[182]Donald C. Clarke, 'Power and Politics in the Chinese Court System, The Enforcement of Civil Judgments', *Columbia Journal of Asian Law*, (1996), Volume 10(1), 1, pp. 41–49; Randall Peerenboom, *China's Long March toward Rule of Law*, (Cambridge University Press, 2002), pp. 311–312.

[183]Article 207 and article 210 of Chinese Civil Procedural Law provides the obligation for the courts to enforce a valid judgment, no matter this judgment is made by the local courts or the courts of other areas. And see, Guang Deng, 'Why is the enforcement of legal judgment difficult: study the way forward', (in Chinese), (民事判决执行难的原因与对策), *Legal and Economy* (法制与经济), (2009) Volume 16; Zuoxiang Liu, 'The criticism of the local protectionism in Chinese judicial system', (in Chinese) (中国司法地方保护主义之批判), *Chinese journal of law* (法学研究), (2003) Volume 1.

authorities create serious obstacles in enforcing the court's judgments.[184] With regards to this practical problem, Yang Xiao, the former president of Chinese Supreme People's court once stated that:

> The difficulty of executing civil and commercial judgments has become a major 'chronic ailment' often leading to chaos in the enforcement process. There were few solutions to the problem … Chinese courts slack the authority and stature to command obedience to their decisions, especially where such decisions affect other government branches and officials.[185]

#### 4.4.2.2 The GDP Worship

The concern of 'local protectionism' might be further aggravated by the governments' GDP worship. Local governments are keen on pursuing a higher GDP record. Government officials attach much importance to GDP that would contribute to their career achievements. In China, the performance of a government official is generally evaluated by the GDP record, which would be problematic and even dangerous. For this reason, a concern might be raised whether the strong pursuance of high GDP record would neglect people's real interests.[186] For example, whether the court (which sides with the government due to the 'inside system' theory) will 'forgive' a company's misbehaviours if it could contribute to a high GDP record. In order to seek higher profits, an enterprise may sacrifice the shareholders' interests and damage the sound corporate governance. For instance, an enterprise may make a short-sighted investment which currently makes money but is essentially harmful to the company.[187] In this case, if the shareholders file a derivative lawsuit, how will the court respond to it? Normally, in light of the rule of territorial jurisdiction, the court governing a derivative lawsuit will be the one in the district where the headquarter of the company is located. Hence, the 'local protectionism' will reinforce the court's reluctance to accept the derivative action concerning a highly profitable enterprise in this area. Even though the local court accepts such a case, the government may interfere in the court's decision for the sake of GDP. Or, this

[184]See Ding Chen, Legal tradition and private securities litigation in China, I.C.C.L.R. 2012, 23 (11), 394–400, p. 397.

[185]China Law and Governance Review (2004) June, No. 2, 'Enforcement of Civil Judgments: Harder than Reaching the Sky (执行难, 难于上青天)', (June 2004) http://www.chinareview.info/issue2/pages/legal.htm#1 (accessed on 30 August 2016).

[186]Higher GDP record does not mean more benefits to the people. See Jie Shen, 'From the adoration of GDP to the care for well-being index: profound turns in the views of development in perspective of theory of development', (in Chinese), (从GDP崇拜到幸福指数关怀—发展理论视野中发展观的几次深刻转折), *Journal of Jiangsu administration institute* (江苏行政学院学报), 2006(3).

[187]For example, a company sells fake goods, which may make money but will damage its reputation in the long run.

case might even be refused at a very early step by the case filing chamber of the court.[188]

#### 4.4.2.3 The Dilemma in State-Owned Enterprises (SOEs) and Public Companies

There is an even more pessimistic situation when a SOE (meanwhile it is also highly profitable)[189] is involved in a given derivative suit. In China, there are many state-owned enterprises and state-holding enterprises due to historical reasons.[190,191] The board of directors and other important senior managers of a SOE usually have strong political background and are generally members of the Communist Party.[192] The management and controlling shareholders of a SOE may

188Sometimes, the courts face pressures from the government or from the Communist Party not only when they judge some cases. As early as the time the court just receives a pleading and decides whether or not accept this case and give continuance to it, the pressure from the local or from the Communist Party might turn up. So in China, some cases with political complexities were dismissed in very initial steps. For example, YAN Hong Versus Directors of Hu Bei Jiang Zuan Co. Ltd case in 2008. Jiang Zuan is a quite profitable public company in Hubei Province. When YAN hong brought the derivative action against the directors in Donghu district People's court in Hubei, the case was refused in the very early stage by the court. The department within a court that decides whether or not accept a given case is called case filing chamber (li'an ting '立案庭').

189Normally, in China, SOEs are highly profitable because of the state support from various aspects. For example, an enterprise with strong state background will win the bidding of some big projects easily than private companies without any political background.

190State-holding enterprises are, in nature, held by the state. The governments at different levels could present the state to hold a majority of shares of the given enterprise. The controlling shareholder or directors of such enterprise are actually controlled by the state (the government). Hence, the operation of the enterprise will be influenced a lot by the state or governments at lower levels.

191The reason why there are lots of state-owned enterprises and state-holding enterprises is because before the reform and opening up policy the planned economy was applied in China. During that period, all companies are state-owned in nature. Private companies run by individuals appeared only after the reform and opening up policy in the 1980s.

192For example, the chief director of Petro China Limited Company is Mr. Jiping Zhou who is a member of the Communist Party; The chief director of Sinopec is Mr. Chengyu Fu, who is also a member of the Communist Party. In some significant SOEs, the chief directors must be the member of the Communist Party. Even though in the past two decades, the government has made lots of effort to reform the traditional SOEs which were plagued by low productivity, unresponsiveness to economic signals, and waste, the reform did not involve privatization or withdrawal of the Party-state block control from the company, and an outright majority of shares within a company were still held by the Party-state. See Donald C. Clarke and Nicholas C. Howson, 'Pathway to minority shareholder protection: derivative actions in the People's Republic of China', in Dan W. Puchniak, Harald Baum and Michael Ewing-Chow (eds), *The derivative action in Asia: a comparative and functional approach*, (Cambridge University Press, 2012), 243, pp. 260–261; And Min Yan, 'Obstacles in China's corporate governance', *Company Lawyer*, (2011), Volume 32 (10), 311, pp. 312–313; See Ming Liu, Xu Zhang et al, 'The Development of Corporate Governance in China', *Company Lawyer*, (2007), Volume 28(7), 195, pp. 196–199.

be governmental or quasi-governmental bodies, or have a close relationship with the Communist Party or its organizations.[193] Even against the background of the market economy, it is still not possible for SOEs to operate their business completely independently without the Party-state's influence. The 'integration of government and enterprise' (政企不分) has been criticized for decades.[194] In the past twenty years, the government has endeavoured to reform SOEs, however, the strategy of corporatization without removing the governments' control did not change the nature of SOEs.[195] When a derivative action is brought against the directors of a SOE, this case will, to a large extent, be politically sensitive and be subject to various kinds of obstacles and interference.[196] Local political power, including the local government, local People's Congresses and the local Communist Party organization, controls the courts informally and formally by means of the personnel appointment and the budget allocation.[197] The court, which is in nature one of the members of the 'inside system', would be reluctant to act in accordance with the principle of judicial independence, which might make a derivative action easily be refused at a very early stage or the judgment be made not in favour of shareholder plaintiffs.

Many Chinese listed companies are state-owned enterprises or *de facto* controlled by the Party-state. The *China Corporate Governance Report 2009* points out that of all companies listed in the Shanghai Stock Exchange Centre, two thirds could be considered as 'state nature' (国家性质).[198] 75% of those 'state nature' companies have a block state holder, meaning the state holds more than 50% of the total shares.[199] The remaining 25% of them are indirectly controlled by the state, meaning that the state holds less than 50% of the total shares but essentially it has a

---

[193]Donald C. Clarke and Nicholas C. Howson, 'Pathway to minority shareholder protection: derivative actions in the People's Republic of China', in Dan W. Puchniak, Harald Baum and Michael Ewing-Chow (eds), *The derivative action in Asia: a comparative and functional approach*, (Cambridge University Press, 2012), 243, pp. 312–313.

[194]Hui Li, *The corruption, the vanity and the relationship between the governments and the state-owned enterprises*, (in Chinese), (腐败,政绩与政企关系), (Fudan University Press , 2011); See Li Hui, *Reports on Chinese governments and the state-owned enterprises*, (in Chinese), (中国政企治理问题报告), (China Development Press, 2003).

[195]Ibid.

[196]Donald C. Clarke and Nicholas C. Howson, 'Pathway to minority shareholder protection: derivative actions in the People's Republic of China', in Dan W. Puchniak, Harald Baum and Michael Ewing-Chow (eds), *The derivative action in Asia: a comparative and functional approach*, (Cambridge University Press, 2012), 243, pp. 275–278.

[197]For instance, the members of the judicial committee which is dealing with significant or influential cases are appointed by the Standing Committee of the People's Congress (article 10 of the Law of the Organization of People's Court) The president of the People's Court is also appointed by the Standing Committee of the People's Congress. (article 34 of the Law of the Organization of People's Court).

[198]'China Corporate Governance Report 2009', (in Chinese), (公司治理报告), Shanghai Stock Exchange Research Centre, (May 2009), pp. 90–93 http://www.sse.com.cn/researchpublications/special/c/special20100312.pdf (accessed on 30 August 2016).

[199]Ibid.

block power on this company.[200] The 2009 report reveals an important finding that the Party-state dominates the shareholding in most of Chinese public companies.[201] When a derivative action involving a public company is launched, it might still be difficult for the court to be judicially independent. For example, the *Sanlian Shangshe 2009* case, which is the first and the only derivative action involving the public company after the promulgation of the 2006 CL, was sued in the Shandong Provincial Higher People's Court. The judgment of this case was made on October 17th 2012, declaring that the claim of minority shareholders was rejected. The reason behind it is obvious: *Sanlian* Group (the defendant) is a significant corporation in Shandong Province and the Shandong government puts it into a core list of enterprises which are strongly supported by the government.[202] In other words, *Sanlian* Group is an influential local enterprise in Shandong province supported by the 'inside system'. Thus, the local court, when dealing with the *Sanlian* case, easily inclined to make a decision in favour of the *Sanlian* Group, for the reason that the government who strongly supports *Sanlian* Group has significant political, administrative, and fiscal control over the local court.[203]

---

[200]Ibid.

[201]When a SOE is listed, the local office of the Bureau of State Asset Management (BSAM) or its subsidiaries called state asset management companies act as the largest shareholder. The chairman of the board of directors is usually a representative from the BSAM. They nominate the managers of the listed SOE and oversee the management. And studies have shown why BSAM officials are poor monitors of the listed SOE. Because they are all civil servants whose pay is not tied to the performance of the companies they oversee. Thus there is no incentive to increase the value of the listed SOE. And also their bosses are the local governments and again this causes them to align their interests with the local government, whose political interests may be to preserve employment rather than increase the efficiency of listed SOEs. The final reason for this poor government by BSAM is that the officials are not experts knowing which decision made by the management is value-enhancing and which is not. They have to oversee hundreds of companies in which the state has an interest. For more, see Lixin Xu, Tian Zhu and Yimin Lin, 'Politician Control, Agency Problems and Ownership Reform: Evidence from China', *The Economics of Transition*, (2002), Volume 13(1), 1, pp. 2–4.

[202]In China, not every case is published. So we cannot find the whole written judgment of this case. But through some interview or media report, we can collect some information of this case. In fact, the trial of the *Sanlian Shangshe* 2009 case is deeply in connection with another *Sanlian Shangshe* case (Sanlian trademark case). The defendants of those two cases are the same (the Sanlian Group). In *Sanlian* Trademark case, the defendant (Sanlian Group) indicated on the court trial on 22 September 2009 that if the plaintiffs won the case, the defendant (Sanlian Group) would suffer severe monetary loss which would lead to the insolvencies of its branch companies and make lots of staffs lose their jobs. Available at http://finance.qq.com/a/20090923/000279.htm (in Chinese) (accessed on 30 August 2016) Through this statement, we could predict that the defendant (Sanlian Group) is a quite significant role in local economic and social development. The court could hardly neglect this fact. Although we cannot get the official written judgment and see the reason why the claim of the minority shareholders was rejected by the court, we suppose that the significant influence of the Sanlian Group is a key reason why the court rejected the shareholders' claim.

[203]Donald C. Clarke and Nicholas C. Howson, 'Pathway to minority shareholder protection: derivative actions in the People's Republic of China', in Dan W. Puchniak, Harald Baum and Michael Ewing-Chow (eds), *The derivative action in Asia: a comparative and functional approach*, (Cambridge University Press, 2012), 243, pp. 284–285.

## *4.4.3 Typical Characteristics of Chinese Judicial System*

### 4.4.3.1 The Lack of Judicial Independence

Influence within the court system cannot be neglected when judicial independence in China is discussed. For instance, the upper courts may give direct instructions to the lower ones in special cases.[204] In 2006, for multiple-plaintiff lawsuits, the Shanghai High People's Court instructed all lower courts in Shanghai not to accept suits with ten or more plaintiffs.[205] This sort of internal instruction within the court system is not rarely found in China. When dealing with complicated or politically sensitive cases, the judge of a lower court can consult the upper court how to deal with the case properly.[206] Lots of scholars as well as legal practitioner have strongly criticized this irrational approach by indicating that the judicial independence will not be completely realized without the abolishment of such internal instructions.[207]

In the last decade, 'building a harmonious society' was adopted by the government as an important ideology.[208] The reflection of this ideology could also be found in Chinese judicial system. During those years, the Supreme People's Court published guidelines to other Chinese courts to emphasize the importance of 'building a harmonious society' by indicating that the achievement of this goal needs the cooperation of the whole judicial system.[209] Therefore, under this

[204]For example, when dealing with complicated cases which have not met before, the lower court may ask for opinions from the upper court which have met similar case before. Donald C. Clarke and Nicholas C. Howson, 'Pathway to minority shareholder protection: derivative actions in the People's Republic of China', in Dan W. Puchniak, Harald Baum and Michael Ewing-Chow (eds), *The derivative action in Asia: a comparative and functional approach*, (Cambridge University Press, 2012), 243, pp. 284–285.

[205]See Nicholas C. Howson, '*Corporate law in the Shanghai People's Courts, 1992–2008: Judicial autonomy in the contemporary authoritarian State*', East Asia Law Review, 5(2010), 303, p. 397.

[206]The consultation with the upper court is not rare and quite typical in China. This internal instruction (个案请示制度) has been strongly criticized by scholars as well as other legal practitioner (lawyers, judges and prosecutors), however, this irrational system which infringes the judicial independence does not vanish until now in Chinese court system.

[207]See Xiutao Han, The judicial independence and contemporary China (司法独立与近代中国 sifa duli yu jindai zhongguo), Qinghua University Press, 2003, p. 207; see Yongmei Sha, 'The abolition of the internal instructions within the court system' (个案请示制度之废除及其功能替代, ge'an qingshi gongneng zhi feichu jiqi gongneng tidai), Hebei law science (河北法学 hebei faxue), 2008(7).

[208]Hu Jintao (the former president of China), 'The importance of building a harmonious society', (in Chinese), (深刻认识构建和谐社会的重大意义), People's Daily (人民日报), (2005-02-19).

[209]Supreme People's Court, *Notice of the Supreme People's Court on Issuing Some Opinions of the Supreme People's Court about Providing Judicial Protection for the Construction of Socialist Harmonious Society*, (in Chinese), (最高人民法院关于为构建社会主义和谐社会提供司法保障的若干意见), (2007-01-15); And see Supreme People's Court, '*Several Opinions of the Supreme People's Court on Further Displaying the Positive Roles of Litigation Mediation in the*

principle, if a complicated and politically sensitive case was brought before the court, the court would hold a very conservative view on it.[210]

#### 4.4.3.2 The Party Control

The Party Control is an even more complicated and tough issue in current Chinese society. It is known that the Communist Party substantially dominates the governments at various levels, and most of the key persons in the central and local governments are members of the Communist Party. And also, for most of SOEs, the chief executives are also members of Communist Party. Since the founding of the People's Republic of China (PRC) in 1949, the Communist Party is the only party that has been ruling the whole state for more than 60 years. In all of the main domains (for instance, the transportation system, the education department, the energy department, the medical service and even the judicial system), the Communist Party holds a direct or indirect control over them. Although the PRC Constitution law has confirmed that judicial independence is a basic principle by indicating that the government cannot interfere in the performance of the judicial system,[211] as analysed before, this principle is hard to be entirely realized in practice.

#### 4.4.3.3 Avoidance of Mass Litigation

It is true that the Chinese courts are reluctant to get involved in mass litigation concerning multiple plaintiffs or the interests of multiple parties, which might be partly caused by the ideology of 'harmonious society'.[212] Several rules and

(Footnote 209 continued)

*Building of a Socialist Harmonious Society', (in Chinese), (最高人民法院关于进一步发挥诉讼调解在构建社会主义和谐社会中积极作用的若干意见), (2007-03-06).*

[210]In recent years (since 2012), the application of this ideology in judicial system has not been mentioned in the official documents. It was recently stated that the use of the ideology of 'building a harmonious society' in judicial system was proved to be a big mistake. See Kaiyu Ouyang, 'insight into the fourth plenary session of the 18th Central Committee of the Communist Party of China 2014, the expected judicial reform' (四中全会前瞻:推进司法改革, 维护公平正义), (in Chinese), available at http://www.chinanews.com/gn/2014/10-16/6686443.shtml (accessed on 30 August 2016).

[211]See article 126 of PRC constitution law: "The people's courts exercise judicial power independently, in accordance with the provisions of the law, and are not subject to interference by any administrative organ, public organization or individual".

[212]For example, if the mass litigation involved a significant local enterprise financially contributing a lot to the local economy (such as a derivative claim brought against directors of such an enterprise), the judgment not in favour of the defendant may affect the business and the reputation of the enterprise, which may further negatively influence the local economy. (for instance, the downside of the share price).

practical guidelines reflecting the state's aversion to such lawsuits reinforce the court's reluctance. Considering the 'internal instruction' between the upper courts and the lower courts as mentioned before, sometimes, the lower ones are directly instructed not to accept multi-plaintiff cases at all. For example, the Supreme People's court has issued instructions to lower courts to strictly limit the acceptance of the securities claims that may have a group of plaintiffs.[213]

In some cases, the courts may require plaintiffs who wish to litigate together to separate their claims into small groups in order to prevent mass litigation. For example, in the first permitted shareholder litigation on false or misleading disclosure, the Harbin intermediate court required the original 381 plaintiffs to break into smaller groups of ten or twenty persons for each.[214]

Restrictions can also be found in lawyers' participation in mass litigation. Lawyers are required to report to the government agencies, and they should also accept the supervision and guidance from them after taking mass litigation.[215] Actually, the Chinese court are not active in hearing corporate and securities cases, making that the enforcement of shareholder protection was confronted with difficulties.[216] Chinese courts are also reluctant to take cases with complicated details

---

[213]See Supreme People's court's notice on temporarily not accepting securities cases involving civil suits for damages, (in Chinese), (最高人民法院关于涉证券民事赔偿案件暂不予受理的通知), issued on September 21st, 2001, available at www.law-lib.com/law/law_view.asp?id=16373 (accessed on 30 August 2016); Also see Supreme People's court's notice on issues relating to the acceptance of civil cases in tort arising out of false representations in securities markets, (in Chinese), (最高人民法院关于受理证券市场因虚假陈述引发的民事纠纷案件有关问题的通知), issued on January 15th, 2002,available at www.law-lib.com/law/law_view.asp?id=16956 (accessed on 30 August 2016); And see Supreme People's court's several provisions on the adjudication of civil suits for damages arising out of false representations in securities markets, (in Chinese), (最高人民法院关于审理证券市场因虚假陈述引发的民事赔偿案件的若干规定), issued on January 9th, 2003, available at www.law-lib.com/law/law_view.asp?id=42438 (accessed on 30 August 2016); One judicial document issued in May 2007 has to be mentioned is that it guided the courts internally to broaden the scope of permissible claims to include market manipulation and inside trading, however, other procedure hurdles established by the aforementioned documents still apply, see Peixin Luo, 'Difficulties over whether to eliminate or keep the precondition procedure', (前置程序去留困境), Finance (财经), 19(2007), 28; Xiaofeng Wu, 'Civil compensation cases for insider trading and market manipulation about to appear', (内幕交易,操纵市场民事赔偿案件呼之欲出), November 18, 2007, available at http://npc.people.com.cn/GB/6543957.html (accessed on 30 August 2016).

[214]See, 'The Daqing lianyi case is pushed forward with difficulties', (in Chinese), (大庆联谊案件难推进), southern weekend (南方周末), (August 4th, 2003), available at http://www.southcn.com/weekend/economic/200308140057.htm (accessed on 30 August 2016); Chao Xi, 'Case Note: Private Enforcement of Securities Law in China: *Daqing Lianyi* Co *v. Zhong Weida and Others* (2004) Heilongjiang Court', Journal of Comparative Law, (2006), Volume 1(2), 492.

[215]In March 2006, the All-China Lawyers Association(a government-controlled body), together with the national Ministry of Justice and its local-government counterpart Judicial Bureau, issued a regulation entitled 'Guidance Opinion on the Undertaking by Lawyers of Mass Cases', which applied to all lawsuits with ten or more plaintiffs.

[216]See Xin Tang, 'Protecting Minority Shareholders in China: A Task for Both Legislation and Enforcement', in Hideki Kanda, Kon-sik Kim, and Curtis Milhaupt (eds.), *Transforming Corporate Governance in East Asia* (Routledge 2008), 141, pp. 152–153.

and powerful defendants for the reason that courts are neither experienced nor politically powerful.[217]

### 4.4.4 The Selection of an Authority Taking Charge of Public Funding

When the Israeli case in public funding was studied, the selection of the authority administrating public funding was a concern. The Israel Securities Authorities (the ISA) is the main authority in charge of public funding. Theoretical concerns are raised that the ISA, as a public regulator, might not be fully shielded from the political and interest group when considering a public funding application.

In the Canadian case, the law foundation of Ontario[218] (LFO) is fully responsible for Class Proceeding Fund. Other than the ISA, the LFO is a non-profit organization created by the 1974 statute.[219] The main aim of it is to improve the access to justice for people in Ontario. In fact, criticism with regards to the Class Proceeding Fund is mainly based on the 10% levy in a successful case which was funded by the Ontario Fund before, but not its possible relationship with political groups. The start-up capital of the Class Proceeding Fund was provided by the LFO, and the members of the Class Proceedings Committee are appointed by the LFO and the Attorney General.[220] But the LFO has firmly claimed that the members of the Class Proceedings Committee are independent from the appointing bodies.[221]

Similar to the Ontario's example, the chairman of the Quebec *Fonds d'aide aux recours collectifs* (the *Fonds*) is appointed by the government after consulting with the Bureau du Québec and the Legal Services Commission.[222] Unlike the Ontario Fund, the *Fonds* is an ongoing financial responsibility of the Quebec government, and the government plays an active role in financially supporting it. From this perspective, compared to the Ontario Fund, the *Fonds* relies more on local government. Being different from China, the concern of 'local protectionism' and 'inside system' does not seem to appear in Quebec.

In China, if public funding were adopted, the most important issue would be which organization would take charge of it. A public authority such as the ISA, or a non-profit organization like the LFO.

---

217 Ibid.

218 The official website of Law Foundation in Ontario is http://www.lawfoundation.on.ca/ (accessed on 30 August 2016).

219 Ibid.

220 The LFO and the Attorney General each appoint one member of the Class Proceedings Committee and jointly appoint the other three, see http://www.lawfoundation.on.ca/class-proceedings-fund/ (accessed on 30 August 2016).

221 http://www.lawfoundation.on.ca/class-proceedings-fund/ (accessed on 30 August 2016).

222 See the official website of the Quebec *Fonds d'aide aux recours collectifs*, http://www.farc.justice.gouv.qc.ca/# (accessed on 30 August 2016).

#### 4.4.4.1 The China Securities Regulatory Commission (CSRC)

Considering the public nature of the CSRC, the same concern appearing in the Israeli case would be raised in China.[223] Such concern might be further enhanced by the fact the ISA does not financially depend on the government,[224] while the CSRC entirely relies on the financial allocation by the central government.

Compared to the ISA, the CSRC established in 1990 has a much shorter history. In the very beginning, the CSRC was founded to regulate the Chinese 'immature' stock market that only had a history of ten years.[225,226] The State Council (Chinese central government 国务院) is the direct supervisor of the CSRC. Therefore, the CSRC is a public institution (事业单位),[227] belonging to the 'inside system'. With

---

223In nature, the CSRC is a public authority being attached to the central government and is led by the Communist Party. http://www.csrc.gov.cn/pub/csrc_en/ (accessed on 30 August 2016).

224The budget of the ISA relies entirely on annual fees payable by entities regulated under the Securities Law and the Joint Investment Trust Law. And this budget is approved by the Minister of Finance and the parliamentary (Knesset) Finance Committee. http://www.isa.gov.il/Download/IsaFile_7411.pdf (accessed on 30 August 2016).

225It should be indicated that the Chinese stock market emerged from a unique background. At the very beginning, the build of the stock market was highly related to the reform of SOES. Like other socialist counterparts, before the 1978 reform and opening-up policy be Mr. DENG Xiaoping, SOEs dominated China's economy, particularly its industrial sector. And almost all of the SOEs at that time were plagued by sloth, inefficiency and waste. After a series of unsuccessful SOE reform, by the end of 1994, more than 50% of approximately 110,000 SOEs in China ran at a loss, and in 1996, the state industry's losses reached a record high of almost 80 billion yuan. Historically, SOEs raised capital primarily through interest-free budgetary grants. Nevertheless, the fall in the Central Government's revenues in the early 1980 s necessitated finding new sources of capital to fund SOEs. In July 1983, the Government started to fund most SOEs' capital expenditures with bank loans. However, since the main banks are also state-owned, many of the loans were more like grants; debt forgiveness and payment deferrals were routinely granted. The persistent loss-making SOEs not only led to high debts to assets ratios for themselves but also accumulated a huge sum of non-performed loans in the banking system. In the end, the Government decided to make use of the stock market as a funding alternative for SOEs. See Chen Ding Chen, 'Legal tradition and private securities litigation in China', *International Company and Commercial Law Review*, (2012), Volume 23(11), 394, p. 398; and see Nicholas R. Lardy, *China's Unfinished Economic Revolution* (Brookings Institution Press, 1998); see Yasheng Huang, *Selling China: Foreign Direct Investment during the Reform Era* (Cambridge University Press, 2005); seeJinglian Wu, *Understanding and Interpreting Chinese Economic Reform*, (Texere 2005).

226In 1992, the *810 Event* happened in Shenzhen gave rise to the birth of the CSRC. On August 6th of 1992, Shenzhen publicly offered 500 million subscriptions of new share, and three days later, all of these were sold out. But the demand of people was more than the supposed amount of subscription, so many people became unsatisfied and created disturbances in the public place on August 10th of 1992. This public event drew attention from the central government. Under such background, the CSRC was established. For more information about the historical background of the establishment of the CSRC, see 'The foundation of the CSRC: how it was established' (in Chinese), (中国证监会的成立:证监会诞生的台前幕后), http://www.china.com.cn/economic/txt/2009-09/29/content_18624019.htm (accessed on 30 August 2016).

227The public institution (事业单位) in China is a unique product generated in the period of planed economy. It financially relies on the budget allocated by the government, and reports to

respect to the personnel in the CSRC, the president of it is appointed by the prime minister, and should report to the appointer.[228] As the most powerful regulatory institution governing Chinese financial and capital markets, the CSRC has a wide range of administrative powers, including, among others, drafting regulations concerning the stock and future market, examining and approving the initial public offering and governing public companies.[229] The CSRC appears to be the most suitable authority to administer public funding for shareholder actions in China in view of its declaration that 'investor protection is the first working priority'.[230] But, unfortunately, this conclusion is not well based for the reason that the CSRC operates within the 'inside system' and the personnel and financial budget of it is substantially controlled by the government. Other Chinese public institutions within the 'inside system' will have a similar problem. In consideration of that, public agencies (for instance, the CSRC) could hardly be the proper authority taking charge of public funding.

#### 4.4.4.2 A Non-profit Organization (NPO)

Perhaps, we could try to figure out the potential for a non-profit organization (NPO, similar to the Law Foundation of Ontario) to administer public funding. In investigating this issue, the first question we need to answer is whether Chinese NPOs are concerned with the 'inside system' like public institutions. To answer this question, we have to examine the nature of NPOs first.

**4.4.4.2.1. The nature of NPOs in China**

It is easy to know from the definition of NPO that it is an organization not aiming at making profits, but at achieving specific goals (for instance, help a certain group of people).[231] In western countries, NPOs function well in the civil society,

---

(Footnote 227 continued)

governments at various levels or their branch department. So it could be regarded that public institution in China also belongs to the 'inside system' (体制内).

[228]The present president of the CSRC is Shiyu Liu, who has held the position since Feb 2016. Since the foundation of the CSRC, there have been eight presidents in total, and six of them once held or is holding the position of member of the central committee (中央委员) or alternate member of the central committee (中央候补委员). Normally, a holding of the position of member or alternate member of the central committee means that the person is appointed as a senior official in Communist Party. Apparently, this person could be regarded as a senior official of the 'inside system' (体制内). From this perspective, the CSRC has a close relationship to the Communist Party and the central government, and undoubtedly, it belongs to the 'inside system'.

[229]See the official website of the CSRC, http://www.csrc.gov.cn/pub/csrc_en/ (accessed on 30 August 2016).

[230]Ibid.

[231]For example, the United Nations Children's Fund (UNICEF) is a non-profit organization to give assistance to children and mothers in developing countries. See its official website http://www.unicef.org/ (accessed on 30 August 2016).

helping to improve people's welfare.[232] The NPOs have been developed into 'the third sector' that is strictly distinguished from the 'first sector' (the governments) and the 'second sector' (the enterprises) in western societies.[233] While in China, NPOs began to develop since the 1980 s, the history of which is comparative shorter than those in western countries. A number of well-known Chinese NPOs, in nature, are government-affiliated rather than independent organizations.[234] For instance, the China Women's Development Foundation (the CWDF),[235] which is a nationwide non-profit social welfare organization, belongs to the government ('inside system'). The first chairman of this foundation was Muhua Chen, who has had hold a series of leading positions within the Chinese governmental system and the Communist Party.[236] Subsequent to Mrs Chen, presidents of the CWDF all have strong political background.[237] Except for CWDF, a number of Chinese public NPOs are actually affiliated to the government. For instance, the Red Cross Society of China (RCSC) is a public NPO affiliated to the state council of China, and its honorary president is Hu Jintao who owns strong political background.[238] Considering the relationship between the public NPOs and the government, scholars have criticized that most of the NPOs can hardly operate independently

---

[232]Some well-known and well-functioned NPOs in the western world include the the United Nations Children's Fund (UNICEF), the Women International Democratic Federation (WIDF), and Hostelling International (HI).

[233]See Helmut K. Anheiner and Wolfgang Seibel, *The third sector: comparative studies of non-profit organizations*, (Walter de Gruyter and Co Publisher 1990), p. 8.

[234]See Taigang Liu, *The legal regulation of non-profit organizations*, (in Chinese), (非营利组织及其法律规制), (China legal publishing house 2009), pp. 20–22.

[235]The Foundation has created a number of public brands since it was established, such as Water Cellar for Mothers (母亲水窖), Health Express for Mothers (母亲健康车) and micro credit programs (母亲小额循环). The Foundation plays a positive role in promoting social welfare for women, including women's development, health, education, training, poverty alleviation and disaster relief. It serves the rights and interests of women and has made positive impact both at home and abroad. See the official website of the CWDF (in Chinese) http://www.cwdf.org.cn/ (accessed on 31 August 2016).

[236]Except for the position of the president of the CWDF, Mrs Chen was the alternate member of the political bureau of the central committee from 1977 to 1987, one of the state councillors of the Chinese state council, and the member of the central committee of the Communist Party. Therefore, Mrs Chen was a senior official of Chinese government and Communist Party as well, and she could be regarded as a politically influential person.

[237]Those following presidents after Mrs Chen were Peiyun Peng, Zhili Chen, Xiulian Gu and Yueyue Shen. All of those four ladies have strong political and governmental background, and they all held senior position inside the Communist Party. For example, the current president (Yueyue Shen) has been the member of the central committee of the communist party of China from 2007 until now; Zhili Chen was one of the state councillors of the Chinese state council from 2003 to 2008; Xiulian Gu was the member of the central committee of the Communist Party of China from 1982 to 2002 and Peiyun Peng was one of the state councillors of the Chinese state council from 1993 to 1998.

[238]See the official website of the Red Cross society of China http://www.redcross.org.cn/hhzh/ (in Chinese). (accessed on 31 August 2016).

without political influence for the reason that they have political background.[239] Therefore, the 'inside system' concern might be likely to appear in the public NPO, making it hardly become a proper organization administering public funding.

Private NPOs called social organizations (社会团体) also exist in China.[240] Although private NPOs are private in nature, they are still subject to state governance to a certain extent. Under Chinese law, social organizations are administered by a 'dual-administration' system. According to the *Regulation on Registration and Administration of Social Organizations* (社会团体登记管理条例), social institutions have to be registered with civil affairs department (民政部门) prior to their establishment.[241] In addition to that, social organizations also need approvals from other 'related department' (有关部门).[242] For example, if a group of people intends to set up a social organization to conduct scientific research on environmental issues, they need to apply for approval from the civil affair department and other 'related department'. In this case, other 'related department' may include the education department (教育部), the science and technology department (科技部) and the environment protection department (环境保护部). Obviously, a long list of departments will create a big disincentive for potential applicants who intend to establish a social organization.[243]

Actually, in recent years, the dual-registration system has been criticized, and it is regarded as a significant obstacle impeding the development of social

---

239See Qiusha Ma, *Non-governmental organizations in contemporary China: paving the way to civil society*? (Routledge 2009); And see Xijin Jia, 'Management systems of the foreign non-profit organizations and their enlightenment for China', (in Chinese) (国外非营利组织管理体制及其对中国的启示), *Journal of Social Sciences* (社会科学), 2004 Volume 4; see Lin Zhen, 'Development of NPO and the policy of Chinese government', (in Chinese), (非营利组织的发展与我国的对策), *Journal of China National School of Administration* (国家行政学院学报), 2002 Volume 1.

240There are less private NPOs than public NPOs in China. A well-known private NPO is Shenzhen One Foundation Charity Fund (深圳壹基金公益基金会), which was founded by Jet Li and was registered on December 3, 2010, as the first private charity in China. See its official website http://www.onefoundation.cn/ (in Chinese). (accessed on 31 August 2016).

241Article 6 of the Regulation on Registration and Administration of Social Organizations provides that 'the Ministry of Civil Affairs (民政部) and local Civil Affairs Departments (民政局) at county level and above are the basic people's government agencies for registration and management of social organizations'.

242The concept and scope of 'related departments' (有关部门) is quite vague and complicated in China. This term appears frequently in the administration regulations. When someone needs to get administrative approval, sometimes the administrative regulation just uses the terms of 'related departments' instead of a specific department that the applicant could resort to. This frequently-used expression has caused lots of practical problems for applicants. And the reason why administrative regulations applies such a vague expression is because administrative department, sometimes, wants to 'pass the buck' (踢皮球 ti piqiu). See Songtao Xu, 'China's Public Administration Reform: New Approaches', http://www.iam.or.jp/asia-pacific_panel/pdfdownloads/athens01-paper4.pdf (accessed on 31 August 2016).

243Perhaps, in this regard, bureaucracy might be a concern for potential applicants if they need to get approval from several government agencies.

organizations.[244] The reason why this 'dual-administration' system is adopted to regulate social organizations in China is thought to be that the government may not be willing to remove all thresholds for the establishment of private NPOs, and it still tries to hold control over these social organizations to a certain degree.[245] Given that, it might be possible to conclude that it may still be hard to shield private NPOs from government's influence, although the concern about the 'inside system' would not be as serious as that in public authorities and public NPOs.

**4.4.4.2.2. The lack of trust in NPOs**

In fact, people may not suppose that NPOs are reliable. A corruption scandal of the Red Cross Society of China (RCSC) happened in 2011 aggravates the loss of public trust in NPOs.[246] Data collected from the internet shows that in 2008 (before the exposure of the serious 2011 scandal), the donation received by the RCSC to financially help the reconstruction after the Wenchun (汶川) earthquake amounted to 43 billion RMB, while the donation after the 2013 Ya'an (雅安) earthquake received by the RCSC only added up to 43 million.[247] In the *weibo* (微博 mini-blog), which is the most popular on-line community with more than 1 billion registered members, people express their dissatisfactions with the RCSC by claiming that they will donate through other ways rather than the RCSC. It is quite obvious that the RCSC has lost most of public trust because of corruption scandal. In fact, criticism regarding the corruption and bureaucracy in public NPOs is not rarely found.[248]

---

[244]See Jun Xu and David Smith, 'Analysis of the development of Chinese social organizations' (in Chinese) (中国非营利组织生存路径探析), *Journal of Chinese academy of governance* (国家行政学院学报), (2012) Volume 5; See Heng Han, 'Reflections of registration of non-profit organization' (in Chinese), (关于非营利组织注册登记的思考), *Research of Administration of NGOs* (社团管理研究), (2008) Volume 6, http://www.sociologyol.org/yanjiubankuai/fenleisuoyin/fenzhishehuixue/zuzhishehuixue/2008-10-09/6261.html (accessed on 31 August 2016).

[245]Heng Han, 'Reflections of registration of non-profit organization' (in Chinese), (关于非营利组织注册登记的思考), *Research of Administration of NGOs* (社团管理研究), (2008) Volume 6, http://www.sociologyol.org/yanjiubankuai/fenleisuoyin/fenzhishehuixue/zuzhishehuixue/2008-10-09/6261.html (accessed on 31 August 2016).

[246]The Red Cross society of China (RCSC) is a public NPO affiliated to the state council of China, and it is the biggest national charity which has been criticized for years due to the non-transparency of its account, the corruption and bureaucracy. In 2011, a serious corruption scandal was exposed to the public through the internet. It is spread out on the internet that a relative of a senior official of the RCSC bought lots of luxuries, which were not financially affordable through their salaries. So the public lost the remaining trust to the RCSC. After that, the RCSC scandal often became the top 10 topic in Chinese internet community, and in Chinese weibo (微博 mini-blog) the corruption of the RCSC has been discussed intensely.

[247]It should be mentioned that most of the 43 million donations after Ya'an earthquake did not come from the public donation. The departments belonging to the 'inside system' assigned the donation task to their personnel. But for the general public, many people who donated in 2008 did not donate for Ya'an through the RCSC because they lost the trust to it. And those people also complaint that they were cheated by the RCSC in 2008.

[248]See Xiaochun Chen, Juhua He and Xiaoyan Pu, 'Building the public trust on Chinese non-profit organizations', (in Chinese), (浅析我国非营利组织的公信力建设), *Journal of Wuyi University* (五邑大学学报) (2007) Volume 8; Hongqing Jiang, 'The information disclosure of the non-profit

As for private NPOs, public trust is also lacking mainly for the reason that valid supervisory mechanism to supervise the operation and the accounts of them is lacking. The One Foundation, which is the biggest private charity in China, was suspected to spend the donation funds on themselves.[249] And also, the One Foundation was challenged by the general public whether it has relationship with the RCSC or other publicly-run charities.[250]

**4.4.4.2.3. Practical difficulties in registering a private NPO to administer public funding**

Provides funding for the commencement of shareholder litigation by a private NPO means, in some cases, it helps shareholder plaintiffs to 'go against' the 'inside system'. Registering such a private NPO with the civil affairs department and other 'related departments' would have practical difficulties. Both the departments administrating private NGOs and the defendants in a politically sensitive shareholder lawsuit are members of the 'inside system', while the private NPO (as a financial sponsor) and the shareholder applicants stand in the opposite side to 'go against' them. Such a practical dilemma may lead to a fact that there is no feasibility of setting up or adopting a private NPO to administer public funding.

In summary, public authorities, public NPOs and private NPOs are not suitable organizations to take charge of public funding in China.

## 4.4.5 Conclusion

Considering the typical characteristics in Chinese judicial system (lack of independence, the 'inside system' theory, the 'local protectionism' and the avoidance of the mass litigation), the features of public institutions and public NPOs (e.g., the CSRC), and practical dilemma regarding private NPOs, it should be quite difficult and even unfeasible for public funding for shareholder litigation to be applied in China. We have to stress that for shareholder litigation not involving significant enterprises and companies with political background, public funding may be applied in spite of the features of Chinese judicial system and the influence of the 'inside system'. Shareholders in big companies, public companies and SOEs are more vulnerable and need to redress losses through litigation mechanism than shareholders in small LLCs. But shareholders in small LLCs may prefer to resolve disputes through personal negotiation rather than to launch a derivative lawsuit.

(Footnote 248 continued)

organization in China', (in Chinese), (非营利组织透明信息的机理和途径分析), *Shandong social science* (山东社会科学), (2012) Volume 2; Xiaochun Chen and Juan Zhang, 'Exploring the social responsibility of the non-profit organizations', (in Chinese), (非营利组织的社会公共责任探析), *Chinese public administration* (中国行政管理), (2007) Volume 12.

[249] 'How the 20 million is used by the One Foundation?' (壹基金:2000万建研究院与红会无关), http://news.ifeng.com/mainland/detail_2013_05/27/25731430_0.shtml (accessed on 31 August 2016).

[250] Ibid.

## 4.5 Summary

This Chapter conducted two case studies: the Israeli public funding to finance derivative actions, and the Canadian approach (the Ontario Fund and the Quebec *Fonds*) to publicly fund class actions. After the empirical study, the potential for transplanting the public funding approach to financially assist shareholder actions in China is investigated mainly through the examination on the China's judicial system and political background. A conclusion that public funding is not suitable for current China is made finally.

Experience drawn from the Israeli and Canadian cases demonstrates that to implement the public funding, a significant problem needs to be resolved is how to finance public funding, by the government or by applicants. The Israeli public funding is fully state financed, while the law Foundation of Ontario is a non-profit organization, which is financially independent from the government. The Ontario fund largely relies on the 10% of recoveries levied from the applicants who finally win the litigation.[251] In fact, the Ontario Class Proceeding Fund does not prove to be a success mostly because the 10% levying rate is too excessive. But on the other hand, if a lower levying rate were set, the financial source of the Class Proceeding Fund would not be sufficient to maintain the functioning of the Fund. The Quebec *Fonds* proves to be much more successful than the Ontario Fund mostly for the reason that it is mainly financed by the government. But no 'public concern' is found in Quebec *Fonds*.

For the Chinese case, the concern of 'inside system' is the most serious one that mainly contributing to the infeasibility of public funding. The relationship between the government and potential institutions administrating public funding is much more complicated than that in many other countries in consideration of the unique political and judicial system. If public funding is introduced into China, the first problem should be solved is to choose a proper organization which can be entirely independent from the government and the Communist Party. Unfortunately, it does not seem to be realistic, as least in current China.

Whether public funding can be applied and well functioned is not an isolated issue. It associates with the judicial system, the political system, and the social background. The public funding is indeed public in nature (we can prove it from the name). When its potential for China is considered, it is extremely necessary to take into account Chinese features in several respects. So far, based on the findings in this Chapter, the potential for public funding in China is limited.

*Last but not least*

Although a negative conclusion regarding the potential for public funding in China was made, from a more cautious perspective, its potential might be possible under certain reforms on Chinese political and judicial system, which might be conducted

[251]The LFO only provides an initial fund of $500,000 to support the Class Proceeding Fund. See http://www.lawfoundation.on.ca/class-proceedings-fund/ (accessed on 31 August 2016).

in the future or is already undergoing now. It is noted that since the second half of 2013, the central government has implemented a series of anti-corruption activities, and reforms on public authorities (including institutions governed by the Communist Party) have also been carried out.[252] Particularly, the fourth plenary session of the 18th Central Committee of the Communist Party of China (四中全会) held in late October 2014 clearly indicated that 'administrative interference in the judicial processes' (行政干预司法) should be forbidden, which might be regarded as a positive signal for the realization of 'judicial independence' in the future. Perhaps, this round of reform may mitigate the concerns discussed in this Chapter (for instance, 'local protectionism').

[252]For example, a special commission of discipline inspection was established and directly led by the central government to deal with corruption in public authorities. See Huaichao Wang, What is it behind the establishment of discipline inspection commission? (单列纪检小组的背后, 'danlie jijian xiaozu de beihou'), in Chinese, available at http://www.dldj.gov.cn/trans.aspx?id=72133 (accessed on 31 August 2016); And in the 'Two Conferences' (National People's Congress和 Chinese People's Political Consultative Conference), lots of proposals about anti-corruptions in public authorities have been proposed. See http://news.ifeng.com/mainland/special/2013lianghui/detail_2013_03/16/23162311_0.shtml (in Chinese) (accessed on 31 August 2016).

# Chapter 5
# Third Party Litigation Funding (TPLF) of Shareholder Litigation

## 5.1 An Overview of TPLF

The most recent development in litigation funding industry is third party litigation funding (TPLF),[1] where an external investor funds the client to commence a civil lawsuit. In recent years, as a growing industry, the TPLF has drawn lots of attention from policymakers, legal practitioners, scholars and potential plaintiffs. Actually, most of opinions hold that TPLF is helpful to solve funding problems with civil litigation, but it should be applied cautiously.[2] Up till now, TPLF has notably spread in Australia and in some European countries (for instance, Austria, Germany, Ireland and the UK).[3] Also in the US, TPLF is a fast-growing industry and is playing an increasingly visible role in financing civil litigation.[4]

The Rand Institute for Civil Justice identifies TPLF as one of the 'biggest and most influential trends in civil justice'.[5] Although TPLF has received lots of positive comments that it facilitates the 'access to justice' for impecunious individuals, there are also counter-arguments holding that potential risk and jurisprudential debates brought by the use of TPLF would negatively affect the public policy.

[1]Strictly speaking, public funding and lawyer's funding are also within the scope of third party funding, because the funding of them also comes externally. But in this chapter, the third party litigation funding excludes the public funding and funding by lawyers, only referring to funding coming from an outside private investor who makes money from investing in lawsuits.
[2]See Jasminka Kalajdzic, Peter Cashman and Alana Longmoore, 'Justice for profit, a comparative analysis of Australian, Canadian and US third party litigation funding', *American Journal of Comparative Law*, (2013), Volume 61, 93, p. 94.
[3]See Christopher Hodges, Stefan Vogenauer and Magdalena Tulibacka, *The Cost and funding of Civil Litigation*, (Hart Publishing, 2010), p. 27.
[4]See US Chamber Institute for Legal Reform, 'Selling Lawsuits, Buying Trouble: Third Party Litigation Funding in the United States', (October 2009), p. 1. http://legaltimes.typepad.com/files/thirdpartylitigationfinancing.pdf (accessed on 31 August 2016).
[5]RAND Corporation, 'Third Party Litigation Funding and Claim Transfer Event Program Details', (2009), available at http://www.rand.org/pubs/conf_proceedings/CF272.html (accessed on 31 August 2016).



W. Chen, *A Comparative Study of Funding Shareholder Litigation*,
DOI 10.1007/978-981-10-3623-1_5

Supporters, citing the need to increase access to the courts and level the playing field between plaintiffs and defendants with sufficient resources, hold the view that TPLF is necessary and should be encouraged to develop further, while opponents suppose that TPLF can 'pose thorny ethical issues'.[6] It is true that TPLF is quite innovative in funding civil litigation, and it indeed provides individual plaintiffs with a new approach to eliminate financial risk in filing civil litigation. However, to conduct a comprehensive evaluation of TPLF, we should examine its shortcomings and potential risk as well. (For instance, moral hazard of the funder, and the complicated funder-lawyer-litigant relationship) As pointed out before, TPLF, as an innovation in funding civil litigation, should proceed with caution.[7]

In this Chapter, first, we will try to anatomize how TPLF functions. Second, experience from selected countries about the use of TPLF will be studies and compared. And finally, the potential for TPLF in China will be investigated and a conclusion will be drawn in this regard.

Prior to the anatomy of TPLF, it should be indicated that, theoretically, all sorts of civil litigation could be funded by TPLF. Actually, it is widely used to finance class actions and other mass litigation in some countries (for instance, in Australia and in the US). The main purpose of this chapter is to analyse whether TPLF could be used to finance shareholder litigation and potential problems with it. As a sub-catalogue of civil litigation, shareholder lawsuits have distinctive features not appearing in general civil litigation (For instance, a higher monetary value involved in shareholder litigation). In consideration of that, when TPLF is discussed in the context of shareholder litigation, problems caused by its distinctive features should be taken into account.

### *5.1.1 The Traditional Avoidance of Champerty and Maintenance*

When discussing the nature and general framework of TPLF, the traditional prohibition of champerty and maintenance should be analysed first.[8] Maintenance is an old common law doctrine which refers to the 'assistance in prosecuting or defending a lawsuit given to a litigant by someone who has no *bona fide* interest in

---

[6]New York City Bar, 'Formal Opinion 2011–2: Third Party Litigation Financing', (2011), http://www.nycbar.org/index.php/ethics/ethics-opinions-local/2011-opinions/1159-formal-opinion-2011-02 (accessed on 31 August 2016).

[7]See Jasminka Kalajdzic, Peter Cashman and Alana Longmoore, 'Justice for profit, a comparative analysis of Australian, Canadian and US third party litigation funding', *American Journal of Comparative Law*, (2013), Volume 61, 93, p. 94.

[8]See Percy H. Winfield, 'History of Maintenance and Champerty', *Law Quarterly Review*, (1919), Volume 35, 50; Max Radin, 'Maintenance by Champerty', *California Law Review*, (1935), Volume 24(1), 48–78.

the case [or] meddling in someone else's litigation.'[9] Champerty is a species of maintenance, which means 'an agreement between a stranger to a lawsuit and a litigant by which the stranger pursues the litigant's claim as consideration for receiving part of any judgment proceeds'.[10] TPLF is an agreement where a third party funder financially assists the impecunious plaintiff to pursue a civil lawsuit, which appears to violate the traditional avoidance of champerty and maintenance. But it should be stated that this traditional prohibition was rooted in the particular social and economic background in the medieval England to preclude frivolous suits. Considering the fundamental changes in today's social and legal situation, the traditional doctrine seems to lose its importance.[11] And also, legal rules should adapt themselves to the social and economic changes by being revised in light of the new social background.[12] In modern society, along with the increasing frequency of commercial activities, disputes between transacting parties arise more often than before, thus resulting in a higher demand for judicial resolution. Considering the fact that resorting to judicial system is quite expensive, the financial risk in a lawsuit may become a big concern to many legal practitioners and litigants. Therefore, some common law jurisdictions began to call for the liberalization of traditional prohibition of champerty and maintenance by exploring exceptions to it.[13]

To investigate how the traditional common law doctrine is relaxed and how TPLF develops to become an exception to it, the Australian experience needs to be studied first. In fact, TPLF started to develop in Australia at the beginning of the

[9]Black's Law Dictionary 224 (8th ed. 2004).

[10]Black's Law Dictionary 246 (8th ed. 2004).

[11]The doctrine developed in the medieval England as the merchant class was growing in importance and the economic power of the feudal nobles was beginning to decline. In particular, the doctrine developed as a judicial and statutory reaction to a practice that was taking place among feudal lords, whereby they would underwrite the costs of suits carried out by others for the recovery of land in exchange for a share of the result. Through this means, the lords could become joint owners of estates at investment prices well below the market value of the land, increasing the size of their retinues and thus aggrandizing their political power. At present, the avoidance of frivolous suits could be achieved by statutory rules but not only through the prohibition of champerty and maintenance.

[12]See Marco de Morpurgo, 'A comparative legal and economic approach to third-party litigation funding', *Cardozo Journal of International and Comparative Law Review*, (2011), Volume 19, 343, p. 388.

[13]For example, in the UK, the Crime Law Act 1967 abolished the liability of crimes and torts generated by the champerty and maintenance; In Australia, the champerty and maintenance have mostly been abolished. In New South Wales, champerty and maintenance were abolished by the Maintenance, Champerty and Barratry Abolition Act 1993, and in Victoria, champerty and maintenance was abolished as a tort by Section 32 of the Wrongs Act 1958. [9] and as a crime by Section 332A of the Crimes Act 1958; In the US, the rise of contingency agreements concluded between lawyers and litigants has, virtually, meant the trend of abolition of champerty and maintenance. In New Zealand, the crime for champerty and maintenance has been abolished, but the torts are still preserved.

1990s.[14] At that time, it was regarded as a statutory exception to the common law prohibition in the exceptional context of insolvency cases.[15] Subsequently, TPLF extended to other areas, but most of them were still within the scope of commercial litigation.[16] The Australian court's tolerant attitude to litigation funding also facilitated the rapid growth of TPLF.[17] In Australia, where TPLF was originated, most of the funded cases are claims with high monetary value. For instance, a commercial case with the monetary value over $500,000 or, for some companies, over $2 million.[18] Claims with comparatively low financial value (for instance, personal injury cases) are, in most of cases, not interest third party funders.[19] The reason for the funder's preference for high-valued commercial cases is generally associated with the fact that such cases, if they are finally won, would bring a big amount of monetary rewards in accordance to 'the funder's share' provided in the TPLF agreement.

It is our opinion of view that in today's world the old doctrine of the prohibition of champerty and maintenance established in a context totally different from today's social and economic background needs to be reformed or abandoned because commercial litigation involving high costs has become common and for many parties external funding would be welcome. In general, in the common law world, there is a trend that the traditional strict prohibition of champerty and maintenance is evolving into a doctrine with flexibility and relaxed interpretation due to the economic development and the changing social context.[20]

---

[14]See Marco de Morpurgo, 'A comparative legal and economic approach to third-party litigation funding', *Cardozo Journal of International and Comparative Law Review*, (2011), Volume 19, 343, p. 390.

[15]See Litigation Funding in Australia, Discussion Paper, Standing Committee of Attorneys General (May 2006), http://www.imf.com.au/docs/default-source/site-documents/discussionpaper standingcommitteeofattorneysgeneral_may2006 (accessed on 30 August 2016); And see Vicki Waye, *Trading in Legal Claims: Law, Policy & Future Directions in Australia, UK & US* (Presidian Legal Publications, 2008), p. 55. For the example for the insolvency case funded by TPLF, refer to Anstella Nominees Pty Ltd v. St George Motor Finance Ltd. [2003].

[16]See Vicki Waye, *Trading in Legal Claims: Law, Policy & Future Directions in Australia, UK & US*, (Presidian Legal Publications, 2008), p. 133.

[17]See Marco de Morpurgo, 'A comparative legal and economic approach to third-party litigation funding', *Cardozo Journal of International and Comparative Law Review*, (2011), Volume 19, 343, p. 390.

[18]See 3.1.2.6.

[19]Ibid.

[20]See Marco de Morpurgo, 'A comparative legal and economic approach to third-party litigation funding', *Cardozo Journal of International and Comparative Law Review*, (2011), Volume 19, 343, p. 392.

### 5.1.2 The Economic Analysis of TPLF

The economic nature of the third party litigation funding could be summarized as follows. The litigant is willing to externalize the financial risk brought by the lawsuit, while the third party funder prefers a case which may bring high monetary returns. If the funded case is won, the funder will share the profits brought from the court order with the litigants. On the other hand, the funder will gain nothing and the financial support provided before will not be refunded in the event that the funded case is lost.

In fact, the professional litigation funder invests money in lawsuits and externalizes risk through a series of investment schemes. For impecunious litigants, the only way to eliminate the financial risk in a lawsuit is to resort to a funder. In a TPLF agreement, the funded litigation can be considered as a commodity. The investor (the funder) purchases the commodity to expect potential proceeds (benefits brought by the judgment or the settlement in favour of the funded litigant). Under this circumstance, a lawsuit, even it has not yet been materialized, is a commodity in the litigation funding market. The sale of an immature claim is equivalent to the sale of legal right.[21] Unlike other commodities, the sale of the claim is unique because it is concerned with public force (the courts) in the transaction of legal right. As a public product, the trial on a case is provided by the judicial system to solve disputes between litigation parties and regulate social orders. Even though most of the countries charge litigants an amount of fees for the use of the courts,[22] the cost of the maintenance and operation of the court system (for instance, the cost of hiring professional personnel, building and maintaining the constructions and money spend on energy) cannot be fully covered by court charges from litigation parties. Taxation levied from the general public also contributes to the maintenance of the court system. If a lawsuit is legally allowed to be transacted as a commodity, it may impose burden on the state tax revenue since more litigation may be brought before the courts with the assistance provided by TPLF.

In light of the abovementioned features of TPLF, it is thus necessary to regulate it in order to prevent excessive use of the court system. It is acknowledged that the regulation of market behaviour can be implemented by the market self-discipline and through external 'intervention' (for instance, statutory rules). The question then is whether the self-regulation of litigation funding market functions well. To answer this question, the cost-and-benefit analysis by the funder should be analysed first.

---

[21]See Keith N. Hylton, 'The Economics of Third-Party Financed Litigation', *The Journal of Law, Economics and Policy*, (2011), Volume 8, 701, p. 702.

[22]Most of the countries in the world applies court charges. France and Sweden are two typical exceptions. In Sweden, the state spends some SEK 4.3 billion on courts annually, and parties pay some SEK 47 million (1% of the total) on applications. Except for France and Sweden imposing no charge in most cases, 28 states in Latin America also adopt no-charge rule. For more, see Christopher Hodges, The costs and funding of civil litigation, p. 13.

In Shavell's opinion,

> Litigation is socially desirable when the deterrence benefit from litigation exceeds the expected cost of litigation. A lawsuit is privately desirable from the plaintiff's perspective when the expected award exceeds the expected cost of litigation to the plaintiff. Thus, the private incentive to litigate diverges from the social incentive.[23]

Shavell's viewpoint demonstrates that the position of a private individual and that of the society as a whole are, in some cases, divergent. A similar divergence also appears in TPLF caused by the different interests of the funder, the funded-litigant and the whole society.

The funder, with the purpose of maximizing profits, tends to financially assist a suit where the expected benefits exceed the costs. Considering that, the potential proceeds (P) brought by a successful funded case will be cautiously evaluated by the funder.[24] From the economic perspective, the model of the funder's evaluation is $(F) = (S1) * (S2) * (R) * (P) - (I)$, where (F) refers to the expected rewards of the funder, (S1) represents the expected success rate of the case, (S2) is the proportion of the reasoning of the plaintiff upheld by the court, (R) stands for the contractually determined sharing rate between the funder and the funded party, (P) denotes the proceeds brought by a favourable outcome of the case where the reasoning of the plaintiff has been 100% upheld by the court and (I) means the funding costs the funder paid before. If the $(F) > 0$ (the benefits exceed the costs), the funder will invest. Otherwise, the case will not interest the funder.

Give an example to clarify the economic model. For instance, a plaintiff files a lawsuit before a court to request an amount of damages of 1 million Euro (P). The funder supposes that the expected success rate of this case is 50% (S1). In many cases, the plaintiff's reasoning (claiming for damages of 1 million Euro in this case) cannot be 100% upheld by the court. Sometimes, the court just partially upholds the plaintiff's reasoning, for example, 70% (S2) in this case. To fund the case, the funder must pay litigation costs amounted at 10,000 Euro (lawyers' fees, court charges, and other relevant expenditures). The TPLF contract provides if the case creates any monetary rewards for the plaintiffs, the funder will get 20% (R) of the damages. In this case, under the economic model, the expected rewards for the funder $(F) = (S1) * (S2) * (R) * (P) - (I) = 50\% * 70\% * 20\% * 1$ million$^{-10}$ thousand = 60 thousand > 0. Therefore, it is a good deal for the funder.

However, it should be pointed out that not all of the determinants in the cost-and-benefit analysis could be precisely predicted by the funder. For example, the most unpredictable elements are the expected success rate of the case (S1) and the proportion of the reasoning of the plaintiff upheld by the court (S2). It is not realistic and even impossible for the funder to figure out accurate (S1) and (S2)

---

[23]See Steven Shavell, 'The Social Versus the Private Incentive to Bring Suit in a Costly Legal System', *Journal of Legal Studies*, (1982) Volume 11, 333, pp. 333–339.

[24]See Marco de Morpurgo, 'A comparative legal and economic approach to third-party litigation funding', *Cardozo Journal of International and Comparative Law Review*, (2011), Volume 19, 343, p. 370.

*ex ante*. Rather, it may be only possible, from the perspective of the funder, to narrow the rate in a range (for instance, 30 to 50%). Generally, the funder evaluates the merits of the case and predicts the scope of (S1) and (S2) to preclude valueless investment. It could be possible for an adventurous funder to finance a case with an extremely high (P) but comparatively low (S1) and (S2) to gamble on the big sum of money brought by a favourable judgment or settlement for the reason that the funder could externalize and eliminate risk through a portfolio of cases varied in success rate.[25] But it should be indicated that, for most of the monetary cases, the litigation costs (I) would rise in proportionate with the monetary value at stake. (P) is generally in proportionate with the financial value at stake in a monetary case. Considering that, the concern of 'adventurous funders' gamble' may not be manifested.

Up till now, there is no strong evidence suggesting that the funder's 'gamble' has led to a bad outcome (mainly refers to the rise in the filing of unmeritorious or frivolous claims). It, however, demonstrates that TPLF increases the scale and complexity of litigation, while frivolous claims and questionable litigation are not encouraged by TPLF.[26] Many countries where TPLF is applied have taken measures to regulate ethical issues of lawyers' and funders' through formulating Codes of Conducts.[27] However, these documents do not mention how to prevent the funder's 'gamble' mainly for the reason that TPLF is an innovative funding method which was originated just a few years ago (for earliest advent of it is in 2006 in Australia), the concern about the funder's 'gamble', thus, has not really been manifested. In this regard, this book holds an opinion that from long-term perspective the prohibition of financing frivolous and unmeritorious claims could be incorporated in the Code of Conduct for funders, although the funder's 'gamble' has not threatened the sound development of TPLF.[28]

---

[25]The funder may invest in some cases with high potential for success to lower the risk brought by other highly risky investment. Through this way, the funder may keep a balance with respect to cost and benefit.

[26]This concern has been stated in many places. For example, US Chamber Institute for Legal Reform, 'Third Party Litigation Financing in Australia: Class Actions, Conflicts and Controversy', (October 2013); Jason Lyon, 'Revolution in Progress: Third-Party Funding of American Litigation', *UCLA Law Review*, (2011), Volume 58, 571, pp. 593–594; Steve Mark (the legal services commissioner, New South Wales), 'Litigation Funding in Australia in Response to Standing Committee of Attorneys-General, Discussion Paper', (September 2006), p. 26, available at http://www.olsc.nsw.gov.au/agdbasev7wr/olsc/documents/pdf/regulation_of_third_party_litigation_funding_march2012_part1.pdf (accessed on 30 August 2016).

[27]For instance, Code of Conduct for litigation funders in England and Wales, (2014), http://associationoflitigationfunders.com/wp-content/uploads/2014/02/Code-of-conduct-Jan-2014-Final-PDFv2-2.pdf (accessed on 31 August 2016); Ohio Revised Code S 1349.55, available at http://codes.ohio.gov/orc/1349.55 (accessed on 31 August 2016).

[28]Interestingly, it is found Juridica (a significant litigation funding company in the UK) declares in its official webpage that 'Juridica does not invest in speculative claims or claims that have not demonstrated economic value and clear merits', see http://www.juridicainvestments.com/about-juridica.aspx (accessed on 30 August 2016); But similar declaration is not found in other funder's place.

### 5.1.3 Ethical Issues in TPLF

Ethical concerns are raised when TPLF is used. For instance, TPLF creates confusion about which party controls the litigation virtually. The funder who provides monetary support or the nominal plaintiff? The participation of a third party funder challenges the traditional law-and-client relationship and raises a question: the lawyer owes fiduciary duty to whom? The funder who financially support the claim or the funded litigant?

#### 5.1.3.1 The Relationship Between the Funder and the Funded Litigant

The relationship between the funder and the funded litigant (the client) has received a number of concerns. For instance, the unscrupulous funder may take advantage of the vulnerable litigants by imposing unfair terms in the funding agreement, or even purposely failing to fully disclose all relevant aspects of the funding agreement to the funded litigant.[29] This concern will be further aggravated in the event that the litigant is impecunious and really needs financial support to pursue a lawsuit.[30]

**5.1.3.1.1. Early Settlements**

The funder's moral hazard could appear as a form of the early settlement. Under some circumstances, the funded litigant tends to await the court's judgment instead of compromising to reach an early settlement with the opposing party. However, the funder prefers an early settlement in order to improve business cash flow.[31] In consideration of that, the conflict of interests between the litigation funder and the funded litigant arises, and the funded litigant's legitimate interest, in this case, is highly likely to be subordinated to that of the funder, which creates chaos in the traditional plaintiff-and-defendant relationship in a lawsuit.[32] Moreover, in some cases, settlements are provided in kind rather than in cash, which may further enhance the concern about the subordination of funded litigant's interests.[33] In this case, the defendant may offer to settle the claim with an offer of products or assets, which are valuable to the claimholder but are of no value to the funder.[34] In general,

[29]The Standing Committee of Attorneys-General in Australia, 'Litigation Funding in Australia: Discussion Paper', (May 2006), p. 8 http://www.imf.com.au/docs/default-source/site-documents/discussionpaperstandingcommitteeofattorneysgeneral_may2006 (accessed on 30 August 2016).

[30]See Litigation Funding in Australia, Discussion Paper, Standing Committee of Attorneys General (May 2006), p. 8. And see Vicki Waye, 'Conflicts of Interests Between Claimholders, Lawyers and Litigation Entrepreneurs', *Bond Law Review*, (2008), Volume 19(1), 225, p. 239.

[31]See Vicki Waye, 'Conflicts of Interests Between Claimholders, Lawyers and Litigation Entrepreneurs', *Bond Law Review*, (2008), Volume 19(1), 225, p. 236.

[32]See Vicki Waye, 'Conflicts of Interests Between Claimholders, Lawyers and Litigation Entrepreneurs', *Bond Law Review*, (2008), Volume 19(1), 225, p. 237.

[33]See Vicki Waye, 'Conflicts of Interests Between Claimholders, Lawyers and Litigation Entrepreneurs', *Bond Law Review*, (2008), Volume 19(1), 225, p. 238.

[34]Ibid.

the litigation funder, who is willing to recoup investment and materialize the profits, prefers to accept a settlement in cash or in the form that could be converted to cash promptly.[35] This concern would be further aggravated by the fact that the lawyer in a lawsuit may side with the funder to reach an early settlement as the lawyer is indirectly paid by the funder who provides funds for the litigant. Under this circumstance, funded litigants are isolated and vulnerable.

But a fact cannot be neglected that the funder, the lawyer and the litigant all expect to get proceeds from an action. The only conflict is that the funder and the lawyer may desire for a quick cash flow, while the litigant, sometimes, may expect for other sorts of proceeds.[36] But what is ascertained is that all of the three parties long for a favourable outcome of the case regardless of the form of the compensation (monetary compensation or non-monetary remedies). Although the funder and the lawyer prefer quick monetary proceeds, while the litigant does not hope for an early settlement, it does not cause fundamental difference in terms of essential benefits since the early settlement bringing quick monetary remedies is also beneficial to the funded litigant. On the other hand, from the perspective of judicial efficiency, the aim of a court proceeding is to realize justice that could also be achieved by an early settlement. In other words, an early settlement which is also beneficial to the litigant, but even more welcome by the funder and the lawyer cannot simply be regarded as an infringement of the litigant's interests. In fact, whether a settlement offer is more beneficial to the litigant or to the funder and the lawyer is very difficult to judge. Although a court's approval is usually required before a settlement comes into effect, it is still difficult for the court to give verdict on this issue.[37] Whether the concern about 'cheap settlement' caused by litigation funders is overstated needs to be considered. A proponent to third party litigation financing indicates that litigation financing encourages 'just' settlements, because the funded litigant, with the provision of funds by the funder, can increase his bargaining power with the defendant when negotiating the settlement agreement.[38] The funder's moral hazard in a settlement could be regulated through the rule of conduct for funders or through the funding agreement by indicating that the funder's interests in a funded case should be subordinated to the funded litigant's, and the funded litigant but not the funder has the right to accept or refuse a settlement agreement.[39]

---

[35]Ibid.

[36]For example, the litigant may expect the dispute in the lawsuit could be fundamentally resolved, but not only compensated with money.

[37]For instance, for a settlement in a derivative lawsuit, the court's approval is required. 23.1 of Federal Rule of Civil Procedure, http://www.federalrulesofcivilprocedure.com/rules/rule-23-1-derivative-actions/ (accessed on 30 August 2016). Chinese law also has similar requirements on the settlement offer. (Article 97 of CPR Civil Procedure Law).

[38]Marial Rodak, 'It's About Time: A Systems Thinking Analysis of the Litigation Finance Industry and Its Effect on Settlement', *University of Pennsylvania Law Review*, (2006), Volume 155, 503, p. 523.

[39]Even though the funder is not satisfied with the settlement offer or does not want to wait for a judgment, he has no right to oppose the funded party's decision. This requirement is suggested to be incorporated in the litigation funding agreement.

**5.1.3.1.2. Confidential Information**
With regards to confidential information in a case, the third party funder will seek access to all confidential and privileged documents of the litigant in order to evaluate the ongoing viability of the litigation.[40] Particularly, in shareholder litigation usually concerned with complicated case details and high monetary value, the funder may be even cautious when evaluating the prospect of the case. However, the litigant may not be willing to provide such access for the funder considering the protection of business confidentiality, which would, thus, deter the cautious funder to invest in such a lawsuit.[41] In practice, the litigant' concern could be eliminated through the provision of a 'confidentiality clause' and the funder's liability of breach of confidence in the TPLF contract.

**5.1.3.1.3. The Lack of Funds in Paying Adverse Fees Under the English Cost-Shifting Rule**
A concern about adverse fees under the cost-shifting rule is also raised when TPLF is applied. A funder's promise to meet all adverse fees in the event that the funded case is lost may turn out to be unfulfillable if the funder does not possess adequate capital or is even on the verge of insolvency. Under this circumstance, the funded litigant is unexpectedly exposed to a substantial liability to pay an amount of adverse fees to the adverse party.

### 5.1.3.2 The Challenge to the Privileged Lawyer-and-Client Relationship

The conflict of interests between parties in a TPLF contract may also involve the lawyer, who is normally in a contractual relationship with the litigant. The lawyer's loyalty duty owed to the litigant is challenged by the fact that the funder rather than the litigant pays the lawyer's fee.[42] Given that, the lawyer, in reality, also has a direct contractual relationship with the third party funder, which may raise a question whether the lawyer's loyalty duty owed to the litigant will be replaced by or subordinated to his contractual duty owed to the funder. For instance, the lawyer may not be able to freely advise the funded litigant provided that this advice negatively affects the funder's interests.[43] As repeat players in the litigation funding

---

[40]Wayne Attrill, 'Ethical issues in litigation funding', (Feb 16th, 2009), p. 8, available at http://www.imf.com.au/docs/default-source/site-documents/ethical-issues-paper-imf09—globalaw-conference (accessed on 25 August 2016).

[41]Ibid.

[42]See US Chamber Institute for Legal Reform, 'Selling Lawsuits, Buying Trouble: Third Party Litigation Funding in the United States', (October 2009), p. 8. http://legaltimes.typepad.com/files/thirdpartylitigationfinancing.pdf (accessed on 25 August 2016).

[43]For example, the lawyer may advise the litigant not to take the funding offered. See Vicki Waye, 'Conflicts of Interests between Claimholders, Lawyers and Litigation Entrepreneurs', *Bond Law Review*, (2008), Volume 19(1), 225, p. 235.

market, it is not rare that litigation funders and lawyers have pre-existing relationship prior to the entry into a given lawsuit. They may mutually support in the exploration of their business.[44] Lawyers may 'tempt' the clients to choose a certain funder, even though the client's particular circumstances suggest a different third party funder would be more appropriate (or third party funding is not necessary), and vice versa.[45] Considering that, the relationship between a funder and a lawyer would be much closer than that between a lawyer and a litigant. In fact, the courts have expressed the worry that 'a lawyer's primary loyalty will, as a practical matter, rest with the person or entity who pays him' even though the attorney is directly retained by the funded litigant'.[46]

## *5.1.4 Externalities Brought by the Use of TPLF*

### 5.1.4.1 Access to Justice

High litigation costs create significant obstacles for impecunious plaintiffs to file lawsuits. Third party litigation funding helps to alleviate this difficulty, thus facilitating the access to justice for them. Also, risk-averse 'non-poor' plaintiffs benefit from the TPLF since litigation risk could be relieved by concluding a TPLF agreement with the funder. The introduction of TPLF, actually, increases the level of equality by increasing all individuals' utilities in term of facilitating the access to justice.[47] Under the classical utilitarian ideology of social welfare, the overall level of social welfare is in direct proportion to the level of each individual's utility.[48]An equal distribution of utilities indeed matters to evaluate the level of the social wellbeing.[49] In light of this theory, the availability of TPLF has a positive external effect that would be helpful to increase the general level of social welfare.[50]

---

[44]Vicki Waye, 'Conflicts of Interests between Claimholders, Lawyers and Litigation Entrepreneurs', *Bond Law Review*, (2008), Volume 19(1), 225, p. 235.

[45]Ibid.

[46]*Oliver v Board of Governors*, 779 SW 2d 212, 215 (Kentuky 1989).

[47]See Steven Shavell, *Foundations of economic analysis of law*, (Harvard University Press, 2004), p. 601.

[48]See Marco de Morpurgo, 'A comparative legal and economic approach to third-party litigation funding', *Cardozo Journal of International and Comparative Law Review*, (2011), Volume 19, 343, p. 380.

[49]See Steven Shavell, *Foundations of economic analysis of law*, (Harvard University Press, 2004), p. 597.

[50]See Marco de Morpurgo, 'A comparative legal and economic approach to third-party litigation funding', *Cardozo Journal of International and Comparative Law Review*, (2011), Volume 19, 343, p. 380.

#### 5.1.4.2 Deterrence Effects

Potential deterrence effect is produced by the use of TPLF. If potential injurers are aware of the fact that victims do not hold sufficient financial resources to support the litigation, they may engage in harmful activities more unscrupulously. Evidently, low costs of misbehaviour cannot deter potential injurers. In this case, if a TPLF is introduced to facilitate the access to justice for impecunious victims, wrongdoers would still be deterred although the judicial way is not actually chosen by the person who suffered wrongdoings.

The deterrence effect will be further enhanced in common law jurisdictions where the doctrine of *stare decisis* is applied. Under this doctrine, a court's opinion in a previous legal case has either binding effects on or be persuasive for cases with similar issues or facts when they are judged by the courts. In light of that, potential wrongdoers could be clearly aware of the court's opinion on a sort of misbehaviours, thus discouraging them from committing such wrongdoings.

#### 5.1.4.3 The Potential Increase in the Overall Volume of Litigation

Counterarguments contend that allowing TPLF will result in the filing of more claims.[51] Lawsuits dropped because of the prohibitive litigation costs or excessive litigation risk now would be initiated with the financial assistance from a third party funder.[52] However, even if the general volume of litigation does increase, it cannot be concluded that 'bad' cases are encouraged by TPLF.[53] If those lawsuits are not frivolous and based on good merits, the increase in the case volume would not be regarded as a negative issue in the sense that more illegal behaviour could be corrected and wrongdoers could be held liable.[54]

Since TPLF is an innovative way to finance civil litigation, there is a dearth of data to demonstrate its effects on litigation. The first article focusing on the empirical study of TPLF was accomplished by David Abrams and Daniel L. Chen in 2009, where the application of TPLF in Australia was analysed in depth. An important finding in this article is that the filing of lawsuits indeed increases in those countries where TPLF is allowed.[55] While in those jurisdictions where TPLF is still

---

[51]See Paul H. Robin, 'Third-party financing of litigation', *Northern Kentuchy Law Review*, (2011), Volume 38, 673, p. 682.

[52]See Jason Lyon, 'Revolution in Progress: Third-Party Funding of American Litigation', *UCLA Law Review*, (2011), Volume 58, 571, p. 590.

[53]See Anthony J. Sebok, 'The inauthentic claim', *Vanderbilt Law Review*, (2011), Volume 64, 61, p. 68.

[54]See Kevin Pennell, 'On the assignment of legal malpractice claims: a contractual solution to a contractual problem', *Texas Law Review*, (2003), Volume 82, 481, pp. 494–496.

[55]See David S. Abrams and Daniel L. Chen, 'A Market for Justice: A First Empirical Look at Third Party Litigation Funding', *University of Pennsylvania Journal of Business Law*, (2013), Volume 15, 1075, p.1090. And this finding could also be found in other articles (both the official

prohibited, a decline in the amount of the lawsuits is observed.[56] However, it is challenged that the empirical study in the article was conducted in Australia where TPLF is largely applied to fund insolvency cases and class actions.[57] In other countries where TPLF is adopted, the situation might be different from the Australian experience.[58] For instance, other than TPLF, contingency fee arrangement is flourished in the US, which provides more options for litigants to lift out the funding obstacle in launching a claim. In Australia where the lawyer's funding is still prohibited, litigants may not have, other than TPLF, effective funding alternatives to finance litigation. In view of that, in the US where there have been other funding alternatives to financially assist litigants, the permission of TPLF may not lead to a noticeable increase in case volume, which might be different from that in Australia.

The question whether the rise in case volume is socially desirable should be analysed in combination with the entire costs and benefits brought by the use of TPLF (as explained in Shavell's theory). The assessment of the merits of the lawsuits and the utility of their outcomes must be determined on a case-by-case basis rather than in a general term.[59] What should be particularly noted is that the filing of frivolous claims and unmeritorious litigation must be prohibited.

#### 5.1.4.4 Frivolous Claims and Unmeritorious Litigation

TPLF is criticized that it encourages frivolous and unmeritorious claims.[60] Providing effective funding ways for plaintiffs makes litigation cheaper and easier,

(Footnote 55 continued)

document and academic literatures), see The Office of the Legal Service commissioner, 'The Regulation of Third Party Litigation Funding in Australia—Discussion Paper', (March, 2012), pp. 5–6, available at http://www.olsc.nsw.gov.au/agdbasev7wr/olsc/documents/pdf/regulation_of_third_party_litigation_funding_march2012_part1.pdf (accessed on 25 August 2016); and see US Chamber Institute for Legal Reform, Third Party Litigation Financing in Australia: Class Actions, Conflicts and Controversy, (October 2013), pp. 3–4.

[56]See David S. Abrams and Daniel L. Chen, 'A Market for Justice: A First Empirical Look at Third Party Litigation Funding', *University of Pennsylvania Journal of Business Law*, (2013), Volume 15, 1075, p. 1090.

[57]See Litigation Funding in Australia, Discussion Paper, Standing Committee of Attorneys General (May 2006), pp. 7–8, http://www.imf.com.au/docs/default-source/site-documents/discussionpaperstandingcommitteeofattorneysgeneral_may2006 (accessed on 25 August 2016).

[58]See Jason Lyon, 'Revolution in Progress: Third-Party Funding of American Litigation', *UCLA Law Review*, (2011), Volume 58, 571, p. 591.

[59]See Deborah R. Hensler, 'Financing Civil Litigation: the US Perspective', in Mark Tuil and Louis Visscher (eds.) *New Trends in Financing Civil Litigation in Europe: A Legal, Empirical, and Economic Analysis* (Edward Elgar Publishing, 2010) 149, p. 169.

[60]See US Chamber Institute for Legal Reform, 'Selling Lawsuits, Buying Trouble: Third Party Litigation Funding in the United States', (October 2009), pp. 5–7 http://legaltimes.typepad.com/files/thirdpartylitigationfinancing.pdf (accessed on 25 August 2016).

but, on the other hand, it might result in the rise of the volume of claims. And even, it has also been argued that "third-party litigation financing particularly increases the volume of questionable actions".[61]

In fact, as a professional litigation funding provider, the funder always conducts a cost-and-benefit analysis prior to financing a case.[62] Rational litigation funders may prefer lawsuits with good prospect of success which could recoup their investment.[63] An empirical research by IMF (the biggest Australian litigation funding company) shows that cases being funded have grown riskier over the past several years.[64] But there is no evidence demonstrating that third party funders would finance truly frivolous or unmeritorious cases since the success rate of those cases is low.[65] In addition to that, even if adventurous funders intend to 'gamble' frivolous cases, it would be difficult to find lawyers who are willing to represent such claims since 'bad' cases might not be profitable for them.

## 5.2 Third Party Litigation Funding: The Australian Case

### *5.2.1 Statutory Exceptions and Access to Justice*

Australia is the country where TPLF started to develop. Historically, champerty and maintenance were regarded as torts and crimes under the Australian law. In 1995, a new statutory exception to the rule against champerty appeared, according to which insolvency practitioners could conclude a TPLF agreement with a third party funder.[66] Therefore, in the very beginning, TPLF was applied in Australia as a statutory exception to the common law prohibition of maintenance and champerty

---

[61]Ibid.

[62]See US Chamber Institute for Legal Reform, 'Selling Lawsuits, Buying Trouble: Third Party Litigation Funding in the United States', (October 2009), p. 19 http://legaltimes.typepad.com/files/thirdpartylitigationfinancing.pdf (accessed on 25 August 2016).

[63]As some data presented, the selection of litigation to be funded is quite stringent. For example, in Australia, the largest litigation funding company (IMF) only funded 5% among the funding applications during 2001–2010. Similarly, in the US, the Juridica Capital Management only funded 6% of the cases considered. See RAND ICJ conference in Washington D.C. Conference: "Alternative litigation finance in the US—where are we and where are we headed with practice and policy?", Washington, D.C., 20–21 May 2010.

[64]See David S. Abrams and Daniel L. Chen, "A Market for Justice: A First Empirical Look at Third Party Litigation Funding", 15 *University of Pennsylvania Journal of Business Law*, (2013), 1075, p. 1091.

[65]Ibid.

[66]See Litigation Funding in Australia, Discussion Paper, Standing Committee of Attorneys General (May 2006), p. 5. http://www.imf.com.au/docs/default-source/site-documents/discussion paperstandingcommitteeofattorneysgeneral_may2006 (accessed on 25 August 2016).

only in the specific context of insolvency cases.[67] Subsequently, TPLF spread to fund other sorts of lawsuits but was still confined within the scope of commercial litigation.[68] At present, the prohibition of champerty and maintenance is abolished in the Australian Capital Territory, such as, New South Wales, South Australia and Victoria.[69] But if a funding agreement is contrary to public policy, it will be held invalid by the courts.[70] In recent years, the litigation funding industry has grown notably in Australia. At present, there are at least five professional commercial litigation funding firms operating in Australia. The largest one is IMF (Australia) Ltd, which is a publicly listed company providing funding for litigation and other relevant services in Australia and overseas.[71]

For the Australian courts, facilitating the access to justice was a main determinant for them in considering the legality of TPLF.[72] Although TPLF agreements outside the scope of insolvency cases were challenged in the past decade, no TPLF agreements, actually, were struck down in the Australian courts.[73]

### 5.2.2 Case Studies

(*Campbells Cash and Carry Pty Ltd v. Fostif Pty Ltd*; *Clairs Keeley v Treacy*; *Spatialinfo Pty Ltd v Telstra Corp Ltd*).

In *Campbells Cash and Carry Pty Ltd v. Fostif Pty Ltd*,[74] the legality of third party litigation funding was considered by the Australian High Court for the first time.[75] One of the reasons why the case came to the High Court is to confirm the issue: whether the proceeding was an abuse of process and could 'the manner of

---

[67]See Vicki Waye, *Trading in Legal Claims: Law, Policy & Future Directions in Australia, UK & US* (Presidian Legal Publications, 2008), p. 55.

[68]See Vicki Waye, '*Trading in Legal Claims Law, Policy & Future Directions in Australia, UK & US* (Presidian Legal Publications, 2008), pp. 55 and 133; and see Litigation Funding in Australia, Discussion Paper, Standing Committee of Attorneys General (May 2006), pp. 4–6.

[69]See Maintenance, champerty and barratry abolition act 1993, ss 3&4 (New South Wales); Criminal law consolidation act 1935, ss 1(3)&3, Sch. 11 (South Australia);Wrong act 1958, s. 32 (Victoria); and Crimes act 1958, s. 332A (Victoria).

[70]For example, see Maintenance, champerty and barratry abolition act 1993, s. 6 (New South Wales); and Wrongs act 1958, s. 32(2) (Victoria).

[71]See IMF's official webpage, https://www.imf.com.au/about-us (accessed on 25 August 2016).

[72]See Litigation Funding in Australia, Discussion Paper, Standing Committee of Attorneys General (May 2006), pp. 5–6. http://www.imf.com.au/docs/default-source/site-documents/discussionpaperstandingcommitteeofattorneysgeneral_may2006 (accessed on 25 August 2016).

[73]Ibid.

[74]*Campbells Cash and Carry Pty Ltd v. Fostif Pty Ltd* (2006) HCA 41.

[75]See Michael Legg and Louisa Travers, 'Necessity is the mother of invention: the adoption of third-party litigation funding and the closed class in Australian class actions', *Common law world review*, (2009), Volume 38, 245, pp. 254–255.

external funding be permanently held'?[76] In this respect, the Court confirmed, by a 5:2 majority, that third party litigation funding was not contrary to the public policy under Australian law, and a litigation funder to finance and control litigation in order to earn profits does not amount to an abuse of the court's process.[77] On the other hand, the minority in the High Court did not support the use of third party funding arrangement.[78] The decision by the High Court in *Fostif* is regarded as a very significant step which boosted the use of TPLF in Australia.[79] The fundamental justification of the permission of TPLF in *Fostif* is that it ensures 'access to justice'.[80]

In *Fostif*, the main issue confirmed is that the third party funding agreement does not violate the public policy and an abuse of the court proceeding was not found in the agreement. But, to a more concrete extent, which elements should be taken into account when the legality of a litigation funding agreement is examined? A proposed standard is the degree of the funder's control over the lawsuit. In other words, whether the funder 'monopolizes' the litigation.[81]

In this regard, the main issue that needs to be investigated is to what degree the control by the funder is permitted in Australia. In case law, the Supreme Court of Western Australia in *Clairs Keeley v Treacy*[82] concluded that the litigation funding agreement was champertous by indicating that 'it is not acceptable for the litigation to be pursued in such a way that the interests of the plaintiffs are subservient to those of the funder, and that would be an abuse of process.'[83] However, then the New South Wales Court of Appeal in *Fostif* disagreed with the viewpoint in *Clairs*

---

[76]See Wayne Attrill, Ethical issues in litigation funding, (Feb 16th, 2009), p. 3, available at http://www.imf.com.au/docs/default-source/site-documents/ethical-issues-paper-imf09—globalaw-conference (accessed on 25 August 2016).

[77]Stuart Clark, 'Case comment: Australia: Civil Proceedings-Litigation Funding', *International Company and Commercial Law Review* (2007), Volume 18(2), N5–6.

[78]In the view of Justices Callinan and Heydon (who are against TPLF) an 'abuse of process' arose out of a combination of factors: the profiteering motive of the funder; the encouragement of persons to sue who would not otherwise have done so; the small size of the individual claims which in any event amounted to a "windfall"; the large profit likely to have been made by the funder; the funder's control of the litigation; the subservience of the claimants' interest to those of the funder; the limited role of the plaintiffs' solicitor; and the monopoly position of the funder. See Jasminka Kalajdzic, Peter Cashman and Alana Longmoore, '*Justice for profit, a comparative analysis of Australian, Canadian and US. third party litigation funding*', p. 106.

[79]See Michael Legg and Louisa Travers, 'Necessity is the mother of invention: the adoption of third-party litigation funding and the closed class in Australian class actions', *Common law world review*, (2009), Volume 38, 245, pp. 254–255.

[80]*Campbells Cash and Carry Pty Ltd v. Fostif Pty Ltd* (2006) HCA 41, at 145.

[81]See Rachael Mulheron and Peter Cashman, 'Third party funding: a changing landscape', *Civil Justice Quarterly*, (2008), Volume 27(3), 312, p. 335.

[82]*Clairs Keeley (A Firm) v Treacy* [2004] WASCA 277.

[83]*Clairs Keeley (A Firm) v Treacy*[2004] WASCA 277 at 71.

*Keeley v Treacy*, and pointed out that the control of the funder was essential to protect the funder's own legitimate interests.[84] Justice Mason P. further mentioned that 'compared to the plaintiffs in *Fostif*, the funder, as a repeat player in litigation market, was better to make the forensic decisions to deal with the defendants'.[85]

In other Australian courts' decisions, the funder's control over the proceeding was allowed.[86] The key issue regarding the funder's control is the permissible degree of it. In *Spatialinfo Pty Ltd v Telstra Corp Ltd*,[87] Sundberg J. made three observations about the permissible degree of the funder's control over the proceeding:

> (a) the funder was entitled to be kept advised of the course of the proceedings, sufficient to enable them to determine what work had been done and whether the invoices rendered by the lawyers were reasonable, and a requirement to be notified of the terms of a proposed settlement, simply constituted (said the court) a protection of their investment[88]; (b) the funder's right to terminate the agreement in their absolute discretion was reasonable, expected, and hardly a threat, given that it had been used in only 3 out of about 210 actions that the funder had funded to that point[89]; (c) the express requirements that the funded claimant should agree not to seek any court order which could adversely affect the funder's rights under the funding agreement were, quite reasonable provisions that may well have been implied in any event.[90]

From these viewpoints, it is found that a proper degree of control by the third party funder is legally permissible. As an external investor, it is reasonable and logical to keep close eyes on the proceeding and secure his own interests in the investment. In fact, whether a TPLF agreement is champertous should depend on the degree of the funder's control over the court's procedure, but could not only rely on a simple fact that the funder's 'control' the lawsuit. For instance, if a funder refuses to allow the direct contact between the funded litigant and the lawyer, the court could hold that the litigation funding agreement is champertous.[91] Similarly, in *Clairs Keeley v Treacy*, the funder controlled the whole litigation procedure by concluding a direct contract with the lawyer and instructing him directly, which could be considered as champerty. In addition to that, the lawyer in that case did not demonstrate that they owed duties to the plaintiff.[92]

---

[84] *Fostif Pty Ltd* v *Campbells Cash & Carry Pty Ltd* [2005] NSWCA 83.

[85] *Fostif Pty Ltd* v *Campbells Cash & Carry Pty Ltd* [2005] NSWCA 83, at 137.

[86] *Trendlen Pty Ltd v Mobil Oil Australia Pty Ltd* [2005] NSWSC 741; *Project 28 Pty Ltd (formerly Narui Gold Coast Pty Ltd) v Barr* [2005] NSWCA 240.

[87] *Spatialinfo Pty Ltd v Telstra Corp Ltd* [2005] FCA 455.

[88] *SpatialinfoPty Ltd v Telstra Corp Ltd* [2005] FCA 455 at 31&32.

[89] *SpatialinfoPty Ltd v Telstra Corp Ltd* [2005] FCA 455 at 33.

[90] *SpatialinfoPty Ltd v Telstra Corp Ltd* [2005] FCA 455 at 34.

[91] See Rachael Mulheron and Peter Cashman, 'Third party funding: a changing landscape', *Civil Justice Quarterly*, (2008), Volume 27(3), 312, p. 337.

[92] See Litigation Funding in Australia, Discussion Paper, Standing Committee of Attorneys General (May 2006), p. 9. http://www.imf.com.au/docs/default-source/site-documents/discussion paperstandingcommitteeofattorneysgeneral_may2006 (accessed on 25 August 2016).

### 5.2.3 Regulations on TPLF in Australia

The first issue needs to be discussed is the protection of vulnerable consumers (funded litigants). Unlike litigation funders and lawyers who are repeat players in litigation market, funded litigants may not always have legal knowledge and not be able to retain adequate control over the court proceeding. It has been suggested from the case law that control over the proceedings by the third party funder should be limited to a certain degree. However, in fact, it is difficult for funded litigants to retain primary control over the whole court proceeding since they are lacking in professional knowledge and practical experience. In most of cases the funded litigants, therefore, rely largely on the funders and lawyers, which necessitates the protection of vulnerable consumers (funded litigants).

In Australia, consumer protection in TPLF is implemented by ensuring that funders are subject to mandatory disclosure requirements.[93] For instance, in the past, litigation funders were required to hold a Financial Services Licence (AFSL) granted by the Australian Securities and Investment Commission (ASIC).[94] Litigation funders holding such a licence were subject to two sorts of pro-active consumer protection obligations.[95] First of all, the licence had requirements with regards to the funders' financial capacities.[96] On the other hand, the funders holding AFSL were obligatorily required to disclose to their clients the risks and benefits of the funding arrangement including fees and commissions, and all other significant features of the agreement.[97] The obligatory disclosure imposed on the litigation funder is to avoid information asymmetry between the funder and their client, thus enabling the litigant to make an informed decision after the awareness of adequate information and key issues in the TPLF agreement.

But in 2012, the High Court's decision in *International Litigation Partners Pte Ltd v Chameleon Mining NL*[98] declared that litigation funders actually provided

---

[93]See Wayne Attrill, 'Ethical issues in litigation funding', p. 10. (Feb 16th, 2009), http://www.imf.com.au/docs/default-source/site-documents/ethical-issues-paper-imf09—globalaw-conference (accessed on 25 August 2016).

[94]In March 2011, the NSW Court of Appeal held that funding arrangements were a 'financial product' because they were a facility for managing risk. The result of this decision was that funders are required to hold an Australian Financial Services Licence (AFSL). If the litigation funding is identified as a sort of financial service, AFSL is obligatory and some other requirement (e.g. information disclosure) should be met by litigation funders as well. See Section 761D and Section 991A of Australian Corporations Act 2001.

[95]See Litigation Funding in Australia, Discussion Paper, Standing Committee of Attorneys General (May 2006), p. 8.http://www.imf.com.au/docs/default-source/site-documents/discussion paperstandingcommitteeofattorneysgeneral_may2006 (accessed on 25 August 2016).

[96]Ibid.

[97]See Chap. 7 of Australian Corporations Act 2001.

[98]*International Litigation Partners Pte Ltd v Chameleon Mining NL* [2012] HCA 45.

credit facility rather than financial service.[99] In light of that, legislative provisions applicable to financial products are not applied to TPLF, meaning that litigation funders are not required to hold an AFSL anymore.

At present, the main document regulating TPLF in Australia is *Regulatory Guide 248: Litigation schemes and proof of debt schemes: Managing conflicts of interest* issued in April 2013 by the Australian Securities and Investment Commission (ASIC), requiring the litigation funders to manage any conflicts in the TPLF.[100] Generally, under the Guide 248, the funder has to identify the pre-existing relationship among any of the funder, the lawyer and the funded litigants, and conduct a review of their business operations relating to the litigation or proof of debt scheme to identify and assess potential conflicting interests.[101] Moreover, they must write procedures for identifying and managing conflicts, and procedures about protecting the interests of members and prospective members must be particularly included.[102]

## 5.2.4 Current Practice and the Way Forward

### 5.2.4.1 The 'Monopolization' of Class Action

As indicated before, current rules regulating TPLF is Guide 248 mainly dealing with the conflict of interests. Compared to the old regime where a AFSL is required to hold by the funder, Guide 248 is light-handed. For instance, there is no requirement in relation to the funder's financial adequacy in Guide 248.[103]

The government justifies the light-handed regulation on funder mainly by stating that such regulation facilitates the access to justice and the industry contributes to

[99]See Jasminka Kalajdzic, Peter Cashman and Alana Longmoore, 'Justice for profit, a comparative analysis of Australian, Canadian and US third party litigation funding', *American Journal of Comparative Law*, (2013), Volume 61, 93, p. 108.

[100]This regulation by ASIC could be downloaded from http://www.asic.gov.au/asic/pdflib.nsf/LookupByFileName/rg248-published-22-April-2013.pdf/$file/rg248-published-22-April-2013.pdf (accessed on 25 August 2015).

[101]See Regulatory Guide 248, RG 248.13 & 248.14.

[102]Ibid.

[103]In fact, a license scheme including financial adequacy requirement for litigation funders is suggested. See Ross Mclnnes, 'Australia: ASIC issues litigation funding guidance to manage conflicts of interests', (June, 8th, 2013), available at http://www.mondaq.com/australia/x/243848/Class+Actions/ASIC+issues+litigation+funding+guidance+to+manage+conflicts+of+interest (accessed on 25 August 2016); and see John Emmerig and Michael Legg, 'Litigation Funding in Australia: More Swings and Roundabouts as Lawyers Withdraw Application to be Funders', (February 2014), available at http://www.mondaq.com/australia/x/292544/Class+Actions/Litigation+Funding+In+Australia+More+Swings+And+Roundabouts+As+Lawyers+Withdraw+Application+To+Be+Funders (accessed on 26 August 2016).

the well-being of the society as a whole.[104] But the 'access to justice' is only facilitated for specific types of claims (class actions, insolvency claims), and only cases with high value and good prospect to win would interest commercial funders.[105] IMF, the largest litigation funding company, has declared that it will not consider claims which are likely to be dependent on oral evidence and claims with a value less than $2 million will not be considered.[106] The facilitation of the 'access to justice' for the general public is hard to be realized considering the funder's business model. In fact, TPLF remains as a driving force behind class actions rather than to enhance the level of 'access to justice'.[107]

#### 5.2.4.2 Lawyers as Funders

Contingency fee arrangements are not legally permitted in Australia.[108] But this prohibition does not apply to non-lawyers. Consequently, law firms may establish its own funding company to contract with litigant in order to circumvent the prohibition. An Australian law firm (Maurice Blackburn) known for its expertise in class actions founded its own funding company (Claims Funding Australia Pty Limited, CFA). Controlling shareholders of CFA are senior principals in the law firm, meaning that the law firm substantially controls the operation of the CFA. On 15 May 2013, CFA and another litigation funder (Argentum) declared to co-fund a class claim (Equine influenza) in which Maurice Blackburn was retained as the lawyers.[109] The request for approval of the CFA's funding agreement in Equine influenza was refused by the Full Federal Court of New South Wales by indicating that the conflict of interests is a big concern because of the relationship between Maurice

---

[104] US Chamber Institute for Legal Reform, 'Third Party Litigation Financing in Australia: Class Actions, Conflicts and Controversy', (October 2013), p. 7.

[105] Ibid.

[106] John Walker, Susanna Khouri and Wayne Attrill, 'Class Actions, Conflicts and Controversy', *University of New South Wales Law Journal*, (2009) 32, 1036, pp. 1049–1053.

[107] John Emmerig and Michael Legg, 'Litigation Funding in Australia: More Swings and Roundabouts as Lawyers Withdraw Application to be Funders', (February 2014), available at http://www.mondaq.com/australia/x/292544/Class+Actions/Litigation+Funding+In+Australia+More+Swings+And+Roundabouts+As+Lawyers+Withdraw+Application+To+Be+Funders (accessed on 26 August 2016).

[108] For example, Section 325 of the Legal Profession Act 2004 (NSW) states,

> 'A law practice must not enter into a costs agreement under which the amount payable to the law practice, or any part of that amount, is calculated by reference to the amount of any award or settlement or the value of any property that may be recovered in any proceedings to which the agreement relates'.

[109] 'Maurice Blackburn to file Equine influenza class action today', (15 May 2013), http://www.mauriceblackburn.com.au/about/media-centre/media-statements/2013/maurice-blackburn-to-file-equine-influenza-class-action-today/ (accessed on 26 August 2016).

Blackburn and CFA, and the waiver of conflicts of interest does not prove to be effective.[110] The attempt to circumvent the prohibition on contingency fees raises discussion about whether rules governing legal profession should be amended to allow the application of contingency fee arrangements. For the research scope of TPLF in this book, we hold an opinion that such circumvent should be prohibited mainly for the reason that the funder's moral hazard and lawyer's fiduciary duty owed to the client is hard to be tackled with. The alliance of the lawyer and funder in a given case (like CFA and Maurice Blackburn) will enhance the interplay between lawyers and funders, and put the funded litigant in an even worse position.

## 5.3 Third Party Litigation Funding: The English Case

In the UK, the experience of TPLF is similar to that in Australia, where TPLF was first used to finance insolvency cases before expanding to other commercial lawsuits.[111] But what is not like the Australian example is that TPLF in the UK has expanded outside the scope of commercial lawsuits and covered non-commercial ones (For instance, personal injury cases).[112] The TPLF industry is growing rapidly in the UK, and there is increasing liberalization of this private and market-based funding mechanism.

### *5.3.1 The Origins of TPLF in England*

Along with the constraints on the legal aid budget by the English government in 1990s, a shift from public litigation funding to a market-based alternative took place. The Access to Justice Act of 1999 conducted a reform where legal aid for all civil claims (including monetary claims) was suggested to be removed.[113] Moreover, the 1999 Act introduced several market-based alternatives to finance litigation, for example, conditional fees agreements and after-the-event (ATE) insurance.[114] Meanwhile, the TPLF, as a private and market-based funding approach, obtained a rapid growth in the UK, particularly, for non-commercial cases that would have been financially assisted by legal aid.

---

[110]Jacques Jacobs, 'Litigation Funders in Australia—Tighter Regulations on the Horizon?', (September 26th, 2013), available at http://www.insuranceflashlight.com/2013/09/26/litigation-funders-in-australia-tighter-regulations-on-the-horizon/ (accessed on 26 August 2016).

[111]See Marco de Morpurgo, 'A comparative legal and economic approach to third-party litigation funding', *Cardozo Journal of International and Comparative Law Review*, (2011), Volume 19, 343, p. 397.

[112]See Vicki Waye, *Trading in Legal Claims: Law, Policy & Future Directions in Australia, UK & US* (Presidian Legal Publications 2008), p. 105.

[113]See Lord Jackson, Review of civil litigation costs: final report, p. 68.

[114]Ibid.

As the country where the traditional common law doctrine (prohibition of champerty and maintenance) was originated, at the beginning of the 1990s, contracts violating the traditional prohibition were void unless they involved the common interests or the statutory exceptions on insolvency cases.[115] The turning point in this respect appeared in *Giles v. Thompson [1994]*,[116] where the House of Lords permitted a rental car provider (the funder) to provide financial assistance for a motorist who had been involved in a car accident and needed to hire a replacement car. In return, the hire charges were paid to the funder. This case brought a fundamental change to the traditional doctrine. The House of Lord did not consider that the funder engaged in 'wanton and officious intermeddling'.[117] It was a breakthrough case where an external entity could provide funding with no pre-existing interest in the subject matter, but just for an amount of commercial proceeds.[118] After *Giles*, the English courts began to relax the old common law principle, and considered that the employment of the TPLF agreements should no longer be confined within certain exceptions. Afterwards, the prohibition of champerty and maintenance was abolished in the English law, however, cases where 'wanton and officious intermeddling' exist were still strictly prohibited.[119]

Coming back to the discussion of the confirmation of the validity of funding agreements, in 2005, the Civil Justice Council (CJC) expressed its support to the TPLF. The civil advisory body published a report which recommended that 'further consideration should be given to the use of third party funding as a last resort means of providing access to justice'.[120] In 2007, the CJC reconsidered the topic of the TPLF, and in a further report, it recommended that

> Properly regulated Third Party Funding should be recognized as an acceptable option for mainstream litigation. Rules of Court should also be developed to ensure effective control over the conduct of litigation where third parties provide the funding.[121]

---

[115]In England, the general position in relation to insolvency office holders such as liquidators or trustees in bankruptcy is that those office holders are exempt from prohibitions of champerty and maintenance. See Vicki Waye, *Trading in Legal Claims: Law, Policy & Future Directions in Australia, UK & US* (Presidian Legal Publications 2008), pp. 106–107.

[116]*Giles v. Thompson*, [1994] 1 A.C. 142.

[117]*Giles v Thompson* [1994] 1 A.C. 142 at 165.

[118]D. Capper and L. Glennon, 'Litigation Funding for 'Big Money' Divorces: An Assessment of Legal Risk', *Civil Justice Quarterly*, (2007) Volume 26, 447, p. 458.

[119]See *Ahmed v. Powell*, [2003] P.N.L.R. 22; *Factortame & Ors v. Sec'y of State for Transport, Local Government and the Regions* (*No. 8*) [2003] Q.B. 381.

[120]*Improved Access to Justice—Funding Options and Proportionate Costs: Report and Recommendations* (August 2005), p. 49 and recommendation 13 at p. 12. http://www.judiciary.gov.uk/wp-content/uploads/JCO/Documents/CJC/Publications/CJC+papers/CJC+Improved+access+to+Justice+-Funding+options+and+proportionate+costs.pdf (accessed on 25 August 2016).

[121]*The Funding of Litigation—Alternative Funding Structures: A Series of Recommendations to the Lord Chancellor to Improve Access to Justice through the Development of Improved Funding Structures* ("CJC 2007 Report") (June 2007), p. 53, recommendation 3 at p. 12. http://www.judiciary.gov.uk/wp-content/uploads/JCO/Documents/CJC/Publications/CJC+papers/CJC+Future+Funding+of+Litigation+Paper.doc (accessed on 26 August 2016).

In *London & Regional (St. George's Court) Ltd. v. Ministry of Defence*[122] (2008), the court summarized the present status of litigation funding in the UK. Justice Coulson explained that when considering whether or not a litigation funding agreement is unlawful on grounds of champerty and maintenance, the primacy issue is to check whether the agreement 'has a tendency to corrupt public justice'.[123] To answer this question, a close examination needs to rest on the nature and surrounding circumstances of a given funding agreement instead of just scrutinizing generally.[124] In *London & Regional*, the court observed that with regards to third party litigation funding agreements, modern authorities demonstrated a flexible attitude towards them and generally enforced these agreements.[125]

Like the Australian case, the key issue in the implementation of TPLF is whether and what type of regulation should be adopted to regulate relevant aspects and to tackle with conflict of interests between stakeholders within an agreement. Mr Robert Musgrove, the Chief Executive of the CJC, indicated that

> It only takes the wrong case by the wrong funder with the wrong lawyer to have a very serious impact upon the market's development. So we're looking at a form of industry-agreed common standards to allow the market to emerge.[126]

In fact, a wide range of opinions with regards to the regulations in the TPLF agreements has been proposed. For instance, establish a new regulator to take on the responsibility for regulating funders[127]; implement a voluntary code of practice or protocol for funders and other parties[128]; require the courts to scrutinize the TPLF agreement on a case-by-case basis.[129]

On top of the confirmation of the legality of TPLF agreements, the *Arkin* principle dealing with the funder's liability of adverse fees needs be discussed also. In *Arkin v. Borchard Lines Ltd*,[130] the Court of Appeal again confirmed the legality of a litigation funding agreement where the funder had no pre-existing interest in the subject matter of the lawsuit. In *Arkin*, the primary issue was to what extent the funder should cover the winning defendant's costs under the English cost-shifting rule in the event that the funding agreement did not lay down any provisions in this

---

[122] *London & Regional (St George's Court) Ltd v Ministry of Defence* [2008] EWHC 526 (TCC).

[123] *London & Regional (St. George's Court) Ltd. v. Ministry of Defence*[2008] EWHC 526 (TCC) para. 103.

[124] See Rachael Mulheron and Peter Cashman, 'Third party funding: a changing landscape', *Civil Justice Quarterly*, (2008), Volume 27(3), 312, p. 330.

[125] *London & Regional (St. George's Court) Ltd. v. Ministry of Defence*, [2008] EWHC 526 (TCC) para. 103&104.

[126] See a report in the Law Society Gazette, (Thursday 17 January 2008), available at http://www.lawgazette.co.uk/features/whatever-you-want (accessed on 26 August 2016).

[127] See Rachael Mulheron and Peter Cashman, 'Third party funding: a changing landscape', *Civil Justice Quarterly*, (2008), Volume 27(3), 312, p. 322.

[128] Ibid.

[129] Ibid.

[130] *Arkin v Borchard Lines Ltd* [2005] EWCA Civ 655.

regard.[131] In other words, as a non-litigation party, should the funder, who did not expressly agree to meet any adverse costs in the funding agreement, be liable for such costs if the defendant is successful? On this issue, Lord Phillips MR stated that

> The fact that the funder is to share in the proceeds of the claim and may thereby derive a large profit from its investment will normally justify an order for costs because the very fact of the funder's stake in recovery represents a risk of interference in the due administration of justice[132]

In the Court of Appeal of *Arkin*, it was also stated that 'it is unjust that a funder who purchases a stake in an action for a commercial motive should be protected from all liabilities for the adverse costs of the opposing party if the funded party fails in the action'.[133] The '*Arkin Principle*', where the funder's liability to pay an adverse costs order should be capped to the extent of the level of funding that the funder provided to his client previously, was established.[134] But Lord Jackson's final report opposes the '*Arkin Principle*' by indicating that third-party funders should be fully exposed to the liability of adverse costs, because a limited scope of liability is unjust to the opposing party (whose costs may not be covered), and to the client who is still liable for the costs that has not been covered by the funder.[135] It is suggested, in Jackson's report, that the extent of the funder's liability should be a matter for the court's discretion on a case-by-case basis.[136] Actually, in *Arkin*, the funder just financed a part of the litigation costs (including the disbursement of expert witness and the cost of organizing the documents) amounted to £1.3 million. It is hard to imagine that the funder should be fully liable for the adverse fees over £6 million, which is disproportionate.[137] In addition to that, the court also stated that the *Arkin* principle could still be applied to a fully-funded case.[138]

On this issue, we agree with Lord Jackson's recommendation that the liability of adverse costs should not be limited to the scope of the funder's investment, and to what extent the adverse fees should be covered by the funder must be determined by the court's discretion on a case-by-case basis. Generally, for professional litigation funders, they could be able to effectively externalize investment risks through a portfolio of cases, or choose to diminish the risk of adverse fees through

---

[131]See George Robert Barker, 'Third Party Litigation Funding in Australia and Europe', *Journal of Law Economics and Policy*, (2011), Volume 8, 451, pp. 453–454.

[132]*Arkin v. Borchard Lines Ltd* [2003] EWHC 2844, paras 71–72.

[133]*Arkin v Borchard Lines Ltd* [2005] EWCA Civ 655, para 38.

[134]For example, if a litigation funder invests £1 million in an unsuccessful claim, he would only be liable for up to an additional £1 million of adverse costs.

[135]Jackson's final report (2009), p. 123.

[136]Ibid.

[137]*Arkin v Borchard Lines Ltd* [2005] EWCA Civ 655.

[138]Ibid.

insurance product (e.g. ATE insurance). But impecunious plaintiffs and defendants are more vulnerable in this regard.[139] The use of the *Arkin* principle would create an uneven playing field leaning to the side of litigation funders.

### 5.3.2 Rules Regarding TPLF

Rules regulating TPLF in the UK are generally voluntary regulations rather than compulsory rules. The Law Society of England and Wales contemplates 'light-handed' regulations on the TPLF industry, pointing out that the main task about TPLF regulation is to ensure that funded litigants are well informed about the funding arrangement they are entering into.[140] It further states that unnecessary regulations on third party funders should be avoided.[141] The reason for the preference of light-handed regulation on TPLF might partly be that English legislators uphold a principle of 'facilitate the access to justice', and do not wish to lay down harsh regulations to impede the development of the new funding industry.[142]

The Civil Justice states a similar opinion with that held by the Law Society that light-handed regulations on TPLF is desired. A Code of Conduct to the third party litigation funder was issued by the CJC in 2011, which was regarded as a very remarkable progress in regulating litigation funding market. Lord Neuberger of Abbotsbury who is also the Chair of the CJC comments that the Code 'is an important development and will help to foster standards of best practice and to promote greater transparency among the providers of litigation funding services to the benefit of the consumers of these services.'[143] For the sake of good enforcement

---

[139]Professional litigation funding may lose investment in one case, but earn money in others, hence the risk of losing money could be diminished by a series of investments. But for plaintiffs and defendants, they are not frequent litigation player. Therefore, if they lose in one case, it may be difficult to gain in other cases. In this regard, plaintiffs and defendants are more 'vulnerable' than professional litigation funders.

[140]See Neil Rose, 'Drive for Transparency on Third-Party Funding' in Law Gazette, February 14, 2008. Available at http://www.lawgazette.co.uk/news/drive-transparency-third-party-funding (accessed on 26 August 2016).

[141]See Neil Rose, 'Drive for Transparency on Third-Party Funding' in Law Gazette, February 14, 2008. Available at http://www.lawgazette.co.uk/news/drive-transparency-third-party-funding (accessed on 26 August 2016).

[142]Tony Guise, Chairman of the Commercial Litigation Association, quoted in 'Regulation of Third Party Litigation Funders Unnecessary', Press Release, March 26, 2007, available at http://www.solicitorsjournal.com/news/commercial/company/regulation-third-party-litigation-funders-unnecessary-says-clan (accessed on 26 August 2016).

[143]See Paul Bannon, 'Recent developments in litigation funding in Australia and the UK' (8 February 2012), available at http://www.mondaq.com/australia/x/163432/Regulatory/Recent+developments+in+litigation+funding+in+Australia+and+the+UK (accessed on 26 August 2016).

of the Code, the Association of Litigation Funders (the ALF) was established in November 2011 to improve the quality of the third party funders by providing them with professional education and training.[144]

In general, the CJC's Code lays down a range of obligations for litigation funders. For instance, to observe the confidentiality of all information and documentation relating to the dispute; maintain at all times adequate financial resources to meet its obligations to fund all of the disputes; not take any steps that cause the litigant's lawyers to act in breach of their professional duties; not seek to influence the litigant's lawyer to cede control or conduct of the dispute to the funder.[145] For the content of the funding agreement, the Code requires it to include the funder's liabilities to meet the adverse costs; to provide security to costs and meet any other financial liability.[146]

The Harbour Litigation Funding, as one of the first professional litigation funders in the UK, confirms the potential positive impacts of the Code on regulating litigation funding market. Particularly, the Code sets provisions with regards to the capital adequacy of the litigation funder in order to prevent an unexpected funding shortage. Regarding the termination of the litigation funding agreement, the Code requires the LFA to indicate strict conditions under which the funder can terminate the agreement.[147] But it has been argued that such strict requirements might create disincentives for potential funders to enter into the market[148] for the reason that it would not be easy for the funder to accelerate cash flow under those strict requirements. Actually, in the UK, the TPLF mainly improves the access to justice for small-to-medium sized companies, while individual plaintiffs do not receive the same benefits.[149] In particular, commercial cases with high monetary value are preferred by third party funders,[150] while consumer cases, personal injury cases and other small-valued claims, on the other hand, do not attract the interests of litigation funders.[151]

[144]See the official website of the Association of Litigation Funders, http://associationoflitigationfunders.com/about-us/ (accessed on 26 August 2016).

[145]See Code of Conduct for Litigation Funders, (January 2014), article 7&9, available at http://associationoflitigationfunders.com/wp-content/uploads/2014/02/Code-of-conduct-Jan-2014-Final-PDFv2-2.pdf (accessed on 26 August 2016).

[146]See Code of Conduct for Litigation Funders, article 10.

[147]See Code of Conduct for Litigation Funders, article 9.

[148]See Civil Justice Council, Consultation Paper on a Self-regulatory Code of Third Party Funding, Summary of Responses, p. 4, available at http://www.judiciary.gov.uk/about-the-judiciary/advisory-bodies/cjc/third-party-funding.htm#pageTitleContainer (accessed on 26 August 2016).

[149]See Nicholas Dietsch, 'Litigation financing in the US, the UK, and Australia: How the industry has evolved in three countries', *Northern Kentucky Law Review*, (2011), Volume 38, 687, p. 702.

[150]See "Elvis Presley case highlights growth of third party funding to back legal claims", (30 November 2012), *The Guardian*, available at http://www.theguardian.com/law/2012/nov/30/elvis-presley-third-party-legal-claims (accessed on 26 August 2016).

[151]Ibid.

Since1 April 2013, contingency fee arrangements have been legally allowed in the English civil justice system. In view of that, it might be possible to predict that low-valued cases that do not interest third party funders might be likely to gain access to justice by the availability of this newly-introduced funding technique. Compared to professional litigation funders, individual lawyers have weaker financial capacity, which deters them to take commercial cases with high monetary value. In addition to that, the court proceeding of a commercial case always lasts longer than a small claim (for instance, contract disputes between two individuals). Normally, a rational individual lawyer would not intent to spend too much time just on one case, because high consumption on time cannot guarantee high monetary rewards and the time would be completely wasted in the event that the case is lost.

As indicated before, the concern is raised that the termination requirements in the Code may disincentivize potential funders to enter into the market.[152] However, such concern is undue because, in fact, litigation funders without abundant capital could hardly compete with their rivals to survive in the litigation funding market even though there are no statutory requirements about a funder's financial capacity. In consideration of the introduction of contingency fee arrangements, the plight of small litigation funders may become even more serious. For instance, a litigant in a small claim (for example, personal injury) may prefer to conclude a contingency fee arrangement with a lawyer but not resort to a third party funder, because directly concluding a contingency fee arrangement without the complicated funder-lawyer-client relationship is an easy and straightforward way for the litigant. If the litigant chooses to enter into a third party funding agreement, he would be confronted with a much more complicated circumstance. For example, the involvement of a third party funder, who is a non-party in the litigation, will increase the agency cost. For reason indicated before, small litigation funders will lose in the competition with lawyers in the field of small claims. Therefore, requirements listed in the Code will not generate real disincentives for funders. Instead, it encourages good competition in litigation funding market by driving out unqualified funders (e.g. without sufficient capital).[153]

---

[152]See Civil Justice Council, Consultation Paper on a Self-regulatory Code of Third Party Funding, Summary of Responses, p. 4, available at http://www.judiciary.gov.uk/about-the-judiciary/advisory-bodies/cjc/third-party-funding.htm#pageTitleContainer (accessed on 26 August 2016).

[153]It should be noted that in the UK, currently, instead of focusing on catering to lower-income individual plaintiffs, the litigation funding industry takes a complex investment approach to financing lawsuits. Hedge funds, insurers, large investment companies and private investors all finance lawsuits in the U.K. In fact, most financing companies are large corporate entities with huge budgets, typically fund lawsuits with very high monetary value. The type of corporate clients who would ordinarily enter into these agreements are usually represented by large law firms, which have now begun to partner with third party litigation finance companies to offer advances to clients. For example, eight of the top ten firms in the U.K. now offer, or are considering to offer external financing to clients in some cases. The cooperation of large law firms and litigation finance companies in the U.K. demonstrates a 'big business' approach to litigation financing, with the industry moving away from access to justice concerns and increasingly towards an investment mindset. See Nicholas Dietsch, 'Litigation financing in the US, the UK, and Australia: How the industry has evolved in three countries', *Northern Kentucky Law Review*, (2011), Volume 38, 687, pp. 701–702.

The advent of the Code, which can be regarded as a guarantee of the development of TPLF, is quite necessary. However, it should be indicated that the Code only applying to the members of the Third Party Litigation Funders Association does not have a binding effect.[154] The litigation market is expanding rapidly and the funders have already planned to extend the use of litigation funding into new markets (for instance, class actions).[155] Therefore, the voluntary code may be unable to adequately cover the growing range and practice of the market.[156] Furthermore, the Code without effective penalties for bad practice is inadequate to deal with rogue funders, thus there are doubts over the adequacy and effectiveness of a voluntary code in this regard.[157] In consideration of a widely-accepted fact that the TPLF in the UK is still in its infancy, self-regulation is the most practical solution at this stage.[158] But it is not sufficient to regulate a fast-growing market, legislations on TPLF are in need.[159]

## 5.4 Third Party Litigation Funding: The American Case

TPLF in the US has a history of a few decades and is still growing rapidly, which, unlike Australia, largely focuses on financing small-scale cases and cases concerning consumer issues.[160]

As a common law jurisdiction, the traditional prohibition of champerty and maintenance is also found in the US.[161,162] Restrictions on maintenance and

---

[154]See article 1 of the Code, http://associationoflitigationfunders.com/code-of-conduct/ (accessed on 26 August 2016).

[155]See Christopher Hodges, John Peysner and Angus Nurse, Litigation funding: status and issues (research report, January 2012), p. 141, available at http://www.csls.ox.ac.uk/documents/ReportonLitigationFunding.pdf (accessed on 31 August 2016).

[156]Ibid.

[157]See Christopher Hodges, John Peysner and Angus Nurse, Litigation funding: status and issues (research report, January 2012), p. 148, available at http://www.csls.ox.ac.uk/documents/ReportonLitigationFunding.pdf (accessed on 31 August 2016).

[158]See Christopher Hodges, John Peysner and Angus Nurse, Litigation funding: status and issues (research report, January 2012), p. 149, available at http://www.csls.ox.ac.uk/documents/ReportonLitigationFunding.pdf (accessed on 31 August 2016).

[159]Ibid.

[160]See Jasminka Kalajdzic, Peter Cashman and Alana Longmoore, 'Justice for profit, a comparative analysis of Australian, Canadian and US third party litigation funding', *American Journal of Comparative Law*, (2013), Volume 61, 93, p. 128.

[161]See Anthony J. Sebok, The Inauthentic Claim, *Vanderbilt Law Review*, (2011), Volume 64, 61, pp. 68–70.

[162]The US Supreme Court defines the traditional doctrines very precisely 'Put simply, maintenance is helping another prosecute a suit; champerty is maintaining a suit in return for a financial interest in the outcome', See Anthony J. Sebok, The Inauthentic Claim, *Vanderbilt Law Review*, (2011), Volume 64, 61, p. 70.

champerty exist to varying degrees across the states. Up till now, almost all of the states permit one form of maintenance—the contingency fee arrangements concluded between lawyers and clients.[163] However, frivolous and unmeritorious suits are strictly prohibited to be funded by lawyers.[164] In the current economic climate, many lawyers and their firms are risk-averse due to the lack of capital,[165] which indirectly creates business opportunities to entrepreneurial litigation funders.

### 5.4.1 The Traditional Prohibition of Champerty and Maintenance

Even as early as the middle of the nineteenth century, the American courts began to challenge the rationale of the doctrine prohibition of champerty and maintenance.[166] Max Radin's study completed in 1935 regarding champerty and maintenance pointed out that 'the doctrines were in practice largely dead and certainly out of step with American thinking about litigation at that time'.[167] Actually, until the advent of the TPLF, the US courts rarely enforced the doctrine of champerty.[168] Even when TPLF appeared in the US, courts expressly held a viewpoint in favour of the abolition of maintenance and champerty on the grounds that those old doctrines no longer responded to the social circumstance at that time.[169]

However, at the beginning of the 21st century, judicial opposition appeared to go against the commercial litigation funding in the US.[170] Quite a few American courts took a negative view of it and applied champerty as a significant obstruction to

---

[163]See Susan L. Martin, 'The litigation financing industry: the wild west of finance should be tamed not outlawed', 10 *Fordham Journal of Corporate and Financial Law*, (2004), Volume 10, 55, p. 57.

[164]See Anthony J. Sebok, The Inauthentic Claim, *Vanderbilt Law Review*, (2011), Volume 64, 61, p. 89.

[165]See Jasminka Kalajdzic, Peter Cashman and Alana Longmoore, 'Justice for profit, a comparative analysis of Australian, Canadian and US third party litigation funding', *American Journal of Comparative Law*, (2013), Volume 61, 93, p. 129.

[166]See Patrick M. Garry, *A nation of adversaries: how the litigation explosion is reshaping in America*, (Springer, 1997), p. 68; And in 1848, the New York Code of Civil Procedure was amended to allow assignments of interests, in nature a form of champerty.

[167]Max Radin, 'Maintenance by Champerty', *California Law Review*, (1935), Volume 24(1), 48, 68.

[168]See Marco de Morpurgo, 'A comparative legal and economic approach to third-party litigation funding', *Cardozo Journal of International and Comparative Law Review*, (2011), Volume 19, 343, p. 394.

[169]For instance, *Hardick v. Homol*, 795 So. 2d 1107 (Fla. 5th Dist. Ct. App. 2001); *Osprey, Inc. v. Cabana Ltd.* P'ship, 532 S.E.2d 269 (S.C. 2000); *Saladini v. Righellis*, 687 N.E.2d 1224 (Mass. 1997).

[170]See Vicki Waye, *Trading in Legal Claims: Law, Policy & Future Directions in Australia, UK & US* (Presidian Legal Publications, 2008), p. 111.

commercial investments in litigation.[171] Actually, litigation funding by a third party is maintenance for profit, which is champerty in nature.[172] In the US, until 2010, twenty-eight states have permitted maintenance in certain forms,[173] and sixteen states have expressly permitted maintenance for profit.[174] The remaining states probably permit champerty, but they do not expressly confirm the investment in a stranger's lawsuit as an allowable form of maintenance.[175]

As a matter of fact, the champerty law in the US is quite complicated, and there is not a uniform practice in this regard. Even in those states where champerty is

---

[171]For instance, *Rancman v. Interim Settlement Funding Corp.*, 99 Ohio St.3d 121 (Ohio 2003).

[172]See Anthony J. Sebok, 'The Inauthentic Claim', *Vanderbilt Law Review*, (2011), Volume 64, 61, pp. 89–91.

[173]See Paul Bond, 'Making champerty work: An invitation to state action', *University of Pennsylvania Law Review*, (2002), Volume 150, 1297; and see Anthony J. Sebok, 'The Inauthentic Claim', *Vanderbilt Law Review*, (2011), Volume 64, 61, pp. 88–90; Case law in those 28 states permiting some forms of maintenance are selected to be listed as follows: Ohio Rev. Code Ann. § 1349.55 (West 2008) [reversing Rancman v. Interim Settlement Funding Corp., 99 Ohio St.3d 121 (Ohio 2003)]; *Landi v. Arkules*, 835 P.2d 458 (Ariz. Ct. App. 1992); *Abbott Ford, Inc. v. Superior Court*, 741 P.2d 124 (Cal. 1987); *Fastenau v. Engel*, 240 P.2d 1173 (Colo. 1952); *Robertson v. Town of Stonington*, 750 A.2d 460 (Conn. 2000); *Kraft v. Mason*, 668 So.2d 679 (Fla. Dist. Ct. App. 1996); *TMJ Hawaii, Inc. v. Nippon Trust Bank*, 153 P.3d 444 (Haw. 2007); *Wright v. Meek, 3 Greene 472* (Iowa 1852); *Boettcher v. Criscione*, 299 P.2d 806 (Kan. 1956); *Martin v. Morgan Drive Away, Inc.*, 665 F.2d 598 (5th Cir. 1982); *Son v. Margolius, Mallios,Davis, Rider & Tomar*, 709 A.2d 112 (Md. 1998); *Saladini v. Righellis*, 687 N.E.2d 1224 (M.A. 1997); *Smith v. Childs*, 497 N.W.2d 538 (Mich. Ct. App. 1993); *Schnabel v. Taft Broad Inc.*, 525 S.W.2d 819 (Mo. Ct. App. 1975); *Green v. Gremaux*, 945 P.2d 903 (Mont. 1997); *Adkin Plumbing & Heating Supply Co. v. Harwell*, 606 A.2d 802 (N.H. 1992); *Polo v. Gotchel*, 542 A.2d 947 (N.J. Super. Ct. Law Div. 1987); *Leon v. Martinez*, 638 N.E.2d 511 (N.Y. 1994); *Odell v. Legal Bucks, LLC*, 665 S.E.2d 767 (N.C. Ct. App. 2008); *Interstate Collection Agency, Inc. v. Kuntz*, 181 N.W.2d 234 (N.D. 1970); *Mitchell v. Amerada Hess Corp.*, 638 P.2d 441 (Okla. 1981); *Brown v. Bigne*, 28 P. 11 (Or. 1891); *Osprey v. Cabana Ltd. P'ship, Inc.*, 532 S.E.2d 269 (S.C. 2000); *Record v. Ins. Co. of N. Am.*, 438 S.W.2d 743 (Tenn. 1969); *Anglo-Dutch Petroleum Int'l, Inc. v. Haskell*, 193 S.W.3d 87 (Tex. App. 2006); *Giambattista v. Nat'l Bank of Commerce of Seattle*, 586 P.2d 1180 (Wash. Ct. App. 1978); and *Currence v. Ralphsnyder*, 151 S.E. 700 (W. Va. 1929).

[174]See Anthony J. Sebok, 'The Inauthentic Claim', *Vanderbilt Law Review*, (2011), Volume 64, 61, pp. 88–90; Case law in those 16 states permiting maintenance for profit are selected to be listed as follows: CO, *Fastenau v. Engel*, 240 P.2d 1173 (Col. 1952); CT, *Robertson v. Town of Stonington*, 750 A.2d 460 (Conn. 2000); FL, *Kraft v. Mason*, 668 So. 2d 679 (Fla. 1996); IA, *Wright v. Meek*, 3 Greene 472 (Iowa 1852); KS, *Boettcher v. Criscione*, 299 P.2d 806 (Kan. 1956); ME, ME. REV. STAT. tit. 9A §12-101 (2009) [partially amending ME. REV. STAT. 17A §516(1) (2009)]; MD, *Son v. Margolius, Mallios, Davis, Rider & Tomar*, 709 A.2d 112 (Md. 1998); MA, *Saladini v. Righellis*, 687 N.E.2d 1224 (Mass. 1997); MO, *Schnabel v. Taft Broad. Co.*, 525 S. W.2d 819 (Mo. App. 1975); NH, *Adkin Plumbing & Heating Supply Co. v. Harwell*, 606 A.2d 802 (N.H. 1992); NC, *Odell v. Legal Bucks, LLC*, 665 S.E.2d 767 (N.C. App. 2008); OH, ORC ANN. 1349.55 (2009) [reversing Rancman v. Interim Settlement Funding Corp. 99 Ohio St.3d 121 (2003)]; OK, *Mitchell v. Amerada Hess Corp.*, 638 P.2d 441 (Okl. 1981); OR, *Brown v. Bigne*, 28 P. 11 (Or. 1891); WA, *Giambattista v. Nat'l Bank of Commerce of Seattle,* 586 P.2d 1180 (Wash. App. 1978); and WV, *Currence v. Ralphsnyder*, 151 S.E. 700 (W. Va. 1929).

[175]See Anthony J. Sebok, 'The Inauthentic Claim', *Vanderbilt Law Review*, (2011), Volume 64, 61, p. 91.

permitted, the practical rules are not identical. For example, Tennessee permits champerty (maintenance for profit) in anything but precludes land transactions.[176] In Texas, where the most liberal view on both assignment and maintenance is held, champerty is not permitted in certain sorts of litigation, such as legal malpractice.[177]

Apart from restrictions on what kind of lawsuits should be regarded as a sort of champerty, a more common limitation is based on how the champerty is performed.[178] It should be noted that those two sorts of restrictions on the application of champerty law in the US are not mutually exclusive, meaning that they can be used in a complementary way.[179] The most common way to control the "how" issue in champerty is to limit the degree of control the investor has over the conduct of the litigation. In this regard, the Australian approach is similar to the American one, where whether or not a champerty is generated depends on whether the third party funder *monopolizes* the litigation.[180]

In the US, sometimes, only *intermeddling champerty* is limited (for instance, a litigation funding agreement allows the third party funder to take too much control over the proceeding).[181] For instance, in Florida, intermeddling means 'offering unnecessary and unwanted advice or services', particularly, in a high-handed way.[182] In practice, *intermeddling champerty* has many forms, and there is not a common test to determine whether the litigation funder intermeddles.[183] But, it could depend largely, as indicated before, on the degree of the funder's control over the proceeding. Actually, the control by the funder over the litigation is diverse, ranging from very basic control (for instance, refer to the documents that do not contain confidential) to quite monopolized control (for example, select a lawyer for the client, and do not allow the client to contact directly with the attorney). In fact, a full (monopolized) control of a lawsuit will collapse the distinction between maintenance[184] and assignment.[185] If a third party funder retained full control of a

---

[176]Ibid.

[177]See Christy B. Bushnell, 'Champerty is still no excuse in Texas: Why Texas courts (and the legislature) should uphold litigation funding agreements', *Houston Business and Tax Law*, (2007), volume 7, 358, pp. 376–377.

[178]See Anthony J. Sebok, 'The Inauthentic Claim', *Vanderbilt Law Review*, (2011), Volume 64, 61, p. 94.

[179]Ibid.

[180]See Rachael Mulheron and Peter Cashman, 'Third party funding: a changing landscape', *Civil Justice Quarterly*, (2008), Volume 27(3), 312, p. 335.

[181]See Anthony J. Sebok, 'The Inauthentic Claim', *Vanderbilt Law Review*, (2011), Volume 64, 61, pp. 92–94.

[182]*Kraft v. Mason*, 668 So. 2d 679, 682 (Fla. App. 4th Dist. 1996).

[183]See Anthony J. Sebok, 'The Inauthentic Claim', *Vanderbilt Law Review*, (2011), Volume 64, 61, pp. 95–96.

[184]Actually, third party litigation funding discussed in this chapter is a sub-section of maintenance, and it is maintenance for profit, which is champerty in nature.

[185]In the event of an assignment, the investor will acquire the whole claim, and bring the claim on his own name. See Anthony J. Sebok, 'The Inauthentic Claim', *Vanderbilt Law Review*, (2011), Volume 64, 61, pp. 90–91.

lawsuit, actually he would be an assignee of the litigation.[186] The contract, under this circumstance, is a contract on assignment, but not maintenance for profit (champerty).[187] In other words, monopolized control by a third party funder over a lawsuit is a form of *intermeddling champerty*, which is impermissible in most of the states.[188] A case in Minnesota can explain more clearly what constitutes 'intermeddling champerty'. The Minnesota Supreme Court voided a maintenance contract because it required the plaintiff to pay the funder an amount of money if the plaintiff settled the case without the funder's permission.[189] Furthermore, some state courts adopts the absence of funder's control over the settlement as a *prima facie* evidence supporting the validation of a litigation funding contract.[190]

As a matter of fact, how to decide whether or not a litigation funding contract is permissible champerty or it is *intermeddling champerty* is quite complicated and there is not a clear standard to test this issue. There are just some circumstances under which the intermeddling champerty can be determined. For example, the power to select the attorney; to accept or refuse a settlement; to decide to terminate the lawsuit.

On the other hand, some American courts incorrectly hold that all third party funding agreements are *intermeddling champerty* in nature.[191] The Ohio Supreme Court indicated that a champerty contract is not legally permissible because the promise to repay the funder would necessarily become an additional factor that would be taken into account by the funded litigant when making the decision whether to settle the case or not.[192] The Ohio court concluded that the funding

---

[186]See Anthony J. Sebok, 'The Inauthentic Claim', *Vanderbilt Law Review*, (2011), Volume 64, 61, pp. 90–91.

[187]See *American Optical Co. v. Curtiss*, 56 F.R.D. 26, 27 (S.D.N.Y. 1971) (holding that an agreement which limited the litigant's control over whether to sue at all violated F.R.C.P. 17(a), which requires the moving party to be the 'real party in interest'), see Anthony J. Sebok, 'The Inauthentic Claim', *Vanderbilt Law Review*, (2011), Volume 64, 61, pp. 90–91.

[188]See Anthony J. Sebok, 'The Inauthentic Claim', *Vanderbilt Law Review*, (2011), Volume 64, 61, p. 90.

[189]*Huber v. Johnson*, 68 Minn. 74, 79 (1897).

[190]*Kraft v. Mason*, 668 So.2d (Fla. 1996), at 683; and *Clifford v. Wilcox*, 175 Wash. 513, 521 (Wash. 1933) (funder did not control the final settlement).

[191]For instance, *Rancman v. Interim Settlement Funding Corp.* 99 Ohio St.3d 121 (2003), para 124 and 125.

[192]*Rancman v. Interim Settlement Funding Corp.* 99 Ohio St.3d 121 (2003). para 125. In this case, the Ohio court noted that the $6000 provided by the funder in advance gave it the right to the first $16,800 of the settlement if the case settled within 12 months. Therefore, the court hypothesized that 'If there had not been any superior liens on [the litigant]'s settlement and her attorney had charged a 30-percent contingency fee, [she] would not have received any funds from a settlement of $24,000 or less. This … gives [her] an absolute disincentive to settle for $24,000 or less because she would keep the $6000 advance regardless of whether she settles … and would not receive any additional money from a $24,000 settlement'. See Anthony J. Sebok, The Inauthentic Claim, pp. 90–91.

agreement between the funder and the litigant intermeddled with the lawsuit because it would prolong the proceeding and reduce the settlement incentives.[193]

Apart from the concern about monopolized control over the proceeding, some states also fear that a champertous contract between the funder and the client is the only cause of a lawsuit that otherwise would not be brought.[194] For example, in *Bashor v. Northland Ins.Co*, the Colorado Supreme Court stated that the control over attorney selection was not an essential element to decide whether or not the funding agreement should be voided.[195] Actually, the court held an opinion that if the cause of the action is meritorious per se, and the plaintiff who needs financial assistance indeed wishes to commence a lawsuit, then the degree of the control maintained by the funder will not be taken into account when determining the validity of the funding contract.[196] Furthermore, the court developed a definition of intermeddling which means a third party funder encourages another person (the plaintiff) to commence a lawsuit 'which otherwise the person would not have brought'.[197] According to this view, the intermeddling of a litigation funding agreement does not stem from the participation of a stranger (the funder) in a given lawsuit, but from the fact that the litigation would have not occurred without the funder's 'encouragement'.[198] Unlike legal practice of champerty (profit maintenance) in other common law jurisdictions, the approach adopted in Colorado is quite unique since it allows the non-party's (a litigation funder's) involvement in a lawsuit. What it concerns is that the desire to commence litigation is indeed from the person whose interests is infringed, but not from a non-party (a funder).

The core issue within a third party litigation funding is that the funder materially helps the impecunious plaintiff who has suffered harm to file a lawsuit to redress wrongs done to him. Regarding the viewpoint held by the Colorado court, it discourages litigation which would not have been brought without the involvement of a non-party (a funder). Actually, for an impecunious plaintiff, without the financial support by a third party funder, he will not be able to initiate a lawsuit. But does this condition fall within the scope of the implication of the Colorado court? The Colorado court might mean to stress that the legality of a litigation funding

---

[193] *Rancman v. Interim Settlement Funding Corp*. 99 Ohio St.3d 121 (2003), para 125.

[194] See Anthony J. Sebok, 'The Inauthentic Claim', *Vanderbilt Law Review*, (2011), Volume 64, 61, p. 94.

[195] *Bashor v. Northland Ins. Co.*, 29 Colo. App. 81, 86 (1970).

[196] See Anthony J. Sebok, 'The Inauthentic Claim', *Vanderbilt Law Review*, (2011), Volume 64, 61, pp. 94–95.

[197] *Casserleigh v. Wood*, 119 F. 308, 312 (8th Cir. 1902 ('[champerty] is committed when a man, with a view of fomenting litigation, encourages another to bring a suit or to make a defense which otherwise he would not have brought or made').

[198] See John C.P. Goldberg, Anthony J. Sebok and Benjamin C. Zipursky, *Tort Law: Responsibilities and Redress, cases and materials*, (Aspen Publishers, 2012), Aspen Publishers, pp. 578–580.

agreement depends on the cause of action in the legal sense but not in financial regard. In other words, it requires the cause of action to be meritorious, and the plaintiff should be *bona fide*. The financial obstacle of a lawsuit is irrelevant when whether or not the litigation would have been brought by the plaintiff is decided. In fact, what the Colorado court attempted to convey is that the litigant would not have developed the desire or interest in pursuing a lawsuit without the funder's 'incitement'.[199] If a plaintiff has been aware of the fact that he is qualified to commence a lawsuit and wishes to do so, the involvement or even 'intermeddling' of a third party funder would not be considered to be unlawful.[200] On the contrary, if the plaintiff per se, does not have any intention to initiate a lawsuit, or he does not want to solve dispute through the judicial way, the litigation is brought simply because of the 'encouragement' of the third party funder. Under this circumstance, the funding contract will be held illegal.[201]

In summary, as analysed before, the TPLF, as a sort of champerty (profit maintenance), has been permitted in some cases, but the legality of TPLF is still uncertain in many states.[202] In many other common law jurisdictions, the governments have issued some policies to widen the access to justice.[203] The US, which is one of the most developed economic entities, has no reasons to reject the use of TPLF. The main issue is not the confirmation of TPLF's legality, but to properly regulate the use of it.

---

[199]See Anthony J. Sebok, 'The Inauthentic Claim', *Vanderbilt Law Review*, (2011), Volume 64, 61, p. 94.

[200]Ibid.

[201]The Colorado approach could be well illustrated by *Casserleigh v. Wood*. In this case, Casserleigh (a stranger) presented the Wood Family with evidence which could prove that the Woods had a valid claim for land that had once been owned by their deceased father. Casserleigh offered the important evidence to the Woods on the condition that, if they used it and they recovered the land (or a sum in compensation for the loss of the land), they would give a portion of that recovery to Casserleigh. The Woods agreed the offer by Casserleigh. However, when the claim was finally successful, the Woods refused to pay Casserleigh from the recovery got from the judgment and claimed that under common law the champertous contract between the Woods and Casserleigh should be voided. But the Colorado court did not view the lawsuit brought by the Woods as unlawful and did not hold that the introduction of the key evidence by Casserleigh made the litigation unlawful. The Colorado court indicated that it would be supremely unjust if the Woods could not pursue the lawsuit just because, although they knew that their rights were being violated, and they wanted to secure their rights, they lacked the resources necessary to sue. See *Casserleigh v. Wood*, 14 Colo.App. 265, (1900), para 271.

[202]See Jason Lyon, 'Revolution in Progress: Third-Party Funding of American Litigation', *UCLA Law Review*, (2011), Volume 58, 571, p. 590.

[203]For example, in the UK, the Access to Justice Act 1999 aimed at widening the access to justice for people; In Ontario and Quebec, class proceeding fund and Fonds d'aide aux recours collectifs also facilitate the access to justice, especially, for plaintiffs in class actions; In Australia, third party litigation funding is quite developed in financing commercial cases.

### 5.4.2 Ethical Concerns

In this regard, in the US like elsewhere, one of the major concerns is the integrity of the lawyer-client relationship.[204] The introduction of a third-party funder (non-party) into this relationship will bring problems in client confidentiality, impartiality, professional judgment and ultimately the client's control over the litigation.[205] For example, in a funded case, it is obvious that the funder instead of the litigant pays the attorney, making it difficult or even impossible for the lawyer to uphold the client-attorney privilege and fully represent his client.[206] The lawyer's duty of loyalty owed to his client is threatened to be undermined by the funder.[207]

The unique relationship created by a TPLF agreement endangers the client's control over the claim. Third party funders, particularly big funding companies, are always interested in direct the claim in order to ensure that the action is managed for the funders' best interests.[208] In fact, this concern has its reflections in White Paper produced by the Working Group of American Bar Association (ABA) stressing that the attorney should exercise independently without the influence of the third party funder, and the attorney must not permit a third party to interfere with the exercise of independent professional judgment.[209] Some states have also issued ethics opinions in order to prevent the funder's control of the court proceeding. For

---

[204] Jasminka Kalajdzic, Peter Cashman and Alana Longmoore, 'Justice for profit, a comparative analysis of Australian, Canadian and US third party litigation funding', *American Journal of Comparative Law*, (2013), Volume 61, 93, p. 135.

[205] See Julia H. McLaughlin, 'Litigation funding: charting a legal and ethical course', *Vermont Law Review*, (2006), Volume 31, 615, pp. 650–654; and see Jasminka Kalajdzic, Peter Cashman and Alana Longmoore, 'Justice for profit, a comparative analysis of Australian, Canadian and US third party litigation funding', *American Journal of Comparative Law*, (2013), Volume 61, 93, pp. 135–136.

[206] Geoffrey Hazard, 'An Historical Perspective on the Attorney-Client Privilege', *California Law Review*, (1978), Volume 66(5), 1061, pp. 1065–1067.

[207] See Julia H. McLaughlin, 'Litigation funding: charting a legal and ethical course', *Vermont Law Review*, (2006), Volume 31, 615, p. 651.

[208] US Chamber Institute for Legal Reform, 'Selling Lawsuit, Buying Troubles: Third-party Litigation Funding in the United State', (2009), p. 7, available at http://legaltimes.typepad.com/files/thirdpartylitigationfinancing.pdf (accessed on 24 August 2016); In a Florida case [Abu-Ghazaleh v. Chaul, 36 So. 3d 691, 693 (Fla. Dist. Ct. App. 2009)], the funder had the right 'to approve the filing of the lawsuit; controlled the selection of the plaintiffs' attorneys; recruited fact and expert witnesses; received, reviewed and approved counsel's bills; and had the ability to veto any settlement agreements'. Cited from Ethics Committee of the Commercial and Federal Litigation Section of the New York State Bar Association, 'Report on the Ethical Implications of Third-Party Litigation Funding', (April, 2013), p. 10.

[209] The American Bar Association Commission on Ethics 20/20 (ABA Commission) 'White Paper on Alternative Litigation Finance', available at http://www.americanbar.org/content/dam/aba/administrative/ethics_2020/20111019_draft_alf_white_paper_posting.authcheckdam.pdf (accessed on 24 August 2016).

instance, New York Rule of Professional Conduct mandates the lawyer to insist that funders not attempt to control the lawyer's professional judgment.[210]

The ethical concerns specifically raised by TPLF include the 'alliance' between the lawyer and the funder. For instance, several state bar associations (e.g. New Jersey, Pennsylvania, Missouri and Maryland state bar associations)[211] expressed opinions on the ethical concerns about the lawyer's recommendation of a funder. For instance, New Jersey Professional Ethics Opinion provides that if the lawyer advises a client to seek litigation funding, the lawyer should also warn the client about the potential loss of attorney-client privilege when a third party funder involves in this case.[212]

The introduction of a third party litigation funder into the primary lawyer-and-client relationship will give rise to concern about the preservation of the client's confidentiality.[213] Rule 1.6(a) of the *Model Rules of Professional Conduct* (the Model Rules) provides that 'a lawyer shall not reveal information relating to representation of a client unless the client gives informed consent.'[214] Under this rule, the client's approval is required prior to the disclosure of confidential information. The lawyer must fully explain to his client the terms of funding agreements, the consequences of the information disclosure to a third party and ensure that the clients are aware of the risks the TPLF agreement presents.[215] The potential waiver

210 New York Rule of Professional Conduct, (2010), S 1.8(f)(2) and 5.4(c), available at https://www.nycla.org/siteFiles/NYRulesofProfessionalConduct4109_362.pdf (accessed on 24 August 2016).

211 See Ethics Committee of the Commercial and Federal Litigation Section of the New York State Bar Association, 'Report on the Ethical Implications of Third-Party Litigation Funding', (April, 2013), p. 3, available at http://www.nysba.org/workarea/DownloadAsset.aspx?id=25665 (accessed on 24 August 2016).

212 New Jersey Advisory Committee on Professional Ethics Opinion 691, (2001).

213 Practically, when a funder 'evaluates' a would-be funded case, he may seek for the access to the information and documents relevant to the case, which may cause a risk that this information would no longer be covered by the lawyer-client privilege. There are some exceptions to this phenomenon, for example, ALFA, Juridica and Oasis Legal Finance have all indicated that they do not seek access to information covered by the attorney-client privilege when performing due diligence prior to funding a claim. See American Bar Association Working Group, Working Group's Issue Paper Concerning Alternative Litigation Financing, American Bar Association Comments (2011), available at http://www.americanbar.org/content/dam/aba/migrated/2011_build/ethics_2020/comments_on_alternative_litigation_financing_issues_paper.authcheckdam.pdf (accessed on 26 August 2016).

214 *Model Rules of Professional Conduct*, Rule 1.6(a), available at http://www.americanbar.org/groups/professional_responsibility/publications/model_rules_of_professional_conduct/model_rules_of_professional_conduct_table_of_contents.html (accessed on 26 August 2016).

215 The American Bar Association Commission on Ethics 20/20 (ABA Commission) 'White Paper on Alternative Litigation Finance', p. 4, available at http://www.americanbar.org/content/dam/aba/administrative/ethics_2020/20111019_draft_alf_white_paper_posting.authcheckdam.pdf (accessed on 26 August 2016). With regards to the information disclosure, the White Paper further states that 'if they are not experienced in dealing with these funding transactions, lawyers who advise clients in connection with alternative litigation finance must become fully informed about the risks and benefits of these transactions, in order to provide competent advice to clients'.

of the lawyer-client privilege regarding information disclosure to a third party litigation funder should also be informed to the client.[216] State bar association, for instance, New Jersey provides that a lawyer must ensure that its client fully understands the risks of information disclosure, including the possible loss of the attorney-client privilege.[217] Philadelphia adopts a 'narrow' approach with regards to the information disclosure, indicating that the lawyer should provide the funder with information which would be discoverable by the lawyer's adversary.[218]

In case law, the Delaware court explored an exception to the lawyer-client privilege by ordering the sharing of the client's information between the funder and the lawyer during their discussion about potential TPLF agreements in a recent case.[219] It means the Delaware court upheld a viewpoint that a disclosure of client's documents to the funder would break the lawyer-client privilege. However, in this regard, a Texas court held that the disclosure of confidential documents to potential funders did not violate the client-attorney privilege.[220]

## 5.5 Concerns and Policy Arguments Brought by the Use of TPLF for Shareholder Litigation

Third party funding of shareholder litigation raises special issues that do not occur, or do not present themselves in the same form when TPLF is used in general commercial cases. Especially in shareholder class actions, it may prove difficult to combine opt-out principles with a TPLF system whereby the funder wants individual agreements with each and every class member, which would defeat the purpose of the class action or in any case leads to a sort of opt-in system.

### 5.5.1 *The Third Party Funder's Financial Adequacy*

Shareholder litigation involving high litigation costs usually creates financial pressure on shareholder plaintiffs and litigation funders.[221] In a funded shareholder

---

[216] The American Bar Association Commission on Ethics 20/20 (ABA Commission) 'White Paper on Alternative Litigation Finance', p. 4, available at http://www.americanbar.org/content/dam/aba/administrative/ethics_2020/20111019_draft_alf_white_paper_posting.authcheckdam.pdf (accessed on 24 August 2016).

[217] New Jersey Advisory Committee on Professional Ethics Opinion 691, (2001), available at http://njlaw.rutgers.edu/collections/ethics/acpe/acp691_1.html (accessed on 24 August 2016).

[218] Philadelphia Bar Association Opinion 99-8 (February 2000), available at http://www.philadelphiabar.org/page/EthicsOpinion99-8?appNum=2 (accessed on 24 August 2016).

[219] *Leader Technologies, Inc. v. Facebook Inc.*, 719 F. Supp. 2d 373 (D. Del. 2010).

[220] *Mondis Technology Ltd. v. LG Electronics, Inc.*, 2011 WL 1714304 (E.D. Tex. May 4, 2011).

[221] Funders here may refer to third party litigation funders and lawyers working on contingent fee basis.

lawsuit, court charges, lawyers' fees, other litigation expenditures on the part of the shareholder plaintiffs and potential adverse fees paid to the opposite party must also be borne by the funder, which may place a higher burden on the funder's financial capacity than that required in an ordinary civil lawsuit. In order to avoid funder's empty promises and the termination of funding during the court proceedings caused by a financial shortage, the funder's financial capacity must be guaranteed. The practical problem here is how the funder's financial capacity should be warranted. In the past (before 2013), Australia tried to do this through prudential regulation, where funders needed a Financial Services Licence prior to the beginning of their practice, and meeting capital adequacy rules was a precondition for getting a licence.[222] However, the new rules contained in Guide 248 do not mention anything with regards to the funder's financial capacity.[223] It might be problematic since it creates uncertainty about the solvency of the funders.[224]

This concern will be further enhanced in the event that the funder is overseas-based and has no assets in the given country.[225] For example, in a Canadian class action, *Dugal v. Manulife Financial Corporation* (2011 ONSC 1785), the funder on the plaintiff's side was Claims Funding International (CFI) based in Ireland and had no assets in Canada. It did not provide any solid evidence concerning its financial capacity to satisfy any cost order that would be made.[226] The Canadian court ordered CFI to pay security into court in stages (an initial payment of $500,000; an additional $1,000,000 after certification; and a

---

[222]The capital adequacy is one of the preconditions that should be met before a Financial Service License is awarded.

[223]Regulatory Guide 248: Litigation schemes and proof of debt schemes: Managing conflicts of interest, (April 2013).

[224]The reason why Australia replaces the AFSL by the Guide 248 to regulate third party litigation funding might be that the Australian legislators want to govern TPLF in the legal but not financial realm. Third party funders are expected to considered as legal service practitioners rather than financial product providers. See the office of the legal services commissioner, 'the regulation of third party litigation funding in Australia—discussion paper', (March 2012), pp. 4–5&10–11; Compared to the requirement for third party funders set out in AFSL, rules and thresholds for funders in Guide 248 are less strict and lowers in Guide 248 which mainly deals with the conflicts of interests in TPLF-funded cases among parties involved. Financial adequacy requirement for funders are not found in the Guide 248. In fact, it has been indicated that the absence of financial capacity requirement is problematic, and it is suggested that such kind of requirement should be incorporated. See Ross Mclnnes, 'Australia: ASIC issues litigation funding guidance to manage conflicts of interests, (June, 8th, 2013), available at http://www.mondaq.com/australia/x/243848/Class+Actions/ASIC+issues+litigation+funding+guidance+to+manage+conflicts+of+interest (accessed on 26 August 2016); and see John Emmerig and Michael Legg, 'Litigation Funding in Australia: More Swings and Roundabouts as Lawyers Withdraw Application to be Funders', (February, 2014), available at http://www.mondaq.com/australia/x/292544/Class+Actions/Litigation+Funding+In+Australia+More+Swings+And+Roundabouts+As+Lawyers+Withdraw+Application+To+Be+Funders (accessed on 26 August 2016).

[225]For instance, in a Canadian class action *Dugal v. Manulife Financial Corporation* 2011 ONSC 1785, the funder on the plaintiff's side is Claims Funding International (CFI) based in Ireland and it has no assets in Canada.

[226]*Dugal v. Manulife Financial Corporation* (2011 ONSC 1785), para 35.

further $2,500,000 90 days prior to trial).[227] This sort of security for cost ordered by the court can also be found in other Canadian cases.[228]

In general, this book suggests that a legal practice regulatory authority could be appointed to control the funder's capital capacity.[229] As indicated later in the part of

---

[227]*Dugal v. Manulife Financial Corporation* (2011 ONSC 1785), supplementary reasons.

[228]For instance, *Labourers' Pension Fund of Central and Eastern Canada v Sino-Forest Corporation*, (2012 ONSC 2937). The funder (CFI) was also ordered to pay security for costs in stages (the amounts in that case were $750,000 initially; $1,500,000 after certification and $3750,000 prior to trial).

[229]There was discussion about whether a financial service regulatory body or a legal practice regulatory authority should be imposed to regulate the industry of third party litigation funding. For example, before 2012 TPLF was considered as financial service and funders were required to hold a financial service license in Australia. But the Australian High Court's decision in *International Litigation Partners Pte Ltd v Chameleon Mining NL* declared that funders could be exempted from holding a financial service license. And litigation funding was no long regarded to be financial service. In April 2013, Australian Securities and Investment Commission (ASIC) issued *Regulatory Guide 248: Litigation Schemes and Proof of Debt Schemes: Managing Conflicts of Interests (Guide 248)* to regulate TPLF. However, the Guide 248 was criticized to be insufficient, which only deals with the 'conflict of interests', but other aspects (i.e. the funder's financial adequacy, and the funder's loyalty duty) are not mentioned. [see, for example, Ross Mclnnes, 'ASIC issues litigation funding guidance', (June 2013), available at http://www.claytonutz.com/publications/edition/6_june_2013/20130606/asic_issues_litigation_funding_guidance.page (accessed on 26 August 2016)]; It is generally though that the Australian government has a famously 'hands off' approach to the regulation of litigation funders. [see Wayne Attrill, 'The Regulation of Conflicts of Interest in Australian Litigation Funding', (August 2013), available at http://www.imf.com.au/docs/default-source/site-documents/the-regulation-of-conflicts-of-interest-in-australian-litigation-funding—wayne-attrill-19-aug-13 (accessed on 26 August 2016)]; It was indicated that for better regulation of TPLF, it should be put into the realm of legal practice instead of financial service. (See The Office of the Legal Service Commissioner, 'The Regulation of the Third Party Funding Litigation Funding in Australia: A Discussion Paper, March 2012, pp. 4–5). It is further indicated that TPLF is indeed in relation to financial service, but it is more closely aligned to the practice of law. It is more reasonable to classify TPLF as legal service in the sense that a fiduciary relationship between the funders, the lawyers, the courts and the funded parties are a key element in TPLF. As a matter of fact, unlike most of other financial service products, litigation funding has potential to impact directly on both the practice of law and the operation of the judicial system. (See The Legal Service Commissioner, 'Litigation Funding in Australia, in Response to Standing Committee of Attorneys-General Discussion Paper', September 2006, p. 30); A financial service license is only appropriate to those entities whose business is only doing so but not relates to other realm. For instance, regulations for financial service only require the disclosure of the financial status of the entity, but not include the disclosure of such things as the relationships between the funder and his client, the rates at which services are to be provided, or the litigant's rights to challenge bills, receive information or advice. More importantly, a litigation funder, as a participant in judicial activities, owed duties to the judicial system. For example, do not corrupt the justice system; ensure the efficient and proper administration of justice. All of these aspects cannot be regulated through rules for financial service. (See The Legal Service Commissioner, 'Litigation Funding in Australia, in Response to Standing Committee of Attorneys-General Discussion Paper', September 2006, p. 30); In fact, classifying TPLF as legal service is not unique. For instance, in the US, third party litigation funders are considered to be legal profession. The regulation on litigation funders (mainly about the ethical issues) is achieved by code from the bar association. For instance, American Bar Association Ethics 20/20; The

'proposal for China' (5.7), litigation funders must hold a licence granted by the Justice Bureau and then register with the Bureau for supervision. The funder's financial capacity is one of the key requirements that should be met before the licence is issued. In a given case, whether or not a security order is required is subject to the court's discretion. In the event that the funder needs to advance security for costs, like the Canadian approach, the deposit money could be paid in stages.

### 5.5.2 *The Opt-in and Opt-out Dilemma in Funded Class Actions*

It is not easy to reconcile TPLF with an opt-out class action system. Take the Australian practice regarding TPLF for class actions as an example to illustrate the practical dilemma. Part IVA of the Federal Court of Australia Act 1976 (Cth) (FCA Act)[230] provides an 'opt-out' class action procedure. Section 33J describes a mechanism for members who are already in a class action to 'opt out' of it at a later stage if they wish, by simply filing a notice to the court of their intention, without providing a reason for the 'opt-out'.[231] When the class action is funded by a third party litigation funder, the normal practice is that the funder requires the funded group to sign a litigation funding agreement where 'opt-in' is applied. The practical dilemma here is could a litigation funding agreement only finance just a group of member plaintiffs but not all? Is it feasible to allow class members who were originally members of the class to opt out after the TPLF has been agreed upon?

Generally, the reason for seeking a third party funder to financially assist a class action is that the group of members is not financially capable to afford the costly litigation. The main purpose of a class action is that a group of persons suffering

(Footnote 229 continued)

Association of the Bar of the City of New York Committee on Professional Ethics, 'Formal Opinion 2011–2: Third Party Litigation Financing'; TPLF in the UK is generally regulated by a voluntary code of conduct for litigation funders. (see Association of Litigation Funders, code of conduct, http://associationoflitigationfunders.com/code-of-conduct/) (accessed on 26 August 2016); and see Civil Justice Council News Release, http://www.judiciary.gov.uk/wp-content/uploads/JCO/Documents/CJC/Publications/CJC+papers/CJC+News+Release++Code+of+Conduct+for+Litigant+Funders.pdf (access on 26 August 2016) It is not found that these voluntary codes regulate litigation funders as financial service provider. Actually, it was suggested that apart from the voluntary code, regulations on legal service could be introduced to monitor the litigation funding industry. (see Jackson's final report 2009, p. 119); and see Christopher Hodges, John Peysner and Angus Nurse, 'Litigation Funding, Status and Issues', (January 2012), pp. 181–182.

[230]Available at http://www.austlii.edu.au/au/legis/cth/consol_act/fcoaa1976249/ (accessed on 26 August 2016).

[231]See Lang Thai, 'Commercial litigation funding: the need to impose regulations to improve the outcome of the shareholder class actions', *Journal of the Australasian Law Teachers Association*, (2011), Volume 4, 1, pp. 12–13.

from the same wrongdoing aggregates together to share litigation costs. All members of a class action are required to afford collectively litigation costs, and share the proceeds brought by a successful outcome. Theoretically, a member of a class action could choose to 'opt out' of a litigation funding agreement but still stay in the class action. Other members accepting the funding agreement can 'contribute' to the case by sharing potential benefits with the funder. However, how do the members refusing the funding agreement make a contribution to the litigation? The first option could be that they would fund themselves, which is not problematic per se. But in practice, how could impecunious members do that? In such a case, it is highly possible that they would become free riders in the class action, which, in fact, violates the principle and policy of the class action. The concern about litigation funding in class actions mainly refers to the second situation, under which impecunious shareholders refuse a litigation funding agreement, but still intend to participate in the class litigation.

In case law, it was proposed that people can join in a class action by signing a funding agreement.[232] But this is substantially an 'opt in' approach instead of the 'opt out' one provided in 33 J of the *Federal Court of Australia Act*, which actually deprives members refusing the funding agreement of the right to participate in the class action. Additionally, defining a group of class action members by reference to persons who have the same contractual relationship with a litigation funder is not in line with the overall aim of a class action (for instance, 'increase the access to justice and judicial efficiency in the form of a common binding decision for the benefit of all aggrieved persons').[233]

Although this so-called closed class mechanism appears to be contrary to the rules established in statutory law, the Australian courts, in fact, have permitted the use of this mechanism in some cases.[234] From 1992 to 2009, closed classes have been adopted in 13 of the 18 funded class actions pursued in the Federal Court.[235] But the closed class mechanism, indeed, produces as a side effect that a sizeable rump of the plaintiffs who have not entered into a funding contract but who otherwise meet the class definition of the initial action may commence a second action (open or closed) after the previous closed one.[236] This phenomenon would

---

[232]*Multiplex Funds Management Ltd v. P. Dawson Nominees Pty Ltd* [2007] 164 FCR 275. (Multiplex II).

[233]Multiplex II [2007] 164 FCR 275.

[234]For instance, Multiplex II [2007] 164 FCR 275.

[235]Vince Morabito, 'An Empirical Study of Australia's Class Action Regimes, Second Report: Litigation Funders, Competing Class Actions, Opt Out Rates, Victorian Class Actions and Class Representatives', (September 2010), pp. 39–40.

[236]For instance, *Anthony Scott & Anor v Oz Minerals Limited* (Federal Court proceeding NSD 1433 of 2010) and *Hobbs Anderson Investments Pty Limited v Oz Minerals Limited* (Federal Court proceeding NSD 1127 of 2009). See US Chamber Institute for Legal Reform, Third Party Litigation Financing in Australia: Class Actions, Conflicts and Controversy, (October 2013), p. 10.

lead to substantial duplication of legal costs and has the potential to undermine the goals of efficiency and certainty underlying the class action regime in Australia.[237]

In fact, litigation funding is a new concept which was only approved by the Australian High Court in 2006 and the Australian class action procedure was enacted in 1991.[238] It is the same in other countries where TPLF is allowed. Therefore, statutory rules concerning the procedures of class actions have no provision concerning funding issues. In this regard, legal scholars indicate that the law needs to explore a way where the traditional opt-out procedure of class action reconciles to the need for introducing litigation funding.[239] For example, statutory rules need to clearly indicate the status of those persons wishing to participate in a class action but not intend to accept litigation funding in a class action. This book holds a view that these people should pay their portion of litigation costs from their own budget, otherwise they should be excluded from the class action in order to prevent free-riding.

### *5.5.3 The Termination of Third Party Litigation Funding*

In England and Wales, the most recent version of the voluntary Code of Conduct for Litigation Funders drafted by the association of litigation funders of England and Wales provides that only under limited circumstances the funder can terminate the funding.[240] For instance, when there has been a material breach of the litigation funding agreement by the funded party. In Canada, *Metzler Investment GmbH v Gildan Activewear Inc*[241] was the first case in Ontario to consider the legality and fairness of a commercial third party funding agreement. The funding agreement of this case provided that the funder (CFI) could terminate the agreement on a seven-day notice, which was considered to be faulty by the court.[242] The reason could be that such short notice is not justified towards the plaintiffs.[243] Because of

[237]See US Chamber Institute for Legal Reform, Third Party Litigation Financing in Australia: Class Actions, Conflicts and Controversy, (October 2013), p. 11.

[238]The origin of Australian class action was introduced in Federal Court of Australia Amendment Act 1991 (No. 181 of 1991).

[239]Michael Legg and Louisa Travers, 'Necessity is the mother of invention: the adoption of third-party litigation funding and the closed class in Australian class actions', *Common law world review*, (2009), Volume 38, 245, pp. 250–252; See Jasminka Kalajdzic, Peter Cashman and Alana Longmoore, 'Justice for profit, a comparative analysis of Australian, Canadian and US third party litigation funding', *American Journal of Comparative Law*, (2013), Volume 61, 93, pp. 99–102.

[240]Code of Conduct for Litigation Funders, (January 2014), article 11 & 12.

[241]*Metzler Investment GmbH v Gildan Activewear Inc* [2009] OJ no 3315 (SCJ).

[242]*Metzler Investment GmbH v Gildan Activewear Inc* [2009] OJ no 3315 (SCJ), para 18.

[243]Aaron Dantowitz, 'Commercial Third Party Funding of Class Actions in Ontario: Eight Early Lessons', in Second Annual Securities Litigation Practice Group Symposium, (September 13rd 2012), p. 14. Available at http://www.stockwoods.ca/wp-content/uploads/2012/01/Third_Party_Funding-Final.pdf (accessed on 26 August 2016).

the short notice of the cancellation, the plaintiffs will suddenly run into a funding shortage, making it difficult to continue the proceeding. Fearing the termination of the funding, the plaintiffs may compromise with the funders in order to satisfy them to avoid a funding cancellation. This means that, to a certain extent, the funder controls the proceeding. This concern would be further enhanced in the special context of shareholder litigation. In consideration of the high litigation costs in shareholder litigation, third party litigation funder, compared to an individual lawyer working on a contingent basis, has a stronger financial capacity and risk externalizing ability to pay a big amount of money to fund such a case.[244] On the part of the plaintiffs, they largely rely on the professional litigation funder in terms of financial adequacy. Therefore, professional funding firms will be highly possible to 'monopolize' the market of high-valued litigation (for instance, shareholder lawsuits). Considering that, an easy termination by funders is not equitable to the plaintiffs and means that the funder will conduct and control the proceeding to a large extent.

In this regard, Lord Jackson, in his final report, holds a view that 'the funder should be obliged to continue to provide whatever funding it originally contracted to provide, unless there are proper grounds to withdraw'.[245] But the final report does not indicate what constitutes 'a proper ground' for the funder's withdrawal. Perhaps, a proper ground for the termination for the funding may include, among others, the funded party contracts with another funder without the consent of the previous funder.[246]

### 5.5.4 *The Risk of Refusal to Share*

If a funded case is won and damages have been awarded to the plaintiff, the funder will claim a share of this award. If the plaintiff refuses to share with the funder, then

[244]See *supra* 5.1.2.

[245]Lord Jackson's Final Report on Civil Litigation (December 2009), p. 119.

[246]For instance, the funded litigant promises in the litigation funding agreement that he will give 50% of the final recoveries to the funder (the previous one). The litigant concludes litigation contract with another funder with the same promise that the funder will get a 50% of monetary recoveries if the funded case is won. (take the Australia's litigation funding company as an example, the commission charged by a funder normally ranges between 20 and 50%) Under this circumstance, the previous funder's interests are likely to be impaired because the funded party's promise to share 50% of the monetary remedies with each of the funder seems unrealistic. In this case, the first funder could terminate the funding. With regards to the termination of the funding, s 11.2 of the Code of Conduct for Litigation Funders in England and Wales (January 2014) provides several proper grounds under which the funder could withdraw his funding 'terminate the LFA in the event that the Funder or Funder's Subsidiary or Associated Entity: (1) reasonably ceases to be satisfied about the merits of the dispute; (2) reasonably believes that the dispute is no longer commercially viable; or (3) reasonably believes that there has been a material breach of the LFA by the Funded Party'.

it is a simple matter of breach of contract which can be resolved before the courts. Nevertheless, attention needs to be drawn to the fact that in China it has happened more than once that lawyers working on a contingency basis are refused by the client to share damages awarded by the court. The same issue may also happen in the context of TPLF-funded case, thus this book recommends that an *ex ante* measure needs to be designed to mitigate such risk. The solution is suggested to be: a rule should be introduced if a judgment or a settlement in favour of the plaintiffs is made, the losing party should pay the monetary compensations to the court first. The court then distributes the damages between the funder and the plaintiffs according to rate agreed previously in the litigation funding contract.

## 5.6 The Potential for TPLF in China

### *5.6.1 The Current Approach to Fund Shareholder Litigation in China*

Chinese law allows two sorts of shareholder litigation—private securities litigation and shareholder derivative actions. However, no statutory rules provide the funding issues with regards to shareholder litigation, which might be considered as a reason why the shareholder litigation is rarely used in China. For instance, from 2006 (shareholder derivative actions were legally introduced) to 2013, only 103 derivative cases were brought into Chinese courts.[247]

At present, apart from self-funding, the only possible approach to finance shareholder litigation in China is through contingency fee arrangements concluded between lawyers and shareholder clients. The law provides, however, that collective litigation (mass litigation) should not be funded by contingency fee arrangements.[248] In light of that, the private securities litigation filed as the form of collective action is excluded from being funded by lawyers.[249,250] On the other hand,

[247]*See* Shaowei Lin, "Derivative Actions in China: Case Analysis", (2014), *Hong Kong Law Journal*, Volume 44, 621, p 638.

[248]In China, the *Measures for the Administration of Lawyers' Fees* (the MALF) enacted in 2006 legally permits contingency fee arrangement in China. (Art. 11 to Art. 13) But it has been indicated that it is prohibited in collective actions, criminal cases and administrative litigation. (Art. 12).

[249]Article 12 of '*The Supreme People's Court: Notice of the Supreme People's Court on the Relevant Issues concerning the Acceptance of Cases of Disputes over Civil Tort Arising from False Statement in the Securities Market*' (关于受理证券市场因虚假陈述引发的民事侵权纠纷案件有关问题的通知) provides that a private securities lawsuit could be brought individually (单独诉讼) and collectively (共同诉讼).

[250]In practice, there are no evidences to show that shareholder derivative actions are regarded as a sort of collective action, and derivative actions could be funded by contingency fee arrangements. See Guanghua Yu and Junhai Liu, 'Legislation and the enforcement of law', (in Chinese), (理性立法和法律实施), commercial law forum no. 330, the minute of this forum could be available at (in Chinese) http://www.civillaw.com.cn/article/default.asp?id=43662 (accessed on 26 August 2016).

the law does not prevent the shareholder derivative action from being funded by contingency fee arrangement, however, this approach is confronted with practical difficulties.[251] For instance, besides lawyers' fees, in China, the plaintiff in a derivative action must pay an amount of court fees (case acceptance fee and application fee) which could not be funded by the contingency fee arrangement. According to the current rules, court fees are charged based on the monetary value at dispute.[252] In fact, a shareholder action usually involves a big sum of money, and accordingly, the court fees paid by the litigant would be high.[253] In light of that, the high court charges will still need to be afforded by the plaintiff shareholders, although the lawyer's fee could be funded by the contingency fee arrangement. And also, the disequilibrium of costs and benefits creates disincentives for potential shareholder litigants. Take a shareholder derivative action as an example. Financial compensation brought by a successful claim directly flows to the company rather than the shareholder plaintiff who commenced the action before. The plaintiffs, particularly minority shareholder plaintiffs, just benefit from a small share of the gains on a *pro rata* basis.[254] On the part of the shareholder plaintiff, the derivative action is likely to be an under-valued claim. For a rational lawyer, he might hesitate to contract with the shareholder plaintiff on a contingent basis for the reason that most of the financial remedies belong to the company but not his client (the shareholder plaintiff).

### 5.6.2 *Why Does China Need TPLF?*

In the chapter regarding public funding, it appears that the main concern is the potential influence from the government which may negatively affect the public

[251]See Guanghua Yu and Junhai Liu, 'Legislation and the enforcement of law', (in Chinese), (理性立法和法律实施), commercial law forum no. 330, the minute of this forum could be available at (in Chinese) http://www.civillaw.com.cn/article/default.asp?id=43662 (accessed on 26 August 2016).

[252]See article 13 and 14 of the *Measures for the Payment of Litigation Costs* (the MPLC).

[253]For example, in *Sanlian Shangshe 2009* case (a shareholder derivative action), the disputed value proposed by the plaintiff was approximately 5 million RMB. Therefore, according to the calculation method stipulated in the MPLC, the court charges will be about 300 thousand RMB. Although this case was rejected by the court, what we want to demonstrate here is the high court charges in a derivative action.

[254]The expected *pro rata* share of monetary compensations is only resulted from a circumstance that the value of the company's shares rises sufficiently after a successful action. But the result whether the share value will rise is far from certain as a successful action may reduce the share value because the company's reputation could be negatively affected by the claim. In general, it lacks incentives for shareholders to launch a derivative action if he is not financed by other funding. See Arad Reisberg, Derivative Actions and Corporate Governance: Theory and Operation, Oxford University Press, (2007), p. 222.

funder's integrity.[255] Unlike the public funding, TPLF is private in nature, and the funders do not belong to the 'inside system'. Although the market of TPLF is and should be regulated through legislations or by public authorities,[256] compared to public funding, TPLF is, indeed, a private funding technique.

China is a country where the doctrine of *stare decisis* is not applied. However, in fact, the Supreme People's Court (SPC) has published a series of guidance books about trials on commercial cases (最高人民法院商事审判指导案例) in order to promote the quality of trials on commercial cases by analysing cases with typical significance.[257,258]

On the other hand, the proper application of legal statutes and interpretation of key issues is expected to be enhanced by the help of the SPC's case reports and case guidance, particularly, in some complicated cases and new cases. For example, in view of the comparatively late promulgation of intellectual property right law, the SPC's case books on intellectual property right lawsuits can provide guidance for complicated cases in this regard to prevent wrong judgments. In consideration of litigation economy, the publication of case books could help to reduce litigation costs and save judicial resources, particularly in high-valued cases (for instance, shareholder litigation, disputes regarding intellectual property right).

In the context of shareholder litigation, the SPC's case books would be of importance both for the courts and for potential litigation parties. First, for the court, the SPC's case guidance will help to deal with shareholder actions more efficiently

[255]See *supra* 4.4.

[256]For example, in Australia, the TPLF is regulated by ASIC (a public authority). In the UK, it is regulated by the Code issued by the ALF (a voluntary association). In the US, it is governed by ABA (a public organization, but not a public authority).

[257]These series of books have been published since 2011. It includes, for example, guidance books about trials of cases concerning contract disputes, cases concerning corporate issues, cases concerning loan guarantee disputes, and financial cases. The most recent one was published in early 2013, and it was specialized in corporate cases and financial cases. See Annual working report of the SPC of 2010, (in Chinese), available at http://www.court.gov.cn/qwfb/sfsj/201105/t20110525_100996.htm (accessed on 26 August 2016).

[258]Apart from commercial cases, the SPC also publishes similar guidance books on trials of cases of intellectual property right. In 2009, the SPC, for the first time, published SPC's annual report on intellectual property right cases (2008) (最高人民法院知识产权案件年度报告2008). Regarding this annual case report, the SPC indicated that it is expected that cases included in this annual report would have potential implication for other cases of the similar type. Case reports on civil litigation was also publicly issued by the SPC. For instance, the understanding and application of judging rules used in guidance cases of the SPC (volume of contract law) in 2012 (最高人民法院指导性案例裁判规则理解与适用:合同卷), see Bixin Jiang and Dongning He, *the understanding and application of judging rules used in guidance cases of the SPC (volume of contract law)*, (China legal publishing house, 2012); In addition to these publicly issued case books, the SPC also internally published case guidelines within the court system (the author once did internship in chamber of criminal cases of the High People's Court of Fujian Province in 2004. There are series of books of analysis of complicated cases in the chamber. These books were only issued within the court system. Now, it is not sure whether there are still such books in the chamber. Perhaps, in the past, those guidance cases were only published internally, but now they have been published publicly).

and more properly. Second, a publicly-published shareholder lawsuit will, indirectly, have deterrent effects on potential wrongdoings in a company. Third, on the part of a shareholder plaintiff, the published case book may help to evaluate the success rate of a lawsuit, and further prevent meaningless effort. Finally, considering the short history of shareholder litigation (either private securities litigation or shareholder derivative actions) in Chinese courts, the issuance of guidance cases in this regard would be helpful to elaborate complicated case issues[259] and improve the qualities of future trials. However, without effective funding techniques, how can 'precedents' of shareholder litigation be established? The lack of effective funding ways of shareholder litigation can even make that Chinese courts have limited opportunities to elaborate unclear and complicated aspects of shareholder litigation. In order to enable the courts to accumulate legal experience in this aspect, it might be possible to conclude that TPLF needs to be introduced in China by being developed at a step-by-step pace with caution.[260]

### 5.6.3 *The Legal Basis for TPLF Under the Current Legal System*

The first chapter of the PRC Civil procedure law (the CPL) provide that one of the purposes of the CPL is to ensure the procedural rights of people.[261] The CPL also aims at maintaining the sound social and economic order by protecting the lawful rights and interests of litigation parties.[262] With regards to the realization of the purpose of 'protecting the people's enforcement of procedural rights', exploring proper techniques to solve funding problems with civil litigation is of significant importance. The reason why Chinese policymakers have not taken further steps to introduce effective funding methods, besides the confirmation of contingency fee arrangements,[263] to finance civil lawsuits mainly caused by the concern malicious

[259]For instance, with regards to the derivative action, how to legally distinguish it from the shareholder direct action; How to determine whether or not a cause of action is tenable; and how to properly apply the 'business judgment rule'. Dan Wang, *Theoretical analysis on shareholders' derivative actions*, (公司派生诉讼论), China legal publishing house (中国法制出版社), 2012, p. 325.

[260]The reason for the 'cautious approach' of TPLF will be illustrated in Chap. 7.

[261]See article 2 of the CPL, available at http://www.lawinfochina.com/display.aspx?id=11161&lib=law&SearchKeyword=&SearchCKeyword=%C3%F1%CA%C2%CB%DF%CB%CF (in Chinese) (accessed on 23 August 2016).

[262]Ibid.

[263]Actually, as indicated before, contingency fee arrangement has not been legally permitted in Law of the People's Republic of China on lawyers (PRC law on lawyers). Theoretically, the law on lawyers is superior to the MALF in legal effect.

actions (恶意诉讼).[264] The 2012 amendment to the CPL adopts several new provisions to avoid malicious actions in order to relieve this concern.[265]

In fact, the appeal for practically implementing the people's procedural rights is very strong in current Chinese society.[266] The basic principles listed in the general provision of the CPL also demonstrates that facilitating the realization of people's procedural rights (for instance, solving funding problems with it), indeed, has jurisprudential basis in the existing law. This book holds a view that TPLF needs be introduced into China to solve funding difficulties, thus practically facilitate the realization of people's procedural rights.

### 5.6.4 *Potential Problems Brought by the Introduction of TPLF in China: From the Perspective of Current Legal System*

#### 5.6.4.1 The Legal Status of the Third Party Litigation Funder

The Chap. 5 of the CPL incorporates rules about litigation participants (诉讼参加人), including litigation parties (plaintiffs, defendants, and the third party 第三人[267]) and litigation representatives (诉讼代理人, usually refers to lawyers).

---

[264]Actually, in China, the prevention of malicious lawsuits has been discussed by legislatures and legal practitioners. Generally, it is thought that malicious actions should be avoided by legislation, and persons bringing such actions should be sanctioned. Particularly, in China, malicious actions in which both parties collude with each other for illegal purposes (e.g. occupy other person's property), need to be strictly prevented by legislations. The 2012 Civil Procedural Law has made new provision in this regard. See Jianhua Xiao, 'Rules On Malicious Prosecution' (论恶意诉讼及其法律规制), *Journal of Renmin University of China*, No. 4, (2012) (in Chinese), p. 13; and see Jianping Lu and Jianghai Ren, 'The Avoidance of Malicious Actions Through Chinese Criminal Law' (恶意诉讼行为刑事规制路径研究), *Journal of Politics and Law*, No. 11, 2012, (in Chinese), p. 2.

[265]One of the most significant aspects of the 2012 amendment to the CPL is that the legislators added some provisions to avoid malicious civil action. For example, article 13 provides that both tow parties in a civil lawsuit should adhere to the principle of good faith in civil proceedings. Article 112 provides that 'where the parties, maliciously in collusion, attempt to infringe upon the lawful rights and interests of other persons by litigation, mediation or any other means, a people's court shall dismiss their claims and impose a fine or detention on the parties according to the severity of the circumstances; and if suspected of any crime, they shall be subject to criminal liability in accordance with law'.

[266]See Weimin Zuo, 'Citizens' right to sue:a study of constitutional and judicial safeguard' (公民诉讼权:宪法与司法保障研究), *Legal Science* 2001 (4); In National People's Congress and Chinese People's Political Consultative Conference of 2013, Weimin Kang (the president of High People's Court of Hunan Province) indicated the importance of practically implementing the people's procedural rights.

[267]The third party (第三人 disan ren) are divided into two catalogues. The first one is a third party with an independent right of claim (有独立请求权第三人 you duli qinqiuquan disan ren), and the

In accordance with the definition of 'the third party' in the CPL, third party funders might be regarded as *the third party without an independent right of claim* (无独立请求权第三人, hereinafter 'the little third party'). CPL provides that the little third party in a civil lawsuit is not entitled to request an independent claim regarding the subject matter of an action between two parties, however, he is *an interested party in law to the outcome of the case.*[268]

In a TPLF agreement, a funder provides an amount of money to financially support the litigant to pursue a lawsuit. A TPLF agreement provides that the funder will be rewarded with an amount of proceeds if the funded case is won. It is obvious that the third party funder has monetary interests in the outcome of the funded case, thus it is easy to understand that the litigation funder can be considered as a little third party in a lawsuit. But, it should be noted that the term applied in the CPL regarding to the little third party is 'an interested party in law to the outcome of the case' (法律上的利害关系). When the legal status of third party litigation funder is considered, it is important to interpret the term—'*an interested party in law*'.

#### 5.6.4.2 How to Interpret the Term of 'an Interested Party in Law to the Outcome of the Case'

Under Chinese law, there is not a precise definition of 'an interested party in law'. Actually, this term is usually interpreted based on legal scholars' opinions from the jurisprudential perspective.[269] Generally, 'an interested party in law' suggests that there is an interested relationship in law between two parties.[270] Contextualizing this interpretation in a TPLF agreement, the essential issue is whether the relationship between the funder and the funded litigant is considered as an interested relationship in law. Prior to answering this question, we should investigate under what circumstance a relationship between two parties could be identified as *an interested relationship in law.*

(Footnote 267 continued)

second one is a third party without an independent right of claim (无独立请求权第三人 wu duli qingqiuquan disan ren). The former one refers to those third parties who deems that he has an independent claim regarding the subject matter of an action between two parties shall have the right to institute an action. And the latter one means those third parties does not have an independent claim regarding the subject matter of an action between two parties but is an interested party in law to the outcome of the case. See article 56 of the CPL.

[268]See article 56(2) of the CPL.

[269]See Xuyong Zhang, 'A new statement of the interested relationship in law', ("法律上利害关系"新表述), *Journal of East China University of Political Science and Law*, 2001(6); See Wei Jiang and Guojun Shan, 'Confirmation of a third party with no independent litigation right for claim' (论民事诉讼中无独立请求权第三人的确定), *Journal of Renmin University of China*, 1997(2).

[270]See Shanghai High People's Court, Explanation of several issues regarding third party in civil litigation (I), (2006).

Under Chinese law, behaviours by human beings could be divided into two main categories: *legal acts* (法律行为) and *factual behaviours* (事实行为).[271] Only the relationship established by a *legal act* could be considered as a relationship in law.[272] Therefore, the main question here needs to be investigated comes down to whether the behaviour of concluding a litigation funding agreement, per se, is a *legal act*. Under the General Principle of the Civil Law of the PRC (the GPCL), article 55 indicates three validity requirements for a *legal act* '(i) the actor should have relevant capacity for civil conduct; (ii) the intention expressed should be genuine; and (iii) the act must not violate the law and the public interest.'[273]

With respect to the three requirements in art. 55, the first two are clear, and it is easy to assess whether those two requirements have been met or not.[274] But how the last requirement—'not violate the law and the public interest' should be examined.[275]

Considering the basic principle of *autonomy of private law* under civil law regime, private individuals could freely engage in any private activities (for instance, conclude a contract) in case that such behaviours are not explicitly banned by law. Different from the common law jurisdiction, there is no traditional prohibition of champerty and maintenance under Chinese law. Hence, concluding a third party litigation funding agreement could not be considered as illegal since it meets the validity requirements for a legal act in art. 55 of the GPCL.

#### 5.6.4.3 How to Regulate the Third Party Litigation Funding Agreement (Contract): From the Perspective of the PRC Contract Law

When the practice of TPLF in other countries (the US, the UK and Australia) is investigated, it is found that TPLF should be properly regulated since several concerns (for instance, ethical concerns, avoidance of unmeritorious claims)are

---

[271]See Ansheng Dong, Juristic Act (民事法律行为 'minshi falv xingwei'), China Renmin University Press, (2012), pp. 159–167; And see Rui Mu, The theory of civil justice act (民法法律行为理论之全部 'minfa falv xingwei lilun zhi quanbu), China University of Political Science and Law Press, (2003), pp. 203–230.

[272]See Xueli Dong and Xiaoyan Wang, 'The requirements of establishment and validity of civil justice act' (论民事法律行为的成立与生效), *Journal of Shandong University (Philosophy and social science)*, 2003(4).

[273]See article 55 of the General Principle of the Civil Law of the People's Republic of China (the GPCL).

[274]See Xueli Dong and Xiaoyan Wang, 'The requirements of establishment and validity of civil justice act', (论民事法律行为的成立与生效), *Journal of Shandong University (Philosophy and social science)*, 2003(4).

[275]Jun Yi, 'Political and philosophical research on clause of the public policy and good morals—focusing on protection of autonomy of will of private individuals' (民法上公序良俗条款的政治哲学思考—以私人自治的维护为中心), *Studies in Law and Business*, 2005(6).

raised by the use of it. As for the regulation of the TPLF in China, we first contemplate to regulate TPLF agreement through PRC Contract Law.

Provisions under PRC Contract Law that could be used to regulate a TPLF contract is article 124, stating:

> Where there are no explicit provisions in the Specific Provisions of this Law or in any other law concerning a certain contract, the provisions in the General Provisions of this Law shall be applied, and reference may be made to the provisions in the Specific Provisions of this Law or in any other law that most closely relate to such contract.[276]

From this article, it could be observed that a TPLF agreement, as a sort of non-specific contract,[277] is regulated by the general provision of the contract law which just provides several basic principles of contract (for instance, a contract should be signed between two *equal* parties), but cannot solve problems specially brought by a TPLF agreement (for instance, the funder's ethical concerns, the damage on the integrity lawyer-and-client relationship). In consideration of that, reforms on the PRC Contract Law need to be carried out to achieve the proper regulation of TPLF. For instance, except for the fifteen types of contracts (for instance, sales contract, leasing contracts), provisions regarding TPLF contract should be added as an independent section of the law, dealing with concerns brought by the TPLF contract. And also, relationship among three participants in a TPLF agreement should be cautiously monitored. For instance, the law should explicitly indicate that the lawyer's duty of loyalty should be owed to the funded litigant but not to the funder. Proposals on the reform of PRC Contract Law will be presented in detail in Chap. 7 of this book.

## 5.7 Summary

The third party litigation funding, as an innovative funding mechanism, has developed for several years in many countries (for instance, Australia, the UK, and the US). Traditionally, it violated the old common law doctrine of prohibiting champerty and maintenance. However, in the wake of fundamental social and economic changes in modern society, this old prohibition has been largely relaxed to allow the use of TPLF.

This Chapter, first gives a general overview of the TPLF mechanism per se, and investigates problems brought by it (such as, ethical concerns, the encouragement of frivolous claims). Then, three typical jurisdictions (Australia, the UK and the US) where the TPLF has been adopted and is rapidly developing are selected to further

---

[276]See article 124 of the PRC Contract Law.

[277]There are specific regulations in the PRC Contract Law for fifteen types of civil contracts, such as sales contracts, gift contracts, contracts for loan of money, and leasing contracts. Other contracts are named 'non-specific' contract (无名合同), which should be subject to article 124 of the PRC Contract Law.

conduct a research on TPLF from an empirical perspective. An examination is also carried out to study how these countries deal with problems brought by TPLF. In addition to that, it is also found that TPLF is subject to regulations in varying degrees in these countries.

Subsequent to the comparative and empirical study, the TPLF's potential for China is examined. Through the studies on relevant Chinese law (for instance, the PRC Civil Procedure Law, the PRC Contract Law), a conclusion is made that TPLF could be used (particularly, fund shareholder litigation in China), but with caution. Reforms in the PRC Contract Law are suggested be carried out for solving potential problems brought by the use of TPLF.

# Chapter 6
# Funding Alternatives Through Fee or Cost Arrangements

## 6.1 Funding by the Company (Indemnity Cost Orders 'ICO' in Shareholder Derivative Actions)

The ICO applied in England is, in nature, a form of litigation funding provided by the company to finance a derivative action. The Civil Procedure Rule 19.9 (E) provides that the court may order a company to indemnify the claimant against liability for costs incurred in a derivative claim which was brought on the name of the company.[1] The rationale for the company's funding is that the company is, essentially, the beneficiary of a successful derivative claim, and the recoveries created by the lawsuit flow to the company directly.[2] Thus, it is reasonable for the company to afford the costs incurred in the proceeding.[3]

---

[1]Civil Procedure Rule (Practice Directions) 19.9 provides 'The court may order the company, body corporate or trade union for the benefit of which a derivative claim is brought to indemnify the claimant against liability for costs incurred in the permission application or in the derivative claim or both'. Available at http://www.justice.gov.uk/courts/procedure-rules/civil/rules/part19#19.9E (accessed on 24 August 2016).

[2]See Arad Reisberg, *Derivative Actions and Corporate Governance: Theory and Operation*, Oxford University Press, (2007), p. 229.

[3]Ibid.



W. Chen, *A Comparative Study of Funding Shareholder Litigation*,
DOI 10.1007/978-981-10-3623-1_6

### 6.1.1 The Origin and Working Mechanism of ICO

The *Wallersteiner v Moir (No 2)*[4,5] case revealed the funding difficulty faced by impecunious shareholder plaintiffs in a derivative lawsuit. In this case, the Court of Appeal held that the company should indemnify Mr. Moir (the plaintiff) for the costs incurred and to be incurred in the forthcoming proceedings.[6] The reasoning by the Court of Appeal was set out as follows:

> Suppose there is good ground for thinking that those in control of a company have been plundering its assets for their own benefit. They should be brought to book. But how is it to be done?… at present there is nothing effective except an action by a minority shareholder. But can a minority shareholder be really expected to take it? He has nothing to gain, but much to lose. He feels strongly that a wrong has been done—and that it should be righted. But he does not feel able to undertake it himself. Faced with an estimate of the costs, he will say: I'm not going to throw away good money after bad'. Some wrongdoers know this and take advantage of it. They loot the company's funds knowing there is little risk of an action being brought against them.[7]

In this case, Lord Denning raised a question why the (impecunious) shareholders would run the risk of filing a derivative claim to safeguard the company's interests if it hardly directly benefited them.[8] According to the fairness doctrine, and also to facilitate shareholder derivative actions, it was desirable to design a mechanism compensating *bona fide* shareholder plaintiffs for the costs incurred in the litigation, regardless of the outcome of the lawsuit in order to remove or at least reduce the formidable funding obstacles for derivative actions.[9]

The only test suggested to be employed when the court decided whether or not to indemnify the plaintiff's litigation costs was that the shareholder plaintiff should

---

[4]*Wallersteiner v Moir (No 2)* [1975] QB 373.

[5]In this case, through a series of manipulative transactions, Dr. Wallersteiner (the defendant), who was a director of the company at issue, had acquired his 80% shares using funds from the company. Mr. Moir (the plaintiff), who was a minority shareholder of the company, had applied to the board of trade to investigate the transaction done by Dr. Wallersteiner, however, he failed. Mr. Moir's request for the disputes to be referred to the shareholders' meeting for decision were also refused by the defendant, therefore, the court was the only place where the transaction could be challenged. At the first stage (Wallersteiner v Moir no. 1), the judgment had been done in favour of the Mr. Moir (the plaintiff), but a further judicial procedure was needed to assess the damages. Dr. Wallersteiner had also applied to appeal to the House of Lords. If the appeal was allowed, Mr. Moir should defend his case in the House of Lords, but Mr. Moir had exhausted all his financial resources through the action for more than ten years. In the Court of Appeal, though it was held that a plaintiff in a derivative claim was not eligible for legal aid, the court ordered the company to indemnify Mr. Moir his costs incurred and to be incurred in the forthcoming proceedings. *Wallersteiner v Moir (No 2)* [1975] QB 373.

[6]*Wallersteiner v Moir (No 2)* [1975] QB 373, at 394.

[7]*Wallersteiner v Moir (No 2)* [1975] QB 373, at 395.

[8]Ibid.

[9]See Arad Reisberg, *Derivative Actions and Corporate Governance: Theory and Operation*, Oxford University Press, (2007), p. 230.

demonstrate *good faith*, and that the claim should be in the company's best interests.[10] Moreover, it was held that the general rule of an indemnity cost order should be that a plaintiff had to apply for this order at the stage when he applied for leave to proceed.[11] But when the court found it appropriate, the indemnity cost order could made at the end of the proceeding.[12] Moreover, it was emphasized that the scrutinize over an indemnity cost order conducted by the court should be 'simple and inexpensive'.[13]

The *Wallersteiner* case considerably influence the subsequent decisions regarding the granting of ICOs.[14] After the *Wallersteiner* case, the rule concerning ICO was further clarified by *Smith v. Croft (No. 1)*.[15] This case started by repeating the principle from *Wallersteiner*, stating that an indemnity cost order could be awarded to impecunious plaintiffs in good faith.[16] However, in *Smith*, Walton J. pointed out that the rule in *Wallersteiner* was oppressive and unfair to the defendant, and the application for the indemnity cost order should not be made *ex post* (at the end of the proceeding), meaning that a stricter judicial scrutiny was actually imposed.[17] Walton J. further suggested an additional test that an indemnity cost order should only be awarded if the court was satisfied that an independent board of directors would have brought the action.[18] Apparently, the test suggested in the *Smith* case would be likely to develop into a mini-trial, which is not in line with the 'simple and inexpensive' principle established in the *Wallersteiner* case and may lower judicial efficiency.[19]

---

[10] *Wallersteiner v Moir (No 2)* [1975] QB 373, at 404.

[11] Previously, there was no requirement that the application for indemnity cost order had to be integrated into the application for leave to proceed. The application was usually made without notice to the other side, shortly after the beginning of the proceeding and on affidavit evidence. But this might lead to a result that the company would thereafter find itself paying for an action which it almost invariably did not want to bring, and which would usually put the whole management under intense pressure. Given that, the application procedure was revised later. And in 19.9 of the Civil Procedure Rule (the CPR), it expressly authorizes the court to give the shareholder plaintiff an order to indemnify the litigation costs out of the company's assets when it thinks appropriate, and also expressly requires the court's approval for the continuance of a derivative action. It means that the application of an indemnity cost order has been integrated into the application for leave to proceed. See CPR 19.9 (3); BG Pette, *Company Law* (2nd edition Longman Law Series, 2005) pp, 219–221; Arad Reisberg, *Derivative Actions and Corporate Governance: Theory and Operation*, Oxford University Press, (2007), p. 231.

[12] *Wallersteiner v Moir (No 2)* [1975] QB 373, at 407.

[13] *Wallersteiner v Moir (No 2)* [1975] QB 373, at 392.

[14] See Qingxiu Bu, 'The Indemnity Order in a Derivative Action', *Company Lawyer*, 2006, 27(1), 2, p. 6.

[15] *Smith v. Croft (No. 1)* [1986] 2 All ER 551.a.

[16] Ibid.

[17] *Smith v. Croft (No. 1)* [1986] 2 All ER 551, at 564–565.

[18] Ibid.

[19] See Qingxiu Bu, 'The Indemnity Order in a Derivative Action', *Company Lawyer*, 2006, 27(1), 2, p. 6.

## *6.1.2 Problems with ICO*

### 6.1.2.1 Does the Financial Ability of a Shareholder Plaintiff Constitute a Bar to Apply for an ICO?

Indemnity cost orders were originally designed to remove funding obstacles for impecunious shareholder plaintiffs.[20] If a shareholder is financially capable of pursuing a derivative lawsuit, whether it is necessary for him to be indemnified by the company for litigation costs. In *Smith v Croft*, Walton J. indicated that the shareholder plaintiff is eligible to apply for an indemnity cost order only if he is in a genuine need of financial aid.[21] It was further stressed by Walton J. that the plaintiff must well establish his genuine need for the indemnification, and indicated

> It therefore appears to me that in order to hold the balance as fairly as may be in the circumstance between the plaintiffs and defendants, it will be incumbent on the plaintiff applying for such an order to show that it is genuinely needed, i.e. that they do not have sufficient resources to finance the action in the meantime. If they have, I see no reason at all why this extra burden should be placed upon the company.[22]

In fact, the 'financial ability test' approach proposed by Walton J. is criticized to be unfair and problematic.[23] According to the principle of equity, the entity receiving the benefits generated by a case should be liable for the costs. Therefore, the company, who is the beneficiary, should pay for the costs incurred in the proceeding regardless of the shareholder plaintiff's financial capacity.

From the practical perspective, in reality, the 'financial ability test' is difficult to be enforced. The wealth bar could be easily circumvented by using a nominal plaintiff who lacks money and who is also willing to act as a representative for a wealthy shareholder.[24] The situation would be even more complicated when a derivative lawsuit has more than one shareholder plaintiff.[25] In such a case, the court cannot clearly identify the impecunious claimant from the other one. It is possible for the court to separate each plaintiff's money precisely, which, however, may prolong the expected 'simple and inexpensive' procedure to a complex and costly mini-trial.[26,27]

---

[20]See Arad Reisberg, *Derivative Actions and Corporate Governance: Theory and Operation*, Oxford University Press, (2007), p. 230.

[21]*Smith v. Croft (No. 1)* [1986] 2 All ER 551, at 567.

[22]Ibid.

[23]See Arad Reisberg, *Derivative Actions and Corporate Governance: Theory and Operation*, Oxford University Press, (2007), pp. 238–239.

[24]*Jaybird Group Ltd v Greenwood* [1986] B.C.L.C. 319, at 328.

[25]Arad Reisberg, *Derivative Actions and Corporate Governance: Theory and Operation*, Oxford University Press, (2007), p. 240.

[26]Ibid.

[27]Walton J.'s 'financial test proposal' was not adopted by the subsequent case law. For example, in *Jaybird Group Ltd v Greenwood* [1986] B.C.L.C. 319, Wheeler Q.C. awarded an indemnity order

#### 6.1.2.2 Under What Circumstances and to What Extent Is an ICO Awarded

In *Smith v Croft (No. 2)*, the indemnity cost order was rejected mainly for the reason that the derivative lawsuit was opposed by a majority of independent shareholders and appeared to have little prospect of success.[28] Walton J. further suggested that an indemnity cost order should not be made before the discovery procedure,[29] at which point it is usually clear whether the plaintiffs are *bona fide* and whether the claim is well established on reasonable grounds and in the company's best interests.[30] In Walton J.'s point of view, the indemnity cost order could be awarded only if the case proved to be a 'clearest, obviously just' one.[31] As a result, the court, actually, owns great flexibility when scrutinizing an application for the indemnity cost in interpreting these unclear standards (for instance, a clearest and obviously just case, for the company's best interests).

It is also unmentioned how generous an indemnity cost order could be when it is awarded: which costs should it cover? Statutory rule (CPR 19.9) provides that 'costs incurred in the permission application or in the derivative claim or both', but it does not further indicate whether adverse fees generated by the English cost-shifting rule in an unsuccessful claim could be indemnified by the company. Given that, guidance needs to be sought from case law. In case law, the courts adopted a pragmatic methodology to grant an indemnity cost order.[32] For example, in *Kiani v Cooper*, Proudman J awarded a limited cost order to cover costs on the side of the shareholder plaintiff (court charges and lawyer's fees), but adverse fees in case of losing would not be indemnified by the company.[33] Proudman J further stated that the applicant should assume part of the financial risk of the litigation.[34] In *Stainer v Lee*, Roth J adopted a flexible and novel approach in granting the indemnity cost order.[35] The expected indemnity cost was first capped at a £40,000

(Footnote 27 continued)

to a wealthy plaintiff. In this case, the court applied the 'necessity' criterion alone, and the decision to award an indemnity cost order to the shareholder plaintiff was made on the basis that the independent and impartial board of directors of the company would have brought the derivative action for the best interests of the company. *Jaybird Group Ltd v Greenwood* [1986] B.C.L.C. 319, at 320.

28 *Smith v Croft (No 2)* [1988] Ch. 114.

29 r.19.9 (7) of the CPR 2000 provides that the application for an indemnity order and the application for the leave to proceed should be integrated together.

30 See Qingxiu Bu, 'The indemnity order in a derivative action', *Company Lawyer*, 2006, 27(1), 2, p. 7.

31 *Smith v Croft (No 2)* [1988] Ch. 114, at 147.

32 Julia Tang, 'Shareholder remedies: demise of the derivative claims?', 1 *UCL Journal of Law and Jurisprudence* 178, (2012), p. 204.

33 *Kiani v Cooper* [2010] BCC 463.

34 Ibid.

35 *Stainer v. Lee* [2011] BCC 134.

limit but with a permission to apply for an extension. The rationale behind this flexible approach is that it prevents an early payment in an unmeritorious case, but still permits the extension for the *bona fide* applicant. The court, in this case, struck a delicate balance between judicial efficiency and cautious scrutiny. The flexible approach also allowed the courts to monitor the progress of the claim at every stage while reassessing the adequacy and rationale of the indemnity costs order to particular circumstances.[36]

#### 6.1.2.3 The Problematic Relationship Between the Application for an ICO and the Application for Leave to Proceed

CPR 19.9 (the statutory rule) does not mention under what circumstances the court could award an ICO to the applicant. The *Smith v Croft* case adopted an approach integrating the application for an indemnity cost order into the application for leave to proceed.[37] However this integrated procedure was criticized be unfair to the company and the shareholders.[38] On the part of the company, an early decision may not be able to screen out frivolous and unmeritorious cases,[39] because it would be difficult to determine whether the case is well-established prior to the discovery and inspection procedure. On the other hand, it is also not easy for the shareholder plaintiff to prove the merits of the case and demonstrate their entitlements because of the limited access to evidence. Even if they succeed in collecting strong evidence, it still cannot guarantee that the court will be convinced to award an indemnity cost order and permit leave for proceed. In light of the risk involved, the shareholder plaintiff may prefer to initiate a shareholder direct action or launch an unfair prejudice petition under 994 of CA 2006 rather than pursue a derivative lawsuit.[40]

In this regard, the approach of a limited indemnity cost order applied in *Kiani v Cooper* is recommended, by which a court could, at an early stage, decide to

---

[36]Julia Tang, 'Shareholder remedies: demise of the derivative claims?', 1 *UCL Journal of Law and Jurisprudence* 178, (2012), p. 205.

[37]*Smith v Croft (No. 2)* [1988] Ch. 114; 19.9 (7) of the Civil Procedure Rule (2000).

[38]Arad Reisberg, *Derivative Actions and Corporate Governance: Theory and Operation*, Oxford University Press, (2007), p. 237.

[39]Ibid.

[40]Unfair prejudice petition in the UK company law is a statutory form of action that may be brought by aggrieved shareholders against their company. Section 994 of the CA 2006 in relation of unfair prejudice remedy provides that the petition could be brought by any member of the company (not only shareholders) on grounds that 'the company's affairs are being or have been conducted in a manner that is unfairly prejudicial to the interests of members generally or of some part of its members; or an actual or proposed act or omission of the company (including an act or omission on its behalf) is or would be so prejudicial.' In general, the statutory requirements for an unfair prejudice petition are lower than those for a derivative action. The comparison between those two mechanisms can be found in Arad Reisberg, *Derivative Actions and Corporate Governance: Theory and Operation*, Oxford University Press, (2007), p. 286.

indemnify the costs incurred in a *prima facie* case within a limited scope without developing the procedure into a mini-trial. As the trial proceeds, if the case proves to be meritorious, the shareholder claimant can apply for an extension of the order. The comparatively moderate attitude held by the court in this 'limited approach' could help to diminish the interplay between the two decisions (leave to proceed and indemnity cost order) to a certain extent.[41]

### 6.1.3 Summary

Under the English law, the traditional way to remove funding obstacles for a shareholder plaintiff to pursue a derivative action is by indemnifying the *bona fide* claimant's litigation costs in the litigation by the company regardless of the result of the lawsuit. Practically, the use of the indemnity cost order is problematic in certain aspects. The most significant reason for the practical difficulty is that the rule of this mechanism is unclear. The financial risk still remains with the shareholder plaintiff because the court has a wide range of discretion when scrutinizing an application for the cost order. Actually, the court, generally, refers to precedents when considering an application. But in England, the number of derivative claims is limited and the judiciary does not have enough opportunities to elaborate relevant issues. Due to this dilemma, up till now, the use of the indemnity cost order still faces practical uncertainties (i.e. whether the financial status of the applicant generates a bar to apply for a cost order).

## 6.2 Funding by Lawyers: The First Option (Conditional Fee Agreements, CFAs)

### 6.2.1 The Nature of CFA

The conditional fee system that consists of a recovery of basic fees and the payment of a reward (the success fee) is most developed in England and Wales.[42] This

[41]The reason why we suppose the court holds a 'comparatively moderate attitude of the court at the early stage' will be explained as follows. In *Kiani v Cooper,* it was indicated that the plaintiff should assume a portion of litigation financial risk instead of relying the indemnity cost order entirely. Although the indemnity cost application was approved to be genuinely-needed, the court could still grant an order in a limited scope. The plaintiff applicant is allowed to apply for an extension of the cost order to cover all the costs incurred in the court proceeding. Considering that, the court's attitude may not be so harsh because if it finds the decision is improper, a correction on the indemnity cost order is still possible to be made.

[42]John Peysner, *'National Reports: England and Wales'*, in Christopher Hodges et al. (eds), *The Costs and Funding of Civil Litigation*, (Hart Publishing, 2010), 289, p. 294.

funding technique employs a principle of 'no win, no fee', meaning that a lawyer is entitled to charge an amount of success fees only if the court finds his client's favour.[43,44] But if the case is lost, the lawyer will not be paid by his client for the work he has done.[45]

It is often assumed that the lawyer working under a CFA evaluates potential risk in advance, making that the lawyer would not be willing to accept a case with a low success rate.[46] Lawyers under CFAs could also be significantly risk-averse, and may tend to drop cases if the success fees cannot justify the risk that lawyers assume.[47] Besides, in order to discourage frivolous claims, it is proposed that the levels of success fee should be set properly and must be capped.[48]

## 6.2.2 *Funding Derivative Actions with a CFA*

### 6.2.2.1 Potential Problems When a CFA Is Applied to Fund a Derivative Claim

Although the CFA is allowed to apply to fund all sorts of civil lawsuits,[49] its application to the derivative action is yet unclear.[50] Derivative actions are different from ordinary civil lawsuits where benefits generated by a settlement or a judgment flow to the claimants directly. In a derivative action, the shareholder claimant is not directly compensated (relief flows to the company) and may only share in a limited (because of his small shareholding) and indirect way, making it difficult to convince the lawyer that he would get the success fees and normal bill from the shareholder plaintiff's pocket.

---

[43]See Jackson's final report: Review of Civil Litigation Costs, (2009), p. 16.

[44]The extra charge (the success fee) by a lawyer could be up to 100% of his normal bill.

[45]See Jackson's final report: Review of Civil Litigation Costs, (2009), p. 8.

[46]It is generally thought that the lawyer is in the best position to know the potential risk involved in a case. Arad Reisberg, *Derivative Actions and Corporate Governance*: *Theory and Operation*, Oxford University Press, (2007), p. 252.

[47]See Sonja Keske, Andrea Renda and Roger Van Den Bergh, 'Financing and Group Litigation', in Mark Tuil and Louis Visscher (eds.) *New Trends in Financing Civil Litigation in Europe: A Legal, Empirical and Economic Analysis*, (Edward Elgar Publishing, 2010) 57, p. 79.

[48]Law Reform Commission of Hong Kong, Consultation Paper on Conditional Fee (2005), Ch. 7, Recommendation 5, paras 7.24 to 7.26, available at http://www.hkreform.gov.hk/en/docs/conditional-e.pdf (accessed on 20 August 2016).

[49]See Sect. 58 of Courts and Legal Services Act 1990, available at http://www.legislation.gov.uk/ukpga/1990/41/section/58 (accessed on 20 August 2016).

[50]See Qingxiu Bu, 'The indemnity order in a derivative action', *Company Lawyer*, 2006, 27(1), 2, p. 13.

#### 6.2.2.2 Disincentives in CFAs Generated by the English Cost-Shifting Rule

Under the English cost-shifting rule, CFA provides, in reality, only a partial solution for the shareholder claimant to alleviate the financial risk of going to court. If the case is lost, the plaintiff is still liable for the opponent's costs incurred in the litigation that would not be covered by the CFA. In practice, a potential claimant usually relieves such risk by using an insurance product to cover the opponent's costs in the event that the action is lost.[51] But in light of the high rate of legal insurance, financial burden still remains with less wealthy shareholder plaintiffs.[52]

Insurance products often used to cover litigation risk includes, among others, before-the-event insurance (BTE, an insurance product purchased before the event that triggers the legal action in order to cover litigation costs on the policyholder's own side and the opponent's litigation expenses in case of losing under the cost-shifting rule) and the after-the-event insurance (ATE, an insurance product bought after the event that triggers the legal claim in order to cover litigation costs on the policyholder's own side and the opponent's litigation expenses in case of losing under the cost-shifting rule).[53] From a practical perspective, however, it is difficult to imagine that prior to investing in a company, a shareholder would purchase either of them just in order to lower the litigation risk in the future.[54] In fact, the legal insurance market is not popular in England, and it is even indicated that the ATE insurance might come to an end partly because it is inevitably expensive.[55] In light of the prohibitive price, it could be impossible for a minority shareholder in a derivative lawsuit to pay the considerable high premium up front.[56] Therefore, employing a conditional fee agreement and a legal insurance product to remove funding obstacle for impecunious shareholders is not practical, and even unrealistic.

In this regard, it was suggested that a shareholder plaintiff could conclude a conditional fee agreement with a lawyer who agrees to pay the premiums for the impecunious shareholder plaintiff in advance.[57] Unfortunately, this approach also

---

[51]For example, after-the-event insurance. See A. Walters and J. Peysner, 'Event-Triggered Financing of Civil Claims: Lawyers, Insurers and the Common Law' (1999) 8 *Nottingham Law Journal* 1, p. 2.

[52]Arad Reisberg, *Derivative Actions and Corporate Governance: Theory and Operation*, Oxford University Press, (2007), p. 254.

[53]Ibid.

[54]See Michael Zander, 'The Government's Plans on Legal Aid and Conditional Fees' (1998) 61 *Modern Law Review* 538, p. 549.

[55]See Jackson's final report: Review of Civil Litigation Costs, (2009), pp. 91–93.

[56]See Zhong Zhang, 'Making Shareholder Derivative Actions Happen in China: How Should Lawsuits be Funded?', 38 *Hong Kong Law Journal* (2008), 523, p. 543.

[57]Ibid.

appears to be unreasonable and impractical for the reason that a lawyer taking over a case under a conditional fee agreement usually believes that the case is likely to be successful before the court and the lawyer would not take over a case where the legal insurance is greatly needed to cover the opponent's litigation costs in case of losing. A rational lawyer must be quite cautious in a case if the client requires him to pay premiums up front.[58]

The conditional fee agreement is often compared with the US contingency fee arrangement. In nature, a contingency fee arrangement grants a lawyer the right to share in the client's compensation brought by a successful claim, while the success fee in a conditional fee arrangement is just a fixed amount of uplift which is not affected by the degree to which a claim succeeds, but only by the fact of success.[59] To shield minority shareholders from financial risk in litigation, it is thought that contingency fees might be more favourable.[60] The reason for it is rooted in the American legal system rather than the funding technique per se. The US does not adopt the cost-shifting rule, which is also the most important reason why derivative actions have flourished in the US, but not in other countries (for example, the UK).[61] Moreover, the rate of the success fee under a CFA may also be a concern, because, in some cases, the basic fees plus the uplifts may exceed or even exhaust the monetary remedies awarded by the court.[62] The Conditional Fee Agreements Order 2013 provides that a 25% cap put on the setting of the success fee under CFAs. For example, in a personal injury claim, 'a lawyer's success fee should be limited to a maximum of 25% of the damages awarded for pain, suffering and loss of amenity and pecuniary loss.'[63]

---

[58]See Zhong Zhang, 'Making Shareholder Derivative Actions Happen in China: How Should Lawsuits be Funded?', 38 *Hong Kong Law Journal* (2008), 523, p. 544.

[59]See Gerald Walpin, 'America's Failing Civil Justice System: Can We Learn From Other Countries?', 41 *New York Law School Law Review*. 647 (1996–1997), p. 656.

[60]See Zhong Zhang, 'Making shareholder derivative actions happen in China: how should lawsuits be funded?', 38 *Hong Kong Law Journal* (2008), 523, p. 544; Arad Reisberg, *Derivative actions and corporate governance: theory and operation*, Oxford University Press, (2007), pp. 255–256; J. Peysner, 'What's Wrong with Contingency Fees?', (2001) 10 *Nottingham Law Journal* 22, p. 46; Winand Emons and Nuno Garoupa, 'The economics of US-style contingent fees and UK-style conditional fees', Managerial and Decision Economics, (2006), Volume 28, Issue 5, 379, p. 381.

[61]See Ian Ramsay, 'Corporate Governance, Shareholder Litigation and the Prospect for a Statutory Derivative Action', (1992) 15 (1) University of New South Wales Law Journal 149, p. 174.

[62]See Geoffrey Woodroffe, 'Loser Pays and Conditional Fees—An English Solution?', 37 Washburn Law Journal. 345, (1997–1998), p. 354.

[63]The Conditional Fee Agreements Order 2013, available at http://www.legislation.gov.uk/ukdsi/2013/9780111533437 (accessed on 20 August 2016).

## 6.3 Funding by Lawyers: The Second Option (Contingency Fee Arrangements, CGFAs)

Traditionally, contingency fee arrangements (CGFAs), which were rejected by the English law, are widely applied in the US.[64] But since April 2013, CGFAs (also known as 'damages based agreements', DBAs) have been legally permitted for contentious work (for instance, litigation and arbitration) in England and Wales, meaning that, for the first time, lawyers are allowed to conduct litigation in return for a share of damages brought by a successful case. On the other hand, in case of losing, the lawyer will not be paid.

### *6.3.1 The Conflict of Interests and the Agency Problem Under a CGFA*

A general debate revolving around CGFAs is about the conflict of interests between the lawyer and his client. It is true that both sides in a lawsuit may have strong incentives to settle the case in order to avoid expensive costs (court charges, lawyer's fees), the time and the uncertainties associated with a trial,[65] and the lawyer may particularly prefer an early settlement that could guarantee a share of recoveries without investing additional time to request for a trial before the court.[66] However, what the lawyer desires, is, in some cases, not in accordance with the objective of the client. For instance, a settlement offer which is optimal for the litigant may not always be an ideal option for a lawyer.[67] In terms of economic theory (cost-and-benefit analysis), the lawyer's net proceeds depend on the share of the damages minus time and efforts spent on the case, while the litigant's net proceeds are damages created by a successful lawsuit minus the part of them shared by the lawyer. Evidently, in view of the different determinants in the economic model, the decision on whether or not to accept a settlement offer may diverge between the lawyer and the funded litigant. To better protect the litigant's interest in

[64]Historically, given the traditional common law prohibition of champerty and maintenance, contingency fee arrangements were prohibited in most of common law nations (But the US is an exception).

[65]Uri Weiss, 'The Regressive Effect of Legal Uncertainty', *Tel Aviv University Law Faculty Working Paper* 30. (2005), pp. 2–5 http://law.bepress.com/cgi/viewcontent.cgi?article=1030&context=taulwps (accessed on 20 August 2016).

[66]See GP Miller, 'Some Agency Problems in Settlement' (1987) 16 *The Journal of Legal Studies*, 189, pp. 192–193; T. Thomason, 'Are Attorneys Paid What They Are Worth? Contingent Fees and the Settlement Process' (1991) 20 *The Journal of Legal Studies*, 187, pp. 191–193.

[67]Hugh Gravellea and Michael Waterson, *No win, No fee: Some Economics of Contingency Legal Fees, The Economic Journal*, (1993), Volume 103 (420), 1025, p. 1026.

a CGFA, regulations on settlements could be found. For instance, for derivative lawsuit, section 23.1 of the US Federal Rule of Civil Procedure requires that the proposed settlement or dismissal of a derivative action should be approved by the court and 'a notice of the proposed dismissal or compromise should be approved by the court', and 'a notice of the proposed dismissal or compromise shall be given to shareholders or members in such manner as the court directs.'[68] Moreover, the judicial approval for a proposed settlement or dismissal has also been adopted by most state law, the Modern Business Corporation Act (MBCA) and the ALI's principles.[69] Additionally, regarding the notice requirement, some states adopt a 'notice-to-shareholders' requirement, while there are also other states giving the court the discretion to decide whether such a notice is required.[70] Generally, settlements in derivative actions are expected to be controlled by the court in order to prevent 'gold-digging' claims which are not in line with the principle of protecting the company's interests.[71]

In reality, the above mentioned rules could help to avoid settlement agreements disadvantageous for plaintiffs. But whether a settlement agreement is more favourable for the litigant than for the lawyer is not easy to be assessed by the court, particularly, in commercial litigation. It is commonly acknowledged that the commercial lawsuit has a 'lawyer-driven feature'.[72] In a derivative action where corporate governance, director's fiduciary duties, and complicated commercial transactions are involved, professional knowledge is needed to instruct the whole court proceeding. In this regard, shareholder plaintiffs (especially minority ones), compared to the company's director and the controlling shareholders, are disadvantaged in terms of accessing the company's documents, getting internal

[68]23.1 of Federal Rule of Civil Procedure.

[69]For example, Rule 23.1 of Rules of the Court of Chancery of the State of Delaware; Section 626 (d) of New York Business Corporation Law; Section 7.45 of the MBCA; Section 7.14(a) of ALI (II).

[70]For example, in Delaware, the notice is required unless the dismissal of the action is without prejudice to the plaintiff. See Deborah A. DeMott, Shareholder Derivative Actions: Law and Practice, Clark Boardman Callaghan (2012); Section 7.45 of the MBCA provides that 'if the court determines that a proposed discontinuance or settlement will substantially affect the interests of the corporation's shareholders or a class of shareholders, the court shall direct that notice be given to the shareholders affected'.

[71]Arad Reisberg, *Derivative actions and corporate governance: theory and operation*, Oxford University Press, (2007), pp. 73–74.

[72]Xiaoning Li, *A Comparative Study of Shareholders' Derivative Actions: England, the United States, Germany and China*, (Kluwer, 2007), pp. 178–179; HM Kritzer, '*The Wages of Risk: The Returns of Contingent Fee Legal Practice*' (1997) 47 De Paul Law Review 267, pp. 268–270; See Eyal Zamir and Ilana Ritov, 'Neither Saints Nor Devils: A Behavioral Analysis of Attorneys' Contingent Fees' (January 22, 2008), pp. 6–8 Available at SSRN: http://ssrn.com/abstract=1085985 or http://dx.doi.org/10.2139/ssrn.1085985; see James D. Dana, Kathryn E. Spier, 'Expertise and Contingent Fees: The Role of Asymmetric Information in Attorney Compensation', *Journal of Law, Economics, & Organization*, 1993, 9(2), pp. 349–367.

information as well as professional knowledge.[73] Thus, the role of the lawyer in such cases would be of great importance since the lawyer, as a repeat player in litigation market and a professional legal practitioner, would be much more familiar with those complex issues indicated above. In fact, the lawyer working on a contingent fee basis combines the role of a professional legal adviser, an advocate, a financier and an insurance broker.[74] In reality, it might not be easy for the litigant to evaluate whether a settlement of agreement is more favourable for the company and himself, or for the lawyer, while on the part of the lawyer, he may clearly know that a settlement agreement is for whose best interest. Compared to CFAs, the conflict of interests in CGFAs is even worse since the fees charged under a CFA are not related to the level of settlement, while fees charged on a contingent basis are in proportion to the level of damages brought by a settlement, which would create more incentive for the lawyer to reach a settlement for his best interests.

Despite the conflict of interests between lawyers and clients, we should also notice an agency problem that the delegation of the company is absent during the negotiation of a settlement agreement of a derivative lawsuit. Although the shareholder plaintiff is supposed to represent the company, in fact, their interests, sometimes, are not consistent with each other in the settlement negotiation.[75]

### *6.3.2 CGFAs and Shareholder Derivative Actions in the US: A Potential Rise in Case Volume*

Although lawyers are traditionally thought to stir up troubles and make money through litigation, it is argued that lawyers under CGFAs turn down cases, at least, as many as those cases they accept, mostly because of the untenable basis for the

---

[73]For example, compared to directors (who are sometimes defendants in a derivative lawsuit), minority shareholders have less professional knowledge with regards to corporate governance. And business operation which is normally professional and complicated may not be easy for shareholders to understand.

[74]See HM Kritzer, '*The Wages of Risk: The Returns of Contingent Fee Legal Practice*', *De Paul Law Review*, (1997), Volume 47, 267, pp. 268–170; and see HM Kritzer, *Risks, Reputations, and Rewards: Contingency Fee Legal Practice in the United States* (Stanford University Press, 2004).

[75]For example, if a shareholder plaintiff sues the director on grounds that the director made a transaction infringing the company's interests. When they negotiate a settlement agreement, the defendant can give an offer which might be less than the company's expectation but is still in favour of the company. For the shareholder plaintiffs, the defendant may give them other benefits outside the company. (which is, actually, not practically prohibited, even though this sort of trade-off must be legally forbidden.) Considering that, it is possible for the shareholder plaintiff and the defendants to conclude a settlement agreement which is more beneficial for the personal interests of the shareholder plaintiffs rather than that of the company. Therefore, it could be said that the interests of shareholder plaintiffs are not always in line with that of the company.

case.[76,77] It's indicated that lawyers under CGFAs are gatekeepers who control the flow of civil cases into the courts.[78]

When discussing third party litigation funding (TPLF) in the previous Chapter, a concern about the increase of case volume caused by the use of TPLF was also investigated. In fact, the volume of cases indeed increased along with the introduction of TPLF, however, there was no evidence demonstrating that the number of unmeritorious and frivolous claims increased.[79] Actually, the increase of the total case volume just indicated that cases that would not have been brought impeded by financial difficulties could be commenced with the funding provided by the third party funder. As for CGFAs, the logic is the same.

The concern about unmeritorious cases would not be manifested in the context of CGFAs mainly for the reason that the individual lawyer's ability of externalizing case risk would be much lower than that of a professional third party litigation funder. For example, within a month, litigation funders may fund ten cases with different rate of success, by which the funders could be able to externalize risk by spreading it through a portfolio of unrelated cases, while an individual lawyer, by contrast, may just take one case during the same period. In this regard, empirical research about CGFA's practice in Canada could suggest that the fear of unmeritorious case is not materialized.[80]

Besides the concern of unmeritorious cases, whether the filing of cases with small probabilities of success but large amounts of monetary recoveries would be encouraged by the speculative lawyer working under a contingent basis needs to be investigated.[81] Empirical study shows that American lawyers turn away a big portion of would-be plaintiffs mainly for the reason that those cases are not winnable, although the potential monetary remedies are high.[82] But it needs to be

[76]See Herbert M. Kritzer, 'Contingency Fee Lawyers as Gatekeepers in the Civil Justice System', *Judicature* Volume 81, Number 1 (1997), p. 22.

[77]In *A Nation Under Lawyers,* the author indicated that 'about half of the practice of the decent lawyer consists in telling would-be clients that they are damned fools and should stop'. See Mary Ann Glendon, *A Nation Under Lawyers: How the Crisis in the Legal Profession is Transforming American Society*, (Harvard University Press, 1996), pp. 37 and 75.

[78]See Herbert M. Kritzer, 'Contingency Fee Lawyers as Gatekeepers in the Civil Justice System', *Judicature* Volume 81, Number 1 (1997), p. 22.

[79]See *supra* 5.1.4.4.

[80]In most Canadian provinces (except Ontario) CGFAs are legally allowed. But it should be mentioned that the cost rule in Canada is mostly followed English cost-shifting rule which make the litigation practice in Canada differ from that in the US. As a matter of fact, in Canada, CGFAs are not used as much as they are in the US. So the fears of CGFAs abuse have not materialized in Canada. See Arad Reisberg, *Derivative actions and corporate governance: theory and operation*, Oxford University Press, (2007), p. 266.

[81]See Arad Reisberg, *Derivative actions and corporate governance: theory and operation*, Oxford University Press, (2007), p. 264. And see Kevin M. Clermont and John D. Currivan, 'Improving on the Contingency Fee' (1978) 63 *Cornell Law Review* 529, p. 570.

[82]See Herbert M. Kritzer, *'The Seven Dogged Myths Concerning Contingency Fees'* (2002) 80 Washington University Law Quarterly, 739, pp. 755–757.

pointed out that the contingent rate should not be set too high since an extravagant rate may induce lawyers to overcome ethical and economic reluctance to take speculative and nuisance lawsuits.[83] But the core problem here stems from the proper setting of the contingent rate, not from the CGFA mechanism per se.[84,85]

### 6.3.3 *Information Asymmetry in CGFAs*

CGFAs, in general, have two types of information asymmetry between lawyers and funded litigants.[86] The first type is when a CGFA is concluded, the client (the potential plaintiff) may be better informed about the facts of the case and the prospect of success than the lawyer.[87] If a client strongly desires to commence a case with few chances to win, he may overstate the fact of a case to the lawyer and try to conclude a CGFA with him.[88] On the other hand, the second type of information asymmetry is that lawyers may be better informed about their own abilities than the potential clients. If a lawyer attempts to conclude a CGFA with a client, he may overstate his ability to get the case.[89] Under this circumstance, the client's 'right to know' may not be well protected because of the information asymmetry. In our points of view, we agree that the second type of information asymmetry is indeed a concern in a derivative lawsuit funded by the CGFA, while the first type of concern might rarely happen. For most of potential plaintiffs, there are not enough incentives for them to commence derivative actions.[90] Effective funding ways (public funding, third party litigation funding or contingency fee arrangements) are expected to remove disincentives for shareholder plaintiffs and facilitate the filing of derivative lawsuits. In consideration of that, it would not be common for a shareholder plaintiff to overstate the case in order to persuade a lawyer to enter into

---

[83]Kevin M. Clermont and John D. Currivan, 'Improving on the Contingency Fee' (1978) 63 *Cornell Law Review* 529, p. 573.

[84]Ibid.

[85]Actually, in the US, the setting of the contingent rate is unregulated in most of states. Lack of regulation prompts some concerns about windfall fees where the level of contingency fee dramatically exceeds the level of effort a lawyer expends on a case. But is has also been stated that regulation of contingency fees through caps would be likely to reduce the access to justice (there is clear evidence that such caps reduce the number of cases brought). See Richard Moorhead, 'Contingency Fees: A Study of the Operation of Contingency Fee Arrangements in the United States of America', (2008), pp. 8–9. http://www.judiciary.gov.uk/wp-content/uploads/2011/06/JCO_Documents_CJC_Publications_CJC+papers_Civil+Justice+Council+Contingency+Fees+Report.pdf (accessed on 20 August 2016).

[86]Daniel L. Rubinfeld and Suzanne Scotchmer, 'Contingent Fees for Attorneys: an Economic Analysis', *The RAND Journal of Economics* Vol. 24, No. 3 (1993), 343, pp. 343–344.

[87]Ibid.

[88]Ibid.

[89]Ibid.

[90]See *supra* 2.3.1.

a CGFA with him. And also, it would be difficult for general shareholder plaintiffs to overstate a case with lots of professional commercial details to a professional and repeat legal practitioner (the lawyer).

### *6.3.4 Lawyers' Ethical Issues in CGFAs*

As indicated before, a proper setting of the contingent rate is important to mitigate the lawyer's moral hazard.[91] Lawyers under CGFAs may collect lawyers' fees amounting to several million dollars, sometimes, just for performing general paralegal work.[92] This section will focus on investigating: how to justify such big amount of lawyer's fees and how to avoid excessive charges mainly through the American experience.

The logic behind the CGFA mechanism, in nature, is that lawyers assume the risk of receiving no fees or low fees in exchange for a share of recoveries generated in the outcome that is in favour of his client.[93] The contingent rate normally ranges between 33 and 50%.[94] Contingent fees received by lawyers are usually higher than ordinary lawyer's hourly charges.[95] Under the hourly-rate charge, regardless of the outcome, lawyers are always awarded with an amount of money calculated based on the time they spent. In a contingency fee arrangement, on the contrary, higher lawyers' fees could be justified by the risk assumed by them. However, in some

---

[91]See *supra* 6.3.2.

[92]U.S. District Court Judge Robert R. Merhige, presiding over the Dalkon Shield Claimants Trust litigation, stated:

> It is to be borne in mind that counsel has already received, in the vast majority of instances, fees of at least one-third of the gross settlement amount, plus costs. These fees, in many instances, exceed $100,000.00 per claim, and the aggregate fees received by some counsel, especially those with hundreds of cases, runs as high as several million dollars per attorney or law firm. Generally, the sole efforts related to such compensation consist of garnering medical records and advising a client whether to accept a non-negotiable settlement offer.

A.H. Robins Co., 182 B.R. 128, 137 n. 10 (E.D. Va. 1995); see Lester Brickman, 'Contingency Fee Abuse, Ethical Mandates, and the Disciplinary System: The Case Against Case-by-Case Enforcement', *Washington and Lee Law Review*, (1996), Volume 53, Issue 4, 1339, p. 1320.

[93]Lester Brickman, 'Effective Hourly Rates of Contingency-Fee Lawyers: Competing Data and Non-Competitive Fees', *Washington University Law Quarterly*, (2003), Volume 81(3), 653, pp. 657–659.

[94]Ibid.

[95]In Olavi Maru, *Digest of Bar Association Ethics Opinions* (1970), it commented that 'where no agreement exists with regard to a fee, it is proper to charge only a reasonable fee, which will ordinarily be less than a fee fixed on a contingent basis'. Therefore, it could be found that Contingent fees usually produce a higher fee than a fixed or hourly fee for the same service. See Lester Brickman, 'Contingency Fee Abuse, Ethical Mandates, and the Disciplinary System: The Case Against Case-by-Case Enforcement', *Washington and Lee Law Review*, (1996), Volume 53, Issue 4, 1339, p. 1347.

cases with low risk, such a high contingent rate may be unjust. Normally, the rate is agreed through a free negotiation between the lawyer and the client. But in the negotiation procedure, the lawyer who is a repeat legal practitioner may be an expert in assessing potential risk in a case. The client, normally, could not be able to estimate the risk involved in a lawsuit precisely since he is not a litigation specialist. Therefore, it was proposed that contingent rate needs to be regulated.[96] Actually, in the US, it has been suggested that the American Bar Association (the ABA) should be the authority administering contingent rate.[97] A standard contingent rate ranged between 33 and 40% of the gross damages has been proposed to prevent lawyer's moral hazard.[98] But counterarguments indicate that the standard contingency fee is unethical when the lawyer bears no meaningful fee risk.[99] The American Trial Lawyers Association (the ATLA) also contends that the proposed standard contingent rate is inappropriate.[100] In this regard, we agree with the ATLA because the application of a standard contingency fee may contradict the purpose of the invention of this technique. Similar with CFAs, CGFAs aim at providing more incentives for lawyers by associating the outcome of a case with the amount of lawyers' fees.[101] The relatively narrow range of 33–40% may not be able to cover

[96]See Richard Moorhead, 'Contingency Fees: A Study of the Operation of Contingency Fee Arrangements in the United States of America', (2008), pp. 8–9; Michael Horowitz, 'Making Ethics Real, Making Ethics Work: A Proposal for Contingency Fee Reform', *Emory Law Journal*, (1995), Volume 44, 173; Lester Brickman, 'ABA Regulation of Contingency Fee: Money Talks, Ethics Works', *Fordham Law Review*, (1996), Volume 65, 247; Lester Brickman, 'Contingency Fee Abuse, Ethical Mandates, and the Disciplinary System: The Case Against Case-by-Case Enforcement', *Washington and Lee Law Review*, (1996), Volume 53(4), 1339.

[97]See Michael Horowitz, 'Making Ethics Real, Making Ethics Work: A Proposal for Contingency Fee Reform', *Emory Law Journal*, (1995), Volume 44, 17.; Lester Brickzan, 'ABA Regulation of Contingency Fee: Money Talks, Ethics Works', *Fordham Law Review*, (1996), Volume 65, 247; Lester Brickman, 'Contingency Fee Abuse, Ethical Mandates, and the Disciplinary System: The Case Against Case-by-Case Enforcement', *Washington and Lee Law Review*, (1996), Volume 53 (4), 1339.

[98]See Lester Brickzan, 'ABA Regulation of Contingency Fee: Money Talks, Ethics Works', *Fordham Law Review*, (1996), Volume 65, 247, p. 248.

[99]Ibid.

[100]In a publication by the ATLA, it urges its members to 'exercise sound judgment in using a percentage in the contingent fee contract that is commensurate with the risk, cost, and effort required'. See American Trial Lawyers Association, *Keys to the Courthouse: Quick Facts on the Contingent Fee System*, (1994), p. 4.

[101]In other words, it means that in contingency fee arrangement the lawyer fee is not calculated on an hourly-rate basis. Instead, the lawyer's fee is calculated in proportion to the damages brought by a successful case. Obviously, compared to ordinary hourly-rate calculation approach, the CGFA will urge the lawyer to work hard to get more rewards. In a conditional fee agreement, the basic theory is the same. The lawyer is motivated to work hard to get 'success fee' which is only available only if the case is won. Compared to hourly rate which is irrelevant with the event, contingency fee arrangements and conditional fee agreements seem to be able to provide more incentives for lawyers.

different levels of risk involved in cases. In fact, caps on contingent fees have come into wide use as a way of regulating fees, especially in medical malpractice litigation.[102] Although the cap on fees was introduced to prevent a drastic increase in litigation volume,[103] it could also achieve an auxiliary purpose to prohibit lawyers from charging excessive fees.[104]

Furthermore, it is suggested that judicial scrutiny should be enforced, where necessary, on a case-by-case basis to solve lawyers' ethical problems.[105] But particularly in the US with its litigation culture, the workload of the courts would increase dramatically, if this approach was adopted. It would be physically impossible for courts to scrutinize even a small number of cases on an *ex ante* basis to determine whether there is meaningful risk at the time of entering into the contingency fee contract.[106] Even if courts sought to assume responsibilities in this aspect by selecting the most egregious case of overcharging, how would they know which case should be chosen for further scrutiny?[107] Therefore, this proposal, from a practice perspective, would be hard to be implemented.

Currently, half of the states in the US have law regulating contingent fees.[108] For instance, Arizona courts take the responsibility to consider the reasonableness of attorneys' fees in medical malpractice cases by taking into account factors such as 'the time and labour required, the novelty and difficulty of the questions involved, and the skill requisite to perform the legal skills properly'.[109] Indiana adopts a fixed 15% fee cap on any award exceeding $100,000 from the Patient's Compensation Fund.[110] Additionally, more states adopt sliding scales to limit attorneys' fees. For example, New York limits contingent fees in medical malpractice cases to 30% of the first $250,000, 25% of the second $250,000, 20% of the next $500,000, 15% of

---

[102]See Richard M. Bimholz, *'Comment: The Validity and Propriety of Contingent Fee Controls'*, 37 UCLA Law Review, 949, pp. 950–951 (1989–1990).

[103]See Patricia M. Danzon, 'Contingent Fees for Personal Injury Litigation', 14 *The Bell Journal of Economics*, 213, (1984), p. 222.

[104]It was proposed that a schedule of permissible contingency fee rates could be a solution to lawyer's overcharging. See Philip H. Corboy, 'Contingency Fees: The Individual's Key to the Courthouse Door', 2 *Litigation* (1975–1976), 27, p. 36.

[105]Lester Brickman, 'Contingency Fee Abuse, Ethical Mandates, and the Disciplinary System: The Case Against Case-by-Case Enforcement', *Washington and Lee Law Review*, (1996), Volume 53, Issue 4, 1339, pp. 1350–1351.

[106]Ibid.

[107]See Philip H. Corboy, 'Contingency Fees: The Individual's Key to the Courthouse Door', 2 *Litigation* (1975–1976), 27, p. 35.

[108]See Centre for Justice Democracy at New York Law School: 'White Paper: Courthouse Cornerstone: Contingency Fees and Their Importance for Everyday Americans', p. 12 & appendix, http://centerjd.org/content/white-paper-courthouse-cornerstone-contingency-fees-and-their-importance-everyday-americans (accessed on 20 August 2016).

[109]Ibid, Appendix.

[110]See Section 34-18-18-1 IND. CODE.

the next $250,000 and just 10% of recoveries over $1.25 million.[111] A most recent movement in this regard is found in Illinois, where a law requiring that contingent fees should be set no higher than one-third of the remedies awarded in medical malpractice cases came into force in January 2013.[112]

Whether it is reasonable to regulate the contingent fee through setting a standard rate or capping it is still under discussion in the US. In 2009, after a survey of 965 plaintiffs' lawyers, the RAND's Institute for Civil Justice (ICJ) concluded that caps on lawyers' fees and limitations on them 'make it harder to retain counsel'.[113] Furthermore, there is a concern that caps on lawyer's fees would make legal assistance available only to those injured persons who are wealthy to afford hourly fees,[114] because lawyers may switch to work on hourly-rate due to caps on contingent fees.

We, in this book, hold a point of view that regulation of contingent fees is necessary, but neither a standard contingency fee nor a fee cap is appropriate. The reason why a standard contingency fee is not recommended is that, as indicated before, the relatively narrow range of standard contingent fees (i.e. 33–40%) would not be sufficient to cover different levels of risk in different cases. And also, caps on contingent fees would likely to create disincentives for lawyers to take risky cases. In fact, the logic behind the technique of contingent fees is that it provides a very free field for lawyers and clients where no minimum and maximum limitations on fees are imposed. Therefore, what the regulation should do is to prevent lawyers' fees which are not proportion to the risks assumed by lawyers rather than the rate of contingent fees per se. For the reasons indicated before, both standard contingency fees and caps on contingent rate just prevent excessive lawyer's charges, they could not, however, fundamentally solve the problem of the disproportionality between the risk the lawyer assume in the case and the amount of lawyer's fees. In this regard, it is proposed that CGFAs could be regulated through lawyers' ethical codes

[111]See Section 474 (a) NY JUD. LAW.

[112]For this reform, the Illinois Governor's spokesperson said, 'Flat rates for contingency fees in medical malpractice cases will provide more consistency and certainty for both malpractice victims and attorneys, while eliminating the awarding of additional attorney compensation by the courts'. See Centre for Justice Democracy at New York Law School: 'White Paper: Courthouse Cornerstone: Contingency Fees and Their Importance for Everyday Americans', p. 13.

[113]Steven Garber et al., 'Do Noneconomic Damages Caps and Attorney Fee Limits Reduce Access to Justice for Victims of Medical Negligence?', 6 *Journal of Empirical Legal Studies*, (December 2009), 637, pp. 640–641.

[114]See American Bar Association Tort Trial & Insurance Practice Section, Report on Contingent Fees in Medical Malpractice Litigation (2004), p. 32. http://apps.americanbar.org/tips/contingent/MedMalReport092004DCW2.pdf (accessed on 20 August 2016).

or lawyers' profession guidelines instead of using standard contingency fee and caps on contingent rate.[115,116]

## 6.3.5 The Potential for CGFAs: The English Experience

In England, as early as the time of *Wallersteiner v Moir (No. 2)*,[117] Lord Denning attempted to explore an exception to permit a CGFA between the plaintiff and the lawyer, which, at that time, was unlawful.[118] But, unfortunately, his proposal was rejected by Lord Buckley and Lord Scarman on the grounds that such an innovation could only be adopted after a comprehensive assessment by a body set up to consider the issue.[119] On the other hand, a strong argument in favour of CGFAs was put forward, stating that the shareholder plaintiff would be in a more secure position in a CGFA than under the indemnity cost order, because the shareholder plaintiff would not be indemnified if the company is insolvent.[120] And also, compared to the indemnity cost order, a CGFA could prevent a lengthy and costly procedure, since, for example, there is no need to consider the applicant's financial status.

But on the other hand, Scarman L.J. in *Wallersteiner v Moir (No. 2)* stated a concern that it would be strange that under a CGFA, a company should share the

---

[115]Actually, the side effects of standard contingency fee and fee caps have been elaborated. In Report on Contingent Fees in Medical Malpractice Litigation (2004) by the American Bar Association Tort Trial & Insurance Practice Section, it was indicated that 'Elimination of, or significant constraints on, contingent fees would make legal assistance available only to those injured persons who are wealthy. The poor, retired, African Americans, and women especially will suffer because they are often unable to afford hourly fees'. And the book *'Two Cheers For Contingent Fees'* by Professor Alexander Tabarrok and Eric Helland also expressed the negative viewpoints towards restrictions on contingent fees. They pointed out that 'restrictions on contingent fees are restrictions on the freedom to contract and, as such, must clear a high hurdle to be justified'. Alexander Tabarrok and Eric Helland, *Two Cheers for Contingent Fees,* (AEI Press, 2006), p. 5. https://www.aei.org/press/two-cheers-for-contingent-fees/ (accessed on 20 August 2016).

[116]The American Bar Association, in fact, urges its members to self-regulate. The principal means of effectuating self-regulation is the promulgation of professional codes. For instance, the *ABA Model Code of Professional Responsibility*. The Standing Committee on Ethics and Professional Responsibility, which focus on the development of ethics standard for lawyers, has made effort to regulate lawyer's work with regards to ethical issues. For more issues about the ABA's role in lawyers' ethical code, see Lester Brickzan, 'ABA Regulation of Contingency Fee: Money Talks, Ethics Works', *Fordham Law Review*, (1996), Volume 65, 247, pp. 255–256.

[117]*Wallersteiner v Moir (No 2)* [1975] QB 373.

[118]*Wallersteiner v Moir (No 2)* [1975] QB 373, at 393.

[119]*Wallersteiner v Moir (No 2)* [1975] QB 373, at 403.

[120]See D.D. Prentice, 'Wallersteiner v Moir: A Decade Later', (1987) *Conveyancer* 167, p. 174; D. D. Prentice, 'Wallersteiner v Moir: The Demise of the Rule in Foss v Hatbottle?' (1976) 40 *Conveyancer* 51, p. 59.

monetary compensation with the plaintiff's lawyer without a prior notice.[121] Actually, this argument may not be reasonable in the sense that a company's consent is never required in the course of a derivative claim. Normally, the commencement of a derivative action is not based on the consent of the company that, at the moment, may be controlled by wrongdoers.[122] In practice, the company's consent is not mentioned in the whole procedure of a derivative action,[123] while the court discretion seems to replaces the consent of the company to scrutinize the 'legality' of the derivative lawsuit. Therefore, it is reasonable that the damages brought by a successful derivative claim could be shared with the plaintiff's lawyer under a CGFA even without the company's consent.

Returning to the discussion about CGFA's application under the cost-shifting rule. It is found that Florida, where CGFA has been traditionally applied, adopts the cost-shifting rule in medical malpractice litigation.[124] An empirical study demonstrated when the US switched to the English cost-shifting rule, there were several changes in litigation but a failure of contingent fee system was not observed.

> (a) Claims are more likely to be dropped without payment; (b) the probabilities of both settlement and litigation decrease; (c) the expenditures by the defendants during trials increase; (d) the win rate of the plaintiff increases; (e) judgments awarded to winning plaintiffs increase; and (f) the amounts of settlement increase.[125]

As for the lawyer's contingent fees under the cost-shifting rule, it should be noted that after the legal adoption of CGFAs, the Ministry of Justice (UK) confirmed that successful litigants using CGFAs will recover their litigation costs (the lawyer's hourly rate fee and disbursements) from defendants in the conventional way, but not be reference to the contingency fees,[126] meaning that the adverse lawyer's fees will be indemnified by the losing party within an amount previously agreed by the

---

[121] *Wallersteiner v Moir (No 2)* [1975] QB 373, at 408.

[122] For instance, the English law does not require the company's consent before the commencement of a derivative lawsuit. And a derivative action is only allowed to be brought on grounds of some causes of actions (e.g. negligence, default, breach of duty). The company's consent is not required. What is needed to proceed the case is the court's permission, see section 261 of UK Companies Act 2006.

[123] For example, in English law there is no relevant provisions dealing with the company's consent in a derivative action.

[124] See Edward A. Snyder and James W. Hughes 'The English Rule for Allocating Legal Costs: Evidence Confronts Theory', (1990) 6 *Journal of Law, Economics, & Organization* 345, p. 367.

[125] These findings were based on data collected during 1980–1985.

[126] 'Successful claimants using DBAs will recover their costs (the lawyer's hourly rate fee and disbursements) from defendants in the usual way, but the claimant will be responsible for paying from their damages any shortfall between the solicitors' costs paid by the losing defendant and the agreed DBA fee and will also be required to pay any shortfall in respect of disbursements.'

See Damages-based agreements (DBAs).

http://www.justice.gov.uk/civil-justice-reforms/main-changes (accessed on 20 August 2016).

two litigation parties rather than the amount calculated on a contingent basis.[127] For instance, if the winning party's lawyer's fees are calculated on a contingent basis (in total 10,000 lb, 20% of the damages), the losing party will not compensate this amount of money. Instead, the losing party will indemnify the wining party's lawyer's fees as the amount of money they agreed before (for instance, they agreed that the losing party would pay 1000 lb as the adverse lawyer's fees). The successful party is still liable for any shortfall between the lawyers' fees covered by the losing party and the agreed contingent fees.[128]

## 6.4 Legal Practice of Funding Alternatives (ICOs, CFAs and CGFAs) in China

### *6.4.1 Legal Practice of CGFAs in China and Its Potential to Fund Shareholder Litigation*

#### 6.4.1.1 Statutory Provisions on CGFAs

Among these funding alternatives (ICOs, CFAs and CGFAs), only CGFAs have been legally confirmed in China (article 13 of Measures for the Administration of Lawyers' Fees, MALF). But article 12 of the MALF indicates that several kinds of cases are not allowed to be funded through CGFAs, including, among others, criminal cases, administrative cases, cases of state compensation and mass litigation. Hence, the potential for CGFAs to finance shareholder litigation depends on whether shareholder litigation is considered as mass litigation under Chinese law. In fact, neither statutory law nor judicial interpretation explain under what circumstances a lawsuit should be regarded as mass litigation. Normally, in practice, a case involving more than thirty plaintiffs or defendants is treated as mass litigation before the court.[129] In reality, in order to get shareholder collective litigation funded by CGFA, injured investors plaintiffs are usually divided into several groups by lawyers (in each group, no more than 30 persons) to circumvent 'mass litigation',

---

[127] See Jackson's final report 2009, p. 133.

[128] Ibid.

[129] There is not a precise provision how many plaintiffs/defendants could be treated as a mass group. The principle is the group should not be too big, and monetary value at stake in each group should not be excessive. From the practical perspective, less than 30 persons for each group and several million RMB monetary value involved is maximum. See 'The future of mass litigation' (群体性诉讼之前景), (in Chinese), available at http://news.sina.com.cn/c/2005-07-22/17007297908.shtml (accessed on 20 August 2016); In the Daqing Lianyi (2004) case, the Harbin intermediate court broke the plaintiffs into several groups, and there were less than 20 persons in each group in order to avoid the 'mass litigation'. See 'The Daqing Lianyi case is pushed forward with difficulties', (in Chinese), (大庆联谊案件难推进), *Southern Weekend*, available at http://www.southcn.com/weekend/economic/200308140057.htm (accessed on 20 August 2016).

and these groups of plaintiffs will file claims separately before the court.[130] If the court 'thinks it fits', these separate claims will be merged into one court proceeding.[131] Considering the fact that a shareholder collective lawsuit has a much longer proceeding (three-five years on average, including the filing of the case, the court proceeding and the enforcement of the judgment)[132] than ordinary civil litigation, the lawyer taking such a case will assume high litigation risk in the sense that all his efforts will be wasted if the case is lost. Even if the case is won, the lawyer's fees might be disproportionate to the efforts made before.[133]

The lawyer's disincentives in such cases would be further enhanced by the unclear procedural rules in PRC Civil Procedure Law. The CPL [article 146(4)] provides that under certain circumstances, the court could postpone the commencement of the trial. For most cases before the court of first instance, the final judgment must be made within 6 months since the court's acceptance of the case. [article 149 (1) of the CPL] With the approval of the president of the court, the court proceeding for complicated cases could be extended from 6 months to 12 months. [article 149 (2) of the CPL] But article 149 (3) is a vague rule, providing that the 12-month period could be further extended in due cases with the permissions of courts of upper level. In reality, a concern that shareholder litigation belongs to the third scenario stated in article 149 (3) of the CPL has proved to be manifested.[134]

---

[130]For instance, in Daqing Lianyi Case, 381 litigants were divided into smaller groups of ten or twenty persons for each. See 'The Daqing Lianyi case is pushed forward with difficulties', (in Chinese), (大庆联谊案件难推进); See also Wuliangye case 2014, a lawyer Mr. Xufeng represents 28 injured investors, and total monetary value at stake in this group is 1.5 million RMB. See, 'Wuliangye, lost costs for the company's false statement', (五粮液,虚假陈述成本太低), (in Chinese), available at http://shipin.people.com.cn/n/2013/0604/c85914-21731032.html (accessed on 20 August 2016).

[131]Article 52 of Civil Procedure Law provides only when the court thinks it fits, separate claims brought by different groups of persons with the same or similar disputed issues could be merged into one case. No further criteria are provided.

[132]No shareholder collective litigation lasting for less than 3 years is found. The lengthiest case is Shengfang Keji (2001) case, which lasted for 12 years. see, 'A Long March of 12 Years: Move Forward with Difficulties in Securities Fraud Litigation', (12年漫漫征途,维权团队负重前行), (in Chinese), (2013), available at http://www.cqn.com.cn/news/cjpd/710456.html (accessed on 20 August 2016).

[133]For instance, in the Daqing Lianyi case, the damages were 9 million RMB. The lawyers' fees were less than 1 million. The case lasted for 7 years, and the principal lawyer Ms Weihua Xuan stated that in order to do investigation, her assistance and she reviewed documents weighted 1 ton in total. Ms Xuan emphasized if she had done this case for earning lawyers' fees, it would have been a bad deal. See Nan Jiang, 'Interview with Ms Weihua Xuan, *Daqiong Lianyi* case will be of historic significance in Chinese securities fraud litigation', (专访宣伟华律师,大庆联谊案件会被写进历史), (in Chinese), available at http://finance.sina.com.cn/stock/y/20061212/19143157928.shtml (accessed on 20 August 2016); See Silu Guo, 'Who will knock the door of shareholder litigation arising from false statement, a ten years' case review', (谁将叩开股东利益保护之门,虚假陈述诉讼十年探讨), (in Chinese), (2014), available at http://www.infzm.com/content/97734 (accessed on 20 August 2016).

[134]In fact, the lengthy court proceeding of shareholder litigation is largely attributed to the vague provision in article 149 (3) of the CPL. For instance, in *Daqing Lianyi* case, the court procedure

Thus, lawyers would be further discouraged by the even lengthy court proceeding of a shareholder lawsuit and uncertainties associated with it. A disappointing finding is that in light of practical difficulties and the lack of incentives, quite few lawyers are willing to devote their time to shareholder litigation.[135]

#### 6.4.1.2 The *Grandall v Weiguan* 2012 Case: The Risk of Refusal to Pay

Since the use of CGFAs in 2006, there have been several cases where the clients refuse to pay the contingent fees to the lawyer after the case is won.[136] A recent case in this regard receiving public attention is *Apple Inc v. Weiguan (Shenzhen)* 2012 case. In this case, the lawyers (the principal lawyer is Mr. Xianghui Xie) from Grandall Legal Group[137] signed a contingency fee arrangement with Weiguan (Shenzhen), providing that Grandall would get 4% of the total monetary compensation brought from a judgment or a settlement in favour of Weiguan.[138] In the Court of Appeal, the two parties (Apple and Weiguan) reached a settlement agreement stating that Weiguan would get an amount of monetary remedies of 60 million US Dollars. In accordance with the previous CGFA agreement between the lawyers and Weiguan, 2.4 million US Dollars (4% of the total compensation) should be paid as lawyer's fees. However, Weiguan refused to pay the lawyer's fee for the reason that it was in an insolvency procedure and the lawyer's fees were not

(Footnote 134 continued)

lasted for more than 2 years (between the court's acceptance of the case and the declaration of the final judgment); An even worse case is *Yinguangxia* (2001) case, which was accepted by the court in 2001 but the judgment came out in 2007. And *Kelong* 2006 case, which was accepted by the court in 2006 and the settlement agreement was achieved and approved by the court in 2009. See 'More than 100 injured investors joined the *Wuliangye* case and damages might exceed 1 billion RMB', (五粮液诉讼再添近百股民,索赔或超十亿), (2009), available at http://finance.sina.com.cn/stock/s/20091106/00036929876.shtml (accessed on 20 August 2016).

[135]See Sufan Guo, 'Pratical difficulties in shareholder litigation', (中国资本市场民事维权缘何艰难), (in Chinese), (2012), available at http://www.kuaiyilicai.com/201202/fbcec86b-a0f4-4555-b3c5-67f00b1b8d5a.html (accessed on 20 August 2016). See Rongbin Cheng and Xiaochuan Jiang, Civil Procedure Law: Cases and Rules, (民事诉讼法案例与法规), (in Chinese), (2006), China Legal Publishing House, pp. 30–40. Ms Weihua Xuan (the principal lawyer of *Daqing Lianyi* case) is now mainly doing project relating initial public offering (IPO), Merge & Acquisition but not shareholder litigation. See her official work page, http://www.grandall.com.cn/zyry/hhr/140327144742.htm (in Chinese), (accessed on 20 August 2016).

[136]For example, Mr. Litai Zhou, a lawyer based in Chongqing, was refused to be paid by his clients after the case was won. The total amount of unpaid lawyer's fee is more than 5 million RMB; And also a lawyer from Jiangsu Zhengda Law Firm was refused by his client to pay the lawyer fee of 1.5 million RMB. http://www.legalinfo.gov.cn/moj/lsgzgzzds/content/2007-12/17/content_763147.htm?node=282 (accessed on 20 August 2016).

[137]Grandall Legal Group (国浩律师集团 guohao lvshi jituan), the official site http://www.grandall.com.cn/index.htm (accessed on 20 August 2016).

[138]See http://tech.sina.com.cn/it/2012-07-23/09227417612.shtml (in Chinese) (accessed on 20 August 2016).

the first priority.[139] In September 2012, the lawyers sued Weiguan in People's Court of Yantian District in Shenzhen (深圳市盐田区人民法院). A judgment, however, not supporting the lawyer's claim, was delivered by the court in September 2013.

This case reveals the risk of refusal to payment face by the lawyers under the CGFA. The question how lawyers can protect their interests in such cases draws the attention from legal practitioners.[140] In fact, there is no specific regulation dealing with risks of non-payment in CGFAs. In this regard, a general resolution for the lawyer is to resort to arbitration or initiate civil litigation to claim for the legal right. But the risk of non-payment will definitely jeopardize the relationship between lawyers and the clients, and lawyers who would enter into CGFAs may be deterred by the risk of non-payment. Therefore, it was suggested that the lawyers association (律师协会) could be appointed as an authority to resolve disputes between lawyers and clients caused by non-payment. The above observations could indicate that CGFAs in China could hardly be considered as a success.

#### 6.4.1.3 Conclusion

This book, in general, does not recommend the use of CGFAs to finance shareholder litigation in China. The reasons are clear: (1) from the practical perspective, procedural ambiguities discourage lawyers from engaging in shareholder lawsuits; (2) lawyers might fear the risk of refusal to pay.

### *6.4.2 Potential for CFAs to Fund Shareholder Litigation in China*

Currently, CFA is not lawful in China. As for their potential for funding shareholder actions, we do not suppose that it could be an effective mechanism for the same reason that appears in the context of contingency fees: (1) procedural difficulties and the lack of incentives; (2) the risk of refusal to pay.

---

[139]This is a disputed issue. When Weiguan received the whole amount of compensation of 60 million US Dollars from Apple, it did not pay the lawyer's fee immediately. When the insolvency procedure began, Weiguan then refused to pay the lawyer's fee based on the reason that it was insolvent. Therefore, Grandall supposed that Weiguan purposely delayed to pay the lawyer's fee and wanted to enter into the insolvency procedure to evade the obligation of affording lawyer's fees. See http://tech.sina.com.cn/it/2012-07-23/09227417612.shtml (In Chinese), (accessed on 20 August 2016).

[140]See Contingency Fee Arrangements Need to be Developed (律师风险代理制度亟待健全), http://www.moj.gov.cn/lsgzgzzds/content/2007-12/17/content_763549.htm?node=287 (in Chinese) (accessed on 20 August 2016).

### 6.4.3 The Potential for ICOs to Fund Shareholder Derivative Actions in China

Indemnity cost orders are not incorporated in existing Chinese law. When this technique is applied in England, procedural rules with it is often criticized to be uncertain and unclear. When investigating the potential for indemnity cost orders in China, apart from making the procedure clearer, this book also suggests that an indemnity cost order should be awarded only if the court grants the leave for the derivative action to proceed before the court.[141] Article 55 of Provisions of the Supreme People's Court about Several Issues Concerning the Application of the Company Law of the People's Republic of China (IV) (the consultation paper)[142] indicates if a shareholder plaintiff launches a derivative action for a company and finally the case is won, reasonable litigation costs (courts fees and lawyer's fees) should be reimbursed by the company.[143] However, in practice, *ex post* monetary compensation might be problematic, because, among others, the plaintiff only finds out at the end of a trial whether he will get funded by the company. It means that financial deterrents of derivative actions are not removed, and shareholder plaintiffs still face high litigation risk.

In fact, the approach in the consultation paper is applied in order to avoid frivolous lawsuits.[144] The logic is only shareholder plaintiffs bringing derivative actions with merits could be financially compensated. But the proposal in the consultation paper employs 'successful cases' instead of 'cases with merits', creating fundamental difference in the sense that a case with merits does not definitely lead to a successful outcome. If a *bona fide* shareholder plaintiff initiates a meritorious derivative action in the company's interests, it is thought that the company should be liable for the proper litigation costs even though the case is lost.[145]

[141]A similar suggestion in this regard could be found in Lihang Geng, 'Cost Assumption and Judicial Approval in Shareholder Derivative Actions' (论我国股东派生诉讼的费用承担和司法许可), *Science of Law*, Volume 1 (2013), 170.

[142]In fact, this document is just a consultation paper without binding effect. 'Higher People's Court of Shanghai Municipality: Several Opinions on Adjudicating Company Litigation' makes a similar provision in this aspect, which provides that if a judgment is made in favour of the shareholder plaintiff, the company should make reasonable monetary compensation to the shareholder plaintiff.

[143]This article uses the word 'reasonable' litigation costs, but it does not further indicate what kinds of litigation costs could be regarded as 'reasonable'. For our points of view, the reasonable costs mean that the shareholder plaintiffs use the money properly, and do not waste money on purpose. But in fact, under this provision, the shareholder plaintiff is only reimbursed after a successful derivative lawsuit. Therefore, we suppose that there is no need to worry that the shareholder plaintiff may waste the money because he pays the costs out of his own pocket and there is no guarantee that the case will definitely succeed in the end.

[144]See Lihang Geng, 'Cost Assumption and Judicial Approval in Shareholder Derivative Actions' (论我国股东派生诉讼的费用承担和司法许可), *Science of Law*, Volume 1 (2013), 170, p. 179.

[145]Ibid.

The strict approach employed in the consultation paper may be useful to prevent frivolous cases, however, on the other hand, it might deter *bona fide* shareholder plaintiffs to initiate meritorious cases.[146] The problem here is how to strike a sound balance between the avoidance of cases without merits and the encouragement of meritorious derivative actions which would improve the level of corporate governance. In fact, existing legal practice suggests that precedents of derivative actions are necessary to be established in the sense that experience regarding trials on derivative lawsuits should be accumulated in order to make this mechanism function well.[147] For instance, what kinds of activities should be considered as 'violation of director's fiduciary duty' in the trial on a derivative lawsuit? In 2003 (derivative actions were not legally confirmed at that time), Xinxian Zhao, the director of *Sanjiu* Medical & Pharmaceutical Company was sued by minority investors for violating the fiduciary duty (the mis-appropriation of the company's assets).[148] No existing laws as well as practical rules at that time and even now has elaborated what kinds of activities by a company's board of directors would be sued for 'violating fiduciary duties'. Therefore, removing funding obstacles for prospective shareholder claimants to commence derivative lawsuits could pave the way for interpreting technical terms (such as the scope of director's fiduciary duty), elaborating practical issues in court trials, and, further, facilitating the functioning of derivative litigation. Considering that, it might be safe to conclude that a reformed indemnity cost order, in which the reimbursement of litigation fees could be awarded to the shareholder plaintiffs as long as the court allows the derivative lawsuit to proceed, could be applied instead of the method suggested in the consultation paper. In this approach, the court's scrutiny is expected to bar unmeritorious lawsuit, and the comparatively relaxed reimbursement requirement could help to remove funding obstacles, to a certain extent, for shareholder plaintiffs.

## 6.5 Summary

An in-depth investigation on three funding alternatives (indemnity cost orders, contingency fee arrangements, and conditional fee agreements) was conducted in this Chapter. As for the indemnity cost order, it is generally criticized because of its unclear procedural rules and practical dilemma. In evaluating funding by lawyers,

---

146 Ibid.

147 Ibid.

148 The case was not accepted by the court because at that time derivative actions were not statutorily confirmed in China, therefore, Chinese courts with conservative attitudes did not want to accept such a case to make an innovation. See 'The Investigation of Sanjiu Medical & Pharmaceutical Co. Ltd: the Eve of Shareholding Reform' (三九医药被查:股改前夜打响清欠第一枪), Shanghai Security News (上海证券报), in Chinese, (27 December 2010), available at http://finance.sina.com.cn/stock/s/20101207/03019064496.shtml (accessed on 20 August 2016).

we prefer contingency fee arrangements (CGFAs) to conditional fee agreements (CFAs), but the moral hazard and the relationship between lawyers and clients are big concerns. Finally, after investigating the current legal practice of these funding alternatives in China and their potential, a conclusion could be reasonably reached that a reformed indemnity cost order could be adopted to fund shareholder derivative actions in China.

# Chapter 7
# Policy Proposals for Solving Funding Problems with Shareholder Litigation in China

## 7.1 Overview

In previous Chapters, we studied funding difficulties with shareholder litigation, and discussed several solutions to these problems. (for instance, third party litigation funding; public funding; indemnity cost orders; contingency fee arrangements) This Chapter will mainly focus on proposals for China—(for instance, which funding technique(s) are suitable for China; how these funding mechanisms should be reformed to cater for present social conditions in China). In general, we suppose that public funding, third party litigation funding (TPLF) and indemnity cost orders all have potential for China, provided certain reforms are carried out.

## 7.2 Option 1—Public Funding

*Para 1. Which authority will take charge of public funding?*

In this regard, we suggest that Chinese courts, rather than other public authorities, would take charge of public funding. Actually, we do not suppose that it is necessary and reasonable to set up a new institution bringing a drain on public budget to administrate public funding.[1] Particularly, at an initial stage, when the prospect of public funding in China has not been clearly predicted, establishing a new institution to take charge of public funding may waste public money.

[1]Public budgets are needed not only to set up and maintain the daily operation of the institution, but also to meet the expenses of administrating it. See Zhong Zhang, *The Derivative Action and Good Corporate Governance In China: Economic Theories And Legal Rules*, Lambert Academic Publishing, (2011), p. 211.


W. Chen, *A Comparative Study of Funding Shareholder Litigation*,
DOI 10.1007/978-981-10-3623-1_7

*Supra* 4.4.4 (the selection of an authority taking charge of public funding) pointed out that public authorities (e.g. CSRC) and non-profit organizations (NPOs) are not suitable to be administer public funding mainly for the reason that it is difficult for them to be shielded from the influences of the Party-State. As for the recommendation that Chinese courts taking charge of public funding, it needs to be stated that in order to shield influence from the local government (the concern of 'local protectionism'), public funding must be financed by special fund allocated by the central government instead of the local government.

In this regard, we suggest that the authority scrutinizing the application of public funding should be an *independent* department within the court. It should be shielded from the influences of other departments within the same court and upper courts.[2,3] Considering that, we suggest that an ad hoc panel could be set up to scrutinize public funding applications. Members of the ad hoc panel could not be permanent, and they should be selected randomly in order to eliminate corruption.[4] The list of the members should be regarded as confidential information that should not be opened to the public as well as prospective judges who will judge the funded cases.[5] Only if the applicant makes an appeal after the refusal of a public funding application, the member list of the panel could be released to the applicant. In general, the main reasons for this proposal (set an ad hoc panel and keep the member list as confidential information) are: (a) it might eliminate corruption; (b) it might eliminate mutual influence between judging tribunals and charging panel of public funding; (c) compared to setting up a permanent department within a court, it could be more flexible and economical.[6]

---

[2]The court is the place where a case is adjudicated. If the independent department within a court takes charge of the public funding, we should guarantee that the future trial on this publicly-funded case would not be affected by the positive decision made by the department approving public funding. The principle applied in deciding which department should be the administering authority of public funding should be that we must eliminate the mutual influence between the two departments (charging authority of public funding and adjudicating tribunal of the court) to the largest extent.

[3]The latter part of this sentence means that the 'internal instruction' between the upper courts and lower ones as mentioned in Sect. 4.4.3.1 does not apply for the public funding department.

[4]In this Chapter, we mainly give proposals for funding shareholder actions in China. Therefore, it is reasonable that the application for public funding to shareholder litigation could be scrutinized by experts who are familiar with corporate law and corporate governance. As for the selection of members of the deciding panel, it could be feasible that a list of experts of corporate law and corporate governance could put into computers, and the random selection could be done by computers. By doing it, we suppose that corruptions might be eliminated.

[5]In this regard, once the random selection has been made, it should be kept as confidential. If an application for public funding is refused and the applicant makes an appeal of the refusal decision, the member list of the panel could be opened to the applicants.

[6]If a permanent department taking charge of public funding was founded, it might use more monetary and human resources. Provided that the charging department was dismissed because of the failure of public funding, those resources might be wasted.

*Para 2. Selection criteria applied in scrutinizing public funding*

When scrutinizing a public funding application, both in Israel and Canada, one of the essential issues is to ensure that the case to be funded should be with merits.[7,8] Except for this requirement, the Israel securities authority (ISA) requires that cases need to demonstrate public significance.[9] Similarly, in Ontario, cases concerning broader public interests would be funded preferentially.[10] In the context of China, we suggest that two criteria (a) cases must be with merits; (b) cases demonstrating public significance will be funded preferentially, meaning that it might be possible that before the potential expansion of the public funding budget, most of publicly funded cases would be those attracting public attention or involving widely dispersed shareholders.[11]

For the first requirement, it needs to be pointed out that the interpretation of 'meritorious' should be an 'easy' one. The applicant only needs to show that it is a *prima facie* case, and there is no need for the applicant to convince the panel further. For instance, in the context of shareholder derivative litigation, the applicant is not required to provide evidence to demonstrate that there is a reasonable prospect the court would grant leave for the lawsuit to proceed as a derivative lawsuit.[12] The main reasons for our suggestion are that: (a) we do not intend to prolong the scrutinize procedure into a costly mini-trial; (b) at an initial stage a strict

[7]For instance, Section 205A of the Israeli Company Law provides that there should be reasonable prospect that the case would be granted leave as a derivative action by the court. Even though a case with merits could be refused by the court as a derivative action, we suppose that this provision is designed to screen out unmeritorious cases. In public funding granted by Ontario Class Proceeding Committee, the merits of a case should be scrutinized by the court when an application is made by the impecunious applicants (Section 59.3(4) of the Law Society Act, RSO 1990).

[8]In the Israeli case, on top of this requirement, the ISA requires that there should be a reasonable prospect that the court would grant leave for the action to proceed as a derivative lawsuit (Section 205A of the Israeli Company Law).

[9]For instance, Section 205 A of the Israeli Company Law provides that there should a public interest in bringing the case.

[10]For instance, in Ontario, the Class Proceeding Committee prefers to grant public funding to the case which represents broader public concerns or cases which will have impact on the improvement of the situation of people who have been historically disadvantaged in society. See David Collins, 'Public Funding of Multi-party Litigation', *Manitoba Law Journal*, (2010), Volume 31, 211, pp. 230–231.

[11]The reason for our proposal is that public funding is, in essence, from the pockets of taxpayers. Therefore, making cases with public significance be preferably funded is reasonable. For instance, in a shareholder lawsuit where many shareholders suffered financial losses because a listed company made misrepresentation about its profitability. For those cases not demonstrating public significance, shareholder plaintiffs may resort to other funding methods to finance the litigation. For instance, they can seek help from lawyers.

[12]Like the Israeli approach, potential grant of leave to a case by the court is regarded to be a selection criterion in awarding public funding. But in China, we suggest that this criterion would not be adopted.

approach may deter potential *bona fide* applicants;[13] (c) as a unique species of civil lawsuits, the procedural requirements for a shareholder lawsuit are more strict than ordinary ones. In light of that, it is highly possible that 'bad' cases could be filtered in the court proceeding.[14]

*Para 3. How could public funding be financed?*

Should public funding be financed by the state budget, by the successful applicants or by others? The Ontario Class Proceeding Fund and the Quebec Fonds d'aide aux recours collectives are financed by different methods. The Ontario funding mainly financially relies on the 10 percent levying from the successful applicants who win the lawsuits afterwards.[15] The set-up capital of the Fund is approximately $500,000, which was provided by the local government. In fact, the Ontario approach has been criticized because of the insufficient governmental financial assistance and sluggish periodic fund flow from the successful applicants, which may lead to a narrow access to the Fund for future applicants.[16] Moreover, in light of the expensive 10 percent levying rate, potential applicants may resort to other funding techniques not requiring a high levy.[17] It was once indicated that the Ontario Class Proceedings Fund does not prove to be a success mainly due to the inadequate financial resource and problematic supplementary funding mechanism.[18] Compared to the Ontario Class Proceedings

---

[13]In our points of view, at a very initial stage, if a strict approach was applied, it would be difficult to see whether public funding could function well in China. For potential public funding in China, we just intend to set an experimental period of one or two years to see the result of public funding of shareholder actions and its function in promote corporate governance. Therefore, during the experimental period, very strict and complicated selection criteria, we suppose, might negatively affect our observation over public funding in China. For example, too strict application requirements may lead potential applicants to resort to other funding sources (e.g. lawyers' funding through contingency fee arrangements) other than public funding. Atthe initial step, what we need (both for the Chinese legislators) is enough practical samples regarding public funding. In fact, it does not mean that we will lift out the floodgate for applicants, but just adopt comparatively non-harsh requirements for potential public funding applicants. If the result after the one-or-two years of experimental period indicated that the requirements were too relaxed and applications should be tightened, it would then reform the requirements to filter unreasonable applications.

[14]Under Chinese law, prior to the grant of the leave for a derivative lawsuit, the court must be satisfied that the shareholder plaintiffs have exhausted all internal remedies, and the claims have been refused by the board of directors. Threshold requirements for shareholder plaintiffs have also been provided in PRC Company Law. For more, see art. 152 of Chinese Company Law 2006 (2006 CCL).

[15]See *supra* 4.3.

[16]The reasons why the periodic capital flow to the Fund is sluggish have been indicated in *supra* 4.3.1.

[17]See Jasminka Kalajdzic, Peter Cashman and Alana Longmoore, 'Justice for Profit: A Comparative Analysis of Australian, Canadian and U.S. Third Party Litigation Funding', *American Journal of Comparative Law*, Volume 61, 93, p. 118.

[18]See Rachael Mulheron, *The Class Action in Common Law Legal Systems, a Comparative Perspective*, Hart Publishing, (2004), pp. 457–458; Garry D. Watson, 'Class Actions: The Canadian Experience', *Duke Journal of Comparative and International Law*, (2001), volume 11, 169, pp. 275–276.

Fund, the Quebec *Fonds* seems to be more successful.[19] One of the reasons should be that the financial resources of the Quebec *Fonds* are more adequate than those of the Ontario Class Proceedings Fund.[20] In fact, the *Fonds* is an ongoing financial responsibility of the Quebec government and the government plays an active role in financially supporting it.[21] Additionally, the *Fonds* is entitled to collect a certain percentage of court-ordered recoveries from any judgment or settlement in class lawsuits (not restricted to the cases funded by the *Fonds* before).[22,23]

In this regard, we suggest that the public funding in China should be wholly financed by the state budget. The reasons for the suggestion are (a) we do not want to repeat the Ontario 'failure' in China (to deter potential applicants because of the high levying rate); (b) we suppose that the Quebec approach is not justified to those successful shareholder plaintiffs who were not publicly funded before.[24]

*Para 4. Conclusion*

In the last four paragraphs, proposals for public funding were delivered in different aspects. Generally, we recommend the use of public funding in China to finance shareholder litigation. From practical perspective, it is suggested that an ad hoc panel in the court, which is expected to avoid corruption and save financial budget, would be established to take charge of public funding. When the public funding is scrutinized, two selection criteria need to be adopted. Namely, the case to be publicly funded should be a meritorious case, and cases demonstrating public significance will be funded preferentially. As for the question how the public funding should be financed, we suggest that it would be totally funded by the state budget.

---

[19]See *supra* 4.3.

[20]See *supra* 4.3.

[21]Jocob Ziegel, 'Class Actions to Remedy Mass Consumer Wrongs: Repugnant Solution or Controllable Genie? The Canadian Experience', *Penn State International Law Review*, Volume 27, 879, p. 891. Unlike Ontario Class Proceedings Fund, the amount of money that the Quebec government provided to support the Fonds was not indicated. However, almost all literatures states that the financial support the Quebec government provided to the Fonds is comparatively adequate and the government plays an active role in supporting the Fonds. For more, see Alan Riley, 'Damages in EC Antitrust Actions: Who Pays the Piper?', *European Law Review*, (2006), Volume 31(5), 748, p. 759.

[22]In fact, the levying percentage varies and mainly depends on the different methods of recovery by the class members. For more, see *supra* Part III Chapter I ('the Canadian experience).

[23]For public funding for derivative actions in Israel, we could not find the financial supplement mechanism of it. So in this section, we do not investigate the Israeli approach in this aspect.

[24]If those successful cases were funded by third party litigation funding or financed by others ways, it is not equal for them to submit an amount of money to the public funding because they had shared the monetary compensation with their funders.

## 7.3 Option 2—Third Party Litigation Funding (TPLF)

*Para 1. General evaluation of the potential for using TPLF to fund shareholder actions in China*

In Chapter 5, after studying the experience of TPLF in three jurisdictions (Australia, the UK, the US), a positive conclusion is finally made that TPLF has potential to finance shareholder litigation in China. In order to facilitate the use of TPLF, certain reforms need to be done in existing Chinese law (for instance, regulating TPLF agreements through PRC Contract Law).[25] When introducing TPLF into China, we propose that at the initial stage strict requirements will be imposed on litigation funders. Only qualified ones could be allowed to enter into litigation funding market. The proposed requirements should include, among other things, the funder's financial capacity.[26] In the following sections, proposals for the working mechanism and regulations of TPLF will be presented in details.

*Para 2. Requirements for third party litigation funders*

Third party litigation funders (litigation funding companies) should be supervised. In this regard, it is recommended that they could be administered by Justice Bureaus (司法局) for the reason that funders, in nature, provide legal service.[27] A similar method with the pre-2012 Australian approach where a qualified third party litigation funder must hold a Financial Service Licence (AFSL) granted by the Australian Securities and Investment Commission (ASIC) could be adopted.[28] It means that, before entering into litigation market, third party funders need to apply for a licence from the Justice Bureau and then register with the Bureau for future supervision.

---

[25]See *supra* 5.7.4.3.

[26]Like in Australia, the Financial Service Licence (AFSL) granted by Australian Securities and Investment Commission (ASIC) should be held by a qualified third party litigation funder. But in 2012, the High Court abolished it and decided that litigation funders were not required to hold AFSLs. See *supra* 5.2.3; However, in this aspect, we suppose TPLF in China could adopt a supervision mechanism similar with AFSLs.

[27]Generally, Justice Bureaus (司法局) are appointed to administer organizations (companies) providing legal service. For instance, law firms are supervised by Justice Bureaus. See *Administrative Measures for Law Firms* (律师事务所管理办法), and *Decision of the Ministry of Justice on Amending the Administrative Measures for Law Firms* (司法部关于修改律师事务所管理办法的决定).

[28]In 2012, third party litigation funding are exempted from the financial service provisions which means that funders are not required to hold a AFSL. The requirement for Australian third party funders in place of it is incorporated in Regulatory Guide 248: Litigation schemes and proof of debt schemes: Managing conflicts of interest (see *supra* 5.2.3).

Requirements for a qualified third party litigation funder should include:

(a) The third party litigation funder must have enough financial resources (for instance, more than 10,000,000 RMB);[29]
(b) The funding company must be equipped with a group of persons who were professional legal practitioners before. For instance, the funding company must have a certain percentage of former lawyers.[30]
(c) The funders should agree if they were found to **seriously** violate the funding agreement, they would be punished or even the licence granted before could be revoked by the Justice Bureau;[31]
(d) The funders should agree if they were found to purposely finance strike suits for their clients, they would be punished or even the licence granted before could be revoked by the Justice Bureau;
(e) The funders should agree if they were found to purposely finance unmeritorious or frivolous suits they would be punished or even the licence granted before could be revoked by the Justice Bureau.

*Para 3. Proposed supplements to PRC Contract Law*

In 5.7.4.3 (how to regulate the third party litigation funding agreement: from the perspective of the PRC Contract Law), we suggested that supplements should be made to present PRC Contract Law (CCL) for a better regulation on TPLF agreements. Under existing law, provisions about non-specific contracts (无名合同) could be applied to administer TPLF agreements.[32] However, specific issues in the context of a TPLF agreement, such as the funder's monopolization on the funded case, are not mentioned. Existing rules, in fact, are not sufficient to tackle with problems particularly caused by TPLF contracts.[33] Proposed supplements to the PRC Contract Law are listed as follows:

---

[29]To fund shareholder litigation, the funder's financial capacity must be even high than other ordinary civil lawsuits.

[30]The reason for this proposal is to make the cost-and-benefit analysis really functions. As indicated before, the prevention of the rise of unmeritorious and frivolous cases could be achieved by the funder's cost-and-benefit analysis, which is highly possible to be implemented by professional legal practitioner than others who did not engage in any professional activities before (see *supra* 5.1.2).

[31]The serious violation may include, for instance, the funder's conspiracy with the lawyer in order to get more interests for themselves.

[32]See *supra* 5.7.4.3.

[33]Rules concerning 'non-specific' contracts are incorporated in article 124 of the PRC Contract Law, only providing that 'provisions in the General Provisions of this Law shall be applied, and reference may be made to the provisions in the Specific Provisions of this Law or in any other law that most closely relate to such contract'. Problems specifically brought by the use of TPLF, such as the funder's moral hazard, are not mentioned in this article, hence, it is not sufficient to regulate TPLF agreements.

(a) It should be stated that funders owe fiduciary duties to their clients (funded parties) but not to lawyers.
(b) It should provide the range of the charging rate (20–40%) by the funder in the event that the funded case is finally won.
(c) Funders, without permissions of their clients (funded parties), are not allowed to contact with lawyers.
(d) Funding applicants are obligatorily required to indicate the case merits.
(e) Confidentiality agreements should be signed between funders and their clients.
(f) The amount of funding budget provided by the funder should be clearly indicated in the funding agreement. Or, if there is no such indication, it should be treated that the funder will continuously provide funding for the case until the final judgment/settlement is achieved. The termination of the funding should be made in limited circumstance. For instance, the funder finds the funded case is unmeritorious or it is a strike suit.

*Para 4. Conclusion*

This book, in general, supports the potential use of TPLF to finance shareholder litigation in China. Then it is suggested that before entering into litigation funding market, funders need to meet several requirements, for instance, the funder's financial capacity. Justice Bureaus would issue licences to qualified funders and supervise their performance (for instance, whether a funder finance a strike suit on purpose). In general, at the very initial stage, we recommend that the industry of third party litigation funding needs to be strictly regulated in order to guarantee a sound market order and disruptive effects should be avoided.

## 7.4 Option 3—Reformed Indemnity Cost Orders

Chapter 6 provided a general analysis of a group of funding alternatives (contingency fee arrangements, indemnity cost orders and conditional fee agreements) other than public funding and TPLF. It finally concludes that reformed indemnity cost orders would be suitable to fund shareholder litigation in China. It is also indicated that the most primary concern with regards to the use of an indemnity cost order is procedural uncertainties. Therefore, what should be reformed regarding this technique is to eliminate procedural uncertainties and make the application requirements more clear.[34] As indicated in Sect. 6.4.3 (potential for ICOs to fund

[34]Procedural uncertainties and unclear application requirements are: when a court scrutinizes an application of an indemnity cost order, it has wide discretion. There are not clear standards under what circumstances an indemnity cost order should be granted by the court. But in fact in England, the number of derivative actions is limited and the court does not have enough experience in elaborating under what circumstances an indemnity cost order should be awarded to shareholder applicants. See *supra* 6.1.2.

shareholder derivative actions in China), it is suggested that once a derivative claim is allowed to proceed before the court, the indemnity cost order could be awarded to the shareholder applicants. In light of this rule, procedural certainties could be achieved without being expanded into expensive mini-trails.[35]

[35]In the practical experience of indemnity cost orders in England, in view of the absence of clear rules, courts hold wide discretion in awarding indemnity cost orders. In fact, the scrutinize procedure is easily developed into an expensive mini-trial.

# Chapter 8
# Conclusion

## 8.1 The Problem of Funding Shareholder Litigation

This book examines the issue of funding shareholder litigation, both in the form of derivative actions and direct actions[1] mainly in the form of class actions. The focus is on litigation for damages, less on injunctive relief. The potential of several funding techniques was investigated in a functionally comparative way. The focus particularly lies with how to effectively fund shareholder derivative actions where shareholder plaintiffs sue wrongdoers on behalf of the company.

There are several reasons why funding of shareholder litigation is an important issue and creates difficulties for the shareholders involved. First, shareholder litigation is often costly in the same way that other litigation is costly: the costs for the plaintiff include court charges, own lawyer's fees, and the adverse fees in case of losing under the cost-shifting rule. Moreover, in a country such as China but also in other countries, such litigation is generally considered as a property lawsuit, where the court charges (a major component of the litigation cost) are calculated on an incremental basis, proportionate with the monetary value involved in the dispute.[2] Shareholder litigation usually involves non-standard, complex cases with intensive fact-finding and high monetary stakes. Both facts have an upward effect on litigation costs. The defendant in shareholder litigation is often either a corporation, or its board or officers (financially) backed by the corporation, or both. The plaintiffs can be large corporations or institutional investors, but often will be retail investors or small minority shareholders. This means it is not uncommon for shareholder litigation to involve a scenario where relatively impecunious shareholder plaintiffs are pitted against a defendant with deep pockets, who can increase the cost of

[1] Being complaints brought by one or several shareholders because they allegedly suffered damage directly, as opposed to 'reflective damage', which is damage to shareholders as an indirect result of damage that was primarily inflicted on the (assets of) the company.

[2] A typical exception in this regard is that the court charge of a derivative lawsuit in Japan is a fixed amount of money which is not relevant to the monetary value. See *supra* 3.1.1.1.



W. Chen, *A Comparative Study of Funding Shareholder Litigation*,
DOI 10.1007/978-981-10-3623-1_8

litigation for the plaintiff by fielding an expensive defense team that the plaintiff to a certain extent needs to match, and by trying to lengthen proceedings, which also increases their costs. Given that, the general litigation costs for shareholder litigation is on average expensive, and this may financially deter shareholder plaintiffs.

At the same time, shareholder litigation often has potential 'positive externalities', but perversely, this creates additional problems for funding shareholder litigation (free riders and collective action problems). For example, if one or a small group of shareholder brings a suit against directors who committed fraud against the corporation, the positive effect of a successful case will benefit all shareholders if the suit is brought in the form of a derivative action, where damages awarded are paid to the company and not to the shareholder who acted as the plaintiff and incurred the risk involved with. This creates a big free rider problem: the risk is borne by the plaintiff(s), the rewards by all shareholders. In consideration of that, if the potential plaintiff in a derivative action is not helped by funding mechanisms that assist him to bear litigation costs or at least limit the risk he is exposed to, he will have a negative incentive to start derivative actions.

But if too few derivative actions or other forms of shareholder litigation take place, the deterrence function of shareholder litigation will not be fulfilled. Shareholder litigation benefits private parties (shareholders) who win the case, but can also contribute to better corporate governance, by enforcing rules for directors or managers. It is a mechanism of 'private enforcement' of corporate law, and we presume that the enforcement of corporate law is good for the legal and economic system of a country. Therefore, if there is a lack of proper funding techniques for shareholder litigation, shareholder litigation may remain below its socially 'optimal level' (Shavell).

A similar problem is that in many cases, shareholder litigation will involve 'negative value claims', that is, the potential damages that the plaintiff would get if the case is won, would probably be lower than the cost of litigation. This is often the case when small investors have lost amounts of money on the stock market as a result of securities fraud by management (e.g. not disclosing price sensitive information in a timely manner), and this amount of money is important for the investor, but litigation is so complex that the cost of litigation will be almost as large or sometimes exceed the damages that are awarded. This negative value problem can be overcome by putting the claims of many shareholders together, so that they can share costs. This still leaves many problems open, like that shareholders often don't know each other. Securities class actions are a technique that can help overcome this negative value and this coordination (collective action) problem.

So funding of shareholder litigation is a problem because shareholder litigation is costly and sometimes there is a 'negative value claims' problem and, particularly in derivative actions, a free rider problem. The funding problem should be solved, because it is only just that shareholders that have been harmed could get compensation, but also because private shareholder litigation also, at least potentially, has a deterrence effect and can help enforce corporate rules, leading to a better economic system.

In this book we looked at several mechanisms to solve the funding problem: public funding (i.e. funding of private litigation by public authorities), third party litigation funding (TPLF), contingency fee arrangements (CGFAs), conditional fee agreements (CFAs) and, more briefly, indemnity cost orders (esp. applied in England and Wales to particularly fund shareholder derivative actions) were discussed.

## 8.2 Public Funding

Our investigation of public funding was based on the Israeli case (public funding of derivative actions) and the Canadian example (the Ontario Class Proceeding Fund and the Quebec *fonds d'aide aux recours collectifs*). The main finding is that public funding could be a useful technique to support shareholder litigation if several practical dilemmas are solved. These include the selection of a proper funding authority, deciding how this authority will be financed (taxes; designing a reimbursement system based on the gains of previous applicants) and laying down clear standards for applicants.

The Israeli public funding is a sort of financial assistance provided by the Israel Securities Authority (ISA) for impecunious shareholder plaintiffs to commence a shareholder derivative action, which was introduced in 2011. The ISA sets out two cumulative preconditions for potential shareholder applicants (1) there should be a reasonable prospect that the case would be allowed to proceed as a derivative lawsuit before the court; (2) the case to be funded needs to demonstrate public interests. It was criticized that the first requirement is vague and, in practice, its determination depends largely on the ISA's discretion. Another issue in this regard is the ISA's decision concerning whether or not the case could be granted leave by the court will have impact on the court's own decision. It might be possible that the court would be partly influenced by the ISA's decision of awarding public funding to finance a derivative action or *vice versa*. With regards to the regulatory authority of public funding (ISA), a theoretic concern is when performing its working task, ISA, as a regulatory agency, might be biased. It is recognized that political and interest groups may have substantial influence on the law-making and law-enforcement process. Considering that, public enforcers may have defects in many cases. The Israeli public funding is a system with a short history of only five years (2011–2016), so it might be too soon to judge whether this theoretic concern appears in the Israeli case. However, the possibility that the public authority might become biased in some cases because of several factors (for instance, political influence, interests of powerful groups and public officers' self-interest) needs to be noticed, particularly when drawing conclusions for China, where it seems clear that there is a possibility of political influence on public agencies.

The Canadian public funding system (Class Proceeding Fund in Ontario and Fonds d'aide aux recours collectifs in Quebec) has a longer history than the Israeli approach (the Ontario one was adopted in 1992 and the Quebec approach was legally confirmed by Bill 80 in 1999[3]). Through the investigation of the Canadian case, the main finding is that the Quebec Fonds proves to be more successful than the Ontario Fund partly due to the different funding reimbursement systems and their respective financial resources. The Ontario Law Foundation provided $500,000 as start-up money to the Fund, and 10% of monetary remedies awarded by the court to the plaintiff must be paid to the Fund in a successfully funded case. In fact, from the perspective of financing, the Fund heavily relies on the 10% levying which is criticized to be excessive.[4] This high reimbursement obligation makes the Fund less attractive to potential applicants (normally those people with a 'strong' case).[5]

In addition to that, the under-utilization of the Fund is perhaps caused by certain procedural requirements set out by the Ontario Law Foundation (the regulatory authority of the Fund). An application for the Fund will not be considered until a statement of defence has been delivered to the court. Normally, the defendants would withhold the filing statement until the certification motion has been determined. But in practice, the availability of the litigation funding will be taken into consideration when the court decided whether the certification motion will be granted. Considering that, the rule provided by the Foundation makes it unpractical for plaintiffs who need financial assistance to satisfy the certification requirement before they get funded. In this regard, the Quebec approach is much more applicant-friendly: the application can be submitted in the very beginning or even before the initiation of a class action. And also, the financial resources in the Quebec Fonds are more adequate than those in the Ontario Fund. Other than in the Ontario's approach, the Quebec government plays an active role in financially supporting the Fonds, and it collects a certain percentage (less than 10%) of the court-ordered recoveries from *any* judgement or settlement in class lawsuits even if they were not previously funded by the Fonds. No evidence suggests that the ongoing government financial assistance has led to the government in Quebec trying to influence cases.

After the investigation of the Canadian and Israeli cases regarding public funding, its potential for China was analysed, with attention focused on the Chinese general legal and social background, the examination of Chinese public authorities and Chinese non-profit organizations (NPOs). For the Chinese case, the main concerns in the political and social area include, among others, the concern of 'inside system' (a group of political and business insiders who are connected among each other), 'local protectionism', the 'GDP worship' and the fact that these issues come together especially in state-owned (sometimes listed) enterprises (SOEs) that are important for the (local) economy. The problems of the Chinese judicial system mainly concern the lack of judicial independence and the judicial aversion against

[3]Bill 80 'An Act to amend the Act respecting the class action', available at http://www.assnat.qc.ca/en/travaux-parlementaires/projets-loi/projet-loi-80-36-1.html (accessed on 20 August 2016).

[4]See *supra* 4.3.1.

[5]Ibid.

mass litigation. In addition to that, when examining the feasibility of public funding in China, potential regulatory authorities (Chinese public authorities and non-profit organizations, NPOs) were also investigated.

The main findings in the Chinese case are:

## *8.2.1 From the Social and Political Perspectives*

### 8.2.1.1 The Concern of the 'Inside System' (体制内)

Chinese courts and governments (both central and local ones) both belong to the 'inside system' which is essentially controlled and heavily influenced by the Party-state. In some shareholder litigation involving significant companies or state-owned enterprises (SOEs), the defendants, who are usually appointed by the Party-state or have a political background, are indeed members of the 'inside system'. Shareholder plaintiffs without strong political background, who are not within the 'inside system', will encounter difficulties to 'go against' those members of the 'inside system'.

### 8.2.1.2 'Local Protectionism' (地方保护主义)

The fiscal budget of a local government depends largely on the tax turned over by local enterprises, which is generally in proportion to their incomes. Considering that, what the local government is concerned about are the incomes and the profitability of local enterprises. Any court orders that would negatively affect the company's profitability may not be favoured by the local government. Under this circumstance, it might be highly possible that the court will side with the government instead of shareholder plaintiffs because both of them are members of the 'inside system' which is controlled and led by the Communist Party.

### 8.2.1.3 The 'GDP Worship'

The concern of 'local protectionism' could be further enhanced by the 'GDP worship' of governments at all levels. In China, the performance of a government official is generally evaluated by his GDP record, which could be problematic and even dangerous. A concern might be raised whether the strong GDP worship leads to the neglect of people's interests. For instance, the court (which sides with the government due to the 'inside system' theory) will 'forgive' a company's misbehaviour if it could contribute to a high GDP record. Under this circumstance, if a group of minority shareholders files a shareholder derivative action involving a high-profitable enterprise in a court, the government may interfere in the court's decision for the sake of high GDP. Or the case might even be refused at a very early stage by the case filing chamber of the court.

#### 8.2.1.4 The Dilemma in State-Owned Enterprises (SOEs) and Listed Companies

Many listed companies are state owned, where the Party-state is the controlling shareholder. When a shareholder lawsuit concerning a listed company/an SOE is launched, it is highly possible that the court will be reluctant to be independent in dealing with the case because of the political sensitivity. For example, the *Sanlian Shangshe* 2009 case, which is the first and the only derivative action involving a listed company, was sued before the Shandong Provincial Higher People's Court. The judgment of this case was made in 2012, declaring that the claim of minority shareholders was rejected. The real reason of the court's rejection was probably that the Sanlian Group (the defendant) is a significant corporation in Shandong Province and the local government had put it into a core list of enterprises which are strongly supported by the government.

### 8.2.2 *From the Perspective of Chinese Judicial System*

#### 8.2.2.1 The Lack of Judicial Independence

First of all, the existence of 'inside system' creates the lack of judicial independence. Within the judicial system, upper courts may officially, as a matter of law, directly instruct lower courts in some complicated but in practice also in politically sensitive cases. The internal instruction has been strongly criticized by Chinese law scholars and legal practitioners. In the last decade, 'building a harmonious society' was adopted by the government as an important ideology, which negatively affected the building of an independent judicial system. During that period, the Supreme People's Court published guidelines to other Chinese courts to emphasize the importance of 'building a harmonious society' by indicating that the achievement of this goal needs the cooperation of the whole judicial system.

#### 8.2.2.2 The Judicial Avoidance of Mass Litigation

Several rules and practical guidelines issued by the Supreme Court limit the commencements of certain sorts of mass litigation. For instance, in 2001 the Supreme People's Court once issued instructions to lower courts to strictly limit the acceptance of securities claims involving multiple plaintiffs. In some cases, the court may require plaintiffs who wish to litigate together to separate their claims into small groups in order to prevent mass litigation. For instance, in the first permitted shareholder litigation on false and misleading disclosure (Daqing lianyi 2006 case), the Harbin intermediate court required the original 381 plaintiffs to break into smaller groups of ten or twenty persons each. Restrictions can also be found in lawyers' participation in mass litigation. Lawyers are required to report to the government agencies, and they should also accept the supervision and guidance from them after accepting a mass litigation. For Chinese courts, we indicated that they are not proactive in hearing corporate and securities cases, because they are neither experienced nor politically powerful in dealing with cases with powerful defendants (for instance, SOEs).

### 8.2.3 *The Selection of Regulatory Authority of Public Funding*

#### 8.2.3.1 A Public Authority (the China Securities Regulatory Commission, CSRC)

Considering the 'inside system' theory, it might be difficult for the CSRC to act unbiased in administering public funding.

#### 8.2.3.2 Chinese Non-profit Organizations (NPOs)

There are generally two sorts of NPOs in China: public NPOs and private NPOs. In fact, many public NPOs in China have a political background and they can hardly operate independently without political interference. It appears that those public NPOs are members of the 'inside system'. Therefore, they are not proper organizations to take charge of public funding.

For private NPOs, there are basically two reasons why they are still not suitable to function as the regulatory authorities administering public funding. First, the registration of a private NPO is greatly subject to the public concern. This means if a private NPO was established to 'go against' the 'inside system' (for instance, help minority shareholders to sue SOEs), it would be practically difficult for it to register. Second, since several scandals happened in private NPOs (for instance, the corruption scandal with the Red Cross), the general public in China has lost trust in private NPOs.

Current social, political and judicial conditions in China do not suggest that public funding is a good technique to finance shareholder litigation. However, in spite of this negative conclusion regarding the potential for public funding in China, from a more cautious perspective, public funding might have potential after certain reforms, which might be conducted in the future or that are already undergoing now, on the Chinese political and judicial system are implemented. It should be noted that since the second half of 2013, the central government has explored a series of anti-corruption activities, and reform on public authorities (including institutions governed by the Communist Party) have also been carried out. More importantly, the fourth plenary session of the 18th Central Committee of the Communist Party of China (四中全会) held in late October 2014 clearly indicated that 'administrative interference in the judicial processes' (行政干预司法) should be forbidden. This might be considered as a positive signal concerning the realization of 'judicial independence', even if it is not a short way forward. In consideration of these developments, we can hope for the potential for public funding in the future. In Chapter 7 of this book, a proposal for public funding in a Chinese context is also presented, which could be summarized as follows:

a. An ad hoc panel inside the court will be set up to scrutinize the public funding application. The funding of this panel should be allocated from the special Fund from the central (and not local) government in order to mitigate political influence. The panel should be independent, meaning that the members could not be permanent (should rotate) and they should be selected randomly. The list of the members should be regarded as confidential information;
b. The fund is wholly financed by the state budget;
c. There are two selection criteria: first, the case should be with merits; second, cases demonstrating public significance will be funded preferentially.

## 8.3 Third Party Litigation Funding

When investigating the potential for third party litigation funding to finance shareholder litigation, this book analyses several core issues through a comparative study of the US, the UK and Australia, three countries that already have got some experience with this funding technique. The use of TPLF brings positive externalities, for instance, it facilitates the access to justice for impecunious litigants; it exerts deterrence effects on potential wrongdoers. On the other hand, concerns with regards to the use of TPLF are also raised. For example, the introduction of TPLF creates the complicated funder-lawyer-litigant relationship: to whom does the lawyer owe duty of loyalty; which party controls the litigation, the funder, the lawyer or the funded litigant; whether the availability of TPLF encourages frivolous and unmeritorious claims; whether the availability of TPLF results in the filing of more lawsuits.

### *8.3.1 Positive Externalities Brought by the Use of TPLF*

#### 8.3.1.1 Access to Justice

High litigation costs may create a significant obstacle for impecunious plaintiffs to file a lawsuit before the court. Apparently, the availability of TPLF is able to solve funding problems and facilitate the access to justice. In addition to that, risk-averse 'non-poor' plaintiffs also benefit from the TPLF which helps them to relieve litigation risk.

#### 8.3.1.2 Deterrence Effects for Potential Wrongdoers

If potential injurers are aware of the fact that victims do not hold sufficient financial resources to support the litigation, they may commit wrongdoings more unscrupulously. The availability of TPLF could be helpful to deter potential wrongdoers even though a lawsuit is not actually commenced by the victims.

### *8.3.2 Concerns Brought by the Use of TPLF*

#### 8.3.2.1 The Complicated Funder-Lawyer-Client Relationship

Ethical concerns in this regard include:

(A) The unscrupulous funders may take advantage of the vulnerable litigants by imposing unfair terms on them in the funding agreement, or even purposely failing to fully disclose all relevant aspects of the agreement to the funded litigants.

(B) Sometimes, the funded litigant tends to await the court's judgment instead of compromising to reach a settlement. However, on the part of the funder, he may prefer an early settlement in order to improve business cash flow. However, the book further indicates that it is not a 'real' ethical concern for the reason that it is ascertained that all the three parties hope for a favourable outcome of the case regardless of the form of compensation (a quick one by an early settlement or remedies brought by a judgment after a long court proceeding). Although the funder and the lawyer prefer quick monetary proceeds, while the litigant does not like an early settlement, this does not cause fundamental differences in terms of the essential benefits, because the early settlement that brings quick monetary remedies is also beneficial to the funded litigant.

(C) In a funded case, the funder will seek access to all confidential and privileged documents of the litigant in order to evaluate the ongoing viability of the litigation. However, the litigant may not be willing to provide such access to the funder considering the protection of business confidentiality, which would deter the cautious funder to invest in such a lawsuit. In practice, such dilemma might be solved by a 'confidentiality clause' in the TPLF contract.

(D) To whom does the lawyer owe his fiduciary duty? To the funder or the funded litigant? In a traditional lawyer-and-client relationship, the lawyer owes fiduciary duties to the litigant. Legally, this remains the same in funded litigation. But in the context of a funded case, this tradition is de facto challenged by the fact that the funder rather than the litigant pays the lawyer's fees.

#### 8.3.2.2 The Fear of Frivolous and Unmeritorious Claims

It's argued by some that the use of TPLF increases the volume of questionable claims. But the funder is in nature an investor whose aim is to make money through an investment. As a matter of fact, cases with a good prospect of success or a high potential rewards would be preferred by the third party funder. The due diligence conducted by the funders could be regarded as a filter to weed out frivolous and unmeritorious claims. Empirical research demonstrates that cases being funded have grown riskier over the past several years, and third party litigation financing increases the complexity of litigation. However, there is no evidence suggesting that third party funders accept truly frivolous suits or groundless cases which may make the funder's investment difficult to be recouped.[6]

#### 8.3.2.3 The Potential Increase in the Overall Volume of Litigation

Opponents hold a viewpoint that the use of TPLF will result in the filing of more lawsuits. In fact, even there is some evidence that the general volume of litigation in certain areas of the law does indeed increase as a result of TPLF, it cannot be concluded that 'bad' cases are encouraged by TPLF. There is no solid evidence suggesting that frivolous or unmeritorious cases were encouraged by the use of TPLF. In Shavell's theory, the rise in the number of lawsuit after the advent of TPLF could not be simply considered as a negative phenomenon. Whether it is socially desirable should depend on the answer whether the general benefits and potential deterrence effect exceed the cost brought by the use of TPLF. In other words, although the general costs (more lawsuits will mean the court is used more frequently) increase because of the rise in the case volume, the total benefits and deterrence effects would also be produced if those cases are 'good' ones that can help to correct wrongdoings.

### *8.3.3 Concerns and Policy Arguments in the Special Context of Shareholder Litigation*

When TPLF is used to finance shareholder litigation, special consideration should be given to:

#### 8.3.3.1 The Third Party Funder's Financial Adequacy

Compared to ordinary civil litigation, shareholder lawsuits involve much higher litigation costs, meaning that the third party funder should allocate more money to

[6]The third party funder's economic analysis before financing a case, see *supra* 5.1.2.

finance a shareholder lawsuit. In order to avoid a risk that the funder falls into funding shortage in the proceeding of a shareholder lawsuit, the funder's financial capacity must be guaranteed. This book, in this respect, suggests that the court's control on the funder's capital capacity could be adopted. It means that the TPLF agreement needs the court's approval regarding the funder's financial adequacy. Under certain circumstances, the funder needs to deposit an amount of money in the court, which is mainly subject to the court's discretion.

#### 8.3.3.2 The Opt-In and Opt-Out Dilemma in Funded Class Actions

In some countries where class action mechanism is used, an opt-out approach is adopted (for instance, Australia and the US). It means when persons do not want become class members, they need to file a notice to inform the court about their intention of 'opting out' of the class. When a class action is funded by a third party funder, the general practice is that the funder requires the funded group to sign a litigation funding agreement where 'opt-in' is applied. Theoretically, a member of a class action who does not sign the funding agreement still stays in the class. Other members accepting the funding agreement can 'contribute' to the case by sharing potential benefits with the funder. However, how do the members refusing the funding agreement contribute to the litigation? It is highly possible that these members become free-riders. In Australia's practice, a closed-class was proposed, where people can join in a class action by signing a funding agreement[7].

#### 8.3.3.3 The Termination of Third Party Litigation Funding

This book suggests that the funder should only be allowed to terminate its funding under limited circumstances. For instance, the funded case proves to be a frivolous case; there is a material breach of the litigation funding agreement by the funded party. In this regard, Lord Jackson's final report on civil litigation holds a similar view with this book by proposing that 'the funder should be obliged to continue to provide funding it originally contracted to provide, unless there are proper grounds to withdraw'.

#### 8.3.3.4 The Risk of Refusal to Share

In high-valued cases (for instance, shareholder litigation), the refusal to share the proceeds will heavily undermine the funder's interests, or even make it financially

[7] *Multiplex Funds Management Ltd v. P. Dawson Nominees Pty Ltd* [2007] 164 FCR 275. (Multiplex II)

collapse. Considering that, an *ex ante* measure needs to be designed to mitigate such risk, which at least in China is real, based on the experience where parties hiring lawyers on a contingency fee basis refused to share the proceeds of a successful action with the lawyer. This book proposes if a judgment or a settlement in favour of the plaintiffs is made, the losing party must turn in the monetary compensation to the court first. The court then distributes the money between the funder and the plaintiffs according to the rate agreed previously in the litigation funding contract.

### *8.3.4 Proposals for China Regarding the Use of TPLF*

In general, this book suggests that TPLF could be used to finance shareholder litigation in China, but certain reform need to be implemented first:

(A) The qualification of funders should be granted by the Justice Bureau (司法局). It means that before entering into litigation funding market, third party funders would need to apply for a licence from the Justice Bureau and then register with the Bureau for future supervision. The requirements for a qualified third party funder should include, for instance, that the funder must have enough financial resources, the funding company must be equipped with a group of persons who were professional legal practitioners before.[8]

(B) Supplements to PRC Contract Law should be added to specifically regulate TPLF agreements. They include, for instance, that it should be clearly stated that funders owe fiduciary duties to their clients but not to lawyers; Funders, without permission of their clients (funded parties) are not allowed to contact with lawyers.[9]

## 8.4 Funding Alternatives

### *8.4.1 Indemnity Cost Orders (ICOs)*

Indemnity cost orders are applied in England and Wales to fund shareholder derivative actions. In this approach, the company indemnifies a *bona fide* shareholder plaintiff for litigation costs incurred in a derivative action. The main problem with this mechanism is its uncertain procedure and the court's requirements for granting an ICO. For instance, does the financial ability of the shareholder plaintiff

---

[8]All requirements for funders are listed in *supra* 7.3.

[9]All proposed supplements to PRC Contract Law are listed in *supra* 7.3.

constitute a bar to apply for an ICO? The English case law suggested that the shareholder plaintiff is eligible to apply for an ICO only if he is in a genuine need of financial aid.[10] But this approach was criticized to be problematic by indicating that there is no reason to risk a shareholder's personal money to commence a shareholder derivative action for the company's interests. Because monetary compensation brought by a successful derivative lawsuit directly flows to the company instead of to individual shareholders. In addition to that, the standard adopted by the court when considering an application for an ICO is vague. In case law, it is found that an ICO could be awarded only if the case proved to be a 'clearest, obviously just' one.[11] This vague standard can easily turn the scrutinizing procedure into a mini-trial which is costly and lengthy. This book proposes a reformed ICO where such an order should only be granted after the court permits the claim to be continued. For instance, if the court allows the claim to proceed as a derivative action, an ICO could be awarded by the court. By this approach, drawbacks in the English law system could be avoided, and the procedure will become more efficient and simple.

### 8.4.2 Lawyers' Funding—Contingency Fee Arrangements

A CGFA is, in nature, based on the 'no win, no fee' basis, where the litigant shares the monetary recoveries brought by a successful claim with the lawyer. If the funded case is lost, neither the funded litigant nor the lawyer will get any money. The main problem in the use of CGFAs is similar with that in TPLF: the conflict of interests between the lawyer and his client. For instance, the concern of early settlement. The final conclusion of this book about the potential for CGFA in China is that we do not recommend the use of it in shareholder litigation. There are two main reasons for our conclusion: (1) procedural difficulties in shareholder litigation—the length of the court proceeding of a shareholder collective lawsuit cannot be predicted in advance, and until now it was very time-consuming in most cases (5 years on average with the lengthiest one until now lasting for 12 years). Moreover, the court's resistance to mass litigation results in shareholder collective actions being easily refused by the court at the very beginning of proceedings; (2) the lack of incentives for lawyers—lawyers taking shareholder collective action should assume higher litigation risk and spend more time. On the other hand, the monetary reward for the lawyer in a successful case is not proportional to the lawyer's efforts; (3) the risk of refusal to pay lawyer's fees which was typically demonstrated in the *Grandall v. Weiguan* 2012 case.

---

[10]Smith v. Croft (No.1) [1986] 2 ALL ER 551, at 567.

[11]Smith v. Croft (No.2) [1988] Ch 114, at 147.

### 8.4.3 Lawyers' Funding—Conditional Fee Agreements

In a CFA, a lawyer is entitled to charge a success fee on top of the basic fees only when the case is successful. For its potential to finance shareholder litigation in China, this book does not suppose that it could be an effective mechanism mainly for the same reasons why CGFAs are rejected for China.

# Bibliography

## Books

American Law Institute (ALI), *Principle of Corporate Governance: Analysis and Recommendations* (American Law Institute Publisher, Minnesota, 1994), Volume 2

American Law Institute (ALI), *Principles of the Law: Aggregate Litigation* (American Law Institute Publishers, 2010)

Andrews, N., *English Civil Procedure: Fundamentals of the new Civil Justice System* (Oxford University Press, 2003)

Anheiner, H. K. and Seibel, W., *The third sector: Comparative Studies of Nonprofit Organizations*, (Walter de Gruyter, 1990)

Bainbridge, S. M., *Corporation Law and Economics* (Foundation Press, 2002)

Bishop, J. W. and Washington, G. T., *The Law of Corporate Officers and Directors: Indemnification and Insurance* (Warren, Gorham & Lamont, 1981).

Bisson, D. and Hamer, D. I. W., *Defending Class Actions in Canada* (third edition, CCH, 2011)

Blundell, J. and Robinson, C. (eds.), *Regulation without the State……The Debate Continues* (Institute of Economic Affairs, 2000).

Bourne, N., *Bourne on Company Law* (Routledge, 2010)

Boyle, A. J., *Minority Shareholders' Remedies* (Cambridge University Press, 2002)

Brickman, L., Horowitz, M. J. and O'Connell, J., *Rethinking Contingency Fees: A Proposal to Align the Contingency Fee System with Its Policy Roots and Ethical Mandates*, (Manhattan Institute, 1994)

Cafaggi, F. and Micklitz, H.W. (eds), *New Frontiers of Consumer Protection: The Interplay between Private and Public Enforcement* (Intersentia, 2009)

Cahn, A. and Donald, D. C., *Comparative Company Law: text and cases on the laws governing corporations in German, the UK and the USA* (Cambridge University Press, Cambridge, New York, 2010)

Cahn, A. and Donald, D. C., *Comparative Company Law: Text and Cases on the Laws Governing Corporations in Germany, the UK and the USA* (Cambridge University Press, 2010)

Cheffins, B. R., *Company Law: Theory, Structure and Operation* (Oxford University Press, 1997)

Chivers, D. QC and Shaw, B., *The Law of Minority Shareholder Power* (Oxford University Press, 2008)

Clark, R. C., *Corporate Law* (Little, Brown, 1986)

Cox, J.D. and Hazen, T. L., *Corporations* (second edition, Aspen Publishers, 2002)

Davies, P., *Principles of Modern Company Law* (seventh edition, Sweet & Maxwell, 2003)

Davies, P. and Worthington, S., *Principles of Modern Company Law* (ninth edition, Sweet & Maxwell, 2012)

DeMott, D. A., *Shareholder Derivative Actions: Law and Practice* (Thomson West Press, 2003)



W. Chen, *A Comparative Study of Funding Shareholder Litigation*,
DOI 10.1007/978-981-10-3623-1

DeMott, D. A., *Shareholder Derivative Actions: Law and Practice* (Clark Boardman Callaghan, 2012)

Dong, A., *Juristic Act* (民事法律行为 'minshi falv xingwei'), (China Renmin University Press, 2012)

Dooley, M. P., *Fundamentals of Corporation Law* (Foundation Press, 1995)

Dunleavy, P., *Democracy, Bureaucracy and Public Choice: Economic Explanations in Political Science* (Harvester Wheatsheaf, 1991)

Ferrara, R. C., Abikoff, K. T. and Gansler, L. L., *Shareholder Derivative Litigation: Besieging the Board* (Law Journal Press, 1996)

Garry, P. M., *A Nation of Adversaries: How the Litigation Explosion is Reshaping in America* (Plenum Press, 1997)

Giraldo, C. A. L., *Factors Governing the Application of the Business Judgment Rule: An Empirical Study of the U.S., U.K, Australia and the E.U.* (Erasmus University, 2005)

Glendon, M. A., *A Nation under Lawyers: How the Crisis in the Legal Profession is Transforming American Society* (Harvard University Press, 1996)

Goldberg, J. C. P., Sebok, A. J. and Zipursky, B. C., T*ort Law: Responsibilities and Redress, Cases and Materials* (third edition, Aspen Publishers, 2012)

Goulding, S., *Company Law* (second edition, Gavendish Publishing, 1999)

Gu, G., *The Protection of Public Shareholders' Rights and Interests* (Beijing University Press, 2009)

Hamer, D. et al, *Defending Class Actions in Canada* (third edition, CCH, 2011)

Hamilton, R. W., *The Way of Corporations in a Nutshell* (Fifth edition, West Group, 2000)

Han, X., *The Judicial Independence and Contemporary China* (司法独立与近代中国 sifa duli yu jindai zhongguo), (Qinghua University Press, 2003)

Hannigan, B., *Company Law* (second edition, Oxford University Press, 2009)

Hao, L., *The Practical Aspect of Shareholder Litigation in China*, (股东诉讼的实施问题研究, gudong susong de shishi wenti yanjiu), (China Legal Publishing, 2012)

Hodges, C., *Multi-Party Actions* (Oxford University Press, 2006)

Hodges, C., Vogenauer, S. and Tulibacka, M., *The Cost and funding of Civil Litigation* (Hart Publishing, 2010)

Howson, N. C., 'Judicial Independence and the Company Law in the Shanghai Courts', Peerenboom, R. (ed.), *Judicial Independence in China: Lessons for Global Rule of Law Promotion* (Cambridge University Press, 2009) 134

Huang, Y., *Selling China: Foreign Direct Investment during the Reform Era* (Cambridge University Press, 2002)

Institute of legal science of Chinese Academy of Social Sciences, *New Development of Legal Studies,* (China Social Sciences Publishing House, 2008)

Jiang, B. and He, D., *The Understanding and Application of Judging Rules Used in Guidance Cases of The SPC (volume of contract law)*, (China legal publishing house, 2012)

Joffe, V. QC et al, *Minority Shareholders: Law, Practice, and Procedure* (fourth edition, Oxford University Press, 2011)

Karlsgodt, P. G., *World Class Actions, A Guide to Group and Representative Actions around the Globe* (Oxford University Press, 2012)

Klonoff, R. H., Bilich, E. K. M. and Malveaux, S. M., *Class Actions and Other Multi-Party Litigation: Cases and Materials* (Second edition, Thomson/West 2006)

Kritzer, H., *Risks, Reputations, and Rewards: Contingency Fee Legal Practice in the United States* (Stanford University Press, 2004)

Kroszner, R. S. and Putterman, L., *The Economic Nature of the Firm* (third edition, Cambridge University Press, 2009)

Lardy, N., *China's Unfinished Economic Revolution* (Brookings Institution, 1998)

Li, H., *Reports on Chinese Governments and the State-Owned Enterprises* (中国政企治理问题报告, zhongguo zhengqi zhili wenti baogao), (China Development Publisher, 2003)

Li, H. et al, *The Corruption, the Vanity and the Relationship between the Governments and the State-Owned Enterprises* (腐败,政绩与政企关系, fubai zhengji yu zhengqi guanxi), (Fudan University Publisher, 2011)

Li, X., *A Comparative Study of Shareholders' Derivative Actions: England, the United States, Germany and China* (Kluwer, 2007)

Liu, G., *A Study on Shareholder Litigation: from the Perspective of Corporate Governance* (公司治理视角中的股东诉讼研究), (China Fangzheng Publisher, 2005)

Liu, T., *The legal Regulation of Non-profit Organizations*, (非营利组织及其法律规制 'fei yingli zuzhi jiqi falv guizhi'), (China legal publishing house, 2009)

Luo, B., *Researches on Securities Class Actions* (Law Press, China, 2011)

Ma, Q., *Non-governmental Organizations in Contemporary China: Paving the Way to Civil Society?* (Routledge, 2009)

Moore, J. W. *et al, Moore's Federal Practice* (third edition, 1997)

Mu, R., *The Theory of Civil Justice Act* (民法法律行为理论之全部 'minfa falv xingwei lilun zhi quanbu), (China University of Political Science and Law Press, 2003)

Mulheron, R., *The Class Action in Common Law Legal Systems: A Comparative Perspective* (Hart Publishing, 2004)

Nagy, D. M. et al, *Securities Litigation and Enforcement: Cases and Materials*, (Thomson/West, 2003)

Pette, B. G., *Company Law* (second edition, Pearson Education, 2005)

Pierre, J., *Bureaucracy in the Modern State: An Introduction to Comparative Public Administration* (Edward Elgar Publishing, 2002)

Pinto, A. R. and Branson, D. M., *Understanding Corporate Law* (third edition, LexisNexis, 2009)

Posner, R. A., *Economic Analysis of Law* (sixth edition, Aspen Publishers, 2003)

Puchniak, D. W., Baum, H. and Ewing-Chow, M. (eds), *The Derivative Action in Asia: A Comparative and Functional Approach* (Cambridge University Press, 2012)

Reisberg, A., *Derivative Actions and Corporate Governance: Theory and Operation* (Oxford University Press, 2007)

Ren, Z., *Securities Class Actions: International Experience And China's Way Out* (Law Press, China, 2008)

Robert H. Frank and Ben S. Bernanke, *Principles of Economics* (fifth edition, Mcgraw-Hill/Irwin, 2012)

Sheikh, S., *A Guide to the Companies Act 2006* (Routledge-Cavendish publisher, 2007)

Shavell, S., *Foundations of Economic Analysis of Law* (Harvard University Press, 2004)

Sime, S. and French, D. (eds), *Blackstone's Civil Practice 2009* (Oxford University Press, Oxford 2008)

Smith, A., *The Wealth of Nations* (Collier, 1902)

Tabarrok, A. and Helland, E., *Two Cheers for Contingent Fees* (AEI Press, 2006)

Toninelli, P. A. (ed.), *The Rise and Fall of State-Owned Enterprise in the Western World* (Cambridge University Press, 2000)

Tuil, M. and Visscher, L. (eds.), *New Trends in Financing Civil Litigation in Europe: A Legal, Empirical, and Economic Analysis* (Edward Elgar, 2010)

Waye, V., *Trading in Legal Claims: Law, Policy & Future Directions in Australia, UK & US* (Presidian Legal Publications, 2008)

Welch, E. P., Turezyn, A. J. and Saunders, R. S., *Folk on the Delaware General Corporation Law* (2010 edition, Aspen publishers, 2010)

Wright, C. A., Miller, A. R. and Kane, M. K., *Federal Practice and Procedure* (second edition, West Publishing, 1986).

Wu, J., *Understanding and Interpreting Chinese Economic Reform* (Thomson, 2005)

Xi, X. (ed), *Annotations to the Provisions in the New Civil Procedure Law* (新民事诉讼法条文释义, 'xin minshi susongfa tiaowen shiyi'), (third edition, People's Court Press, China, 2010)

Xi, X., *The Supreme People's Court's Analysis of Civil Cases* (*Construction Project Cases*), (Legal Press China, 2010)

Zhang, Z., *The derivative action and good corporate governance in China: Economic theories and legal rules* (Lambert Academic Publishing, 2011)

Zhao, J. et al, *Case Materials on Shareholder Representative Litigation* (股东代表诉讼:中国律师办案实录, gudong daibiao susong: zhongguo lvshi ban'an shilu), (China Law Press, 2007)

Zhu, J. (ed.), *Report on the Chinese Law Development, Database and Indicators* (中国法律发展报告:数据库和指标体系 'zhongguo falv fazhan baogao: shujuku he zhibiao tixi) (Press of Renmin University of China, 2007)

## Articles

Abrams, D. S. and Chen, D. L., 'A Market for Justice: A First Empirical Look at Third Party Litigation Funding' (2013) 15 *University of Pennsylvania Journal of Business Law* 1075

Alexander, J. C., 'Do the Merits Matter? A Study of Settlements in Securities Class Actions', (1991) 43 *STAN L. Rev.* 497

Andrews, N., 'Multi-Partv Proceedings in England: Representative and Group Actions', (2001) 11 *DUKE J. Comp. & Int'l L.* 249

Arsalidou, D., 'Objectivity vs Flexibility in Civil Law Jurisdictions and the Possible Introduction of the Business Judgment Rule in English law' (2003) 24(8) *Company Lawyer* 228

Bainbridge, S. M. and Gulati, G. M., 'How Do Judges Maximize? (The Same Way Everyone Else Does—Boundedly): Rules of Thumb in Securities Fraud Opinions' (2002) 51 *Emory Law Journal* 83

Bimholz, R. M., 'The Validity and Propriety of Contingent Fee Controls', (1989-1990) 37 *UCLA L. REV.* 949

Black, B. S. and Kraakman, R., 'A Self-Enforcing Model of Corporate Law', (1996) 109 *Harvard Law Review* 1911

Black, B. S., 'Agents Watching Agents: The Promise of Institutional Investor Voice', (1992) 39 *UCLA L. REV.* 811

Bond, P., 'Making Champerty Work: An Invitation to State Action', (2002) 150 *U. PA. L. REV.*1297

Brandi, T. O., 'The Strike Suit: A Common Problem of the Derivative Suit and the Shareholder Class Action'(1993) 98 *Dickinson Law Review* 355

Bratton, W. W. and Wachter, M. L., 'The Political Economy of Fraud on the Market', (2011) 160 *U. PA. L. REV.* 69

Brickman, L., 'ABA Regulation of Contingency Fee: Money Talks, Ethics Works', (1996) 65 *Fordham Law Review* 247

Brickman, L., 'Contingency Fee Abuse, Ethical Mandates, and the Disciplinary System: The Case against Case-by-Case Enforcement', (1996) 53(4) *Washington and Lee Law Review* 1339

Bronsteen, J. and Fiss, O., 'The Class Action Rule', (2002) 78 *Notre Dame Law Review* 1419

Bu, Q., 'The Indemnity Order in a Derivative Action', (2006) 27(1) *Company Lawyer* 2

Bushnell, C. B., 'Champerty is Still No Excuse in Texas: Why Texas Courts (and the Legislature) Should Uphold Litigation Funding Agreements', (2007) 7 *Hous.Bus. & Tax. L. J.* 358

Capper, D. and Glennon, L., 'Litigation Funding for 'Big Money' Divorces: An Assessment of Legal Risk' (2007) 26 *C.J.Q.* 447

Chao X., 'Private Enforcement of Securities Law in China: Daqing Lianyi Co v Zhong Weida and Others (2004) Heilongjiang High Court' (2006) 1(2) *Journal of Comparative Law* 492

Cheffins, B. R. and Dine, J. M., 'Shareholder Remedies: Lessons from Canada', (1992) 13 *Company Lawyer* 89

Chen, D., 'Legal tradition and private securities litigation in China', (2012) 23(11) *I.C.C.L.R.* 394

Chen, X. and Zhang, Z., 'Exploring the social responsibility of the non-profit organizations', (非营利组织的社会公共责任探析, feiyingli zuzhi de shehui gonggong zeren tanxi), (2007) 12 *Chinese Public Administration* 78.

Chen, X., He, J. and Pu, X., 'Building the public trust on Chinese non-profit organizations', (浅析我国非营利组织的公信力建设, qianxi woguo feiyingli zuzhi de gongxinli jianshe), (2007) 8 *Journal of Wuyi University*

Chen, Y., 'The Introduction of Class Litigation in China should be Cautious', (中国引入集团诉讼应当缓行) (2010) 30 *Economic Research Guide*

Chiu, I. H., 'Contextualising Shareholders' Disputes: A Way to Reconceptualise Minority Shareholder Remedies', 2006 (14) *Journal of Business Law* 312

Choo, P. M., 'The Statutory Derivative Action in Singapore: a Critical and Comparative Examination' (2001) 13 *Bond L. Rev.* 64

Clark, S. S., 'Case comment: Australia: Civil Proceedings-Litigation Funding' (2007) 18(2) *International Company and Commercial Law Review* N5-6

Clarke, D. C. and Howson, N. C., 'Pathway to minority shareholder protection: derivative actions in the People's Republic of China', in Dan W. Puchniak, Harald Baum and Michael Ewing-Chow (eds), *The Derivative Action in Asia: A Comparative and Functional Approach*, (Cambridge University Press) 215.

Clermont, K. M. and Currivan, J. D., 'Improving on the Contingency Fee' (1978) 63 *Cornell Law Review* 529

Coffee, J. C. and Schwartz, D. E., 'The Survival of the Derivative Suit: an Evaluation and a Proposal for Legislative Reform', (1981) 81 *Colum. L. Rev.* 261

Coffee, J. C., Jr., 'Litigation and Corporate Governance: An Essay on Steering between Scylla and Charybdis', (1983) 52 *GEO. WASH. L. REV.* 789

Coffee, J. C., Jr., 'New Myths and Old Realties: The American Law Institute Faces the Derivative Action', (1993) 48(4) *Business Lawyer* 1407

Coffee, J. C., Jr., 'Reforming the Securities Class Action: An Essay on Deterrence and Its Implementation', (2006) 106(7) *Columbia Law Review* 1534

Collins, D., 'Public Funding of Multi-party Litigation' (2010) 31 *Manitoba Law Journal* 211

Corboy, P. H.,'Contingency Fees: The Individual's Key to the Courthouse Door', (1976) 2(4) *the Economics of Litigation* 27

Cox, J. D., 'Making Securities Fraud Class Actions Virtuous', (1997) 39 *ARIZ. L. Rev.* 497

Cox, J. D., 'The social Meaning of Shareholder Suits', (1999) 65 *Brook. L. Rev.* 3

Dana, J. D. and Spier, K. E., 'Expertise and Contingent Fees: The Role of Asymmetric Information in Attorney Compensation', (1993) 9(2) *Journal of Law,Economics & Organization* 349

Danzon, P. M., 'Contingent Fees for Personal Injury Litigation', (1984) 14 *BELL J. ECON.* 213

David, C., *'Public Funding of Multi-Party Litigation'* (2010) 31 *Manitoba Law Journal* 211

de Morpurgo, M., 'A Comparative Legal and Economic Approach to Third-Party Litigation Funding', (2011) 19 *Cardozo Journal of International and Comparative Law* 343

Demyanyk, Y. and Van Hemert, O., 'Understanding the Subprime Mortgage Crisis' (2011) 24(6) *Rev. Financ. Stud.* 1848

Deng, G., 'Why is the enforcement of legal judgment difficult: study the way forward' (民事判决执行难的原因与对策, minshi panjue zhixing nan de yuanyin yu duice), (2009) 16 *Legal and Economy* (法制与经济, fazhi yu jingji)

Dietsch, N., 'Litigation financing in the US, the UK, and Australia: How the industry has evolved in three countries', (2011) 38 *N. Ky. L. Rev.* 687

Dong, X. and Wang, X., 'The requirements of establishment and validity of civil justice act' (论民事法律行为的成立与生效 'lun minshi falv xingwei de chengli yu shengxiao'), (2003) 4 *Journal of Shandong University* (Philosophy and social science)

Dykstra, D. J., 'The Revival of the Derivative Suit', (1967) 116 *U. Pa. L. Rev.* 74

Erickson, J., 'Corporate Governance in the Courtroom: An Empirical Analysis', (2010) 51 *WM. & MARY L. REV.* 1749

Fisch, J. E., 'Class Action Reform, Qui Tam, and the Role of the Plaintiff', (1997) 60 *LAW & CONTEMP. PROBS.* 167

Fisch, J. E., 'Class Action Reform: Lessons from Securities Litigation', (1997) 39 *Ariz. L. Rev.* 533

Fisch, J. E., 'Teaching Corporate Governance through Shareholder Litigation', (2000) 34 *Georgia Law Review* 745

Gan, P., 'Potentials For Derivative Actions In China', (论股东派生诉讼在中国的有效适用, lun gudong paisheng susong zai zhongguo de youxiao shiyong), (2002) 39(5) *Journal of Peking University (Humanities and Social Science)* 17

Gao, Z. and Yang, Z., 'Rethinking the litigation culture in China—under the ideology of harmonious society', (和谐社会视野下厌诉之反思, hexie shehui shiyexia yansu zhi fansi), (2008) 1 *QiuSuo* (求索) 117

Garber, S. et al., 'Do Noneconomic Damages Caps and Attorney Fee Limits Reduce Access to Justice for Victims of Medical Negligence?' (2009) 6 *J. Empirical Legal Stud.* 637

Garry, P. M. et al, 'The Irrationality of Shareholder Class Action Lawsuits: A Proposal for Reform' (2004) 49(2) *South Dakota Law Review* 275

Geng, L., 'Cost Assumption and Judicial Approval in Shareholder Derivative Actions' (论我国股东派生诉讼的费用承担和司法许可, lun woguo gudong paisheng susong de feiyong chengdan he sifa xuke), (2013) 1 *Science of Law* 170.

Gibbs, D., 'Has the statutory derivative claim fulfilled its objectives? A prima facie case and the mandatory bar: Part I', (2011) 32(2) *Comp. Law.* 41

Glover, M., 'The Structural Role of Private Enforcement Mechanisms in Public Law' (2012) 53 *William & Mary Law Review* 1137

Gravellea, H. and Waterson, M., 'No win, No fee: Some Economics of Contingency Legal Fees', (1993) 103*The Economic Journal* 1206.

Gray, A. M., 'The Statutory Derivative Claim, an Outmoded Superfluousness', (2012) 33(10) *Comp. Law.* 295

Guo, F., 'The Construction Of Chinese Securities Class Actions: A Case Study Of Daqing Lianyi Shareholder Litigation' (从大庆联谊股东诉讼案谈中国证券民事赔偿制度的构建, 'cong daqing lianyi gudong an tan zhongguo zhengquan minshi peichang zhidu de goujian'), (2006) 1 *Law Science Magazine* (法学杂志, 'faxue zazhi')

Hale, C., 'What's Right with the Rule in Foss v. Harbottle?' (1997) 2 *Company Fin. Insolvency L. Rev.* 219

Han, H., 'Reflections of Registration of Non-Profit Organization' (关于非营利组织注册登记的思考, guanyu feiyingli zuzhi zhuce dengji de sikao), (2008) 6 *Research of administration of NGOs* (社团管理研究, shetuan guanli yanjiu)

Hannigan, B., 'Board Failures in the financial Crisis: Tinkering with codes and the need for wider corporate governance reforms: Part 2', (2012) 33(2) *Comp. Law.* 35

Hazard, G. C., 'An Historical Perspective on the Attorney-Client Privilege', (1978) 66(5) *California Law Review* 1061

Heck, R. C., 'Conflict and Aggregation: Appointing Institutional Investors as Sole Lead Plaintiffs under the PSLRA', (1999) 66(4) *University of Chicago Law Review* 1199

Hensler, D. R., 'The future of mass litigation: Global class action and third-party litigation funding', (2011) 79 *George Washington Law Review* 306

Hornstein, G. D., 'The Shareholder's Derivative Suit in the United States', (1967) *J. Bus. L.* 282

Horowitz, M., 'Making Ethics Real, Making Ethics Work: A Proposal for Contingency Fee Reform', (1995) 44 *Emory Law Journal* 173

Houseman, A. W., 'Civil Legal Assistance for Low-Income Persons: Looking Back and Looking Forward', (2002) 29 *Fordham Urb. L. J.* 1213

Howson, N. C., 'Corporate law in the Shanghai People's Courts, 1992-2008:Judicial autonomy in the contemporary authoritarian State', (2010) 5 *East Asia Law Review* 303

Huang, H., 'The Statutory Derivative Action in China: Critical Analysis and Recommendaations for Reform', (2007) 4 *Berkeley Bus. L.J.* 227

Hughes, J. W. and Snyder, E. A., (1998), 'Allocation of Litigation Costs: American and English Rules', in Newman, P. (ed.), *The New Palgrave Dictionary of Economics and the Law,* (Palgrave Macmillan, 2004) 51.

Hurst, P., 'The New Costs Rules and Practical Directions', (2013) 32(2) *C.J.Q.* 153

Hylton, K. N., 'The Economics of Third-Party Financed Litigation', 12 December 2011, *Boston Univ. School of Law, Law and Economics Research Paper* No. 11-57, available at http://ssrn.com/abstract=1971229 or http://dx.doi.org/10.2139/ssrn.1971229

Issacharoff, S., 'Regulating after the Fact' (2007) 56 *DePaul Law Review* 375.

Jia, X., 'Management systems of the foreign non-profit organizations and their enlightenment for China', (国外非营利组织管理体制及其对中国的启示, guowai feiyingli zuzhi guanli tizhi jiqi dui zhongguo de qishi), 2004(4) *Journal of Social Sciences* (社会科学 shehui kexue)

Jiang, H., 'The information disclosure of the non-profit organization in China',(非营利组织透明信息的机理和途径分析, feiyingli zuzhi touming xinxi de jili he tujin fenxi), (2012) 2 *Shandong social science*

Jiang, W. and Shan, G., 'Confirmation of a third party with no independent litigation right for claim' (论民事诉讼中无独立请求权第三人的确定 lun minshi susong zhong wu duli qingqiuquan disanren de queding), (1997) 2 *Journal of Renmin University of China*

Jones, T. M., 'An Empirical Examination of the Resolution of Shareholder Derivative and Class Action Lawsuits' (1980) 60 *Boston University Law Review* 542

Kakalik, J. S. et al, 'Just, Speedy, and Inexpensive? An Evaluation of Judicial Case Management under the Civil Justice Reform Act' (1997) 49 *Ala. L. Rev.* 717

Kalajdzic, J., Cashman, P. and Longmoore, A., 'Justice for Profit: A Comparative Analysis of Australian, Canadian and U.S. Third Party Litigation Funding', (2013) 61 *Am. J. Comp. L.* 93

Kamar, E., 'Shareholder Litigation under Indeterminate Corporate Law', (1999) 66 *U. CHI. L. REV.* 887

Kaplan, W. and Elwood, B., 'The Derivative Action: A Shareholder's Black House?' (2003) 36 *University of British Columbia Law Review* 443

Keay, A. and Loughrey, J., 'Something Old, Something New, Something Borrowed: an Analysis of the New Derivative Action under the Companies Act 2006' (2008) 124 *Law Quarterly Review* 469

Kilian, M., 'Alternatives to Public Provision: The Role of Legal Expenses Insurance in Broadening Access to Justice: The German Experience', (2003) 30 *Journal of Law and Society* 42

Kobayashi, B. H. and Ribstein, L. E., 'Class Action Lawyers as Lawmakers', (2004) 46 *Ariz. L. Rev.* 733

Koh, P., 'Directors' Fiduciary Duties: Unthreading the Joints of Shareholder Ratification' (2005) 5 *Journal of Corporate Law Studies* 363

Koniak, S. P. and Cohen, G. M., 'Under Cloak of Settlement', (1996) 82 *VA. L.REV.* 1051

Kritzer, H. M., 'Lawyer Fees and Lawyer Behavior in Litigation: What Does the Empirical Literature Really Say?', (2002) 80 *Texas Law Review* 1946

Kritzer, H. M., 'Contingency Fee Lawyers as Gatekeepers in the Civil Justice System', (1997) 81 (1) *Judicature* 22.

Kritzer, H. M., 'The Seven Dogged Myths Concerning Contingency Fees' (2002) 80 *Washington University Law Quarterly* 739

Kritzer, H. M., 'The Wages of Risk: The Returns of Contingent Fee Legal Practice' (1997) 47 *De Paul Law Review* 267.

La Porta, R., Lopez-de-Silanes, F., Schleifer, A. and Vishny, R., 'Investor protection and corporate governance', (2000) 58 *Journal of Financial Economics* 3

Landsman, S., 'The History of Contingency and the Contingency of History,' (1998) 47(2) *DePaul Law Review* 261

Lee, E. G. III and Willging, T. E., 'Defining the Problem of cost in Federal Civil Litigation', (2010) 60 *Duke Law Journal* 765

Legg, M. and Travers, L., 'Necessity is the mother of invention: the adoption of third-party litigation funding and the closed class in Australian class actions', (2009) 38 *Common Law World Review* 245

Legg, M. J., 'Shareholder class actions in Australia—The perfect storm?', (2008) 31(3) *UNSW Law Journal* 669

Liebman, B. L., 'Lawyers, Legal Aid, and Legitimacy in China' in Alford, W. P. et al (eds.) *Raising the Bar: The Emerging Legal Profession in East Asia* (Harvard University Press, 2006) 311.

Liebman, B. L., 'Legal Aid and Public Interest Law in China,' (1999) 34 *Texas international Law Journal* 211

Lightman, D., 'The Role of the Company at the Permission Stage in the Statutory Derivative Claim' (2011) 30 *Civil Justice Quarterly* 23

Lin, S., *'Derivative Suits in China: One Step Forward, Two Steps Back?'*, (2012) 23(6) *I.C.C.L.R.* 197

Lin, Z., 'Development of NPO and the policy of Chinese government', (非营利组织的发展与我国的对策, feiyingli zuzhi de fazhan yu woguo de duice), (2002) 1 *Journal of China National School of Administration* (国家行政学院学报 guojia xingzheng xueyuan xuebao)

Lin, Z., Liu, M. and Zhang, X., 'The Development of Corporate Governance in China', (2007) 28 (7) *Company Lawyer* 195

Liu, Z., 'The criticism of the local protectionism in Chinese judicial system', (中国司法地方保护主义之批判, zhongguo sifa difang baohu zhuyi zhi pipan), (2003) 1 *Chinese journal of law* (法学研究 faxue yanjiu)

Lockwood, B. L. and Barsch, K. L., 'United States', in Campbell, D. (general editor) and Buckley, S. (editor), *Protecting Minority Shareholders*, (Kluwer Law International, 1996) 656.

Loewenstein, M. J., 'Shareholder Derivative Litigation and Corporate Governance', (1999) 24(1) *Delaware Journal of Corporate Law* 1

Loughrey, J., 'Directors' Duties and Shareholder Litigation: the Practical Perspective' in Loughrey, J. (ed) *Directors' Duties and Shareholder Litigation in the Wake of the Financial Crisis* (Edward Elgar, 2013) 239

Lu, J. and Ren, J., 'The Avoidance of Malicious Actions through Chinese Criminal Law' (恶意诉讼行为刑事规制路径研究, 'eyi susong xingwei xingshi guizhi lujing yanjiu'), (2012) 11 *Journal of Politics and Law* 2

Lyon, J., 'Revolution in Progress: Third-Party Funding of American Litigation', (2011) 58 *UCLA L. Rev.* 571

Macey, J. R. and Miller, G. P., 'The Plaintiffs' Attorney's Role in Class Action and Derivative Litigation: Economic Analysis and Recommendations for Reform', (1991) 58 *U. CHI. L.REV.* 1

Manne, H. G., 'Our Two Corporation Systems: Law and Economics', (1967) 53(2) *Virginia Law Review* 259

Martin, S. L., 'The litigation financing industry: the wild west of finance should be tamed not outlawed', (2004)10 *Fordham J. Corp & Fin. L.* 55

McKenna, J. A. and Wiggins, E. C., 'Empirical Research on Civil Discovery', (1998) 39(3) *Boston College Law Review* 785

McLaughlin, J. H., 'Litigation funding: charting a legal and ethical course', (2007) 31 *Vt. L. Rev.* 615

Melamed, P., 'An Alternative to the Contingent Fee? An Assessment of the Incentive Effects of the English Conditional Fee Arrangement', (2006) 27 *Cardozo L. Rev.* 2433

Meng, F., 'Funding Derivative Actions in China: Lessons from Wallersteiner v Moir (No.2) for the Court', (2010) 31(1) *Comp. Law.* 29

Metcald, C., 'Litigating Environmental Quality: An Economic Approach', (2004) 13 *J. Env. L. & Prac.* 293

Miller, G. P., 'Some Agency Problems in Settlement' (1987) 16 *The Journal of Legal Studies* 189

Moll, D. K., 'Minority Oppression & the Limited Liability Company: Learning (or Not) from Close Corporation History' (2005) 40 *Wake Forest Law Review* 883

Molot, J. T., 'A Market in Litigation Risk', (2009) 76 *U. Chi. L. Rev.* 367

Moore, N. J., 'Who Should Regulate Class Action Lawyers?' (2003) 5 *U. Ill. L. Rev.* 101

Moorhead, R., 'Conditional Fee Agreements, Legal Aid and Access to Justice' (2002) 33 *U. Brit. Colum. L. Rev.* 471

Morrisey, D. L., 'Shareholder Litigation after the Meltdown', (2011) 144 *West Virginia Law Review* 531
Mulheron, R. and Cashman, P., 'Third party funding: a changing landscape', (2008) 27(3) *C.J.Q.* 312
Mulheron, R., 'From Representative Rule to Class Action: Steps rather than Leaps' (2005) 24 *C.J. Q.* 424;
Olson, J. F., Mahaffey, D. C. and Casy, B. E., 'Pleading Reform, Plaintiff Qualification and Discovery Stays Under the Reform Act', (1996) 51 *Bus. Law.* 1101
Pennell, K., 'On the assignment of legal malpractice claims: a contractual solution to a contractual problem', (2004) 82 *Tex. L. Rev.* 481
Peysner, J., 'National Reports: England and Wales', in Hodges, C., Vogenauer, S. and Tulibacka, M. (eds), *The Costs and Funding of Civil Litigation* (Hart Publishing, 2010) 294
Peysner, J., 'What's Wrong with Contingency Fees?', (2001) 10 *Nottingham Law Journal* 22
Polinsky, M. and Shavell, S., 'The Theory of Public Enforcement of Law', (2000) 38(1) *Journal of Economic Literature* 45
Prentice, D. D., 'Wallersteiner v Moir: A Decade Later', (1987) 51 *Conveyancer* 167
Prentice, D. D., 'Wallersteiner v Moir: The Demise of the Rule in Foss v Harbottle?' (1976) 40 *Conveyance* 51
Pritchard, A. C., 'Markets as Monitors: A Proposal to Replace Class Actions with Exchanges as Securities Fraud Enforcers', (1999) 85 *VA. L. Rev.* 925
Puri, P., 'Financing of Litigation by Third-Party Investors: A Share of Justice', (1998) 36 *Osgoode Hall L. J.* 515
Rabinovich-Einy, O., 'Beyond Efficiency: the Transformation of Courts through Technology', (2008) 12(1) *UCLA Journal of Law & Technology* 1
Radin, M., 'Maintenance by Champerty' (1935) 24(1) *California Law Review* 48
Ramsay, I., 'Corporate Governance, Shareholder Litigation and the Prospect for a Statutory Derivative Action', (1992) 15 (1) *University of New South Wales Law Journal* 149
Reisberg, A., 'Access to Justice or Justice Not Accessed: Is There a Case for Public Funding of Derivative Suits?' (2012) 37(2) *Brooklyn Journal of International Law* 1037
Reisberg, A., 'Corporate Law in the UK after Recent Reforms: The Good, the Bad and the Ugly' (2010) 63 *Current Legal Problems* 315
Reisberg, A., 'Shadows of the past and back to the future: Part 11 of the UK Companies Act 2006 (in)action', (2009) 6 *European Company and Financial Law Review* 219
Reisberg, A., 'Derivative Claims Under the Companies Act 2006: Much Ado about Nothing?' in Armour, J. and Payne, J. (eds.) *Rationality in Company Law: Essays in Honour of DD Prentice* (Hart Publishing, 2009)
Reisberg, A., 'Funding Derivative Actions: A Re-examination of Costs and Fees as Incentives to Commence Litigation', (2004) 4 *J. CORP. L. STUD.* 345
Richard, M., 'Conditional Fee Agreements, Legal Aid and Access to Justice', (2000) 33 *U. Brit Colum. L. Rev.* 472
Richmond, D. R., 'Other people's money: the ethics of litigation funding', (2005) 56 *Mercer Law Review* 669.
Riley, A., 'Damages in EC Antitrust Actions: Who Pays the Piper?' (2006) 31(5) *E.L Rev.* 748
Robin, P. H., 'Third-party financing of litigation', (2011) 38 *N. Ky. L. Rev.* 673
Ridaj, M., 'It's About Time: A Systems Thinking Analysis of the Litigation Finance Industry and its Effect on Settlement' (2006) 155 *University of Pennsylvania Law Review* 503
Romano, R., 'The shareholder Suit: Litigation without Foundation?' (1991) 7(1) *The Journal of Law, Economics and Organization* 55
Rowe, T. D., Jr., 'Shift Happens: Pressure on Foreign Attorney-Fee Paradigms from Class Actions' (2003) 13 *Duke J. Comp & Int'l L.* 125
Rubenstein, W. B., 'Why Enable Litigation: A Positive Externalities Theory of the Small Claims Class Action', (2006) 74 *Umkc L. Rev.* 709

Rubinfeld, D. L. and Scotchmer, S., 'Contingent Fees for Attorneys: An Economic Analysis', (1993) 24(3) *The RAND Journal of Economics* 343

Schmidt, V. A., 'The European Union's Eurozone Crisis and What (Not) to Do about It', (2011) 17 *Brown J. World Aff.* 199

Sebok, A. J., 'The Inauthentic Claim', (2011) 64 *Vand. L. Rev.* 61

Sha, Y., 'The abolition of the internal instructions within the court system' (个案请示制度之废除及其功能替代,ge'an qingshi gongneng zhi feichu jiqi gongneng tidai), (2008) 7 *Hebei Law Science* (河北法学 hebei faxue)

Shavell, S., 'The Level of Litigation: Private Versus Social Optimality of Suit and of Settlement', (1999) 19 *INT'L REV. L. & ECON.* 99

Shavell, S., 'The Social Versus the Private Incentive to Bring Suit in a Costly Legal System', (1982) 11 *J. LEGAL STUD.* 333

Shen, J., 'From the adoration of GDP to the care for well-being index: profound turns in the views of development in perspective of theory of development', (从 GDP 崇拜到幸福指数关怀—发展理论视野中发展观的几次深刻转折, cong GDP chongbai dao xingfu zhishu guanhuai—fazhan lilun shiye zhong fazhanguan de jici shenke zhuanzhe), (2006) 3 *Journal of Jiangsu administration institute* (江苏行政学院学报)

Sherman, E. F., 'Group Litigation under Foreign Legal Systems: Variations and Alternatives to American Class Actions', (2003) 52 *DePaul L. Rev.* 401

Siems, M., 'Private Enforcement of Directors' Duties: Derivative Actions as a Global Phenomenon', in Wrbka, S., Van Uytsel, S. and Siems, M. (eds.) *Collective Actions: Enhancing Access to Justice and Reconciling Multilayer Interests?* (Cambridge University Press, 2012) 93

Snyder, E. A. and Hughes, J. W., 'The English Rule for Allocating Legal Costs: Evidence Confronts Theory', (1990) 6 *Journal of Law, Economics, & Organization* 345

Steinitz, M., 'Whose Claim Is This Anyway? Third Party Litigation Funding' (2011) 95(4) *Minnesota Law Review* 1268

Swanson, C. B., 'Juggling Shareholder Rights and Strike Suits in Derivative Litigation: the ALI Drops the Ball', (1993) 77 *MNLR* 1339

Sykes, J. P., 'The continuing paradox: a critique of minority shareholder and derivative claims under the Companies Act 2006', (2010) 29(2) *C.J.Q.* 205

Tang, J., 'Shareholder remedies: demise of the derivative claims?'(2012) 1 *UCL Journal of Law and Jurisprudence* 178

Tang, X., 'Protecting Minority Shareholders in China: A Task for Both Legislation and Enforcement', in Kanda, H., Kim, K. and Milhaupt, C. (eds.), *Transforming Corporate Governance in East Asia* (Routledge, 2008) 141

Thai, L., 'Commercial litigation funding: the need to impose regulations to improve the outcome of the shareholder class actions', (2011) 4 *Journal of the Australasian Law Teachers Association* 1

Thai, L., 'How Popular are Statutory Derivative Actions in Australia? Comparisons with United States, Canada and New Zealand', (2002) 30 *AUSTL. BUS. L. REV.* 118

Thomas, R. S., 'A Theory of Representative Shareholder Suits and its Application to Multijurisdictional Litigation' (2012) 106(4) *Northwestern University Law Review* 1753

Thomason, T., 'Are Attorneys Paid What They Are Worth? Contingent Fees and the Settlement Process' (1991) 20 *The Journal of Legal Studies* 187

Thompson, B. H., Jr., 'The Continuing Innovation of Citizen Enforcement' (2000) *U. ILL. L. REV.* 185

Thompson, R. B. and Thomas, R. S., 'The Public and Private Faces of Derivative Lawsuits', (2004) 57 *VAND. L. REV.* 1747

Thompson, R. B. and Thomas, R. S., 'The New Look of Shareholder Litigation: Acquisition-oriented Class Actions', (2004) 57(1) *Vanderbilt Law Review* 134

Veljanovski, C., 'Third Party Litigation Funding in Europe' (2012) 8 *Journal of Law, Economics and Policy* 444

Walker, J., Khouri, S. and Attrill, W., 'Class Actions, Conflicts and Controversy' (2009) 32 *University of New South Wales Law Journal* 1036

Walpin, G., 'America's Falling Civil Justice System: Can We Learn From Other Countries?', (1997) 41 *N. Y. L. Sch. L. Rev.* 647

Walters, A. and Peysner, J., 'Event-Triggered Financing of Civil Claims: Lawyers, Insurers and the Common Law' (1999) 8 *Nottingham Law Journal* 1

Wang, B. and Huang, H., 'China's New Company Law and Securities Law: An overview and assessment', (2006) 19 *AUSTL. J. CORP. L.* 229

Wang, D., *Theoretical analysis on shareholders' derivative actions*, (gongsi paisheng susong lun '公司派生诉讼论'), (China legal publishing house, 2012) (zhongguo fazhi chubanshe '中国法制出版社')

Watson, G. D., 'Class Actions: The Canadian Experience', (2001) 11 *Duke Journal of Comparative & International Law* 269

Waye, V., 'Conflicts of Interests between Claimholders, Lawyers and Litigation Entrepreneurs', (2007) 19(1) *Bond Law Review* 2005

Weiss, E. J. and Beckerman, J. S., 'Let the Money do the Monitoring: How Institutional Investors Can Reduce Agency Costs in Securities Class Actions', (1995) 104 *YALE L.J.* 2053

Weitzel, P. D., 'The End of Shareholder Litigation? Allowing Shareholders to Customize Enforcement through Arbitration Provisions in Charters and Bylaws' 2013 *BYU L. Rev.* 65

Wilson, J. D., 'Attorney Fees and the Decision to Commence Litigation: Analysis, Comparison and an Application to the Shareholder's Derivative Action', (1985) 5 *Windsor Yearbook of Access to Justice* 177.

Winfield, P. H., 'History of Maintenance and Champerty', (1919) 35 *L. Q. Rev.* 50

Woodroffe, G., 'Loser Pays and Conditional Fees—An English Solution?', (1998) 37 *Washburn L. J.* 345

Xiao, J., *'Rules On Malicious Prosecution'* (论恶意诉讼及其法律规制, 'lun eyi susong jiqi falv guizhi'), (2012) 4 *Journal of Renmin University of China*

Xu, J. and Smith, D., Analysis of the development of Chinese social organizations (中国非营利组织生存路径探析, zhongguo fei yingli zuzhi shengcun lujin tanxi), (2012) *5 Journal of Chinese academy of governance* (国家行政学院学报,guojia xingzheng xueyuan xuebao)

Xu, L., Zhu, T. and Lin, Y., 'Politician Control, Agency Problems and Ownership Reform: Evidence from China' (2005) 13(1) *Economics of Transition* 1

Yan, M., 'Obstacles in China's corporate governance', (2011) 32(10) *Comp. Law.* 311

Yi, J., 'Political and philosophical research on clause of the public policy and good morals—focusing on protection of autonomy of will of private individuals' (民法上公序良俗条款的政治哲学思考—以私人自治的维护为中心, 'minfa shang gongxuliangsu tiaokuan de zhengzhi zhexue sikao—yi siren zizhi de weihu wei zhongxin'), (2005) 6 *Studies in Law and Business*

Zakaib, G. M. and Martin, J. M., 'International Class Actions in the Canadian Context: Standing, Funding, Enforceability and Trial', (2012) 79 *Def. Counsel J.* 296

Zander, M., 'The Government's Plans on Legal Aid and Conditional Fees' (1998) 61 *Modern Law Review* 538

Zhang, X., 'A new statement of the interested relationship in law' ("法律上利害关系"新表述, falv shang lihai guanxi xin biaoshu), (2001) 6 *Journal of East China University of Political Science and Law*

Zhang, Z., 'Making Shareholder Derivative Actions Happen in China: How Should Lawsuits be Funded?', (2008) 38 *Hong Kong L.J.* 523

Ziegel, J., 'Class Actions to Remedy Mass Consumer Wrongs: Repugnant Solution or Controllable Genie? The Canadian Experience', (2009) 27 *Penn St. Int'l L. Rev.* 879

Zuo, C. and Yu, G., 'Rationale Law Making and Enforcement Efficiency: the Case of Derivative Action' (2011) 3 *Law Review of the Chinese Capital Market* 377

Zuo, W., 'Citizens' right to sue:a study of constitutional and judicial safeguard' (公民诉讼权:宪法与司法保障研究, 'gongmin susong quan: xianfa yu sifa baozhang yanjiu'), (2001) 4 *Legal Science*

## Other Sources

American Bar Association Tort Trial & Insurance Practice Section, 'Report on Contingent Fees in Medical Malpractice Litigation (2004)', available at http://apps.americanbar.org/tips/contingent/MedMalReport092004DCW2.pdf

American Bar Association Working Group, Working Group's Issue Paper Concerning Alternative Litigation Financing, American Bar Association Comments (2011), available at http://www.americanbar.org/content/dam/aba/migrated/2011_build/ethics_2020/comments_on_alternative_litigation_financing_issues_paper.authcheckdam.pdf

American Bar Association, 'Model Rules of Professional Conduct', available at http://www.americanbar.org/groups/professional_responsibility/publications/model_rules_of_professional_conduct/model_rules_of_professional_conduct_table_of_contents.html

American Trial Lawyers Association, *Keys to the Courthouse: Quick Facts on the Contingent Fee System* (1994)

Annual report 2010 of the Class Proceeding Fund by Ontario Law Foundation, available at http://www.lawfoundation.on.ca/pdf/annual_reports/LFOAR2010_Book3.pdf

Annual Report of the Ontario Class Proceedings Fund, 2009-2010, available at http://www.lawfoundation.on.ca/pdf/annual_reports/LFOAR2010_Book3.pdf

Annual working report of the SPC of 2010, (in Chinese), available at http://www.court.gov.cn/qwfb/sfsj/201105/t20110525_100996.htm

Armour, J., 'Enforcement Strategies in UK Corporate Governance: A Roadmap and Empirical Assessment', April 2008, ECGI - Law Working Paper No. 106/2008, available at http://ssrn.com/abstract=1133542

Arnold, P. and Stewart, P., 'United Kingdom, England Embraces Contingency Fees', 10 October 2013, available at http://www.mondaq.com/x/268388/trials+appeals+compensation/England+Embraces+Contingency+Fees

Attrill, W., 'Ethical Issues in Litigation Funding', February 2009, available at http://www.claimsfunding.eu/fileadmin/Documents/Ethical_Issues_Paper.pdf

Bannon, P., 'Recent developments in litigation funding in Australia and the UK', 8 February 2012, available at http://www.mondaq.com/australia/x/163432/Regulatory/Recent+developments+in+litigation+funding+in+Australia+and+the+UK

Barker, G. R., 'Third Party Litigation Funding in Australia and Europe', 13 December 2011, available at http://ssrn.com/abstract=2034625

Calihan, R. B., Dent, J. R. and Victor, M. B., 'The Role of Risk Analysis in Dispute and Litigation Management', American Bar Association 27th Annual Forum on Franchising, October 2004, available at http://www.litigationrisk.com/Paper%20on%20Risk%20Analysis%20for%20ABA%20Forum%20on%20Franchising.pdf

Centre for Justice Democracy at New York Law School: 'White Paper: Courthouse Cornerstone: Contingency Fees and Their Importance for Everyday Americans', available at http://centerjd.org/content/white-paper-courthouse-cornerstone-contingency-fees-and-their-importance-everyday-americans

China Law and Governance Review (2004) June, No2, 'Enforcement of Civil Judgments: Harder than Reaching the Sky (Zhixing nan, nanyu Shangqingtian)' (June 2004), available at http://www.chinareview.info/issue2/pages/legal.htm#1

Civil Justice Council, Consultation Paper on a Self-regulatory Code of Third Party Funding, Summary of Responses, available at http://www.judiciary.gov.uk/about-the-judiciary/advisory-bodies/cjc/third-party-funding.htm#pageTitleContainer

Compere, L., 'litigation funding in China', 7 May 2012, available at http://www.legalfunding.com/news/litigation-funding-in-china/

'Contingency Fee Arrangements Need to be Developed' (律师风险代理制度亟待健全, lvshi fengxian daili zhidu jidai jianquan), http://www.legalinfo.gov.cn/moj/lsgzgzzds/content/2007-12/17/content_763147.htm?node=282 (in Chinese)

Emons, W. and Garoupa, N., 'The Economic of US-style Contingent Fees and UK-style Conditional Fees', July 2004, CEPR Discussion Paper No. 4473, available at http://ssrn.com/abstract=574542

Flood, J., 'The Transformation of Access to Law and Justice in England and Wales 60 Years on', 21 November 2009, U. of Westminster School of Law, Research Paper No. 10-14, available at http://papers.ssrn.com/sol3/papers.cfm?abstract_id=1574869

Fu, H., 'Access to Justice in China: Potentials, Limits, and Alternatives', 15 September 2009, available at http://ssrn.com/abstract=1474073

Gan, P., 'Overview on Shareholder Derivative Action in Chinese Company Law', (简评中国公司法对股东派生诉讼制度的借鉴 'jianping zhongguo gongsifa dui gudong paisheng susong zhidu de jiejian'), available at http://www.civillaw.com.cn/Article/default.asp?id=25127

Green Paper Contingency Fees (Cm 571) (January 1989)

Hensler, D. R. et al, 'Compensation for Accidental Injuries in the United States', Rand, 1991, available at http://www.rand.org/content/dam/rand/pubs/reports/2006/R3999.pdf.

Hodges, C., Peysner, J. and Nurse, A., 'Litigation funding: status and issues', Oxford Legal Studies Research Paper No. 55/2012, January 2012, available at http://papers.ssrn.com/sol3/papers.cfm?abstract_id=2126506

http://www.lpclrd.lawlink.nsw.gov.au/agdbasev7wr/lpclrd/documents/pdf/litigationfundingdiscussionpapermay06.pdf

Hu, H. and Zhang, X., 'Civil Compensation System and Shareholder Representative Actions in Listed Companies', Working Paper Series published by Shanghai Stock Exchange Centre. http://www.sse.com.cn/cs/zhs/xxfw/jysjs/researchDir/mspc.pdf

Institute for the Advancement of the American Legal System, 'Preserving Access and Identifying Excess: Areas of Convergence and Consensus in the 2010 Conference Materials' (2010), available at http://www.uscourts.gov/uscourts/RulesAndPolicies/rules/Duke%20Materials/Library/IAALS,%20Preserving%20Access%20and%20Identifying%20Excess.pdf

Jackson, R., 'Review of Civil Litigation Costs: Final Report', December 2009, available at http://associationoflitigationfunders.com/wp-content/uploads/2014/02/Jacksonfinalreport140110.pdf

Klöhn, L., 'Private Versus Public Enforcement of Laws—A Law & Economics Perspective', Ludwig-Maximilians-Universität Munich Working Paper, 2010, available at http://papers.ssrn.com/sol3/papers.cfm?abstract_id=1730308

Law Council of Australia, 'Regulation of third party litigation funding in Australia', June 2011, available at http://www.lawcouncil.asn.au/shadomx/apps/fms/fmsdownload.cfm?file_uuid=FDE54AA6-C860-A078-ED07-5BB15F2A31E3&siteName=lca

Law Reform Commission of Hong Kong, Consultation Paper on Conditional Fee, September 2005, available at http://www.hkreform.gov.hk/en/docs/conditional-e.pdf

'Lawyers' Contingent Fees' (律师风险代理 lvshi fengxian daili), http://www.chinalawinfo.com:81/chyzl/detail.asp?id=518&cid=63 (in Chinese)

Le Sueur, A., 'A Report on Six Seminars about the UK Supreme Court', December 2008, *Queen Mary School of Law Legal Studies Research Paper* No. 1/2008, available at http://ssrn.com/abstract=1324749

Lee, E. G. III and Willging, T. E., 'Litigation Costs in civil Cases: Multivariate Analysis Report to the Judicial Conference Advisory Committee on Civil Rules', Federal Judicial Center, March 2010, available at http://www.fjc.gov/public/pdf.nsf/lookup/costciv1.pdf/$file/costciv1.pdf

Legal Service Corporation, 'Documenting the Justice Gap in America: The Current Unmet Civil Legal Needs of Low-Income Americans', September 2005, available at www.lsc.gov/press/documents/LSC%20Justice%20Gap_FINAL_1001.pdf

Lindeman, R., 'Third Party Investors Offer New Funding Source for Major Commercial lawsuits', BNA Daily Report for Executives, 5 March 2010, available at http://www.fulbrookmanagement.com/2010/03/05/third-party-investors-offer-new-funding-source-for-major-commercial-lawsuits/

Lord Chancellor's Department, 'Access to Justice with Conditional Fees', 1998, available at https://www.jspubs.com/experts/ext_rep/lcd_main.htm

McGovern, G. et al, Third Party Litigation Funding and Claim Transfer: Trends and Implications for the Civil Justice System, RAND conference proceedings series, 2009, available at http://www.rand.org/content/dam/rand/pubs/conf_proceedings/2010/RAND_CF272.pdf

McInnes, R., 'Australia: ASIC issues litigation funding guidance to manage conflicts of interest', 8 June 2013, available at http://www.mondaq.com/australia/x/243848/Class+Actions/ASIC+issues+litigation+funding+guidance+to+manage+conflicts+of+interest

'Measures for managing intellectual property right subsidy funds in Guangzhou' (in Chinese), available at http://www.sskc.gov.cn/HTML/NEWS_ZHENGCE/37.html

'Measures for managing patent subsidy funds in Ningbo new and hi-tech industrial development zone' (in Chinese), available at http://xxgk.nbhtz.gov.cn/govdiropen/jcms_files/jcms1/web1/site/index.html

Ministry of Justice, 'Legal Aid: Funding Reforms', Consultation Paper CP 18/09,August 2009, available at http://www.clsa.co.uk/assets/files/general/legal-aid-funding-reforms.pdf

Molot, J. T., 'Theory and Practice in Litigation Risk', Burford Whitepaper, 2012, available at http://www.burfordcapital.com/wp-content/uploads/2012/11/Burford_Whitepaper11.pdf

Moorhead, R. and Hurst, P.,'"Improving Access to Justice", Contingency Fees: A Study of their Operation in the United States of America', a research paper informing the Review of Costs, November 2008, available at http://www.judiciary.gov.uk/wp-content/uploads/2011/06/JCO_Documents_CJC_Publications_CJC+papers_Civil+Justice+Council+Contingency+Fees+Report.pdf

Napier, M. et al, 'Improved Access to Justice – Funding Options and Proportionate Costs: Report and Recommendations', August 2005, available at http://www.judiciary.gov.uk/wp-content/uploads/JCO/Documents/CJC/Publications/CJC+papers/CJC+Improved+access+to+Justice+-Funding+options+and+proportionate+costs.pdf

Napier, M. et al, 'Improved Access to Justice – Funding Options and Proportionate Costs: The Future Funding of Litigation – Alternative Funding Structures', Civil Justice Council's paper, June 2007, available at http://www.judiciary.gov.uk/related-offices-and-bodies/advisory-bodies/cjc/costs-and-funding/

Pagano, M., Panetta, F. and Zingales, L., 'Why do companies go public? An Empirical Analysis', National Bureau of Economic Research (NBER) Working Paper Series 5367, November 1995, available at http://www.nber.org/papers/w5367

Palmer, M. and Xi, C., 'Collective and Representative Actions in China', 2007, available at http://globalclassactions.stanford.edu/sites/default/files/documents/China_National_Report.pdf

Pastre, F., 'How Shareholder Litigations Deter Directors and Officers: U.S. and Italy, A Comparative Analysis', 14 July 2011, available at http://ssrn.com/abstract=1921754

Polinsky, A. M. and Rubinfeld, D. L., 'A Note on Settlements under the Contingent Fee Method of Compensating Lawyers', March 2002, Stanford Law and Economics Olin Working Paper No. 224, available at http://ssrn.com/abstract=286055

Ramsay, I. M.andSauners, B. B., 'LitigationbyShareholdersandDirectors:An EmpiricalStudyof The StatutoryDerivativeAction',CenterforCorporateLawandSecurities Regulation,Universityof Melbourne,2006, available at http://www.law.unimelb.edu.au/files/dmfile/Statutory_Derivative_Action_Research_Report__15_03_06_21.pdf

Reese, W. A., Jr. and Weisbach, M. S., 'Protection of Minority Shareholder Interests, Cross-listings in the United States, and Subsequent Equity Offerings', NBER Working Paper No. 8164, 17 November 1999, available at http://ssrn.com/abstract=194670

Rose, N., 'Drive for Transparency on Third-Party Funding' in Law Gazette, 14 February 2008, available at http://www.lawgazette.co.uk/news/drive-transparency-third-party-funding

Schepens, T., 'Bridging the Funding Gap - The Economics of Cost Shifting, Fee Arrangements and Legal Expenses Insurance and Their Prospects for Improving the Access to Civil Justice', German Working Papers in Law and Economics: Vol. 2007, Article 1, available at http://www.bepress.com/cgi/viewcontent.cgi?article=1196&context=gwp

Shanghai Securities News (in Chinese), 'Majority shareholders of Lianhua Weijing were sued by a minority shareholder because of the misappropriate companies' assets', available at http://finance.sina.com.cn/roll/20040722/0627890447.shtml;

Shanghai Security News (in Chinese), *'The Investigation of Sanjiu Medical & Pharmaceutical Co. Ltd: the Eve of Shareholding Reform'* (三九医药被查:股改前夜打响清欠第一枪, sanjiu yiyao beicha: gugai qianye daxiang qingqian diyiqiang), 27 Dec 2010.

Shanghai Stock Exchange Research Centre, 'China Corporate Governance Report 2009' (gongsi zhili baogao '公司治理报告'), May 2009, available at http://www.sse.com.cn/researchpublications/special/c/special20100312.pdf

Shareholders Lawsuits and Enforcement', China Law & Practice, May 2006, available at http://www.chinalawandpractice.com/Article/1692125/Channel/9930/Corporate-Governance-under-the-New-Company-Law-Part-2-Shareholder-Lawsuits-and-Enforcement.html

Silver, C., 'Dose Civil Justice Cost Too Much?',Public Law and Legal Theory Research Paper No. 37, June 2002, available at http://ssrn.com/abstract_id=314964

Standing Committee of Attorneys General, 'Litigation Funding in Australia', Discussion Paper, May 2006, available at

The American Bar Association Commission on Ethics 20/20 (ABA Commission) 'White Paper on Alternative Litigation Finance', available at http://www.americanbar.org/content/dam/aba/administrative/ethics_2020/20111019_draft_alf_white_paper_posting.authcheckdam.pdf

The Company Law Review Steering Group, 'Modern Company Law for a Competitive Economy: Final Report', Volume I, available at http://webarchive.nationalarchives.gov.uk/20070603164510/http://www.dti.gov.uk/cld/final_report/prelims.pdf

The World Bank, *Doing Business: Protecting Investors in Israel* (2012, 2013), available at http://www.doingbusiness.org/data/exploreeconomies/israel/#protecting-investors

Trebilcock, M., 'Report of the Legal Aid Review', submitted to the Attorney General of Ontario, 2008, available at http://www.attorneygeneral.jus.gov.on.ca/english/about/pubs/trebilcock/legal_aid_report_2008_EN.pdf

U.S. Chamber Institute for Legal Reform, 'Selling Lawsuits, Buying Trouble: Third Party Litigation Funding in the United States', October 2009, available at http://www.instituteforlegalreform.com/sites/default/files/thirdpartylitigationfinancing.pdf

UK Law Commission Report No 246, 1997, 'Shareholder Remedies', available at http://lawcommission.justice.gov.uk/docs/lc246_Shareholder_Remedies.pdf

Walker, J., 'IMF's Submissions on State Regulation of Litigation Funding', submission for consideration by officers in the Attorney-General's Department of NSW, 16 September 2005, available at http://www.imf.com.au/docs/default-source/site-documents/20050916_submissionsonregulationoflitigationfunding

Wang, H., 'What is it behind the establishment of discipline inspection commission?' (单列纪检小组的背后, 'danlie jijian xiaozu de beihou'), in Chinese, available at http://www.dldj.gov.cn/trans.aspx?id=72133

West, M. D., 'Why Shareholders Sue: The Evidence from Japan', November 2000, *Michigan Law and Economics Research Paper* No. 00-010, available at http://ssrn.com/abstract=251012

Xi, X., 'New Development of Trial of Intellectual Property Right Cases' (努力实现知识产权审判工作新发展 nuli shixian zhishi chanquan shenpan gongzuo xinfazhan), a public speech on the conference on the research of the trial of intellectual property right cases, (在全国法院知识产权审判工作座谈会上的讲话), available at http://www.court.gov.cn/zscq/dcyj/201205/t20120509_176766.html (in Chinese)

Xu, S., 'China's Public Administration Reform: New Approaches', available at http://www.iam.or.jp/asia-pacific_panel/pdfdownloads/athens01-paper4.pdf;

Yu, G. and Liu, J., 'Analysis of Shareholder Derivative Actions', Commercial Law Forum No.330, the minute of this forum could be available at (in Chinese) http://www.civillaw.com.cn/article/default.asp?id=43662

Zamir, E. and Ritov, I., 'Neither Saints nor Devils: A Behavioral Analysis of Attorneys' Contingent Fees', *22* January 2008, available at http://ssrn.com/abstract=1085985

# List of Selected Cases

## Australia

ABC v Lenah Game Meats Pty Ltd [2001] HCA 63; 208 CLR 199; 185 ALR 1; 76 ALJR 1 (15 November 2001)
Anstella Nominees Pty Ltd v. St George Motor Finance Ltd. [2003] FCA 466; 21 ACLC 1347
Campbells Cash and Carry Pty Ltd v. Fostif Pty Ltd (2006) HCA 41
Clairs Keeley (A Firm) v Treacy [2004] WASCA 277
Fostif v Campells Cash and Carry [2005] NSWCA 83
International Litigation Partners Pte Ltd v Chameleon Mining NL [2012] HCA 45 (Oct. 5, 2012).
Jenkins v Enterprise Gold Mines NL (1992) 6 ACSR 539;
Multiplex Funds Management Ltd v. P. Dawson Nominees Pty Ltd (2007) 164 FCR 275
Niord Pty Ltd v Adelaide Petroleum NL (1990) 2 ACSR 347.
Project 28 Pty Ltd (formerly Narui Gold Coast Pty Ltd) v Barr [2005] NSWCA 240
Spatialinfo Pty Ltd v Telstra Corp Ltd [2005] FCA 455
Trendlen Pty Ltd v Mobil Oil Australia Pty Ltd [2005] NSWSC 741

## Canada

Edwards v Law Society of Upper Canada (2000), 188 DLR (4th) 613, 48 OR (3d) 329 (CA)
Gagne v Silcorp Ltd (1998), 41 OR 3d (417) (CA)
Garland v Consumers' Gas Co (1995), 22 OR (3d) 767 (Gen Div)
Garland v Consumers' Gas Co (1998), 165 DLR (4th) 385, 40 OR (3d) 479 (SCC)
Parsons v. Canadian Red Cross Society [1999] OJ No 3572
Pearson v Inco Ltd (2002), 33 CPC (5th) 264
Turner v Mailhot (1985) 50 OR (2d) 561
Wong v Second Cup Ltd, (2005) OJ No. 2897



W. Chen, *A Comparative Study of Funding Shareholder Litigation*,
DOI 10.1007/978-981-10-3623-1

## The United Kingdom

Ahmed v. Powell, [2003] P.N.L.R. 22
Alexander v Automatic Telephone Co [1990] 2 Ch 56
American Cyanamid Co v Ethicon Ltd [1975] AC 396 (HL)
Arkin v Borchard Lines Ltd [2005] EWCA Civ 655
Arkin v. Borchard Lines Ltd [2003] EWHC 2844
Assurance Co Ltd v Newman Industries Ltd (No 2) [1981] Ch 257
Clark v Cutland [2003] 2 BCLC 393
Cook v Deeks [1916] 1 AC 554
E.M.I. Records Ltd. v. Riley, 1 W.L.RI 923 (Ch. 1981)
Eastford Ltd v. Gillespie [2009] CSOH 119
Factortame & Ors v. Sec'y of State for Transport, Local Government and the Regions (No.8) [2003] Q.B. 381
Foss v Harbottle (1843) 67 ER 189
Franbar Holdings Ltd v Patel & Ors [2008] EWHC 1534 (Ch), [2008] BCC 885; [2009] 1 BCLC 1; [2009] Bus LR D14
Giles v Thompson [1994] 1 A.C. 142
Hill v Archbold [1968] 1 Q.B. 686
Jaybird Group Ltd v Greenwood [1986] BCLC 319
Kiani v Cooper [2010] BCC 463
Lesini v Westrip Holdings Ltd [2009] EWHC 2526 (ch); [2010] BCC 420
London & Regional (St George's Court) Ltd v Ministry of Defence [2008] EWHC 526 (TCC)
Lowe v Fabey [1996] 1 BCLC 262; Anderson v Hogg [2002] BCC 923
Mission Capital plc v Sinclair case ([2008] EWHC 1339 (Ch), [2008] BCC 866
Pennock v Hodgson [2010] EWCA Civ 873
Prudential Assurance Co Ltd v Newman Industries Ltd (No 2) [1982] 1 Ch 204
Re a Company (No 005827 of 1985) [1986] BCLC 68
Re Stewarts (Brixton) Ltd [1985] BCLC 4
Roberts v. Gill & Co & Anor [2008] EWCA Civ 803; [2008] WTLR 1429; [2009] 1 WLR 531; [2009] CP Rep 3; [2009] PNLR 2
Smith v Croft (No 1) [1986] 1 WLR 580
Smith v Croft (No 2) [1988] Ch 114
Society Ltd v CUFC Holdings Ltd & Ors [2010] EWCA Civ 463
Trendtex Trading Corp v Credit Suisse [1980] 1 Q.B. 629; [1982] A.C. 679
Wallersteiner v Moir (No 2) [1975] 1 ALL ER 849; [1975] QB 373
Wisbart v Castlecroft Securities Ltd [2010] BCC 161

## The United States

American Optical Co. v. Curtiss, 56 F.R.D. 26 (S.D.N.Y. 1971)
Aronson v. Lewis, 473 A.2d 805 (Del. 1984)
Auerbach v Bennett 47 N.Y.2d 619,393 N.E.2d 994,419 N.Y.S.2d 920 (N.Y.1979)

Bashor v. Northland Ins. Co., 29 Colo. App. 81, 480 P.2d 864 (1970)
Basic Inc. v. Levinson, 485 U.S. 224 (1988)
Bates v. State Bar of Arizona. 433 U.S. 350 (1977)
Bokat v Getty Oil Company, 262 A.2d 246 (Del. 1970)
Brehm v. Eisner, 746 A.2d 244 (Del. 2000)
Burks v. M Lasker 441 U.S. 471 (1979)
Casserleigh v. Wood, 119 F. 308, 312 (8th Cir. 1902)
Casserleigh v. Wood, 14 Colo.App. 265 (1900)
Clifford v. Wilcox, 175 Wash.513; 27 P.2d 1087 (Wash. 1933)
Davis v. Comed,Inc.,619 F.2d 588 (6th Cir. 1980)
Deephaven Risk Arb Trading, Ltd. V. UnitedGlobalCom, Inc., C.A. No.379-N (Del. Ch. July 13, 2005)
Elster v. American Airlines, Inc., 34 Del. Ch. 94, 100A.2d 219 (1953)
Fogel v. Chestnutt, 533 F.2d 731 (2d Cir. 1975)
Fradkin v. Ernst, 98F.R.D. 478 (N.D.Ohio 1983).
Gall v Exxon Corp., 418 F Supp 508 (SDNY 1976)
Grimes v Donald, 673 A.2d 1207 (Del. 1996)
Guenther v. Pac. Telecom., Inc., 123 F.R.D. 341 (D.Or.1998)
Hall v. State, 655 A.2d 827 (Del. Super. Ct. 1994)
Hardick v. Homol, 795 So. 2d 1107 (Fla. 5th Dist. Ct. App. 2001);
Hawesv.CityofOakland,104U.S.450(1882).
Hillson Partners Ltd. P'ship v. Adage, Inc., 42 F.3d 204 (4th Cir. 1994)
Huber v. Johnson, 68 Minn.74 (1897)
I. Meyer Pincus & Assocs. v. Oppenheimer & Co., 936 F.2d 759 (2nd Cir. 1991);
In re A.H. Robins Co., 182 B.R. 128 (E.D. Va. 1995)
In re Donald J. Trump Casino Sec. Litig., 7 F.3d 357 (3d Cir. 1993).
In re New Valley Corp. Derivative Litigation. C.A. No. 17649-NC (Del. Ch. June 28, 2004).
In re the Dow Chemical Company Derivative Litigation, Del. Ch. Civ. No. 4349-CC (Jan. 11, 2010)
Johnson v. Wrught, 682 N.W.2d 671 (Minn. Ct. App.2004)
Kalmanovitz v. G.Heileman Brewing Co., 595 F. Supp. 1385 (D. Del.1984), aff'd,769 F.2d 152(3d Cir.1985).
Kraft v. Mason, 668 So. 2d 679 (Fla. App. 4th Dist. 1996)
Kramer v. W. Pac. Indus., Inc., 546 A.2d 348 (Del. 1988)
Leader Technologies, Inc. v. Facebook Inc., 719 F.Supp. 2d 373 (D. Del. 2010)
Lewis v. Anderson, 477 A.2d 1040 (Del. 1984)
Lewis v. Curtis, 671 F.2d 788 (3d Cir.1982)
Mazzetti v. Shepherd, C.A. No. 8198, slip op. at 7 (Del.Ch.Aug.26, 1986)
Miller v Register and Tribune Syndicate, Inc., 336 N.W.2d 709 (Iowa 1983)
Mondis Technology Ltd. v. LG Electronics, Inc., 2011 WL 1714304 (E.D. Tex. May 4, 2011)
Moses v. Burgin, 445 F.2d 369 (1st Cir.1971),
Nathenson v. Zonagen, Inc., 267 F.3d 400 (5th Cir. 2001);
Oliver v Board of Governors, 779 SW 2d 212 (Ky, 1989)

Oran v. Stafford, 226 F.3d 275 (3d Cir. 2000);
Osprey, Inc. v. Cabana Limited Partnership, 532 S.E.2d 269 (S.C. 2000).
Parnes v. Gateway 2000, Inc., 122 F.3d 539 (8th Cir. 1997)
Parnes v Bally Entertainment Corp., 722 A.2d 1243 (Del. 1999)
Perlman v. Feldmann,219 F.2d 173 (2d Cir. 1955),
Polin v. Conductron Corp., 552 F.2d 797 (8th Cir. 1977)
Rancman v. Interim Settlement Funding Corp., 99 Ohio St.3d 121 (Ohio 2003)
Romani v. Shearson Lehman Hutton, 929 F.2d 875 (1st Cir. 1991);
Rosenfeld v Black 445 F.2d 1337 (2d Cir.1971)
Rotstein v. Reynolds & Co., 359 F. Supp. 109 (N.D. III. 1973)
Saladini v. Righellis, 687 N.E.2d 1224 (Mass. 1997)
Shields v. Smith, No. C-90-0349 FMS, 1991 WL 319032 (N.D. Cal. Nov. 4, 1991)
Sinay v. Lamson & Sessions Co., 948 F.2d 1037 (6th Cir. 1991);
Smith v. Van Gorkom, 488 A.2d 858 (Del. 1985)
Tooley v Donaldson, Lufkin & Jenrette, 845 A.2d 1031 (Del. 2004)
TSC Indus., Inc. v. Northway, Inc., 426 U.S. 438 (1976)
United States v. Bilzerian, 926 F.2d 1285 (2d Cir. 1991)
Zapata Corp. v. Maldonado, 430 A.2d 779 (Del. 1981)
Zerman v. Ball, 735 F.2d 15 (2d Cir. 1984);

## China

Daqing Lianyi (2004)
Lianhua Weijing (2004)
Sanjiu (2003);
Sanlian Shangshe (2009)
York Point Science & Technology Co (亿安科技) (2001)
Grandall v. Weiguan (2012)
Wuliangye (2009)
Apple Inc v. Weiguan (2011)
Yinguangxia (2004)

# List of Selected Legislation

## The United Kingdom

UK Companies Act 2006

Part 11; 30; Section 172; 239; 994

Civil Procedure Rules 1998 (CPR)

Part 19

Practice Direction

19C

The Rules of Supreme Court (UK)

Part 7

Access to Justice Act 1999 (UK)

Sched.2, para.1

## The United States

Model Business Company Act

Section 7.4; 7.42; 7.45

Delaware General Corporation Law

Section 220; Section 327

Pennsylvanian Business Corporation Law

Section 1782(b)

California Corporation Code 1977

Section 800



W. Chen, *A Comparative Study of Funding Shareholder Litigation*,
DOI 10.1007/978-981-10-3623-1

Federal Rule of Civil Procedure

Section 23.1

Securities Exchange Commission

Rule 10b-5.

Securities Act. See 17 C.F.R. § 230.175 (1997)

Rule 175

Private Securities Litigation Reform Act (PSLRA 1995)

Section 21E(c) 21E(c) (1) (A) (i) 21E(c) (1) (A) (ii) 21E(c) (1) (B)
27 (a) (3) 27 (a) (3) (B) (vi)
21D (a) (2) (A) (i) to 21D (a) (2) (A) (vi)
27 (a) (3) (B) 27 (a) (3) (B) (v)

**China**

Company Law (2014)

Chapter 2 & 3; Chapter 4 & 5; article 71; 75; 146-152;

Civil Procedure Law

Article 3;17; 53; 54(2); 54(4); 55; 56; 89; 91; 193(1); 207; 210

Contract Law

Article 124

The Opinions of the Supreme People's Court on Some Issues Concerning the Application of the Civil Procedure Law of the PRC (2008)

Article 43; 46; 47; 50; 52; 55; 56; 59; 60; 62; 63; 64

The Judicial Interpretation of the Supreme People's Court on Some Issues Regarding the Application of Security Law of the PRC (2000)

Article 124, 128

General Principles of the Civil Law of the People's Republic of China

Article 55; 135

The Supreme People's Court: Notice of the Supreme People's Court on Refusing to Accept Civil Compensation Cases Involving Securities For the Time Being(2001)

Article 4

The Supreme People's Court: Notice of the Supreme People's Court on the Relevant Issues concerning the Acceptance of Cases of Disputes over Civil Tort Arising from False Statement in the Securities Market (2002)

Article 12

The Supreme People's Court: Some Provisions of the Supreme People's Court on Trying Cases of Civil Compensation Arising from False Statement in Securities Market (2003)

Article 13; 14; 15

Zhejiang High People's Court in 2002 (Understandings on Several Difficult Issues Regarding the Application of the Company Law)

Beijing People's High Court in 2004 (The Guiding Opinions of Beijing High People's Court on Several Issues on Adjudicating Corporate Disputes Cases)

Measures on the Payment of Litigation Costs (2006)

Article 6; 9; 10; 12; 13(d); 14(1)(2)(3)(6); 15; 20; 29

Measures for the Administration of Lawyers' Fees (2006)

Article 11; 12; 13

Regulations on Legal Aid (2003)

Article 3; 10

Guangdong Provincial Rules on Legal Aid

The municipal government heightened the minimum income eligibility level for legal aid to let more people access to the court

Shanghai High People's Court, Explanation of several issues regarding third party in civil litigation (I), (2006)

**Israel**

Israeli Companies Law 1999

Article 205(A)-(C); 209

## Canada

Law Society Act (Ontario)

Section 59.1-59.5; 59.3 (1) (2) (4); 59.4 (1)

Solicitors Act R.S.O. (Ontario, 1990)

Section 15 to 33

British Columbia Class Proceedings Act

Section 37

An Act Respecting the Class Action, RSQ,c R-2.1 (Quebec)

Section 23; 31

Quebec Code of Civil Procedure

Section 1050(1)

## Others

Australian Corporation Act 2001.

Section 237(2)

Hong Kong Companies Ordinance

Section 168(B) (C)

New Zealand Companies Act 1993

Section 165(1) (b)

FSC
www.fsc.org
MIX
Papier | Fördert gute Waldnutzung
FSC® C083411

Kolibri 360 GmbH
Ferdinand-Jühlke-Straße 7
99095 Erfurt, Deutschland
produktsicherheit@kolibri360.de